RELIGION
What Is It?

Religion
What Is It?

Second Edition

WILLIAM CALLOLEY TREMMEL
University of South Florida

HOLT, RINEHART AND WINSTON

New York Chicago San Francisco Philadelphia Montreal Toronto
London Sydney Tokyo Mexico City Rio de Janeiro Madrid

Library of Congress Cataloging in Publication Data

Tremmel, William C.
 Religion, what is it?

 Bibliography: p. 304
 Includes index.
 1. Religion. I. Title.
BL48.T7 1983 200′.1   83-12976

ISBN 0-03-062834-2

CBS COLLEGE PUBLISHING
Holt, Rinehart and Winston
The Dryden Press
Saunders College Publishing

Acknowledgments

Page 78: "Theology and Verification" by John Hick, published in *Theology Today* (April 1960), Princeton, N.J.

Page 157: "The Creation" from *God's Trombones* by James Weldon Johnson copyright © 1927 by Viking Press, Inc; copyright renewed 1955 by Grace Nail Johnson. Reprinted by permission of Viking-Penguin, Inc.

Page 217: "The Cargo Cult Mentality in America," by Ruben Mettler, quoted from the September 22, 1980, issue of *Business Week* by special permission; © 1980 by McGraw-Hill, Inc., New York. All rights reserved.

*This book is dedicated to my teacher
William Henry Bernhardt,
who aimed me in this direction,
and to my wife
Opal Mitchell "Mike" Tremmel,
who has accompanied me the full distance.*

FOREWORD

The aim of this book is to introduce students to the phenomenon of *Religion: What Is It?* A number of basic questions are asked: (1) Why do people "do" religion? What is it about people that makes them the "religious animals"? (2) What are the central concepts that guide the beliefs and actions of religion? (3) What are the procedures and techniques employed in doing religion? (4) What human benefits are available in religious life and experience?

To get the answers to such questions, I have employed basically a method of functional analysis (including the sacred-experience aspect of religion), which I have found in my own introductory courses to have considerable explanatory power. This functinal procedure also leads to viewing religion not only from a single faith system, but from the perspectives of any number of world religions. Such viewing fosters an appreciation of the richness of non-Western religions and, at the same time, while distancing students from their Western religious traditions, gives them a new perspective from which to view their own more familiar traditions.

The book is divided into four parts. Each part concentrates attention on one of the four parts of the functional definition of religion presented on page 7: Part I deals with the human animal as a religious animal; Part II, with the concept of divine power; Part III, with the ways people "do" religion; Part IV, with religion as a rewarding and renewing experience.

The structure of the book is flexible enough for instructors to concentrate time and attention on one part or another of the four parts of the book, if they so choose. Breadth and depth, beyond that possible in a relatively brief and primarily introductory work such as this, can be achieved by using other readings, such as those recommended for each chapter in the bibliography at the end of the book. There is also an extensive biography and glossary section at the end of the book.

Religion: What Is It? second edition has been deliberately written so that it can be read by students just beginning a serious study of religion. At the same time, the book is more than just a cursory excursion through what is actually a highly disciplined subject matter—as well as a profoundly significant human phenomenon. I hope this book will serve students as a comprehensible and meaningful guide to an understanding of what religion is, and was, and apparently always will be.

I want to thank several professional colleagues who read the manuscript and offered many helpful suggestions: Robert Esbjornson, Gustavus Adolphus College; Robert D. Linder, Kansas State University; Charles S. Milligan, Iliff School of Theology; Robert C. Smith, Trenton State College.

Special thanks to my students, who keep me working always at being a better teacher; to Kandy Jill Lones, a fine secretary who keeps me from forgetting all my appointments and such things; and to Pat Schuster, who patiently put all of this on that new marvel of book-writing tools—a floppy disk.

Tampa, Florida   W.C.T.
October 1983

CONTENTS

Afterword: Getting It in Shape   277

Appendix 1   Data Bank for Religious Studies   281

Appendix 2   How We Know—Empirically, Rationally, Intuitively   300

Appendix 3   The Ontological Argument Assailed   302

PART ONE

Speculations on the Origins of Religion

Do not imagine that these great mysteries
are completely and thoroughly known to
any of us.

Maimonides°

I. Religion is a complex form of human behavior whereby a person (or community of persons) is prepared intellectually and emotionally to deal with those aspects of human existence that are horrendous and non-manipulable. [See page 7]

Chapter 1

A DEFINITION

The true meaning of a term is to be found by
observing what a man does with it, not what
he says about it.

P. W. Bridgman[1]

In a study of *religion—what is it?* a good working definition would be helpful.
But a good definition of religion is hard to come by, mostly because it must
incorporate an enormous array of beliefs and activities all the way from magic
to mysticism, from private prayer to sacred community. Not that we are short
of definitions of religion. All sorts of persons, eminent and otherwise, can
come up with a good definition of religion. For example, the important
nineteenth- and early-twentieth-century anthropologist Edward Tylor°*
defined religion as "belief in Spiritual Beings."[2] In more recent times the
philosopher Alfred North Whitehead° declared religion to be "what an individual does with his own solitariness."[3] That giant among eighteenth-century
philosophers, Immanuel Kant,° declared that religion is "the recognition of
our duties as divine commands."[4] And the German theologian Friedrich
Schleiermacher,° a generation after Kant, discerned "the common element of
religion" to be "the consciousness of ourselves as absolutely dependent."[5]
The late Paul Tillich° identified religion as "mankind's ultimate concern."[6]
Someone, perhaps not as intellectually formidable as the above-cited company but exercising an equal right to answer the question, has said that
"religion ain't doin' nobody no harm; leastwise not intentionally; and any-
ways not very often." We might add our own one-line definition calling
religion a form of human behavior in which people: (1) exorcise the demonic
elements of life (its horrendous finitudes), and (2) experience the divine
elements of life (the transcendence of finitude). But like the other one-line
"parcel" definitions this, too, appears to be more an incidental comment than
a definitive pronouncement.

The obvious thing about these several answers to *religion—what is it?* is that
they all sound good, but all obviously need large amounts of "unpacking" to
give them sufficient scope and sufficient precision to be adequate as defini-

*Names and terms marked by ° are identified and defined in the Biographical Notes and Glossary
section at the end of the book.

3

tions of religion. Whatever is wrapped up in these parcel definitions is only partly apparent from the shape of the package. About any one of them much more needs to be said. When there are too many answers, there really is no answer at all. When answers to complicated questions come too easily, we may suppose exactly that—they are *too easy*. What we need for our purpose is a description and an explanation much broader and at the same time more precise than can be accomplished in any capsule comment, no matter how insightful that comment might be.

TOWARD A FUNCTIONAL-EXPERIENTIAL DEFINITION OF RELIGION

Admitting that an adequate definition of religion is difficult to accomplish, we shall still try for a *working definition* that will direct us in our explorations—all the way from magic to sacred community. We shall use this working definition as an outline of our study. It will address two aspects of religious phenomena: (1) the functional aspect—which deals with the question of *why* people do religion, the question of *what they do* when they do religion, and the question of *what benefits* accrue to their doing it; and (2) the "sacred" aspect—which deals with the experience of something mysterious and magnificent that reportedly happens to people when they do religion, or even, sometimes, before they start doing it. Religion can be understood as a phenomenon° in the life of humans by observing it from one or *both* of two directions: (1) as something special that people do in order to achieve benefits—a functional approach; and (2) as something that happens to people—an existential approach.

First – The Functional Mode (The *Wherefore* Aspect)   On January 6 each year in the Greek community of Tarpon Springs, Florida, there is a religious festival both solemn and joyous. The community gathers to celebrate the ancient festival of Epiphany°* and the not so ancient festival of "casting the cross." First a solemn mass is conducted by the Greek Orthodox archbishop of North and South America in the Greek Orthodox Church of St. Nicholas of Tarpon Springs. After a lengthy and highly ornate mass, a marvelous parade forms outside the church. Men, women, and children, dressed in traditional Greek costumes, march to blaring bands from the church, around through the main street, and down to the bayou, where a contingent of young men is waiting in boats a few yards off shore. The crowd, having followed the parade,

---

*The Epiphany service celebrated by the Greek Orthodox church is mainly a commemoration of Jesus' baptism in the Jordan River. But it is also, in various Christian communities, a celebration symbolizing the revelation of Jesus as Christ to the Gentiles through the coming of Gentiles (the Zoroastrian priests/the Magi) to visit the Holy Family at the time of Jesus' birth.

gathers around the shoreline, where another solemn service begins. This one includes the blessing of a silver cross, and the casting of that cross into the bayou waters. The archbishop dips the cross three times into the water, then tosses it into the bayou to symbolize Christ's triple immersion into the Jordan River, and immediately the young men in the boats erupt into a frenzy of action. Out of the boats they go—diving for the cross. *The one who gets it will be blessed with good fortune*. They dive and surface, dive and surface, until finally one of them comes up, arm held high, displaying the cross he has rescued. The people applaud enthusiastically; some of them shout and cheer. A small child releases a dove from a cage. It flies upward and free. Then the archbishop raises his hand in one more blessing. After that there is a festive social celebration that begins with food, good and ample, followed by Greek dancing that continues all day and, according to reports, throughout most of the night.

This is all marvelous fun. It is also very religious. The people celebrate not just for a good time, but both to commemorate the ancient Christian festival of Epiphany *and to bring a blessing and good fortune on the community and on one young man in particular*—the one who rescued the cross.

What is it in people that causes them to do such things? What is it that makes us the only animals who hold religious festivals, say prayers, build churches, bury our dead ceremonially, and even, occasionally, dance in ecstatic God-intoxicated frenzy, or speak in tongues? A study of *religion—what is it?* must explore not only why people do such things, but also what they expect to gain from such behavior. To see why people do religion, and what they do when they do it, and what benefits they get from doing it is to see religion functionally, according to the functions it performs in human life. This will be one dimension of our definition of religion and of our exploring that definition.

Second – The Existential° Mode (The *Happening* Aspect)   Besides its functional dimension, we shall also examine religion in its sacred° experience aspect, in its existential mode, as something that happens to people.

According to Rudolf Otto° in his book *The Idea of the Holy*,[7] human beings are capable of a *numinous°* state of mind; that is, a consciousness of holiness, an awareness of divine power that comes surging up in them, or sweeping over them (at times terrifyingly, at times joyously, at times grisly and demonic, at times divinely gentle) from out there—the experience of something mysterious, or as William James° called it: "something there"[8]—*something more*. Robert Ellwood° calls this experience (as do many other persons) "mystical experience" and defines it as ". . . experience in a religious context that is immediately or subsequently interpreted by the experiencer as encounter with ultimate divine reality in a direct nonrational way that engenders a deep sense of unity and of living during the experience on a level of being other than the ordinary."[9]

John Taylor,° in his book *The Go-Between God*, considers the numinous experience as more than simply an "encounter with God." It is a consciousness of spirit calling to life in many, even quite ordinary, ways. Taylor writes, "I am not thinking of what is narrowly described as 'encounter with God,' but of quite unreligious commonplace experiences. . . . The mountain or the tree I am looking at ceases to be merely an object I am observing and becomes a subject, existing in its own life, and saying something to me—one could almost say *nodding* to me in a private conspiracy." Taylor points out that this nodding conspiracy targets close to the meaning of the word "numinous," which, according to Taylor, comes from the Latin *nuo*, which means to "nod" or "beckon." "The truly numinous experience is not marked only by primitive awe in the face of the unknown or overwhelming, but occurs also when something as ordinary as a sleeping child, as simple and objective as a flower, suddenly *commands* attention."[10]

Taylor calls his numinous experience an ordinary conspiracy. William James reports the experience of another person who identified his "numinous" encounter not as an ordinary experience but as an extremely non-ordinary experience—one of divine presence. Quoting an unnamed person, James reports:

> I remember the night, and almost the very spot on the hilltop, where my soul opened out, as it were, into the Infinite, and there was a rushing together of the two worlds, the inner and the outer. It was deep calling unto deep—the deep that my own struggle had opened up within being answered by the unfathomable deep without, reaching beyond the stars. . . . The ordinary sense of things around me faded. For the moment nothing but ineffable joy and exultation remained. . . . The darkness held a presence that was all the more felt because it was not seen. I could not any more doubt that *He* was there than that I was. Indeed, I felt myself to be, if possible, the less real of the two.[11]

Whether the numinous experience is an ordinary conspiracy of nodding, or a non-ordinary experience of divine presence, it is something that happens to people in religion and is important for our definition and study.

These two dimensions (the functional dimension and the sacred experience dimension) are sometimes regarded as separate and discrete, and there are some authorities who define religion strictly according to one dimension or the other. For example, the sociologist of religion J. Milton Yinger° has formulated a definition of religion that stresses the functional dimension.

> Religion . . . can be defined as a system of beliefs and practices by means of which a group of people struggles with [the] ultimate problems of human life. [It] is the refusal to capitulate to death, to give up in the face of frustration, to allow hostility to tear one apart from one's human associations.[12]

This is obviously a functional definition: Religion is what people do to deal with the horrendous and uncontrollable dimensions of human existence—with such things as death, suffering, guilt, meaninglessness.

But other scholars go the other route. They concentrate on a "sacred experience" definition. They say that the essential feature of religion is an awareness of sacredness. Objecting to the functionalists' definitions, the history of religions scholar Mircea Eliadé° insists that to define religion as primarily a method of dealing with human needs is to ignore "the one unique and irreducible element in it—the element of the sacred."[13]

In fact these principles for defining religion do not exclude each other, for religion is both something that people do to deal with certain elements of their own finitude and something that happens to them that is mysterious, tremendous, and wonderfully renovating. Indeed, the "sacred experience" aspect of religion is one of its functions. It is one of the things, perhaps the most desired thing, that people are trying to achieve when they do religion. The functional and the experiential aspects of religion are compatible, and both should be included in any attempt to understand what religion is.

Affirming that a definition of religion must include both the "functional" and the "sacred experience" aspects of religion, we shall begin with the following *working definition* and then proceed through the rest of the book to flesh out our definition with more detailed examination and analysis.

THE DEFINITION: Functional-Experiential

I.   Religion is a complex form of human behavior whereby a person (or community of persons) is prepared intellectually and emotionally to deal with those aspects of human existence that are horrendous and nonmanipulable.

II. Doing so from the conviction that there is at the center of human experience, and even of all reality, a being, or beings, or process (a divine reality) in which and through which a person (or community of persons) can transcend the life-negating traumas of human existence, can overcome the sense of finitude.

III. And doing so by the employment of various religious techniques: (a) a belief system (myths, doctrines, and theologies); (b) a ritual system (reverent behavior and dramatic performances); (c) a moral system (ethical doctrines and rules).

IV. With all of this (and especially in the conviction that there is a divine order basic to life) religion turns out to be for people not simply a method of dealing with religious problems (those horrendous, nonmanipulable circumstances of life), but also is itself an experience of great satisfaction and immense personal worth. Religion is not only something people "do" and "use"; it is also something that happens to them. It is an experience—a highly treasured experience, and even, at times, an experience of sheer ecstasy.*

---

*Parts I and III of this definition are re-formations of the functional definition of religion given by William H. Bernhardt° in his *Functional Philosophy of Religion*, where he states that "religious behavior is a complex form of individual and group behavior whereby persons are prepared intellectually and emotionally to meet the nonmanipulable aspects of existence positively by means of a reinterpretation of the total situation and with the use of various techniques." (Denver, Colo.: Criterion Press, 1958, p. 157.)

STYLES OF RELIGIOUS STUDIES

Kerygma *(kērugma)* is a Greek word that means "proclamation," "preachment," or "message." Phenomenon *(phaenomenon)* is a Latin word that means "any occurrence or fact observable by the senses." These two concepts (to preach and to observe) categorize two approaches to the study of religion—two reasons for studying religion: one is to get the message; the other is to understand the phenomenon of religion as a human experience.

When Paul, in his letter to the Romans 1:17, wrote: "For in the gospel is revealed the justice of God which begins and ends with faith; as the Scripture says, 'the just man shall live by faith, ' " he was speaking kerygmatically. He was proclaiming a "truth" for salvation. But when we simply report without value judgment that Paul in his letter to the Romans wrote "For in the gospel . . . ," we are speaking phenomenonistically. We are not proclaiming his salvation message, but simply observing that he proclaimed it. One style is parochial-theological; the other is academic-historical.

The Romans quote is from *The New Testament,* New American Bible (NAB).

The Kerygmatic Method   The kerygmatic method is concerned with the study or presentation of religion as a saving message. The function is to uncover true theology and appropriate religious practice for contemporary people. It is aimed at making persons truly religious no matter what historical era they happen to be living in. The kerygmatic method studies religion as a "saving message," a preachment, meaningful *today,* whenever today happens to be. It alters the message to fit the time. For example, St. Augustine° (A.D. 354–430), who was steeped in Greek philosophy, wanted to be a Christian and also wanted to hold to the Greek philosophy (Neo-Platonism°) popular in his day. So he Christianized Plato,° or Platonized Christianity; that is, he interpreted Christianity in Platonic terms. He "modernized" Christianity for the fifth century. He made it make sense in his day. In the thirteenth century, St. Thomas° Aquinas did the same thing with Aristotelian philosophy. Later Martin Luther° and John Calvin° "modernized" Christianity (re-stated the kerygma) for their times. Each generation, indeed, each culture in each generation reinterprets its saving message in the language of its day. Preachers, rabbis, priests, holy men everywhere, present their religious truths and practices kerygmatically. A contemporary presentation of the kerygma (that is, the proclamation of a particular set of religious doctrines for salvation purposes) is a proper thing. It is what Christian churches and Jewish synagogues, and Muslim mosques, and Buddhist temples, and Japanese zendos* are all about. It is, indeed, the job of ministers and priests and Sunday school teachers, and religious professionals everywhere to persuade, to propagandize, to convince, to save, by proclaiming and preaching what they and their theological circle hold to be *the* message. This is legitimate, but it is not the method that will be employed in this book. We shall opt for another style— the more academic, prosaic method, which we are calling the *phenomenistic method*.[14]

The Phenomenistic Method The phenomenistic (or historical) method is employed by academicians who want to examine the data of religion as objectively and even-handedly as possible. The concern is to observe, describe, and analyze the phenomena of religion not only objectively but also *empathetically*.°

In the phenomenistic method questions concerning value and truth are suspended, that is, bracketed out. The interest is in what people sincerely believe and do in the name of religion, not whether what they believe and do is "true." It is enough to observe that it is "true" for them. The effort is to appreciate the validity of religion, in any of its forms, as seen by the people who embrace it.

Certainly observing and talking about religious experience is different from experiencing that religious experience, but this does not negate an understanding for and an appreciation of the person whose behavior indicates having had such an experience. We can, without disparaging judgments, observe religious phenomena in their functional dimensions—as they serve human needs—psychological, social, and spiritual. And we can also, without disparaging judgments, listen to accounts of sacred experience, and we can try to imagine empathetically what such experiences mean to the "true believers" reporting them.

In the phenomenistic method one is interested in describing and defining, not, as in the kerygmatic method, proclaiming and persuading. The object is not to save, but only to understand.

NOTES

[1] P. W. Bridgman, *The Logic of Modern Physics* (New York: Macmillan, 1958), p. 7.
[2] Edward B. Tylor, *Primitive Culture* (New York: Gordon Press, 1974), vol. 1, p. 383.
[3] Alfred North Whitehead, *Religion in the Making* (Cleveland: World, Meridian Books, 1969), p. 16.
[4] See Immanuel Kant, *Religion within the Limits of Reason Alone*, tran. T. M. Greene and H. H. Hudson, 2nd ed. (LaSalle, Ill.: Open Court Publishing, 1960), pp. 142–151.

*A zendo is a Zen Buddhist meditation hall where, in disciplined meditation, persons seek and wait upon the "sacred experience" they call "*satori*."°

In both *Religion with the Limits of Reason Alone* and *The Critique of Practical Reason*, Kant (1724–1804) made his case for morality as the basis and essence of religion. All revelation, all theology, all scriptural truth is to be judged by one standard: How do they contribute to people's moral stature? Consciousness tells me that I ought to perform certain actions, and a little thought convinces me that *oughtness* is universal. Everyone *ought* to behave in a moral fashion. There is a moral law, and it is autonomous; it is not founded on anything else. One ought to be good not because it is expected, but because it is right. "Nothing," said Kant, "can be called good without qualification except a good will"—that is, the will to perform with perfect morality. Kant taught that the will is free. He taught that the moral law (so apparent to us in the fact that we all have consciences) is not simply made by humans, but is a transcendental, universal affair. Furthermore, the moral law postulates something whose nature is not only supreme, but is also complete (*consummatum*), an embodiment of that perfect holiness that is the sum of all the conditions implied in a transcendent moral order; which means, the moral law implies God. God is the embodiment of the universal moral order; thus, religion is obeying God—accepting our moral duties (as written in our hearts) as God's commands.

⁵See Freidrich Schleiermacher, *The Christian Faith*, ed. H. R. Mackintosh and J. S. Stewart (Edinburgh: T. & T. Clark, 1928), pp. 5–18.

⁶The idea of Ultimate Concern as the definition and matrix of religion appears throughout Tillich's works, especially in his three volumes titled *Systematic Theology*. In volume 1 of that work he states:

> Ultimate concern is the abstract translation of the great commandment: "The Lord, our God, the Lord is one; and you shall love the Lord your God with all your heart, and with all your soul and with all your mind, and with all your strength." (Mark 12:29, Revised Standard Version [RSV]) . . .
> *The object of theology is what concerns us ultimately. Only those propositions are theological which deal with their object in so far as it can become a matter of ultimate concern for us.* [Chicago: University of Chicago Press, 1951, pp. 11, 12]

By defining religion as Ultimate Concern, Tillich opened the definition to cover a vast range of human belief and activity. It would appear that just as the writer of the Gospel of Matthew had an ultimate concern, had an almost infinite passion, for Jesus Christ and the coming of the kingdom of God, so Karl Marx had an ultimate concern, had an almost infinite passion, for the emancipation of the workers and the coming of the communistic kingdom of mankind. Apparently by Tillich's definition they are both religions—although Tillich would surely regard one of them as bogus religion. Indeed, if ultimate concern is the hallmark of religion, the amassing of money as an end in itself, which so ultimately concerns some people, constitutes the religion of such people, *à la* Tillichian theology.

⁷Rudolf Otto, *The Idea of the Holy*, tran. J. W. Harvey (London: Oxford University Press, 1923).

⁸William James, *Varieties of Religious Experience* (New York: Modern American Library, 1902), p. 58. This volume is composed of The Gifford Lectures delivered at Edinburgh by James in 1901–1902.

⁹Robert Ellwood, Jr., *Mysticism and Religion* (Englewood Cliffs, N.J.: Prentice-Hall, 1980), p. 29.

[10] John V. Taylor, *The Go-Between God* (New York: Oxford University Press, 1979), pp. 11–12.

[11] William James, *Varieties of Religious Experience* (New York: Random House, Modern Library, ©1902), p. 66.

[12] J. Milton Yinger, *Religion, Society and the Individual* (New York: Macmillan, 1957), p. 9.

[13] Mircea Eliadé, *Patterns in Comparative Religion* (New York: World Press, 1963), p. xiii.

[14] What I am calling "phenomenistic method" might be called phenomenology,° but because phenomenology represents not only a methodology, but (despite disclaimers) a contemporary philosophical system as well, I chose the less colorful, and less controversial, term "phenomenistic."

Chapter 2

THE RELIGIOUS ANIMAL

*Every child comes with the message that God
is not yet discouraged of mankind.*
                              Rabindranoth Tagore°

Apparently mankind is the only animal that does religion. This makes us
special animals: religion-doing animals.* Of course we are also the only
animals that do quite a number of things—philosophy, science, retail mer-
chandising, plumbing—but for our purposes here the specialty in religion will
suffice. First, we want to know why we do religion. What motivates us to this
kind of thinking and acting? We suspect that the answer is somewhere in the
statement: Humans do this because they have special kinds of minds. But
precisely what kinds of minds? With Aristotle we might say, "Rational
minds," and that is certainly part of it, but not all of it. We do think about
religion. We try to be reasonable in our faith. But there is something more
visceral than reason in our urge to do religion. That something lies in the fact
that we have the kind of mind that presents us with a vivid and immediate
awareness of *our*self. Not only do we have cool, problem-solving (rational)
minds, but we also have disturbing (self-conscious) minds that tell us *that* we
are and *where* we are. And knowing that we are and where we are is disturbing, even horrendous, because it informs us accurately that we are living in a
self-defeating world. The self (that is, any person) is disturbed because once
old enough to have much sense, it gets the sense of the true situation into
which it has been born. All humans are involved, even trapped, in a world, in a
human environmental condition, that sooner or later defeats and annihilates

*To say that mankind is the religious "animal" does not imply that human beings are not very
special beings. It does not decry the contention that people are made just a little less than perfect,
a little less than angels (a Jewish-Christian claim), and crowned with glory and honor. Indeed, all
religions, no matter how they malign the present condition of humans, hold finally that human
beings are infinitely worthy and capable of direct communion with divinity. When we say that
mankind is the religious animal, we are saying that people are not *just* animals. They are animals
of special qualities and qualifications.

12

all selfhood. Put simply, this is to say that none of us ever gets out of life alive, and none of us ever gets out of life half of what we want; *and humans are the animals who really know this*. We know that things are not as good for us as they should be, or perhaps even could be. We think about ourselves, and such thinking is bad for happiness, or if not happiness, bad for tranquility. And we think about ourselves not necessarily because we want to, but because we have to. Humans have to think, if they want to survive, because they are the animals most deficient in DNA° knowledge. They are deficient in the instinctive responses sufficient to the essential life-support acts that are genetically built into other animals. The only alternative to genetically established support responses is thinking. The human animal, far more than any other animal, has to learn how to keep itself alive. We have to think about ourselves in this world or we will not make it. The basic problem of human life, which sets humans on the path to *Homo sapiens*° ("wise man") instead of *Homo naturalis*° ("natural man"), is that humans are all born short on instinctive "know-how."

THE NONPROGRAMMED ANIMAL

To say that humans are the animals deficient in DNA knowledge, short on instinctive "know-how," is to say that they are the nonprogrammed animals: the ones for whom life and meaning depend not on simple maturity but on instructed maturity. We cannot just grow up and be ourselves (wise man); we must grow up instructed, educated. The existentialist° philosophers are on target when (according to Sartre's account)[1] they observe that human beings are the only animals whose existence precedes their essence. The essential nature of other animals is instructed, programmed, built into the genetic structure. Ours is not. A duck is always a duck. It is born that way. It can never be anything but a duck and exactly that kind of duck. All of the instructions, even, apparently, the migratory routes, are put down in the beginning of a duck's time. But this is not the case with humans. It is true that at birth, even at conception, there is an instructed part laid down in human beings: their physical existence. The body begins, and the instructions for its physical maturity are all there; but not humanity, not mind, not language, not attitudes, loves, antipathies, sadness, religion. All this—and all else that makes one a person, a personality, a human being—is yet to be learned, yet to be created. So, humans are different because of the absence of certain instructed regulations in their genetic equipment. As Erich Fromm° puts it:

> The first element which differentiates human from animal existence is a negative one: the relative absence in man of instinctive regulation in the processes of adaptation to the surrounding world. . . . The less complete and fixed the instinctual equipment of animals, the more developed is the brain and therefore the

ability to learn. The emergence of man can be defined as occurring at the point in the process of evolution where instinctive adaptation has reached its minimum.[2]

But this deficiency in programming is far from tragic, for it is the deficiency out of which burgeons a person's self-consciousness, memory, foresight, language, reason, and imagination. Or, as Fromm puts it:

> He emerges with new qualities which differentiate him from the animal: his awareness of himself as a separate entity, his ability to remember the past, to visualize the future, and to denote objects and acts by symbols; his reason to conceive and understand the world; and his imagination through which he reaches far beyond the range of his senses.[3]

All that constitutes mankind's created humanness is important to the doing of religion, but for our purpose here we need observe only two especially human qualities: self-consciousness and imagination.

SELF-CONSCIOUSNESS AND IMAGINATION

To say that a person is self-conscious is to say that that person *sees himself*. He sees himself as involved in a past, a present, and a future. Largely through the mechanism of speech and play,* made possible by a distinctive physiological and neurological inheritance. Mr. Jones knows himself to be Mr. Jones. He is an object of himself. He is at the same time both an object and a subject. He may not see himself exactly as others see him, but he definitely sees himself. He sees himself in his own immediate awareness, and he sees himself in his imagination. That is to say, he is a *self*-conscious being, and a being who sees himself as here and now (acting in the present), and sees himself as there and then (acting in the past), and sees himself where he yet may be (acting in the future).

Perhaps other animals have some degree of self-consciousness and imagine themselves in other places doing other things, but if they do, they do not do so very effectively, because generation after generation they go on living in the same old way. If things are imagined differently, changing modes of operation and ways of life ought to occur. But nonhuman animals rarely change their modes and ways. Apparently other animals live in the immediate world, with some memory of the past, but with little thought about, or imagination of, themselves living (or dying) in the future. In this, of course, humans are really different. A person is extremely aware of the future—tomorrow, next month, next year, retirement, eternity. Indeed, people often seem to do more of their living, or try to, in the future than in the present. People, especially modern people, endlessly worry and want for tomorrow. They look at their immediate world and imagine how it could be different, how, in fact, it will be different

---

*Identified by George Herbert Mead° as the basic mechanism in the creation of the human mind.

tomorrow. Because they possess the power of self-consciousness and imagination, they want what is not and are afraid of what is not. They live positively and negatively, not only in their actual world, but in their "wished-for" world and in their "afraid-of" world. Positively they imagine what is not and desire it, sometimes passionately. Negatively, they imagine what is not and fear it, sometimes desperately. This puts them in the condition of estrangement. Wherever they are, indeed in the world itself, they feel as if they do not belong. They are constantly aware that things are not to their liking. Life never measures up to their expectations, and it never could, because that is the character of the expectations of a self-conscious, imaginative human being. Whoever we are, whatever we are, whatever we have, it is not enough. We want to be more than we are; we want to be somewhere else; we want to have greater possessions. If only I were eleven (the age when some of us were to get our first bicycles), I would be happy and not need anything else . . . if only I were twenty-one, through college, had a good job, were married to Susie, were famous, rich, richer. There is no end to it. Even when one rebels and turns against "this rat race," it is the same. The only thing that changes, important as that may be, is the style of the self-consciousness and imagination, the style of imagining ourselves as we are not and where we are not.

NEW WORLDS

Because things are not to our hearts' desires, because we can imagine them differently and want them so, we strive to make our lives different; and people always have so striven. They are always building new worlds for themselves. Motivated by their desires for a better life (desires that arise naturally in each person's self-disturbing mind), humans go to work imaginatively and create fantastic artificial worlds, wherein one finds central plumbing, air conditioning, rapid transit, $E = MC^2$,° the Roman papacy, the law of parsimony,° the Republican party, the Pietà,° hospitals, faith healing, stereophonic noise, and television commercials to remind them of what they do not have and keep them wanting it. What is being said here is that all human enterprises—especially those of significance, such as science, philosophy, religion—arise in human need, in our awareness of the inadequacies in ourselves and our world, and work to accomplish human welfare, or what is believed to be human welfare, or, at least, things closer to our hearts' desire.

Because the world does not measure up to our wants and expectations, and because we have the kind of minds to know this, we try to reform the world with technology and science; we try to make it reasonable, less mysterious and frightening, with philosophy and theology; and we try to relate to it adequately or transcend it successfully with religious beliefs, devotions, and commitments. Religion, so regarded, is the way one believes and behaves in an effort to overcome and transcend the existential estrangement, the horrendous, nonmanipulable aspects of human existence, the sense of finitude—which is to say, the *human condition*.

THE HUMAN CONDITION

Special consideration should be given this phrase, "the human condition," for it lies at the base of religious motivations. The human condition is the condition of estrangement. Just below the surface of tranquilizers and other superficial distractions, it is the condition of humans to feel estranged from their own world and in disharmony with their own lives. Humans are a part of nature and at the same time are divorced from nature. This dichotomy, as we observed, occurs because humans, unlike other animals, know their destiny in nature. They are caught in an impossible split: being subject to nature and transcendent to nature. Possessing a body that wants to stay alive, each person possesses at the same time a mind that says the body's wish is doomed. As an innocent part of nature, the heart beats as if it would never stop, but the mind knows better. Other animals find their fulfillment in simply repeating the patterns of their species, but human beings are not so fulfilled. Evicted from innocence (from instinctive almost thoughtless existence even as it was experienced prenatally), mankind is doomed to work forever at a problem no one can possibly solve. As Fromm put it, "having lost paradise, the unity with nature, [man] has become the eternal wanderer (Odysseus, Oedipus, Abraham, Faust),"[4] endlessly searching to restore a unity with the rest of nature that was irreparably ruptured on the day of birth. In an attempt to repair the rupture, Fromm tells us, humans first construct all-inclusive world hypotheses, that is, world views within which they can answer the question of where they stand in the midst of life and what they ought to do. But, Fromm explains, such thought systems are not adequate. If humans were only thinking animals, their minds would be sufficient; but each human is also endowed with a body. Thus they must respond not only by thinking, but also with feelings and actions. According to Fromm, a person "has to strive for the experience of unity and oneness in all spheres of his being in order to find a new equilibrium. Hence any satisfying system of orientation implies not only intellectual elements but also elements of feeling and sense to be realized in action in all fields of human endeavor. Devotion to an aim, or an idea, or a power transcending man such as God, is an expression of this need for completeness in the process of living."[5]

Doing Religion   Fromm goes on to point out that these systems of orientation, these world views, vary depending on the culture in which they happen, but they are nevertheless all concerned with the same thing: to give mankind a framework of meaning in which to find its own personal meaning. They are, in fact, reinterpretations of the world (theologies) developed so that the horrendousness of life may be mitigated, or perhaps even denied. For example, one might say, with the Hindu: This is only an illusory world (maya); search behind the appearances of it for the real world. Or one might say, with the Christians: This is only a preliminary world, a testing place for eternity; beyond is Heaven, or, if you are not careful, Hell. Fromm admits that he would like to call such orientation systems religion, but because some of these systems are not theistic (centered in a personal God), he backs away, saying: "For lack of a better word I therefore call such systems 'frames of orientation and devotion'."[6] It is our intention not to back away, because constructing such frames of orientation and devotion is exactly what people do when they do religion, whether or not they do it with reference to a theistic/personalistic God.

Horrendous and Nonmanipulable   We have asserted that religious behavior is a complex response to those aspects of human existence that are horrendous and nonmanipulable. By "horrendous" we mean to convey the sense not simply of fright and frightening things, but of the deeper-seated dread that arises in the face of those things that threaten to destroy basic human values, to destroy essential life-styles, and even life itself. Religious responses are not evoked at horror movies—although a person may be "half scared to death" by them—or by walking through a graveyard at night, or by hearing an eerie sound coming through the fog, but by circumstances that put in peril the life and meaning of the person involved. An example of this kind of horrendousness is the dread that accompanies death. Death is not only a universal problem—everybody has to face it sooner or later—but it is also, except sometimes when given an adequate religious interpretation, a horrendous problem. In its blunt factuality, death terrorizes people. The death of another person, the death of a loved one, one's own death, is horrendous both in fact and contemplation, and it evokes religious responses.

Death is a classic example of the horrendousness of religious problems. But it is not the only one. Living can also be horrendous. Indeed, for many people death is not the most terrible thing a person ever has to face. Much worse for some people is facing life. The fact that some people commit suicide indicates that for them death is the lesser of two evils. And even among those who do not commit suicide or even contemplate it, many people find the really difficult problem is not how to die well, but how to live well. Many discover that Thoreau's quiet desperation, or even a screaming desperation, is the really devastating thing in their lives. For those who live past the tender years, the basic tragedy of living may not be in death, but in disillusionment, in the discovery that life must be lived in picayune ways far beneath the expectations of youthful dreams and ambitions. For many sensitive people, the trauma of life, the horrendousness, comes in the lost beauty of life, the lost ecstasy of living, in the dulling of expectancy by the hard facts of mundane existence, in the general loss of youthful ideals before the calculating motion of the years. The real frustration is not that life must end, but that it must be lived in little ways. The religious question is not whether to make "a quietus" with the "bare bodkin,"° but to decide whether life is indeed shattered by the slings and arrows of fortune, by the grunt and sweat of weariness, by the cowardly conscience, sicklied with pale thoughts and terrified of dreamful sleep—or if it need be. Death is merely a convenient, Everyman illustration of the kind of frustration that evokes religion, the kind of frustration that is religiously horrendous.

Religious problems are horrendous problems. They are also nonmanipulable problems. John O'Hara took the title for one of his novels, *Appointment in Samarra,* from a parable by W. Somerset Maugham in which with startling clarity both the inimical (horrendous) character and the inevitable (nonmanipulable) character of death are exemplified.

> Death speaks: There was a merchant in Bagdad who sent his servant to market to buy provisions and in a little while the servant came back, white and trembling, and said, Master just now when I was in the market-place I was jostled by a woman in the crowd and when I turned I saw it was Death that jostled me. She looked at me and made a threatening gesture; now, lend me your horse, and I will ride away from this city and avoid my fate. I will go to Samarra and there Death will not find me. The merchant lent him his horse, and the servant mounted it, and dug his spurs in its flanks and as fast as the horse could gallop he went. Then the merchant went down to the market-place and he saw me standing in the crowd and he came to me and said, Why did you make a threatening gesture to my servant when you saw him this morning. That was not a threatening gesture, I said, it was only a start of surprise. I was astonished to see him in Bagdad, for I have an appointment with him tonight in Samarra.[7]

The point of this story, so far as we are concerned, is not the overtone of fatalism, not the precision of the appointment, but the final inevitability of such an appointment for all of us, sometime, somewhere, if not today, tomorrow, if not in Samarra, then in Bagdad. Also, there is no denying that when death gestures at us, we are threatened. It is an enemy, and it cannot finally be outflanked. It is horrendous and it is nonmanipulable.

By nonmanipulable we mean circumstances that are beyond direct human control. By religiously significant nonmanipulables, we mean nonmanipulable circumstances that are also horrendous.* The phases of the moon, the rising and falling of the tides, the progression of our galaxy toward Andromeda are all nonmanipulables, but they do not evoke religious responses because they do not threaten human life or essential life-styles. An

---

*"Nonmanipulable" is an adjective. It has no noun form. However, it is convenient at times to treat it as a noun. We shall do this occasionally, using it to mean a thing that cannot be altered, changed, or reordered by humans.

ocean cannot be manipulated, but it does not become a religious problem until, in a storm, it threatens to swamp your boat, and your life along with it. At that moment the nonmanipulable becomes horrendous and religiously significant.

There are, it appears, two kinds of religiously significant nonmanipulables: first, those *of incompetence,* which are temporary, and, second, those *of condition,* which are permanent.

First, *of incompetence:* This class of religiously significant nonmanipulables includes all those uncontrollable, horrendous circumstances that cannot be manipulated simply because one does not know how to manipulate them *at the moment.* They are temporarily nonmanipulable. Take, for example, famine: Some people's lives are threatened by famine, not because famine is nonmanipulable, not because we do not have the know-how and technological skill to banish famine, but only because *those* people do not yet have the know-how and skill. The situation is nonmanipulable for them, simply because of ignorance. Again, as with famine, such diseases as diphtheria, scarlet fever, small pox, poliomyelitis, can be controlled. Yet in certain places they are not controlled and for the people of those places they remain religiously significant nonmanipulables. Again, certain kinds of social ills are nonmanipulables of incompetence. In many situations where life and lifestyles are threatened, we simply do not know enough to do what should be done or how to persuade people to do so even if we did know. Thus the world is plagued with war, racial prejudice, human deprivations, crimes, broken homes, broken persons, and ten thousand other social ills, all of which are theoretically solvable, but not immediately or practically so.

In the horrendous nonmanipulables of incompetence, religion gets involved and remains involved until the nonmanipulable is solved and becomes manipulable; with that, technology replaces religion in that situation. If this were all there were to it, we could expect that the kinds of problems that drive people to religion might eventually all disappear, and religion along with them. Once incompetence was overcome, through the accomplishments of science and technology and perhaps some applied social ethics, the need for religion would end and all people would live happily in a prayerless everafter. But this is not all there is to it. There are certain kinds of religiously significant problems that are apparently permanently nonmanipulable. Such problems we shall designate as nonmanipulables of condition.

Second, *of condition:* This second type of nonmanipulable is characterized by permanance. These are the horrendous circumstances of life that will not go away with a little more know-how. These are the nonmanipulables of the human condition. As long as people are people such conditions will continue to frustrate them and drive them to the "hope" of religion rather than the manipulations of technology. These nonmanipulables have ontological status—that is, they are essential to the nature of people's being people. For example, it appears that no amount of scientific knowledge or technological skill will ever change the basic self-disturbing character of mankind's self-conscious, imaginative mind, as we noted earlier. The only possibility of ending this normal condition of estrangement would be to tranquilize people to the point at which they would no longer be anything like authentic humans. As long as they are real people, they will live forever wanting things better and expecting them worse. To the degree that there are permanent horrendous problems in human existence there are nonmanipulables of condition. The difference is that the "of incompetence" type is manipulable at least in principle, whereas the "of condition" type is not.

What nonmanipulables of condition basically do to humans is threaten their very being—threaten them with nonbeing. Nonbeing here means the denial or loss of those conditions that are essential to genuine human life—such things as life itself, a sense of personal worth, an awareness of moral integrity. Paul Tillich,° in his insightful little book *The Courage To Be,* identifies these permanent threats to man's being as fate and death, emptiness and meaninglessness, guilt and condemnation. Fate and death threaten a person's *ontic* self, that is, his existence as a being. Emptiness and meaninglessness threaten the spiritual self. Guilt and condemnation threaten the moral self. It is the condition of a person to be born at a moment in time, at a place in time, and possessing certain genetic equipment. Human life is thus set in a definite matrix. This matrix is more or less fixed. Within the boundaries of individual time, space, and genetics, one must strive to find or create a meaningful life, for, as we have noted, people cannot live satisfactorily, or with satisfaction, simply performing animal functions. Each person must somehow fulfill the demands of his or her own human ego. Each one must effect a sense of personal, individual worth. Each must find a way to "belong" in spite of the normal estrangement. Each person must acquire a spiritual status that makes him or her worthy of respect, especially self-respect, and this is not easy to do. Every person, no matter who, will experience times of depression and emptiness, times of quiet desperation. Indeed, just below the surface of all of an individual's activities, the anxiety of emptiness/meaninglessness lurks disquietingly, for, as we noted, estrangement is the natural condition of mankind, and anxiety is the persistent symptom of that condition. When the sense of emptiness becomes extreme, it slides into the horrendous experience of meaninglessness—a life without purpose or worth, a life worse than death.

Accompanying the anxiety of emptiness/meaninglessness is the equally permanent anxiety of guilt/condemnation. After a while it becomes impossible to go on blaming others for our own faults and failures. We may say that we are "worthless bastards" because of bad toilet training, but we know better. It is not somebody else's fault; it is my fault. *I* am guilty. *I* have failed others. *I* have failed myself. *I* have failed life. *I* have failed God. *I* am responsible and no one else. God help me! When this anxiety of guilt spreads and colors the whole of one's life, the condition of condemnation asserts itself. I am not only guilty, but I am condemned. God forgive me! And, of course, during this whole living process, we are dying, and at least part of the time we know it. The condition of "fate" accelerates to the extreme and death happens. To a spiritual nonbeing and a moral nonbeing is added the final nonbeing—the ontic, the nonbeing of the self.

Tillich's threats to being (fate/death, emptiness/meaninglessness, guilt/condemnation) are examples of nonmanipulables of condition. No amount of know-how will change them. Religion is the only answer, for religion is an admission of the worst, and a stance of courage in spite of it. Before the threat of nonbeing, religion gives people "the courage to be."

To the several examples on nonmanipulables of condition given so far, one or two more might be added. First there is the condition of social ignorance. Social ignorance can be viewed partly as a nonmanipulable of incompetence instead of a nonmanipulable of condition. The problems of racial injustice, crime and rehabilitation, poverty and urban blight, and the like, all arise out of social ignorance. They are all solvable and are, thereby, nonmanipulables of incompetence. But on a deeper level, social ignorance has a permanent structure, and in its horrendous dimensions must be dealt with as a nonmanipulable of condition. Here we are dealing with the ontology° of human societies and recognizing that ignorance is a permanent feature of the structure (being) of society. It is a sad fact that vast numbers of people always have been ill informed and ignorant and have acted in stupid ways, and apparently they always will. Especially in times of cultural change, the structure of social life is simply too complicated to be understood adequately by most of the people involved. And even if the masses of mankind had the reasoning power to understand all they would need to understand, there is no evidence that they would choose to act reasonably. To be sure, people do make rational choices part of the time, but more of the time, and often in the critical issues of life, they choose willfully, passionately, irrationally. How else are we to account for the mob's concurrence in the crucifixion of Jesus, the lynching of blacks in Alabama, the Nazi Holocaust, the years of war in Vietnam, the enormous overkill of modern nuclear armaments, the poverty of urban slums surrounded by suburban affluence? The cutting edge of each day, each year, each generation is always running ahead of the institutions, customs, convictions, education, and morality that determine and govern the life of each day, each year, each generation. There is little reason to believe that the masses of mankind will ever be a spearhead for any social progress whatsoever; that their education will ever match the complexities of their times; that enough of them will at any time be wise enough and cool headed enough to allay the enormous social ills that endlessly spawn in the muck of human ignorance. Like death, social ignorance seems destined to plague humans to the end of time.

In private correspondence, Charles Milligan° extended the conversation of ignorance as a nonmanipulable of condition with this excellent observation:

> Although the unknown can be intriguing and invite exploration, it may in other ways be a threat, like the darkness that encircles the campfire light's circumference. The awareness of the fact of the boundaries of knowledge is itself a nonmanipulable. That applies to the sum total of human knowledge and also to the individual's knowledge within that totality.
>
> Now if one's area of knowledge grows, the number of points where ignorance impinges upon it—and one is aware of that boundary—increases by something like geometric proportion. The very provincial person is not nearly as aware of the extent of the unknown as the very learned one. Often a college student is simply overwhelmed by the size of the library and the realization of how much he will never know. In this way—as the circle of knowledge increases, the circumference of ignorance increases dramatically—the sheer fact of ignorance is a nonmanipulable that will not ever be conquered, but in fact ever becomes more poignantly brought home to us, especially in a time of knowledge explosion.
>
> A second part of ignorance is that it pervades the future. No amount of information enables us to know in advance which of two good paths to follow is the better when there are unknown developments ahead, and possibly one of them will turn out to have a disastrous fortuitous consequence. Indeed, the more we know, the more tantalizing it is that in real life decisions the unknowable aspects of future developments are beyond our grasp. I think of Robert Frost's° "The Road Not Taken" in relation to this.* Religion functions here by providing an underlying stance of trust.

Milligan's observations have a shocking ring to them—outside the campfire light of right now, and every right now, there stands mystery on mystery, night on night, threat on threat, fear on fear—the dimension of "one more dimension of ignorance."

And again, as Milligan observes, ignorance dominates our adventure ahead. The future may be planned for, prepared for, worked for, but it can never be known or controlled. One may eat, drink, and be merry today because tomorrow he dies—but then he may not die. Or one can, in work and study, sacrifice today to the conquest of tomorrow—and die before the next sunrise.

This form of nonmanipulable is sufficiently critical to evoke a religious response. Indeed, we might cover our heads with our ignorance and pretend there is no mystery or future to worry about; but wisdom advises us to take a more religious stance and invite "God's will be done"—decide to trust to luck, or God, or something, that the mystery somewhere, some way, makes sense, and that the future is not only probable, but promising.

---

*In his poem "The Road Not Taken," Robert Frost reports that he came upon two roads in a woods one day. He would like to have traveled both, but couldn't. He had to choose one way or the other. He chose the one that seemed less traveled, but he wondered if he should have. It made all the difference, but the difference it made he would never know.

A DIFFERENT SIDE OF THE COIN

But human beings are not only self-conscious, imaginative, making endless emotional, intellectual, technological adjustments to their worlds, they are also playful-aesthetic-exotic animals, with a passion for self-stimulation and many talents to effect that stimulation. We paint pictures. We build cathedrals. We like music. We laugh. We weep. We write it all down in poems and plays; and in stories—scary stories, funny stories, stories with a moral, and some stories to intrigue our "almost intuition" that there is *something more*.

The Sufis° tell such a story. It goes something like this: once there was a "holy man" named Hajj.° He had made pilgrimage. He was a dervish. He recited Qur'an diligently. But everybody knew that he was also a little crazy—touched in the head. His "peculiarities" were humorously commented on by the townspeople when they saw him riding his donkey because he rode it backward, sitting facing the tail. Partly because he was a holy man, but, perhaps, more because he was a familiar "joke," he was made a member of the council of town elders. He sat with them deliberating and dealing with town problems, but mostly he just deliberated and rode his donkey backward. Until one day when all the other elders were away from town and a thief was caught stealing in the marketplace. Judgment would have to be rendered, and punishment; but there were no elders in town except Hajj. Then Hajj would have to act as judge.

The problem of justice here involved was not a serious one. There was ample law and precedent. The Book (the Qur'an) clearly states that the offending hand of the thief shall be cut off. Hajj, the holy man, knew the Book. He recited it prayerfully day on day. Let him then render the judgment, announce the punishment. And he did. He said they should let the thief ride his donkey. So they did. And the thief rode it out of town.

And that is the end of the story; although one suspects there must be more to it than "meets the ear."*

Try another story, equally curious, but with perhaps a more definite conclusion drawn. This is the story of a monk named Jean Jacques Beaumont. He lived in a monastery in Belgium. Brother Jean was a gentle man who loved all God's gentle creatures, birds and squirrels, oxen and sheep, the peaceful things of the countryside.

One day as Brother Jean walked through the fields he heard a lark singing and stopped to listen, enchanted, until the bird flew away.

Jean Beaumont then returned to his monastery, but, to his surprise, he did not recognize the doorkeeper, nor did the doorkeeper recognize him. Indeed, no one at the monastery recognized him, nor he them!

---

*For starters—maybe the ordinary "book way" is not the only way to the heart of faith.

Finally the abbot solved the mystery. Searching the records he found that a monk by the name of Jean Jacques Beaumont had lived at that monastery 100 years before.

You see, for Jean Beaumont time stood still while he listened to the singing of the lark.*

As I recall, it happened to me the first time (that sacred peak experience) not in a field but on a mountain trail when I was a small boy. Suddenly I "knew" an overwhelming sense of *something more*. The whole world around me sang in a melded harmony. It was as if the whole thing stood still in a moment of eternal perfection. I still go "home" each year to those same mountains just to make sure that *something more* still happens.

Recently when I confessed the meaning of my annual pilgrimage to my son, he nodded his head understandingly. "But," he said, "with me it happens on a beach at the edge of an ocean."

The Granny Story

There is a widespread belief (and one that runs back beyond the memory of man) that there is more going on out there than meets the eye.

After my mother died several years ago, I inherited the old family home, the place where I grew up. It was in need of some repairs and I prevailed upon my son Michael to do some interior decorating. He did. And then, because my daughter Susan had chosen to go to Colorado to live, I was pleased to have her take over the house and live there. Recently while visiting her I was told this story. She told it quite matter of factly.

"For a long time," she said, "after I moved into this house, Granny was still here. I'd get the feeling that someone was in the house, in the room with me; then when I turned, I'd just catch a glimpse of her slipping away down the hall."

Susan said that a young woman roommate also had seen Granny. And a young man staying alone in the house one day reported that he, too, had seen her.

All agreed that Granny was not at all threatening in her "appearances." Rather, she seemed unsure, hesitant, a little bewildered.

Susan then reported that once she told her brother Michael (the one who had decorated the house and who "peaks-out" on beaches) of her experience and he responded: "I wasn't ever going to tell anybody, but when I was there decorating, I saw her too."

I asked when Granny had last "appeared" and Susan said, "Not since the night you stayed here and we had the party and you were happy and said, 'This is a happy house.' I think Granny was satisfied then that everything was all right."

---

*For starters—"In a sacred moment, anything can happen."

Now, dear reader, be assured that this account has been presented not because I believe that "Granny" was really there, or because I do not believe it. It is written here simply to report that at least four modern, intelligent, generally skeptical young people had an experience of something more than is typical in an ordinary day.

We all have a capacity (if we let it loose) sometimes to suspect *something more,* sometimes to be awe-struck, and sometimes to shiver. And all of this surely contributes to mankind as the religious animal.

The biologist Julian Huxley° insists that humans have an innate capacity to experience sacredness: "Not only does the normal man have this capacity for experiencing the sense of the sacred, but he demands its satisfaction."[8] More recently Abraham Maslow,° a psychologist, began saying a similar sort of thing. He proposes that for human beings sacred experiences are very normal sorts of experiences. He argues that "peak experiences," as he calls them, are common among people not simply as religious experiences, but as experiences that occur in art, love, and music as well. Indeed, Maslow believes that people who do not have such experiences are, in fact, persons who, because they fear such experiences, suppress them.[9]

Various attempts to quantify intense religious experiences have been made in recent years.[10] Andrew Greeley,° in 1974, made a national survey and found that more than three out of ten Americans sampled (35 percent) had had intense spiritual experiences.[10] In Great Britain, D. Hay and A. Morisy report similar findings: 36 percent of English people sampled reported intense spiritual experiences.[11] C. Kentzer found a considerably higher percentage of American college students (65 percent) claiming to have had "transcendent experience."[12]

However, none of these studies of religious experience defined very precisely the experience they were examining. What was meant by "intense religious experience," or "peak experience," or "transcendent experience," or "mystical experience"? Eugene Thomas and Pamela Cooper, in their 1980 study, addressed themselves to the need for a more precise definition. They devised an open-ended sampling tool in which the respondent not only reported having or not having an intense religious experience— "Have you ever had the feeling of being close to a powerful spiritual force that seemed to lift you outside yourself?"*—but was invited to describe that experience. The respondents were permitted "to define the terms in their own way. A content analysis provided a typology of kinds of spiritual experiences. . . ."[13] The typology is as follows:

Type 0: No experience reported.

Type 1: *Uncodable:* Insufficient information was given on which to base a coding decision, or respondents gave irrelevant experiences.

*The same question asked by Andrew Greeley in his 1974 national sampling.

Type 2: *Mystical:* Response included expressions of awesome emotions, a sense of the ineffable, feeling of oneness with God, nature, or the universe. May also have included description of changed perceptions of time and surroundings and a feeling of "knowing," coupled with a reordering of life priorities.

Type 3: *Psychic:* Respondent described an "other worldly" experience in which an extraordinary or supernatural element was present (e.g., ESP, telepathy, out-of-body, contact with spirits). Experiences which were vicarious in nature or which contained mention of religiosity or spirituality in addition to these elements were included.

Type 4: *Faith and consolation:* Experience described mentions religious or spiritual elements, but no indication of the extra-ordinary or the supernatural is given. Experiences were often of a traditional church-related nature.

Thomas and Cooper found that 1 percent of their respondents had had "a genuine mystical experience" (type 2); 8 percent had had the "psychic" (type 3) experience; 16 percent had had the "faith and consolation" (type 4) experience. Of their findings, Thomas and Cooper concluded, among other things, that:

The study provided an almost exact replication of Greeley's (1974) findings, in which over a third of a national sample (35%) believed that they had had an intense spiritual experience. The content analysis from this study suggests that the vast majority of this number could hardly be called mystics. Nevertheless almost 1% of the total sample gave responses which indicated a true mystical experience.* Further, these data indicate that roughly one in 13 persons . . . had undergone some type of intense spiritual experience of the type defined as 'faith and consolation.'[14]

The holy is both known and hidden. It is revealed to human experience, but is not definable in human categories/words/language. The Lakota Sioux Black Elk expressed this paradox. He said:

And while I stood there I saw more than I can tell and I understood more than I saw; for I was seeing in a sacred manner the shapes of all things and the shape of all shapes as they must live together like one being.

John G. Neihardt, *Black Elk Speaks: Being the Life Story of a Holy Man of the Oglala Sioux* (New York: Pocket Books, 1972), p. 36.

---

*For more on mystic and mysticism see pages 272–275.

That the sacred experience can be fearful and imperative was a major theme in a powerful poem written by Francis Thompson°:

> I fled Him down the nights and down the days;
> I fled Him down the arches of the years;
> I fled Him down the labyrinthine ways
>   Of my own mind: and in the midst of tears
> I hid from Him and under running laughter,
>   Up vistaed hopes I sped;
>   And shot, precipitated
>   Adown titanic glooms of chasmed fears,
> From those strong Feet that followed, followed after,
>   But with unperturbed pace,
>   Deliberate speed, majestic instancy
>   They beat—and a Voice beat
>   More instant than the Feet—
> "All things betray thee, who betrayest Me."

For the rest of this poem, see Francis Thompson, "The Hound of Heaven," in *The World's Great Religious Poetry,* ed. Caroline Miles Hill (New York: Macmillan, 1942), pp. 45–49.

NOTES

[1] Jean-Paul Sartre, "Existentialism Is a Humanism," in *Existentialism from Dostoevsky to Sartre,* ed. Walter Kaufmann (Cleveland: World, Meridian Books, 1965), pp. 287–311.

[2] Erich Fromm, *Man for Himself* (New York: Fawcett World Library, 1973), p. 48.

[3] Ibid.

[4] Ibid., p. 50.

[5] Ibid., p. 55.

[6] Ibid., p. 56.

[7] W. Somerset Maugham, "*Sheppey*" (Garden City, N.Y.: Doubleday, 1934). A play.

[8] Julian S. Huxley, *Religion without Revelation* (New York: Harper & Brothers, 1957), p. 110.

[9] Abraham Maslow, *Religious Values and Peak Experiences* (Columbus: Ohio State University Press, 1964), pp. 19–29. See also Maslow's "Lessons from Peak Experiences," *Journal of Humanistic Psychology,* 2 (1962):9–18.

[10] Andrew M. Greeley, *Ecstasy: A Way of Knowing* (Englewood Cliffs, N.J.: Prentice-Hall, 1974).

[11] D. Hay and A. Morisy, "Reports of Ecstatic, Paranormal, or Religious Experience in Great Britain and the United States: A Comparison of Trends," *Journal for the Scientific Study of Religion* 17 (1978):255–268.

[12]C. Kentzer, ''Whatever Turns You On: Triggers to Transcendent Experiences,'' *Journal of Humanistic Psychology* 18 (1979):77–80.

[13]L. Eugene Thomas and Pamela E. Cooper, ''Incidence and Psychological Correlates of Intense Spiritual Experiences,'' *Journal of Transpersonal Psychology* 12 no. 1 (1980):78.

[14]Ibid.

Chapter 3

RELIGIOUS ORIGINS – PRIMITIVE

> ... if oxen and horses ... had hands, and
> could paint with their hands, and produce
> works of art as men do, horses would paint
> the forms of the gods like horses, and oxen
> like oxen ...
>
> *Xenophanes*[°1]

Perhaps a helpful way to approach *religion–what is it?* would be, first, to see how various scholars view its origins among primitive people;* and, second (in the next chapter), how other scholars view its origins in ordinary social structures, or in the peculiarities of the human psyche, or as something started by "God-Himself"—that is, as a sociogenetic phenomenon, or as a psycho-genetic phenomenon, or as a theogenetic phenomenon.

SPECULATIONS OF PRIMITIVE ORIGINS

Animism—A Mistaken Interpretation of Natural Phenomena In the second half of the nineteenth century a number of scholars interested in anthropology and sociology began to zero in on not only the artifacts of ancient primitive people, but, especially, on the societies of living primitives.† Immediately it was recognized that primitives were very religious people. Their worlds were literally full of Gods. In ancient Greece, Thales° (c.624–546 B.C.), the father

---

*The term "primitive" is used in this book not in a pejorative sense. Primitive religions are not "bad religions" or even wrongheaded religions. They are, rather, earlier religions, primordial religions. They are the religions of preliterate people and differ from "high" religions (which we shall subsequently call "consummate" religions) only in style, not in function. In other words, primitive or primordial religions do for preliterate people just what high, or advanced, or consummate religions do for literate people, and often much more directly and effectively.

† There are, according to some estimates, as many as 200 million primitive people alive today, living primarily in Central Africa, South America, North Asia, and the Pacific Islands. See David G. Bradley, *A Guide to the World's Religions* (Englewood Cliffs, N.J.: Prentice-Hall, 1963), p. 10.

29

of Western philosophy, once said that "All things are full of Gods." But according to the discoveries of F. Max Müller° and Edward B. Tylor,° two nineteenth- and early-twentieth-century scholars, this really got said much earlier—in the dawn of human history.

Professor Müller became convinced that religion began in nature worship—that the first humans developed their religions from observing the forces of nature. They observed the regularities in nature—night following day, the seasons rotating, the tides rising and falling, the phases of the moon, the progression of the stars. They responded by sacralizing° and personalizing° these phenomena. They gave names to the sun, moon, stars, days, nights, seasons, years, and began to tell stories about these phenomena. The stories became myths explaining the origin, meaning, and destiny of both world and humans, and why things happened the way they happened. For example, Müller "discovered" that the Greek myth of Apollo and Daphne (wherein Daphne fled from her would-be lover), was a myth about the sun (Apollo) and the dawn (Daphne). Müller concluded that the original primitive story (from which this Greek myth developed) was simply a story of how the sun chases away the dawn each morning. Getting this kind of mythological clue, Müller was convinced he had found the secret to the origin of religion. Primitives observed the forces of nature, personified those forces, told stories about them, and eventually built religion around those stories.

Once, so the story goes, Apollo who was arrogant like his father Zeus (king of the Gods), and like his father inclined to amorous affairs with various females, was observing Daphne, the daughter of the river God Peneus, when Cupid, son of Venus, came by. Apollo, perhaps provoked by the unwelcome intrusion of Venus's cherub son, referring to Cupid's bow and arrows, said sarcastically, "What are you doing with a *man's* weapon? Can't you find something more appropriate for a child to play with?" Angered, Cupid made reply with the very weapon Apollo was decrying, only this time he plucked from his quiver not just a golden love arrow, but also a leaden hate arrow. The golden dart he sent piercing into Apollo; and immediately the great sun God was stricken not with simple desire, but with passionate love for the daughter of Peneus. But Cupid sent the hate arrow flying at the young and beautiful Daphne. Thus did the God Apollo love and the girl Daphne hate. Apollo pursued his new love, but she was too fast for him and disappeared into the forest. The next day Apollo returned, but again Daphne got away, and the next day, and the next. But one day she did not get away. She fled again, her hair streaming out behind her head, her bared legs flashing in the sunlight, but Apollo was gaining on her. He came faster and faster until, when he was about to overtake her, Daphne cried out to her father for help. The river God responded. He transformed his daughter into a laurel tree. But even then Apollo's love for Daphne continued and the laurel tree became his sign forever more.

With this thinking, Müller placed himself in the camp of those who identify the origins of religion with *animism* (a Latin word that means breath or soul), a position that holds that religion started when primitive mankind, all the way back to Neanderthal man,° populated the world with spirits and Gods. According to Müller, primitives populated the world with spirits; then told stories about those spirits. In civilized antiquity those stories became the myths about which more elaborate religions were formed.

Like Müller, Edward B. Tylor promoted animism as the source of religion. Religion originated, he held, when primitive people mistook natural objects and events as "acting subjects," and then proceeded to give those subjects human attributes and personal names. For example, prehistoric humans might look upon the wind as alive, even as people were alive, and sometimes the wind was "happy" and sometimes it was "angry," even as people were happy and angry.* Like Müller, Tylor contends that religion began when primitives rationalized the forces of nature and gave those forces feelings, emotions, passions, thoughts, and names—when manlikeness was erroneously read into nature. Tylor then further proposed[2] that primitives had trouble distinguishing between dreams and reality, and from this difficulty and confusion the ideas of souls and life after death emerged. Primitive people came to believe that there was something in living things that went out of them when they died. That something was not like a stick or a stone, which could be touched and held, but was like smoke or breath. When that something, that breath, that soul, departed the body permanently, the body never lived again. But that something might leave the body only temporarily, as when it went adventuring in dreams but was back in the morning. Furthermore, even when the soul departed the body permanently, the souls of the dead sometimes came back in dreams and visions. They could be seen and heard, and they looked like, or almost like, the body they formerly inhabited. They were ethereal duplicates—ghosts.

Tylor correctly observed that once people grasped the idea that human life was composed of two parts (physical and spiritual), it was but a short step to spiritualizing not only human life, but all life, and all sorts of nonliving things as well. The animation seen in humans and nonhumans was caused by souls. The world was full of souls—full of Gods.

Whether or not Müller and Tylor were right that religion actually originated from prehistoric humans' endowing natural phenomena with human characteristics and names does not alter the fact that religious people still often "rationalize" the world and endow it with living, spiritual agents—with

---

*People still sometimes humanize and personalize nonhuman things and events. No man with a tiller of his own ever thinks of his boat as "it" or doubts that "she" is as emotional and capricious and self-willed as any real woman ever was. Annually we characterize the passing year as an old man, and the new year as a diapered infant. The biological environment in springtime is a mother. And, according to Carl Sandburg, "fog comes in on little cat feet."

spirits, souls, demons, Gods and/or God, saints, angels, and other supernatural beings.

Animism is by many scholars no longer held to be the earliest form of religion, the genesis of religion, (as Tylor and Müller thought), but religions, old and new, primitive and modern, have not discarded the notion that humans are composite beings, both physical and spiritual, and that the soul animates and survives and that, if not always in nature itself, there is behind nature, causing and animating it, something spiritual called by such names as Brahman or Heaven or Tao or God.

> To many North American Indians, Thunderbird is the Great Spirit of storm clouds, lightning, thunder, and rain. Lightning is the flashing of his eyes; thunder the noise of his wings.
>
> He is assisted by other birds, especially hawks and eagles. One in particular is Dew Eagle (Oshadages), who puts out forest and prairie fires. When fires rage, Dew Eagle finally comes carrying water on the feathers of his back, as dew gathers on the grass. He flaps his wings, the water falls, the fire is put out, and the forest and prairie can begin again.
>
> Thunderbird himself has an even more significant role in the life of the world, for without Thunderbird, bringer of rain, the earth would parch, the forests wilt, the grass die.

Mana—A Response to Power In both Müller's and Tylor's contentions, religion began when primitive people "rationalized" some of their experiences. It was a "logical inference" drawn from experiences. Other students of primitive anthropology believe that religion came before theology, before rational explanation. It was prelogical. Religion predated logical inferences and arose originally simply as the emotions of awe and fear *felt* by prehistoric people as they confronted "the powers" in their world. Such people did not live in a "universe," in a world where order has been discerned in, or imposed upon, nature. They lived in a world where "out there" were wildness and destruction and chaos and perpetual danger. They lived in a world where everything devoured everything else—where only the fit survived, and even the fit eventually fell to be devoured by scavengers and rot. They lived amid powers, and they responded to the powers, propitiating, avoiding, using those powers in any way they possibly, pragmatically could.

In 1891 Bishop Codrington[3] reacted against the idea that religion had begun in logical speculations about the character of man and nature. From Codrington's encounter with the religious expressions of living primitives, people of the Melanesian Archipelago, he concluded that religion originated prelogically in man's response to the experience of impersonal power in his world. The Melanesians had a word for this power—*mana*.* Mana, and functionally equivalent terms in other cultures, is a word for the power or the powers that made things special: the power in hurricanes and storms, in charismatic men, in seductive women, in great artists and warriors, in medicine men and prophets—in all marvelous and awesome things. Mana was not a living spirit, was not good or bad, was not friendly or unfriendly. It was just power—sheer, special power. Codrington observed that mana was not something that people "concluded" about nature, but something they encountered in special circumstances.

Concurring with Codrington, Professor R. R. Marett,° in 1900, wrote a widely read and influential article entitled, "Pre-Animistic Religion."[4] In that article he forcefully contended that religion predated rational speculations about humans and nature. It began in the sense of awe felt by early people as they experienced the impersonal powers encountered everywhere in their world—those powers causing things to be, sometimes intriguing, sometimes terrifying, usually dangerous, often desirable, and always awesome. Not inferred souls or assigned names, but experienced power, Marett held (as did Codrington), was the genesis of religion.

Whether or not mana was the genesis of religion and the "father" of the Gods may be argued, but the fact is that mana, differently named and extremely theologized, remains a central dynamic† of religion. When Rudolf Otto speaks of the *numinous* experience he is surely talking about what various primitives call *mana, orenda, wakanda, ngai, kalou,* and other equivalent names.†† And when Paul Tillich speaks of the Power of Being, or Being Itself, or the Ground of Being, and a Hindu philosopher speaks of Brahman, one might seriously ask, how, except in sophistication, does their God behind the Gods differ from mana?

The Prelogical Character   It is important to take special notice of the prelogical, prerational aspect of religious phenomena. People act before they think. They are alive before they are rational. They are, as existentialists, such as

---

*Later it was discovered that primitive people in many other places had equivalent terms for such a power: in North America Eskimos (Inuits) called it *Inua;* Iroquois called it *Orenda* when good and *Otgon* when bad; Hurons called it *Oki;* Siouans called it *Wakanda;* Algonquins called it *Manitou* (or *Manitu*). Among the Malagasy the term is *Anadriamanitra;* the Masai call it *Ngai,* the Fijians call it *Kalou.* According to Hartley B. Alexander in *The Mythology of All Races: North American* (New York: Cooper Square, 1964, p. 8), these words all mean power, mystery, magic, or, more commonly, spirit of medicine.

† Manaism is also called dynamism.

†† The German theologian Rudolf Otto applied the idea of mana to theology and proposed that religious experience tends to prove the existence of unseen force—the *numinous* (mana) before which people stand in awe and with which they interact.

Sartre, tell us, in existence before their essence (humanness) is accomplished. Thinking and reasoning come after experience or, at least, concurrent with experience—and this is so not only where individual humans are concerned, but it must have been so in the emergence of mankind. Let us enter a fictitious time machine for a few moments and be transported back in time a half-million years or so, to a primeval forest somewhere on the continent of Europe, perhaps in what is now called France or Spain. We see a man or near man, fleeing from some enemy. Our man stumbles. Where he falls there is, quite by accident, a broken tree branch of hand-size diameter and about three feet long. He seizes it, turns and bashes in the head of his attacker. Having slain his enemy, he looks at the club and thinks, "That's a good thing for bashing heads."

This simple little fictitious account makes a fundamental point not only about the genesis of weaponry, but also about the genesis of religion. Observe: The man did not think to himself, "That tree branch over there will make a good weapon," and then pick it up and use it. He picked it up first, used it, and then thought about it. He was in the condition of weaponry, before he comprehended weaponry.

On another day, with his trusty club in hand, our man went forth to bash a bear for dinner, or anything else he could find. He guessed that the bear might be in the rocks where the bear caves were. The rocks were beyond the swamp. He did not like the swamp. It was full of powers—full of frightening and dangerous "things." Not things like bears or wolves, but things you could not really see. Things that suddenly opened their mouths and sucked you in. Things that got inside you and made fire in your gut—things weird, demonic, unseen. He would prefer to avoid the swamp. But it was a long way around the swamp, and only a little way through it. As he hesitated, he observed that he had come to the edge of the swamp at a point he had never been before, at a place where there was a most fantastic tree, very old, very gnarled and wind-bent, but very strong, very powerful, full of mightiness. He sensed that it was a *special tree*. A tree afraid of nothing. A tree stronger than the swamp things. He did not think such things exactly; he felt them along his spine. Coming closer to the tree he saw a place on the trunk where the bark had been rubbed smooth by passing animals, perhaps. He touched the smooth place. It was good to touch, to slide his hand over. Somehow it made him feel strong—like the tree. After a short time spent gazing at the tree and touching it, he continued his journey through the swamp to the other side, without mishap, unassailed by the things. And on the other side he had good luck. He did not even have to fight a bear. He found and bashed a ram instead. After that he crossed the swamp many times, but always first he went to the place of The Tree and touched the smooth spot. At first he did not think of why he sought The Tree, he just did so. Later, maybe, he started to think about it but only after The Tree had, in fact, become a thing of "religion," and his performance a "religious act."

Our primitive man, or near man, was in the "condition of religion" (as well as the "condition of weaponry") before he ever comprehended it, before he rationalized it. Primitive people may have *happened* into religion before they ever happened to understand it. Primordial people must have been terrified by lightning, stricken with diseases, and devastated by death before they ever began to comprehend these extraordinary powers and began to give them names and explanations, and to devise ways to deal with them in some hopeful, spiritual fashion.

Magic—Introducing Extranatural/Supernatural Power into Natural Processes   One method that primitive people used (and still use) to deal with "the powers" in their world is called magic. Magic is the direct control of nature by the employment of extranatural/supernatural power. It is ubiquitous in primitive religion and not unknown in "civilized" religions, even the religions of modern, scientific cultures. There is obviously some kind of affinity between magic and religion, so it seems reasonable to ask how they are alike and different, and how they are related to each other.

The Scottish classicist and anthropologist Sir James George Frazer° (1854–1941) who, in his multivolumed work *The Golden Bough,* presented pioneering investigations on the nature of magic and religion, concluded that magic (being the simpler form) was the forerunner of religion. The basic difference between magic and religion, he observed, was in the attitude and expectation of the person using each. In magic it was believed and expected that desired results could be accomplished by a direct manipulation of the environment through the direct employment of supernatural or extranatural techniques. Men (usually special men—magicians or shamans) who were privy to the supernatural techniques for controlling the powers of nature could control or coerce those powers to accomplish desired human ends. Thus, according to Frazer's calculations, magic was for primitive mankind not only the forerunner of religion but a form of science and technology. Like science and technology, magic understood the laws governing nature and could directly manipulate those laws for human benefit. Thus magic, Frazer held, was different from religion. Religion did not attempt directly to control the powers of nature; rather, it made an appeal to those powers or, more correctly, to the supernatural agents that controlled those powers. Frazer believed that religion developed when primitive people: (1) grew dissatisfied with the accomplishments of magic, and (2) advanced in their thinking to the point where they began to conceive of their world animistically, as being dominated by spirits in nature (animism) and, to some extent, by the souls of departed humans (ancestors). They began to perform rites intended to propitiate the Gods, not coerce them. They began to behave in ways that amounted to worship and genuine religion. Magic continued, but religion moved to center stage. It became the dominant actor in the drama of life and death in a menacing world.

This claim that magic predated religion has been generally discredited by modern anthropologists. However, Frazer's recognition of a difference between magic and what he called "religion," but what we shall later call "rogation," is legitimate and valuable in understanding that aspect of religion we shall later call "metatechnology,"* which is a term that stands for all attempts to go beyond (meta) technology and introduce extranatural/supernatural power into natural processes. In magic one gets a shaman to bring about (or attempt to bring about), through a direct manipulation of extranatural/supernatural power, a desired result. In rogation, which means "to beseech," one attempts (usually through a priest) to get the Gods or spirits to bring about a desired result.

*See pages 60–66.

Magic is employed where human desire outruns human ability. If natural skill cannot suffice, is it possible that extranatural/supernatural skill can? Magic is one attempt to answer in the affirmative. So thought and still think, primitive people, and many people not called primitive. With magic one expects to control mana, and sometimes even, perhaps, spirits. Ancient Hindu priests, for example, came to think that a rightly performed ritual contained the power (Brahmanaspati) to coerce both people and Gods.

Magic, then, is a matter of knowledge and skill. If one knows the rules of magic and employs them correctly, supernatural coercion occurs. This sort of magical control can take several forms, for example, imitative magic, or black magic, or fetish magic.

Imitative magic functions on the principle of look alike, act alike. If one draws a picture of a stag being shot down with arrows, and, perhaps, conducts a special sacred performance imitating a successful hunting exploit, a live stag in the forest will be, may be, is hoped to be, assailed by not only human hunters, but also by supernatural power. A successful hunt is thus assured. When bad hunting means hunger, good magic is exceedingly important.

Other examples of imitative magic are to be seen in the practice of going out into the fields and jumping straight up, up, up, up, in order magically to induce the crops to grow tall—as tall as a man can jump. Also, there are those primitive people who end a drought by throwing pebbles down a hill and at the same time shout, "Boom! Boom!" imitating raindrops falling and thunder booming. (If one performs this way long enough success is guaranteed. Given enough time the rain always comes; at least, it always has.)

And then, of course, there is *black magic*—bad magic used to cripple or destroy a human enemy. Pins in voodoo* dolls, one sometimes hears, are still sometimes employed in this sort of magic, as is the "evil eye." Pins in dolls is imitation black magic. There is also contagious black magic where

*More correctly spelled vodum.

bits of purloined hair or fingernail parings or clothing are utilized to bring dark happenings to a designated victim. On display in the British Museum in London is a "pointing bone," a long, slender bone with a thong of hair attached. When a magician points this bone at a person and chants a death spell, that person is supposed to die. People who believe in the power of the pointing bone, and see and hear the magic performed against them, may do just that—die.

There is also *fetish magic*. The term "fetish" properly means any sort of power in inanimate objects. The fetish objects may be natural, such as a special stone or a bone or a rabbit's foot. They may also be manufactured, such as amulets, love potions, lucky coins.

In all this the thing to note is that magic is controlled by people. Magicians (shamans) make the magic all by themselves. They manipulate supernatural power. They need no spirits or Gods to assist them. When people go beyond magic and begin to appeal to spirits or Gods, or both, they are engaging in something other than magic.

Frazer's hypotheses that magic preceded religion and that it was the primitive person's substitute for science and technology were soon seriously challenged by other students of primitive life. It was pointed out that there was no evidence that magic came first, or that religion evolved when magic failed. Primitive people practiced both magic and religion, and they did so often in the same magico-religious rite. The primitives often propitiated and coerced in the same breath, so to speak. Indeed, Wilhelm Schmidt° tried to reverse Frazer's contention and argued that the religion of primitive people began in the experience and worship of a High God,* and that only later did their religion devolve into the religious beliefs and practices called animism, ancestor worship, and magic.

Paul Radin presents two images of the High God found among American Indians. One image is of God as supreme deity, just and rational, but far away. The other image is of God as a trickster, who is not always just or fair, and is not remote, but intervenes in the lives of humans. For example, to the Crow Indians of Montana, the sun is the supreme deity, but Coyote, the trickster, is also a God, and his activities are important, and often times capricious.

See Radin's article "Monotheism Among American Indians," in *Teachings from the American Earth*, ed. D. Tedlock and B. Tedlock (New York: Liveright, 1975), pp. 224ff.

*Father Wilhem Schmidt, an Australian, pointed out in his book *Der Ursprung der Gottesidee* (The Origin of the God-Idea) that many primitive religions in Australia and Africa held a common belief in a distant High God.

Schmidt's theory of the origins of primitive religion has been generally less acceptable than Frazer's. Probably the most reasonable position to take for the moment is to say that both magic and religion (rogation) should be viewed as two associated ways in which primitive people saw themselves and their world and tried to cope.

That magic was the primitive's science and technology was also challenged. Bronislaw Malinowski,° reporting on the religion of the Trobriand Islanders,° made a special point of the fact that Trobrianders employed both magic and natural technology (science) in their programs for food getting and health, and that they never mistook the one for the other.[5] When it was time to build a canoe for deep-sea fishing, or to plant a garden, or to medicate for a simple ailment, they did so "scientifically," that is, by rules and procedures based on natural law and technological know-how. When, however, they wanted to infuse their boats and farm plots with extranatural powers, or deal with serious illnesses, they suspended their technology for the performance of magic. Protection from bad storms at sea, from droughts and insect infestation, and from deadly maladies (none of which was understood or directly controllable by their normal technology) demanded different, more potent forms of belief and action. Those beliefs and actions were not scientific (dealing with natural laws), but supernaturalistic (dealing with the supernatural powers in and behind nature). Science and technology dealt with natural order, and magic dealt with the supernatural order. One was not the other, and Malinowski's Trobrianders never mistook the one for the other, or used the one for the other, or identified the one with the other.

Frazer's distinction between magic and religion (rogation) as direct and indirect methods of effecting change in the life and world of human beings invites further consideration. He points out that magic was used to alter natural situations by the direct, human-manipulated employment of special "lawful" powers. In this it has a real affinity with science and technology. In science the laws are viewed as natural, in magic as supernatural, but in both cases humans are the direct agents controlling the change. Religion as rogation operates indirectly, appealing to the Gods to change things, which, unlike in magic and scientific technology, people cannot change by their own manipulation of law and power.

Observe, however, that the important "human" thing occurring here is not some nice distinction between methodologies but the fact that desired changes are being made, or are believed to be being made. This is the real and basic affinity between magic and rogation. Things that cannot be altered naturally can be altered supernaturally.

NOTES

[1] From the "Fragments of Xenophanes," quoted in W. T. Jones, *A History of Western Philosophy* (New York: Harcourt Brace, 1952), p. 41.

[2] Edward B. Tylor, *Religion in Primitive Culture* (New York: Harper & Row, 1958; first published, 1871).

[3] R. H. Codrington, *The Melanesians* (New York: Dover, 1972).

[4] See R. R. Marett, *The Threshold of Religion* (London: Methuen and Co., 1909; Ann Arbor, Mich., and London: University Film International, 1979). This document contains lectures delivered by Marett on various occasions; "Pre-Animistic Religion" (1900) is among them. Other important essays in the book are: "From Spell to Prayer"; "Is Taboo Negative Magic?" (a *Festschrift* article celebrating Edward B. Tylor's seventy-fifth birthday, October 2, 1907); "The Conception of Mana"; and "A Sociological View of Comparative Religions."

[5] See Bronislaw Malinowski, *Magic, Science and Religion* (Glencoe, Ill.: Free Press, 1948), pp. 1–18.

Chapter 4

OTHER SPECULATIONS

. . . religion, when it is being examined within the framework of science, is dealt with as part of the natural world, subject to the laws of cause and effect and the rules of logic.

J. Milton Yinger[1]

Religion exists not as a dull habit, but as an acute fever.

William James[2]

SOCIOGENETIC PHENOMENON

Much of what we have said so far, especially with reference to religion as emerging from mankind's reading of its own emotions into nature (Müller), or from misreading dream persons as being disembodied souls (Tylor), or from magic as a technique for coercing nature (Frazer), seems to base religion in faulty primitive thinking. These speculations (animism, mana, magic) saw religion as originating in fantasies and unreality. It arose out of human illusion. But the sociologist Émile Durkheim (1858–1917) flatly rejected such a notion. Religion, he said, is based in the solid facts of social experience. It is, in all its various forms, the product of "social consciousness." Humans everywhere (and this is critical to religion) regard some things as sacred and some things as profane; sacred being behavior essential for social survival, profane being ordinary behavior for individual accommodation. Durkheim stated, "Sacred things are those *representations* [that] society itself has fashioned. . . . Profane things, conversely, are those things which each of us constructs from our own sense data and experience."[3] In order to survive society lays demands on people, for example, respect for authority, obedience to laws, adherence to moral rules, honor of the home place. There is also a sense of mysterious forces binding together the community, be it tribe or nation, into something very special, even sacred. All of this, and more, is simply "writ large" and becomes the transcendent divine community: the

40

basis for religious beliefs and practices, the community's faith and ritual. Secular (social) experience is given transcendent value. It is given sacred status. This sort of thing makes it possible to explain such questions as, Where did we come from? Why are we as we are? If, for example, someone would ask, "How come some of us are chiefs and some Indians?" the answer for the status quo could be readily forthcoming: "Because long ago in the *dream time,* when the Old One created the earth and the sky and our people, he decreed it that way—some chiefs, some Indians." Of course, Durkheim would say that actually this explanation has the cart before the horse. The cause-effect is in reverse. First came the essential aspects of the society (the items and attitudes necessary for social survival), which were then, partly because they were mysterious, given sacred status. And they were mysterious because they were learned not as ordinary things are learned in direct, critical experience, but as the teaching lore of the culture, be it primitive or civilized. Because the learning is in this fashion, the question about chiefs and Indians would probably never be asked. In the learning of childhood and puberty the young person would already have been told that things are as they are, as everyone knows, because of the Gods.

From his study of Australian primitives (the Aruntas), Durkheim believed he had discovered that the "elemental task" of even the "most simple religions is to maintain in a positive manner, the normal course of [social life],"[4] which means among other things, that just as religion gains its form and structure from the social setting, so also it works to preserve that social setting. On the one hand, for example, the hierarchical form of the Roman Catholic Church is no accident. It is a direct parallel to the totalitarian form of the Roman government existing at the time of Constantine,° the first Roman emperor who was a Christian. He ruled from 306 to 337. Even the elaborate garb worn by Catholic bishops and archbishops was patterned after the Roman governors and other high government officials. Society structures religion, but on the other hand, religion also plays a major role in the formation and conservation of social structures. In *The Elementary Forms of the Religious Life,* Durkheim argues:

> It can be said that religion has played a strategic part in the human enterprise of world-building. . . . Religion implies that human order is projected into the totality of being. Put differently, religion is the audacious attempt to conceive of the entire universe as being humanly significant.[5]

The basis for religion, then, according to Durkheim, was society. Religious beliefs and practices had their origins in social forces. It was society itself that first aroused the experience of divinity in the minds of its individual members. From the forces of society in controlling its individual members arose the notion of superior power and inversely the notion of personal dependence. The moral authority of society over its members engendered a sense of sacred demand controlling each individual life. Society dominated individual members in spiritual ways effecting attitudes of reverence and submission and veneration. It was to the society that one must turn to find nurture and self-meaning. And all of this led to the feeling that there were forces and "active causes from which [man] gets the characteristic attributes of his nature, and which, as benevolent powers, assist him, protect him, and assure him a privileged fate."[6]

Society established religious attitudes, sentiments, and concepts which in turn rewarded society by effecting cohesiveness in the system and by giving sustenance and courage to society's human participants. It was religion that sacralized certain structures within the sociocultural system and thus endowed that system with cohesiveness and spiritual power. It was religion that constrained people and curbed antisocial passions, often with the threat of divine punishment. On the other hand, it was religion that assisted individual persons in finding themselves and fulfilling themselves within the confines, protection, warmth, and nurture of an essential communal life.

There is no doubt that society is basic to human life. Humans cannot begin to exist or survive, or even become "human," as George Mead° has made so emphatically evident, except in a structure of sociality. There is, also, no doubt that religion is affected by (in Durkheim's terms, produced by), and affects, the social structure. Society informs religion. The religious expression is always connected with the language, science, and mores of the social culture where it resides. On the other hand, religion sanctifies society. It idealizes the social system and makes it, or some important part of it, more than ordinary; makes it sacred.

With Durkheim one views religion as a sociogenetic phenomenon—a phenomenon produced by society or social forces—which is different from seeing it as arising in animism or manaism or magic. This perspective does not dispense with the insights we have observed in the work of the anthropologists of religion. It simply adds to them, and clues us to the possibility of viewing religion from still other perspectives for other possible insights.

Actually the first modern thinker to state clearly that religion is a projection of the human self-consciousness and self-image into the nature of things was the German philosopher Ludwig Feuerbach° (1804–1872). Especially in his *The Essence of Christianity* (1841), he asserted that our religious life depends on our wishes. We project our own human qualities into the "supernatural." We believe in love and justice; ergo, God is the essence of love and justice. This anthropomorphism is especially strong, Feuerbach argued, in the Old Testament (Jewish Bible) in which Yahweh merely represents the tribal traits of the ancient Hebrews. Religion, he claimed, actually represents our inner urges and desires that we try to impose upon the cosmos. At the core of all religions there are God images that are really (as Xenophanes° long before had suggested) human images projected, as in a Japanese lantern, into the supernatural world. Religion is really no more than "the relation of man to himself, or more correctly to his own nature."

Ludwig Feuerbach, *The Essence of Christianity* (New York: Harper & Row, 1957), p. 5.

Religion is more than a simple projection of the social structure on the human image into the supernatural. It is also a projection of the aspirations of humans. It represents not only the *actual* situation, but also the religious community's dream of ideal possibilities. When Yahweh was depicted as a "man of war" (Exodus 15:3), he represented the character of Hebrew life at that ancient time; but when Micah envisioned a time when in God's power swords would be plowshares and spears would be pruning hooks and no one would "learn war anymore" (Micah 4:3), he was seeing religion as a fantastic potential of the human character. Again when in the first John letter in the New Testament it is stated that "God is love," we have an affirmation that even though love is not the central dynamic of this contemporary world, it can be the hope and the dream and the religious expectation of another someday world.

Max Weber° (1864–1920) was another sociologist who, like Durkheim, examined the interdependence of religion and society—the mutually inter-creative and intercontrolling aspects of the sacred and the profane dimensions of human life. He especially noted the intricate involvement of religion and economics. In his *Sociology of Religion* he stated that "[t]he ends of religious actions are predominantly economic."[7] It is from the economic activities of a people that their symbols and creeds about the nature of religion and the Gods are derived. For example, a nomadic people such as the ancient Israelites had a nomadic, hunting, traveling-with-them-God—God Yahweh.° Ancient agrarian people had farmer (fertility) Gods, as did the Israelites once they settled in Palestine and became farmers. There they added to their nomadic God Yahweh, an array of Canaanite° fertility Gods called Baals.

In his outstanding work *The Protestant Ethic and the Spirit of Capitalism* especially, Weber pointed out how the central concepts, attitudes, and practices of Protestant Christianity (for example, the priesthood of each individual, distrust of hierarchal authority, austere living, hard work) laid the ground for the emergence of the modern industrial state and modern capitalism. After all, God expected each person to be responsible for his or her own life, to work hard, to be frugal, to save, to take concern for others, and to be religious as well. Put this all together and you are on your way to free enterprise, profits, millionaires, philanthropy, as well as "pie-in-the-sky"—which epithet itself implies the affinity of religion and economics.

Durkheim, Weber, and others* were right at least about the close connection between religion and the socioeconomic structures of human societies. Religion, whether or not it started as a sociological projection, has certainly acted as a power directing society, and as a controlling dynamic in political systems, and this is certainly not new. It is at least as old as those primitive societies in which the social structure and political power is said to have been established by The-Old-One-In-The-Sky-Far-Away who long ago created the tribe and set its social and political structures. Again, history records religion as a controlling dynamic in the magnificent theocracy of ancient Israel, in the Christian political-social domination of medieval Europe, in the pristine dominance of Islam in the Near East, and more recently, in the Protestant ethic that so affected the spirit of modern capitalism.

PSYCHOGENETIC PHENOMENON

One fruitful perspective is the view of religion that sees it as a psychogenetic phenomenon. William James° (1842–1910), a pioneer thinker in the field of modern psychology of religion, held that all our knowledge of ourselves and our world begins in our own experience, in consciousness. Sigmund Freud° (1856–1939), of psychoanalytic fame, insisted that we are what we have experienced. And Edmund Husserl° (1859–1938) created a method of philosophical analysis called phenomenology,° which purports to lay bare the very essence of experience—our basic consciousness, which he called the transcendental ego. In each case—in James's radical empiricism, Freud's psychoanalyzed personality, and Husserl's transcendental ego—religion appeared as a primary datum.

William James argued that on both psychological grounds and philosophical (pragmatic) grounds we have ample reasons for endorsing religion as valid and worthy, and for pursuing its benefits. First, James offered demonstrations that people have a capacity for genuine religious experience. They have experiences that assure them of a "something there," a something more, that is extraordinary—mysterious, awesome, frightening, divine. Second, through religion people experience transformation of personal life. And third, through religion one can be "turned-on" to dynamic, exciting, joyous life.

First then—the "something there." James opens his chapter "The Reality of the Unseen," in his *Varieties of Religious Experience,* with a statement declaring that in the broadest sense, religion "consists of the belief that there is an unseen order, and that our supreme good lies in harmoniously adjusting ourselves thereto."[8] For many people, James observes that this belief is experienced primarily as an idea (as a belief), but for others it is an existential

*See especially Peter Berger's *Sacred Canopy* (New York: Doubleday, 1969).

experience sometimes so vividly presented that it is reported as a sensible vision.

From an examination of reports concerning this phenomenon of an "unseen order," made especially by persons who declared their encounters with the "divine presence" to be direct experiential encounters, James stated:

> . . . the whole array of our instances leads to a conclusion something like this: It is as if there were in human consciousness a *sense of reality, a feeling of objective presence, a perception* of what we may call "something there," more deep and more general than any of the special and particular "senses" by which the current psychology supposes existent realities to be originally revealed.[9]

As noted earlier on page 6, John Taylor calls his numinous experience an *ordinary* conspiracy, a nodding of life to life. James identifies it as being at times not ordinary, but remarkably extraordinary. We cited one such experience as recorded by James. Many other similar reports can be found in *The Varieties*, but perhaps two more short accounts of this remarkable sense of "something there" will suffice. From the *Journal of Psychical Research* James quotes:

> 'I had read,' the narrator says, 'some twenty minutes or so, was thoroughly absorbed in the book, my mind was perfectly quiet, and for the time being my friends were quite forgotten, when suddenly without a moment's warning my whole being seemed roused to the highest state of tension or aliveness, and I was aware, with an intenseness not easily imagined by those who had never experienced it, that another being or presence was not only in the room, but quite close to me. I put my book down, and although my excitement was great, I felt quite collected, and not conscious of any sense of fear. . . .'[10]

Again, from E. Gurney's *Phantasms of the Living,* James quotes:

> Quite early in the night I was awakened. . . . I felt as if I had been aroused intentionally, and at first thought some one was breaking into the house. . . . I then turned on my side to go to sleep again, and immediately felt a consciousness of a presence in the room, and singular to state, it was not the consciousness of a live person, but I can only tell you the facts as they occurred to me. I do not know how to better describe my sensations than by simply stating that I felt a consciousness of a spiritual presence. . . .[11]

First then, James observes that many people have, or intensely believe they have, extraordinary experiences that assure them of the reality of an unseen order. Second, James observes that this kind of experience and belief can and does transform human lives. It reorganizes the "psychic set"[12] so that persons become, as it were, new persons. They experience and respond to situations in a totally different manner. James makes this argument most persuasively in his two chapters on conversion in *The Varieties*. He opens his argument saying:

To be converted, to be regenerated, to receive grace, to experience religion, to gain an assurance, are so many phrases which denote the process, gradual or sudden, by which a self hitherto divided, and consciously wrong inferior and unhappy, becomes unified and consciously right superior and happy, in consequence of its firmer hold upon religious realities.[13]

James then proceeds to give reports of persons whose lives have been so transformed. Several could be selected as examples, but one, perhaps, will suffice—that of S. H. Hadley, reported first in Hadley's pamphlet *Rescue Mission Work,* published at the Old Jerry M'Auley Water Street Mission in New York City. It depicts vividly the transformation of Hadley's life from a drunken, bumbling disorder, to one of poise and control through the psychic power of religious belief and experience.

"One Tuesday evening I sat in a saloon in Harlem, a homeless, friendless, dying drunkard. I had pawned or sold everything that would bring a drink. I could not sleep unless I was dead drunk. I had not eaten for days, and for four nights preceding I had suffered with delirium tremens, or the horrors, from midnight till morning. I had often said, 'I will never be a tramp. I will never be cornered, for when that time comes, if ever it comes, I will find a home in the bottom of the river.' But the Lord so ordered it that when that time did come I was not able to walk one quarter of the way to the river. As I sat there thinking, I seemed to feel some great and mighty presence. I did not know then what it was. I did learn afterwards that it was Jesus, the sinner's friend. I walked up to the bar and pounded it with my fist till I made the glasses rattle. Those who stood by drinking looked on with scornful curiosity. I said I would never take another drink, if I died on the street, and really I felt as though that would happen before morning. Something said 'If you want to keep this promise, go and have yourself locked up.' I went to the nearest station-house and had myself locked up.

"I was placed in a narrow cell, and it seemed as though all the demons that could find room came in that place with me. This was not all the company I had, either. No, praise the Lord; that dear Spirit that came to me in the saloon was present, and said, Pray. I did pray, and though I did not feel any great help, I kept on praying. As soon as I was able to leave my cell I was taken to the police court and remanded back to the cell. I was finally released, and found my way to my brother's house, where every care was given me. While lying in bed the admonishing Spirit never left me, and when I arose the following Sabbath morning I felt that day would decide my fate, and toward evening it came into my head to go to Jerry M'Auley's Mission. I went. The house was packed, and with great difficulty I made my way to the space near the platform. There I saw the apostle to the drunkard and the outcast—that man of God, Jerry M'Auley. He rose, and amid deep silence told his experience. There was a sincerity about this man that carried conviction with it, and I found myself saying, 'I wonder if God can save *me*?' I listened to the testimony of twenty-five or thirty persons, every one of whom had been saved from rum, and I made up my mind that I would be saved or die right there. When the invitation was given, I knelt down with a crowd of drunkards. Jerry made the first prayer. Then Mrs. M'Auley prayed fervently for us. Oh, what a conflict was going on for my poor soul! A blessed whisper said, 'Come'; the devil said, 'Be careful.' I halted but a moment, and then, with a breaking heart, I said 'Dear Jesus, can you help me?' Never with mortal tongue can I describe that moment. Although up to that moment my soul had been filled with indescribable gloom, I felt that glorious brightness of the noonday sun shine into my heart. I felt I was a free man. Oh, the precious feeling of safety, of freedom, of resting on Jesus! I felt that Christ with all his brightness and power had come into my life; that, indeed, old things had passed away and all things had become new.

"From that moment till now I have never wanted a drink of whiskey, and I have never seen money enough to make me take one. I promised God that night that if he would take away the appetite for strong drink, I would work for him all my life. He has done his part, and I have been trying to do mine."[14]

Religion can make a tremendous psychological difference. It can and does transform human life.

James was not only a psychologist concerned with the psychology of religion, but a philosopher concerned with religion. He was one of the three or four founders of the American philosophy called Pragmatism.* Pragmatism is, according to James, "first a method, and second, a generic theory of what is meant by truth."[15] The aim of Pragmatism is to understand things, not according to their essences or ideal or transcendent forms, but according to their functions and values. In his essay "What Pragmatism Means," James wrote that Pragmatism is "*[t]he attitude of looking away from first things, principles, 'categories,' supposed necessities; and of looking towards last things, fruits, consequences, facts.*"[16] In Pragmatism one tries to arrive at conclusions "by tracing" the pertinent "practical consequences" of the subject involved. In religion, for example, the primary question would not be "Does there exist a God we can believe in?" but "What are the human consequences of believing that God exists?" In other words, what difference does it make in practical living whether or not one believes in God's existence; and in the existence of a particular kind of God? If believing makes a difference, the question is *real*. If believing makes a substantial difference, the question is *momentous*. If believing one way or another cannot be avoided, the question is *forced*.

In his philosophical essay, "The Will to Believe," James, among other things, addressed the question of sufficient evidence for belief. There are those who insist that we should not believe anything unless we have sufficient empirical (scientific) evidence to prove it. James agreed partly. Don't believe anything where there is sufficient evidence to the contrary (for example, don't believe that you can jump out of a tree and not fall; or trust a liar to tell the truth; or a barking dog not to bite; in each case there is sufficient evidence to the contrary). But in those live, momentous, forced circumstances (where a

*Other leading figures in the establishment of Pragmatism were Charles Peirce, John Dewey,° George Mead,° Edwin Starbuck.

decision must be made, such as whether there is a God) where there is insufficient evidence to the contrary, we have a right to believe what we need to believe in order to live life to the fullest.

Our passional nature not only lawfully may, but must, decide an option between propositions, whenever it is a genuine option that cannot by its nature be decided on intellectual grounds; for to say, under such circumstances, "Do not decide, but leave the question open," is itself a passional decision—just like deciding yes or no— and is attended with the same risk of losing the truth. [17]

[W]e have the right to believe at our own risk any *hypothesis that is live enough to tempt our will.* [18]

Before William James did so, Blaise Pascal° (1623–1662), an eminent French mathematician, had also proposed the inevitability of choosing either for God's existence or against it (either for religion or against it). The decision not to make up your mind is, in fact, a decision against God's existence (against religion). Pascal then went on to argue that one could not choose for or against God on rational grounds. The proofs for God simply do not prove, but a decision has to be made. How shall we choose then? How shall we wager? Well, Pascal argued, wager to win. If God exists, and you choose the religious life, you win eternity. If God does not exist, what do you win? You don't win anything—which is exactly what you win if you vote against God's existence in the first place. This sort of arguing is called Pascal's Wager: If a person wagers *for* the existence of God (and he must wager because a decision has to be made) and God exists, then the individual gains the infinite (Heaven). If God does not exist, there is no loss. On the other hand, if a person wagers *against* God's existence and God does exist, then there is infinite loss (damnation). So by wagering for God's existence one has everything to lose and nothing to gain.

For the text of this argument see Blaise Pascal's *Pensées,* published in New York by E. P. Dutton and Co., 1958, Section III, pp. 52–70.

James felt that the logical and empirical evidence for belief in God, and therefore support of the religious commitment, was not sufficiently commanding either to demand belief and commitment or to deny it. There is, indeed, evidence supportive of a belief in God, but, at the same time, there is much evidence to justify considerable doubt on the subject. Why then should one choose to be a religious person? Why choose for God and religion instead of against God and religion?* James found the legitimacy for believing in religion's capacity to trigger the "strenuous mood,"[19] a mood that he

---

*And choosing, James insisted, had to be done, because to choose not to choose was pragmatically the same as choosing not to believe. In both cases, whatever benefits are available through religion would not be forthcoming.

regarded as healthy and exciting. It meant living life to the hilt. James identified another general attitude or style of life, which he called the "easy-going mood." This mood causes one to be cautious, unadventuresome, preferring to avoid difficulty than to provoke excitement. One can live out his life "from 9 to 5" without ever courting "the wilder passions," the lustier life. But James believed that we are all tempted at times to "go the limit," to turn it all on; yet most of the time when such excitement tempts us we back off and take the safer path. The strenuous mood lies slumbering in every one of us, but in some of us it is just more difficult to awaken. "It needs the wilder passions to arouse it, the bigger fears, loves, and indignations; or else the deeply penetrating appeal of some one of the higher fidelities, like justice, truth, or freedom"[20]—and especially religion. A life lived in the conviction that one is responding to an infinite expectation and demand is infinitely greater—more alive, more momentous—than one lived simply for "me, my wife, and my son John, and maybe John's wife," for ordinary, everyday, mundane things. If one believes that God is there and God wants and expects "you!" then the strenuous mood can really be roused. As James put it:

> The more imperative ideals now begin to speak with an altogether new objectivity and significance, and to utter the penetrating, shattering, tragically challenging note of appeal. They ring out like the call of Victor Hugo's alpine eagle, *"qui parle au precipice et que le gouffre entend"* [who speaks to the precipice, and whom the abyss understands] and the strenuous mood awakens at the sound. It saith among the trumpets, ha, ha! it smelleth the battle afar off, the thunder of the captains and the shouting. Its blood is up; and cruelty to the lesser claims, so far from being a deterrent element, does but add to the stern joy with which it leaps to answer to the greater. . . .[21]

James found religion to be a psychically healthy response that loosened the "strenuous mood" in a person and set that person on the high road to dynamic, unconquerable, spiritual living. James informed us that religion was a primary value in a person's inner nature, for it released "every sort of energy and endurance, of courage and capacity for handling life's evils." Indeed, James argued that if there were no other grounds for believing in God, "Man would postulate one simply as a pretext for living hard, and getting out of existence its keenest possibilities of zest."[22]

Sigmund Freud, like James, believed that religion was an effective element in psychical life, but unlike James, Freud saw it as anything but healthy and desirable. Religion, Freud held, was a sign of man's inability to face life in any genuine fashion. Religion was the product of emotional immaturity, a surrogate for facing reality. It was the way that adults, by employing disguised childhood mechanisms, sought to deal with the threatening conditions of their everyday living. Freud wanted people to "grow up" and get over the need for religion, which was, in its basic psychic origins, simply "wish fulfillment."

Some people, especially people who take religions seriously, may find Freud's notions on religion distressing. But Freud's genius is not to be denied. It demands attention. His insight and imagination "invented" psychoanalysis. He discovered the unconscious, and the fact and dynamic of childhood sexuality. He identified psychological mechanisms of projection and regression, and the psychic dimension of "id" and "ego." He was acutely aware of disguised sex drive motivating important segments of human behavior. He not only pegged the neuroses of individuals in the libido,° but originated religion there as well. Regarding Freud's contributions, Eliot Slater states: "It was above all Freud's discovery that the springs of human action lie deeply buried in functional levels of nervous activity of which the individual himself is unconscious, and the discovery of a method of penetrating to those levels, that have transformed both medical and lay views of the interpretation of human behavior."[23]

In *The Future of an Illusion* (1928), Freud was "close-hauled" in his speculation on the Oedipus complex° (on sexual desire) as the origin and nature of religion, but already in his earlier *Totem and Taboo* he had let his imagination loose on the subject.[24] According to Freud religion began in the ambiguous relationship between parent and child and particularly between the father and the son. The ambiguity was actually a hate-love paradox: (1) The son hated (was jealous of) the father because the father interfered with the son's incestuous desires for the mother. Freud called it the Oedipus complex.* But at the same time, (2) the child had need of the protection and affection of the father without which it could not survive physically or develop morally and spiritually. In *Totem and Taboo* Freud gave his paradigm of the hate relation. In *The Future of an Illusion* he gave voice to the love/need relation.

In *Totem and Taboo* Freud proposed that in the beginning there was the "primal horde," a community dominated by one male who possessed all the females and drove off the male sons as they grew old enough to threaten the father's exclusive sexual rights to all the females. According to Freud's fantasy, "One day the brothers [joined forces and] killed the . . . father." And they not only killed him, they ate him. "The primal father had doubtlessly been the feared and envied model of each one of the company of brothers; and in the act of devouring him they accomplished their identification with him, and each one of them acquired a portion of his strength."[25]

But now other problems emerge: (1) Who would possess the women? Which brother? Indeed, were they not still confronted with the same old dominant-male power struggle? Would they not have to fight with each other until one

*See box on Oedipus story, p. 51–52.

drove off all the others? And (2) in addition they were now plagued with a sense of guilt for having killed their father upon whom they had formerly depended for protection and moral nurture.

At this point in the new conflict Freud proposed that the father returned as once again the dominant controlling force. But now he was no longer a physical force. He was back even more potently as a spiritual force. He returned as the totem figure (often symbolized in the form of an animal) who was the "father of the tribe," and who controlled all marriage relations. Now the "equal brothers" were constrained by the rules of totem exogamy. Members of the same totem could not marry. It was forbidden. It was taboo. In other words, the authority of the dead patriarch was still recognized, and in addition there now existed a sense of guilt because of the rebellion. This guilt was somewhat allayed by venerating the spirit of the slain father, now in the form of the totem, and by restraining the sexual activities of the group to the same rules that had existed before the rebellion.

Freud proposed that the worship of the slain father persisted in the primitive religion of totemism; that is, in the religion in which the particular animal that represented the patriarchal father was venerated as too sacred to kill. However, all was not yet solved because the old sexual repressions were still there. So on special occasions the "brothers" (the people of the tribe) again killed and ate the "father"—the totem animal, and therewith permitted a time of wild festivity in which the normal social rules were suspended and people unleashed their pent-up passions in riotous behavior (in a sort of New Orleans Mardi Gras fashion).

In totem worship (surrogate ancient father worship), according to Freud, humans learned to submit to a superior divine authority. This deity kept social behavior (especially sexual behavior) in check, more so even, perhaps, than in the beginning. In totemism that emerged from a sexual conflit between father and sons in the primal horde, religion was born—*à la* Sigmund Freud. And it was in Freud's opinion something to be disposed of as soon as possible. We should grow up and stop being primitive children.

Oedipus was the son of Laius, king of Thebes, and his wife Jocasta. At Oedipus's birth an oracle foretold that Laius would be killed by his son. The infant was given to a herdsman who was to expose him to death, but, rather, the herdsman gave Oedipus to another herdsman, who gave him eventually to Polybus, king of Corinth, who reared Oedipus as his own beloved son.

When grown, having been warned by a different oracle that he would kill his father and have an incestuous relationship with his mother, Oedipus, believing the Corinthian royal pair to be his true parents, left home to avoid the oracle's threat.

On his journey, Oedipus met Laius, his real father, unknown to him, who was traveling incognito, not in the trappings of the king of Thebes. They quarreled and Oedipus killed Laius.

Later Oedipus solved the riddle of the Sphinx, thereby freeing Thebes from a plague, and was for this made king of Thebes. He took Jocasta, his mother, unknown to him, as his wife. With her he had several children— Etecoles, Polynices, Antigone, and Ismene.

Eventually after Polybus died and the throne of Corinth was offered to Oedipus, an old shepherd revealed that Oedipus was not the real son of Polybus but had been a foundling. Upon close inquiry Oedipus discovered exactly where Laius had been killed, and what he had looked like, and how many servants (four in all) had been with him when he died. Then Oedipus knew the oracles had foretold the truth—he had, indeed, slain his father and married his mother. In the horror of this discovery, Oedipus tore out his eyes, and Jocasta hanged herself.

Freud is not to be understood as condemning religion on the basis of genetic fallacy. That it might have started in the reprehensible behavior of a "primal horde" would not make it, thereby, invalid. He condemned religion because it permits humans to refuse to outgrow childish neuroses, that is, their immature reliance on something other than themselves for fullness of living. This observation is penetratingly insightful and not to be summarily dismissed. In *The Future of an Illusion* Freud argued that just as a child is necessarily neurotic, so was the childhood of the human race neurotic. In growing up, the child usually outgrows most of its neuroses. But in the maturing of human culture, the races of mankind have been less successful. They are still trapped in the neurosis of religion. Children are neurotic because they cannot deal with many of their instinctual impulses by rational mental effort. They must, under various threats of parental punishment, repress their impulses and thereby effect anxiety tensions. But, said Freud, "[m]ost of these child neuroses are overcome spontaneously as one grows up." But this is not the case with religion. Using the child's neuroses as an analogy, Freud turned his attention to mankind and stated:

In just the same way one might assume that in its development through the ages mankind as a whole experiences conditions that are analogous to neuroses . . . because in the ages of its ignorance . . . it achieved by purely affective means the instinctual renunciations, indispensable for man's communal existence. And the residue of these repression-like processes [with religion as a prime example,] which took place in antiquity, has long clung on to civilization. Thus religion would be the universal obsessional neurosis of humanity. It, like the child's, originated in the Oedipus complex, the relation to the father.[26]

Freud held that worship of God is a dead giveaway of man's inability to resolve even as adults "the helplessness of his own childhood," and is a leading clue to the origin of religion in "the childhood of the human race."

Concerning religion, Freud addressed himself primarily to the religions of the West, especially Judaism and Christianity, and he saw them as unfortunate answers to people's immature, neurotic needs. He said:

> . . . a store of ideas is created, both from man's need to make his helplessness tolerable and built up from the materal of memories of the helplessness of his own childhood and the childhood of the human race. . . . Everything that happens in this world is an expression of the intentions of an intelligence superior to us, which in the end, though its ways and byways are difficult to follow, orders everything for the best. . . . Over each of us there watches a benevolent Providence which is only seemingly stern. . . . Death itself is not extinction, is not a return to inorganic lifelessness, but the beginning of a new kind of existence. . . . In the end all good is rewarded and all evil punished, if not actually in this form of life then in the later existences that begin after death. In this way all the terrors, the sufferings and the hardships of life are destined to be obliterated. . . .
>
> These, which are given out as teachings, are not precipitates of experience or end-results of thinking: they are illusions, fulfillments of the oldest, strongest and most urgent wishes of mankind.[27]

Like James and Freud, the phenomenologists (after Edmund Husserl) also see religion as arising out of the psychic character of humans, but they are not interested in evaluating the religious condition, as were James and Freud. Phenomenologists just want to try to describe and understand the experiences and behaviors that are called religious.

Phenomenology is a method of doing philosophy.* The aim of this philosophical method is to expand human understanding by describing with subjective concern humans in their world. Giving up what they regard as an impossible task—the solution of the debate over what things in themselves are—phenomenologists are concerned to report as exactly as they can the world as experienced by humans. In religious studies this means to report as faithfully as possible religious beliefs and behavior as experienced by "true believers."

The method of doing this includes at least three salient features: radical empiricism, descriptive analysis, the suspension of truth/value judgments.

First, radical empiricism. All knowledge about the world begins in extremely personal experience and analysis. Immanuel Kant° had identified this fact in his *Critique of Pure Reason* (1781). William James had used it as his data base and named it "radical empiricism." Radical empiricists argue that there is no such thing as innate (in-born) knowledge. All knowledge is from experience. The real is what is experienced.

In religious studies, then, phenomenology insists that religious knowledge is to be based directly on first-person data—on what a person thinks and feels when thinking and feeling religion.

*The idea for phenomenology was initiated by Georg Hegel° in his *Phenomenology of the Mind* (1807). The method has been developed more recently by Edmund Husserl.

Second, descriptive analysis. In proper relation with its radical empiricism, phenomenology is concerned to present descriptions—descriptions of what people feel in their religious commitments; descriptions of their mythology; descriptions of their rites and rituals. Careful attention is given to what a person means (existentially means) when he uses words like God, faith, immortality, salvation. (A phenomenological examination of the salvation concept, as we shall observe, is extremely helpful in seeing *religion—what is it?* from this point of view.)

Third, on truth and value. Philosophy, which means love of wisdom, has always been keenly concerned with truth and value. What is truth? What is value? These are central questions in philosophy, and they are important in phenomenological philosophy also, but with a difference. Phenomenology is concerned with what people believe to be true and valuable, not with whether their judgments are in fact somehow abstractly true and valuable. Questions of truth as truth and value as value are "bracketed out" of consideration. In religious studies, for example, the question of God, from phenomenological perspective, is not, "Does God exist?" but "What do people mean by, and how do they experience, what they call God?" In phenomenology questions about the truth of faith are suspended. What is noted and held of critical importance is a knowledge of, and an empathy for, the commitments and beliefs of the persons whose religion is being observed. Believers are committed to the truth of their faith. This, in phenomenology, is to be recognized and appreciated.

As we observed, both James and Freud made value judgments about the origins of religion (indeed, about religion itself). Husserl and his phenomenological disciples would have them and us refrain from such judgments. The question in phenomenology is not: Is the religious experience good or bad, healthy or psychotic, or even is it about anything "real," but simply, what is it for anything to be an instance of religion? When one pursues religion in this fashion, it becomes increasingly obvious that when the consciousness is laid bare (either by phenomenological analysis or by mystical contemplation) it is found that religion is simply there—an innate part of human nature. For example, as an instance of religion we can look at the religious experience called "salvation." The phenomenologist Peter Koestenbaum[28°] points out that the desire for salvation is situated within the basic structure of human consciousness. It is human to seek salvation, to yearn for perfection. Koestenbaum argues, "Man's condition is to reach for some perfection, some otherness, some solution to this yearning, that leads to a region beyond his personal ego."[29] The center of his being reaches outward to some external reality. His nature is to transcend himself. The ultimate symbol for such outreach is the word God. To characterize this we might appropriate Jean-Paul Sartre's[°] apt phrase, "Man's project is God." This outreach, this passion to transcend, this God project, this religiousness, is not because it is good for him (James) or bad for him (Freud), but because it is his nature, his condition, his consciousness.

Another illustration of religion as the condition of human consciousness can be seen in the phenomenological discovery of the inner core of consciousness, or as Husserl called it, the "transcendental ego." This ego is the consciousness of consciousness: our center, our soul, which experiences our experiences. As expressed in mysticism (which is pure phenomenological experience) the soul "has close affinity and may be considered as even identical with the Transcendental Realm or the totality of Being."[30] Which is to say, also, that human consciousness possesses a direct consciousness that behind all "things" there is essential "is-ness"—that is, a necessary ground of being, that is, God.

However accurate are the judgments of James and Freud, or however adequate the method of phenomenological analysis, the insight of importance remains: Religion is based in and arises from the psychic nature of human beings. They are by nature the religious animals—the only religious animals.

THEOGENETIC PHENOMENON

Thus far we have noted theories on the origin of religion that are anthropocentric, that is, arising out of human origins. But one might shift to the opposite pole and consider religion as a God-imposed phenomenon. Religion begins not with people but with God. Certainly St. Augustine° saw it this way. He opened his *Confessions* saying, "Great art Thou, O Lord, and greatly to be praised . . . Thou madest us for Thyself, and our heart is restless, until it rest in Thee." In the sixteenth century, John Calvin° was of the same persuasion, holding that "God himself, to prevent any man from pretending ignorance, has endowed all men with some idea of his Godhead, the meaning of which he constantly renews and occasionally enlarges. . . ."[31]

More recently, in 1898, Andrew Lang° wrote a book, *The Making of Religion,* which, he believed, "exhibits religion as probably beginning in some kind of Theism, which is then superseded, in some degree, or even corrupted, by Animism in all its varieties."[32]

Wilhelm Schmidt° also proposed, in 1912, that the most primitive of contemporary people (for example, the Pygmies of Africa) have beliefs and practices that indicate that the earliest form of religious expression was the worship of a high being—an original monotheism. Today, the respected history of religion scholar, Mircea Eliadé,° holds that the most primitive of people do have a belief in a supreme being, but that this High God does not play an important role in the religious life of the people who affirm it.

Such observations may suggest to us that it may be that God and not man is the genesis of religion—that is, religion is an experience "inflicted" on man from an outside source—from a God "out there."

One can speculate that this imposition of religion from without is primarily a rational affair, or that it is primarily an existential encounter. The French philosopher René Descartes° (1596–1650) proposed the former; the German theologian Rudolf Otto° (1869–1936), the latter.

In his "Third Meditation," Descartes made an argument for the existence of God, which also argues on the grounds of epistemology° that our knowledge of God's existence is innate, given in the human mind. The idea of God could not be in our minds if God had not put it there. Descartes made this claim by reaffirming an old Aristotelian axiom that a cause must have as much reality (actuality) as the thing it causes. You cannot, so to speak, have more water in your bucket than you had in the well. You cannot get something from nothing. In his own words Descartes put it thus:

> It is obvious . . . that there must be at least as much reality in the total efficient cause as in its effect, for whence can the effect derive its reality, if not from its cause. . . .
> And from this it follows, not only that something cannot be derived from nothing, but also that the more perfect—that is to say, that which contains in itself more reality—cannot be a consequent of the less perfect.[33]

People have in their minds the idea of an infinitely perfect being, "an infinite substance, external, immutable, independent, omniscient, omnipotent"[34] God. But nowhere in humans or in their world is there anything absolutely perfect that could cause them to have such an idea. Yet they have the idea—an idea that as an effect must have come from a cause equal to or greater than itself; therefore, it must have come from God, the absolutely perfect being. It must have been imposed on the human mind from out there somewhere. And it follows, then, that (1) God exists, and (2) that our knowledge of God's existence is not something that people have invented, or found in their world, but is something God given.

Like Anselm° before him, Descartes demonstrated the reality of the "philosopher's God": the God of cognition, the God of intellect, the God of thinking, which is to say, the fascinating God of speculation; but hardly the God of a shaman, or of Abraham, or Gautama Buddha, or Jesus, or anyone else who stands in awe and wonder, in fear and trembling, before the incalculable mysteries of life and death, before the horrendous nonmanipulables of human existence. The philosopher's God seems a bit cerebral to be the source of religion. If religion is of theocentric origins, it appears that one must look elsewhere (outside the operations of philosophical speculation) for evidence. And this Rudolf Otto does.

In looking at the primitive origin of religion, and the sociogenetic and psychogenetic origins, we have seen religion interpreted as arising totally within the human condition: religion as anthropocentric. But Otto rejects this. Religion is, he believes, not something invented by humans but something given to them, revealed to them, but not, as with Descartes, as primarily a rational affair. It goes far beyond reasoning; it is predominantly a *feeling* that is aroused by the impact of a sense of holiness that sweeps over us and evokes an awareness of our createdness, and of the existence of a *Holy Other*—that is also wholly other.

There is an experience of awesomeness and dread, of wondrousness and spiritual excitement, which arises in people as they encounter a quality of overpowering mystery and might that comes to them from "out there." Otto calls this experience the "*numinous* state of mind," and it is evoked by a de facto numinous reality outside of humans. In primitive people we see this numinous state reflected in their dread of demons. In ourselves we can sometimes feel something like it when we shudder at a ghost story, or when our flesh creeps at a howl or at hysterical laughter coming to us out of the night, but it can be infinitely more than fear and creepiness. This mysterious and tremendous feeling can also come sweeping into us

> like a gentle tide, pervading the mind with a tranquil mood of deepest worship. . . . It may burst in a sudden eruption from the depths of the soul with spasms and convulsions, or lead to the strangest excitements, to intoxicated frenzy, to transport, and to ecstasy. It has its wild demonic forms and can sink to an almost grisly horror and shuddering . . . again it may be developed into something beautiful and pure and glorious. It may become a hushed, trembling and speechless humility of the creature in the presence of—whom or what? In the presence of that which is *Mystery* inexpressible and above all creatures.[35]

We have thus far accumulated a number of insightful observations about religion and religious behavior:

1. We have observed the proposal that religion began when people mistakenly read their own emotions into nature (Müller)
2. and mistakenly concluded from their dream life that the world was full of souls (Tylor).
3. We have observed the primitives' awareness and religious response to mana power (Codrington)
4. and Frazer's observations about the place of magic in primitive life.
5. We have observed the proposal that religion is simply society writ large (Durkheim, Weber)
6. and the proposal that it is the inner psychological dynamic in adventuresome living (James)
7. and that it is a sickness to be cured as soon as possible (Freud).
8. We have observed the phenomenological analysis that sees religion as an innate aspect of the human condition
9. and the proposal that it is (a) an intellectual and (b) an emotional response to a divine reality self-disclosing itself to humans.
10. And running through all of these observations we can discern that religion functions especially for people in their personal distresses by giving them

transcendence and even infinite assurances in the face of immediate, traumatic circumstances. Religion gives people something to hang onto when their lives go devastatingly awry.

NOTES

[1] J. Milton Yinger, *Sociology Looks at Religion* (New York: Macmillan, 1963), p. 12.

[2] William James, *Varieties of Religious Experience* (New York: Mentor, 1958), p. 24.

[3] W. S. F. Pickering, *Durkheim On Religions* (London: Routledge & Kegan Paul, 1975), p. 95. Durkheim's statement was first published in 1899 in *L'Année sociologique*, under the title "De la Définition des phénomènes religieux."

[4] Émile Durkheim, *The Elementary Forms of the Religious Life* (New York: Collier Books, 1961), p. 43.

[5] Ibid., p. 28.

[6] Ibid., p. 212.

[7] Max Weber, *The Sociology of Religion*, tran. Ephriam Fishoff (Boston: Beacon Press, 1963), p. 1.

[8] William James, *The Varieties of Religious Experience* (New York: Random House, Modern Library), p. 53.

[9] Ibid., p. 58.

[10] James, *The Varieties of Religious Experience*, p. 61, quoting from *Journal of Psychical Research*, February, 1895, p. 26.

[11] Ibid.

[12] For more on the nature of the psychic set, see W. C. Tremmel, "The Converting Choice," *Journal for the Scientific Study of Religion*, 10, no. 1 (1971): pp. 17–25.

[13] James, *The Varieties of Religious Experience*, p. 186.

[14] Ibid., pp. 198–199.

[15] William James, "What Pragmatism Means," in *Essays in Pragmatism*, ed. Alburey Castell (New York: Hafner Library of Classics, 1948), p. 151.

[16] Ibid., p. 147.

[17] William James, "The Will to Believe," in *Essays in Pragmatism*, ed. Alburey Castell (New York: Hafner Library of Classics, 1951), p. 95. Author's italics.

[18] Ibid., p. 107.

[19] See William James, "The Moral Philosopher and the Moral Life," in *Essays in Pragmatism*, ed. Alburey Castell (New York: Hafner Library of Classics, 1951), pp. 84–86.

[20] Ibid., p. 85.

[21] Ibid., pp. 85–86.

[22] Ibid., p. 86.

[23] Eliot Slater, in his "Introduction" to a report, "The International Congress on Mental Health," August, 1949; printed in *The British Medical Bulletin*, 6, no. 1, and quoted by Julian Franklyn in *Death By Enchantment* (New York: G. P. Putnam's Sons, 1971), p. 16.

[24] *Totem and Taboo* was first published in two volumes under the title *On Some Points of Agreement Between the Mental Lives of Savages and Neurotics*.

[25] Sigmund Freud, *Totem and Taboo*, tran. James Strachey (London: Routledge & Kegan Paul, 1961, second edition), p. 142.

[26] Sigmund Freud, *The Future of an Illusion*, tran. W. D. Robson-Scott (New York: Liveright, sixth edition 1953), pp. 75–76.

[27] Sigmund Freud, *The Future of an Illusion* (Garden City, N.Y.: Doubleday, Anchor Books, 1964), pp. 25–27, 47. For a carefully considered answer to Freud, see Charles Hartshorne and William Reese, *Philosophers Speak of God* (Chicago: University of Chicago Press, second edition 1963), pp. 478–486.

[28] See Peter Koestenbaum, "Religion in the Tradition of Phenomenology," in *Religion in Philosophical and Cultural Perspective*, ed. J. C. Feaver and W. Horosz (New York: Van Nostrand Reinhold, 1967), pp. 174–214.

[29] Ibid., p. 181.

[30] Ibid., p. 191.

[31] John Calvin, *Institutes of the Christian Religion*, tran. Henry Beveridge (Grand Rapids, Mich.: Wm. B. Erdman Publishing, 1953), vol. 1, p. 43.

[32] Andrew Lang's 1898 edition was reprinted by AMS Press, New York, in 1968.

[33] René Descartes, *Meditations on First Philosophy* (Indianapolis: Bobbs-Merrill, 1960), p. 39.

[34] Ibid., p. 43.

[35] Rudolph Otto, *The Idea of the Holy*, tran. J. W. Harvey (London: Oxford University Press, 1924), pp. 12–13.

Chapter 5

RELIGIOUS RESPONSES TO THE HUMAN CONDITION

They shall mount up with wings as eagles.
Isaiah (40:31)

People respond self-consciously and imaginatively to the finitudes of life in a number of ways. They may do so, for example, by (1) attempting to exorcise the demonic elements of life, (2) by living in a transcending hope, (3) by being sometimes extraordinarily grateful for gifts not earned, (4) by giving themselves in total commitment to promising faith systems, (5) by living in the expectation that there is, in fact, a power and grace that transforms it all—that salvation is real.

In our attempt to compose (in Chapter 1) a succinct definition of religion, we proposed that religion is mankind's most effective weapon in its "conquest of finitude." We shall now further propose that this conquest is accomplished by the dual-polar modes of exorcism and ecstasy. Religion is a form of human behavior in which persons attempt to exorcise the demonic elements of life—its horrendous finitudes; or to experience the divine elements of life— the transcendence of finitude; or to do both. The first we shall call "metatechnology"; the second is "divine encounter."

Of the five examples stated above, the first—exorcising the demonic—is metatechnology. Examples two, three, four, and five—transcending hope, extraordinary gratitude, total commitment, power and grace—are all directed to effecting divine encounter.

METATECHNOLOGY

When we considered Sir James Frazer's° notions of magic and religion, we introduced William Bernhardt's° term "metatechnology"* and observed that metatechnology is employed both as magic and rogation.

*Metatechnology is any attempt to introduce extranatural or supernatural power into natural processes.

60

In magic, people themselves manipulate the supernatural powers to effect desired changes in natural processes. But we also noted that people often, perhaps more often, try to get God or the Gods to intervene and effect the desired changes for them. What people cannot do for themselves, they often attempt to get the powers (Gods) or *the* power (God) to do for them. We are calling this second form of metatechnology "rogation," from the Latin *rogare,* which means "to beseech."* By rogation we shall mean any sacrifice or prayer or other performance, by anybody, that makes appeal for divine intervention to alter the natural conditions; for example, praying for rain, or to be given victory in battle, or to be cured of disease. Rogation is a form of metatechnology different from magic in form but like magic in intention.

We need, now, to introduce another term into our considerations: *metapsychological response,* a term to designate those inner psychological changes that are effected by religious beliefs, actions, and experiences— especially those religious responses that go "beyond" normal, expected, psychological responses. For example, when martyrs face death serenely, praying for their slayers, or when people respond to personal tragedy courageously and even serenely *because* they believe that there is in God's plan reason for their suffering, they are evidencing not normal psychological responses, but metapsychological responses.

Metapsychological response must be further delineated as (1) self-conscious or intentional, and as (2) subconscious or unintentional. As self-conscious, it is intended; as subconscious, it is accidental—a by-product. In self-conscious metapsychology persons do not expect to change "things," but to change themselves. They attempt to go beyond the usual, normal psychological response and establish a courage-to-be-in-spite-of response. In self-conscious metapsychology one turns to religion to find wisdom and courage in order to take whatever happens, which cannot be changed, and to do so with dignity and even serenity. This is what the biblical Job finally discovered. He was supposed to trust God and accept life, no matter what. It is what the Chinese Taoist (of the quietist variety) does when choosing to practice *wu-wei,* that is, quiet, nonaggressive, nonresisting action. It is the very essence of a commonly spoken prayer: "God grant me the serenity to accept the things I cannot change, courage to change the things I can, and wisdom to know the difference."† This prayer is obviously a self-consciously metapsychological prayer. In it one is asking not for the world to change, but for oneself to change. On the other hand, when the President of the United States asked the nation to pray for the safe return of the astronauts in the damaged Apollo 13 spaceship, the concern was obviously metatechnological. The prayers were to get supernatural intervention into a natural process. The

---

* In the early Christian church, rogations were performed in times of disaster. Those rogations might involve processions, litanies, fasting, penitence, prayers, all beseeching God to alleviate the calamity. An instance of this occurred in 590 when Pope Gregory the Great ordered a rogation ritual called *litania septiformis* to be performed in an attempt to get divine succor during a pestilence that followed an inundation in Rome.

† Reinhold Niebuhr° is credited as the author of this prayer.

prayers were to get God to make *things* right. Whether or not God answered the prayers and assisted in getting the craft back, a lot of people felt better for having done their part. They got some psychological benefits out of the "religious exercise." In a mild way at least, they experienced some subconscious metapsychology.

The second form of metapsychology is subconscious metapsychology. In this form the religious inner change takes place not so much by request as by accident. It is a sort of by-product of faith; the releasing, as James suggests, of the strenuous, courageous, adventuresome mood as a result of one's religious conviction that the magic works, or that God is on our side. This aspect of metapsychology will become more obvious as we turn now and ask, How are metatechnology and metapsychology related in religion?

Metatechnology versus Metapsychology   To understand how these two aspects of religion relate to each other, we should first make clear the relationship between technology and metatechnology. William Bernhardt, in his *Functional Philosophy of Religion,* establishes that there is a concomitant° relation between technology and metatechnology: The more technology one has, the less metatechnology one uses. From an examination of the religious practices of a primitive society, the religious practices of the Romans during the Augustan Age, and the religious practices of some modern Christians, Bernhardt concludes that in the areas of food supply and human health, metatechnology is extensively used in prescientific cultures where good production techniques and medical skills are minimal, and is rarely used by people who have attained advanced technologies in food supply and scientific capacity in medicine.

Bronislaw Malinowski,° in his *Magic, Science and Religion,* illustrates the relationship of technology to metatechnology in the culture of the Melanesian primitives of the Trobriand Islands.° The Trobrianders use both technology and metatechnology (mostly of the magical type) and they know in each case what they are doing and why. The Trobrianders are, among other things, fishermen. They venture out beyond the safe reef-protected lagoons of their islands into the deep not always pacific waters in search of fish. They do this in outrigger dugout canoes. With long-established technologies, they build fine seaworthy boats in a straightforward technological fashion. As artisans they use technology, not metatechnology. But a good sailing craft is not the last word in deep-sea fishing. One needs not only a good boat to ride the waves but also a lucky boat to get through or avoid storms and to find fish. The sea is big and dangerous, and fish are where you find them. Something more than good boat building and smart fishing is involved. This "something" takes special handling, and so along with their technology, the Trobrianders employ metatechnology. Malinowski tells us:

Canoe building has a long list of spells, to be recited at various stages of the work, at the felling of the trees, at the scooping out of the dugout; and towards the end, the painting, lashing together and launching.[1]

He reports the same kind of technology/metatechnology in the Trobrianders' farming enterprises. They use farming techniques, but because crop failure means hunger and perhaps starvation, they also employ metatechnology to deal with those aspects of farming that seem to need something more than ordinary know-how. Also, Malinowski reports that the Trobrianders use metatechnology to ward off or cure serious illnesses. They have no modern medical practices. They do employ some natural remedies for minor afflictions, but in all serious illness they employ metatechnology extensively. What the Trobrianders cannot manipulate technologically, they try to manipulate metatechnologically. They get God, or the Gods, or just plain magic to protect them from horrendous nonmanipulables, to fix it so they can survive, and even prosper.

An obvious question to ask at this point is: Does it work? Do they get it fixed? Is the "nonmanipulable" really manipulated for them? We can answer by saying that it is obvious what the natives think they are getting. They think they are getting extranatural or supernatural assistance in the face of nonmanipulable aspects in their existence. They believe they are getting control in those areas that are precarious and in which important values are threatened. They use their religion to restore, or preserve, or promote vital values they believe are in danger.

Of course, what they are getting, as seen by an outsider, might be something else altogether. An observing outsider might conclude that the Trobrianders are mistaken. They are not really getting a guaranteed harvest, or a safe and successful fishing voyage, or protection from, or cure of, diseases. They just think they are. But one might also conclude that despite a metatechnological impotence in their activities, they are getting something else quite valuable: a by-product. Believing in the efficacy of their metatechnological techniques, they are getting an inner surety, a sense of assurance, a fund of courage. They are getting subconscious metapsychological benefits. Through their religious activities, they are going beyond the fear that normally arises at the prospect of famine or drowning or serious illness, and are securing for themselves a courage, a morale, they would not otherwise have. If their world has not really changed, at least they have.

Although we might regard the metatechnological practices of the Trobrianders as only subjectively beneficial, we may not be willing to be so restrictive when viewing our own metatechnological practices. Surely many of the enlightened, scientifically cultured people who prayed for the astronauts' return believe that their prayers did assist with more than psychological benefits. If, for example, we ask, Does prayer change *things*? we find voices in the modern world declaring an emphatic *yes*.

Of course, we hear denials also. William Bernhardt voices his denial as follows:

Historically . . . religious behavior was essentially metatechnological. Persons sought for supernatural or magical aid in their attempts to conserve their values.

Present day information leads one to believe that all such metatechnological activities were futile so far as objective results were concerned. . . . At the same time, religious behavior continued despite its metatechnological impotence because it served man in other ways. It had subjective success which more than compensated for its objective failures. . . . Religious behavior, in other words, aided individuals to make subjective adjustments to situations not subject to objective control at the time, and to do so without loss of morale.[2]

The evidence would indicate that Bernhardt writes the "minority opinion" in this case. Prayer for health, for rain, for the security and preservation of tangible, physical values is still widely practiced and ardently defended. It is still something people do when they do religion, and they justify their doing so usually based on two types of arguments: It is reasonable, and it works.

Peter Bertocci° argues that it is reasonable. If God is a person, as Bertocci believes, and a person whose very essence consists in his concern for increase in value, then it is reasonable to expect that he will take every opportunity to help people increase values. In his *Introduction to the Philosophy of Religion*, Bertocci argues that the laws of nature are themselves evidences of God's loving concern for humans. Without a minimum of physical, biological, and mental laws, the world or communal life could not exist. God shows his care for us through these "impersonal" laws.

But is that all? Does this exhaust God's concern for the individual? Bertocci insists that the answer is definitely, *no*. God's general providence is just the basis for his special providence. God listens and responds. Within, but not in conflict with, the laws necessary for an orderly nature and a communal life, there is no reason, argues Bertocci, why God cannot or would not respond to human invitation and initiate or preserve the existence of some prayed-for essential, human value.

Bertocci is, actually, a rather cautious protagonist for metatechnology. Much more radical and passionate statements are available for those who wish to believe that divine intervention really happens. But the more usual grounds for holding to the effectiveness of metatechnology, for believing that prayer changes things, is not an argument at all. It is an experience. If you want *the word*, ask the man who prayed for rain and got it; ask the man who was healed by faith; ask the man who "felt" the power of God invade his being. For such persons, there is no arguing; there is only affirmation.

That metatechnology actually affects changes in the environment is questionable, but that metapsychology changes people is not questionable. It is a demonstrable fact. People's lives are changed because they believe in the claims and engage in religious forms of behavior. William James,° in his essay "The Moral Philosopher and the Moral Life," makes this point with his usual inimitable style. He declares

that even if there was no metaphysical or traditional grounds for believing in God, men would postulate one simply as a pretext for living hard, and getting out of the game of existence its keenest possibilities of zest. Our attitude towards concrete evils is entirely different in a world where we believe there are none but finite demanders, from what is in one where we joyously face tragedy for an infinite demander's sake. Every sort of energy and endurance, of courage and capacity for handling life's evils, is set free in those who have religious faith. For this reason the strenuous type of character will on the battlefield of human history always outwear the easy-going type, and religion will drive irreligion to the wall.[3]

The Trobriander who believes that his boat sails with supernatural luck sails with confidence, and probably even with more skill. In a storm he is less likely to be incapacitated by a sense of his own helplessness. He can count on more than himself. As James puts it, for those who have faith, "every sort of energy and endurance is set free." Better to sail with that man than with the other kind. What is true of primitives in this regard is not less true of their sophisticated, civilized brothers. Courage, someone has said, is fear that prayed, and for the millions who know from experience what this means, nothing more need be said.

The prayer that Jesus is reported to have prayed in the Garden of Gethsemane appears to have been about half metatechnological and half metapsychological. He prayed for God to change the circumstances and spare his life, but if this would not be done, then in his prayer he resolved to accept God's will. He prayed, first, for the cup to pass him by, and, second, if not pass him by, for the courage to take it, no matter what it was. The cup did not pass. The prayer did not "change things," but, if we can trust the account of how he behaved during those last hours of his life, we may surely conclude that the prayer changed him. The man who was terrified when he went into the garden (who fell on his face and sweat blood) became a man walking with courage and dignity and transcendence to the top of The Skull,° and beyond it into the hearts and lives of countless millions ever since.

Magic and Rogation in the Twentieth Century

Many people see themselves in a scientific age that in principle renders magic and rogation as superfluous. But the fact is that this scientific age has neither ended metatechnology, nor many other more primitive ideas that one might have expected it to end. Indeed, there seems to be a revival of archaic religious beliefs and practices. During the 1940s and '50s, when some of us went to college, such subjects as magic, angels, demons, astrology, witchcraft, life after death, did not receive much attention, certainly not in any academic context. There were some early explorations in extrasensory perception, but even those were side issues not to be taken especially seriously. Then something happened. The scientific-humanistic optimism of nineteenth- and early twentieth-century liberalism appeared to founder on the rocks of wars and the rumors of wars, on dislocations and violence, in a century in which the word "crisis" is too mild an epithet for the times. Bronislaw Malinowski once said, "Magic appears in those phases of human action where knowledge fails man." He was talking about primitives. He was (although in the first years of this century when he was doing his major work he might not have guessed it), also, apparently talking about us as well.

The amount of popular concern for occult subjects (evidenced on popular bookstands, TV shows, movies) and the lack of classroom discussions on magic, witchcraft, satanism, glossolalia,° and other such gifts, as well as visitors from outer space, is evidence of a cultural gap between older college professors and students. However, the tide may be turning for classes in the occult are being introduced into the curriculums of colleges and universities. In some places, perhaps, the gap between what professors want to say and students want to hear is, indeed, closing.

RELIGION AND TRANSCENDING HOPE

Attempts to exorcise the demonic are not the only responses people give to the finitudes of life. The courage afforded by religion is not simply grit-the-teeth-and-bear-it courage. It is courage characterized by transcending hope. As noted earlier, Jean-Paul Sartre tells us that "man's project is God," which we employed as a paradigm expression for the fact that human nature—both affective and cognitive—is to transcend itself, to ride above its human condition, to overcome its finitudeness. Humans need to be (or need to be with) God; just a little lower than the angels; born again, Christ-man rather than Adam-man. Religion does not prepare persons by having them cringe, whimpering before death, or flee to suicide before the slings and arrows of outrageous fortune. Rooted in horrendous frustrations, it is nonetheless directed optimistically to the transcending of those frustrations. Religion is not so much a running away as it is a rising above. In a voice that is not only authentically religious, but also more excitingly so than a prayer for rain, the Prophet Isaiah sings:

> They that wait upon the Lord
> Shall renew their strength.
> They shall mount up with wings as eagles.
> They shall run and not be weary.
> They shall walk and not faint.
>
> *Isaiah 40:31, King James Version (AV)*

If human need is the rootage of religion, great expectations are its bud, and great aspirations its flower. On all levels of human need, religion speaks. When life is trapped in physical needs, when hunger and danger are constant companions, the major religious concerns of people are also concentrated upon the physical, and on how to manipulate it to their welfare. They will employ all they know (technologically, metatechnologically, metapsychologically) to better their lot. As soon as they succeed at this, they will discover other needs, which can be just as important, and just as threatened. As soon as they get enough bread, they discover that bread alone is not enough. More sophisticated needs (personal, social, intellectual, aesthetic, moral, spiritual) thrust upon them demandingly. And they will cry out for the needs of their souls just as ardently as they ever cried out for the needs of their bodies.

Spiritual needs create a dimension of religion that can transcend the desperation in which religion has its roots. The nonmanipulable remains. It is still horrendous. The anxiety is still there. The man who, for example, strives for sainthood is motivated by anxious need just as surely as the frightened man praying for deliverance from wild waves, but the direction of their expectations is not the same. One person aspires to something; the other flees from something. Religion is not fear only; it is fear transcended. It is characterized by hope quite as much as despair, by courage quite as much as fear, by laughing quite as much as crying, by living quite as much as dying. Religion not only has the preciseness of need; it also has the scope of aspiration. Alfred North Whitehead,° who zeroed in on a narrow target and called religion "what an individual does with his own solitariness,"[4] just as emphatically reversed the narrowness and opened the scope to an infinite breadth.

> Religion is the vision of something which stands beyond, behind, and within, the passing flux of immediate things; something which is real, and yet waiting to be realized; something which is remotely possible, and yet the greatest of present facts; something that gives meaning to all that passes, and yet eludes apprehension; something whose possession is the final good, and yet is beyond all reach; something which is the ultimate ideal, and the hopeless quest.[5]

RELIGION AS EXTRAORDINARY GRATITUDE

Another religious response can be, should be, extraordinary gratitude. Religion can be seen, should be seen, especially by young adults making their move from childhood dependence to mature independence and responsibility, as more than a device for making miracles (metatechnology) or overcoming distress (metapsychology), and even different from having "wings" for spirits' soaring. It is a new awareness and stance in the wonder of simply being alive. Proper religious perspective should evoke in us an attitude of enormous gratitude—a gratitude big enough to give balance to all that is horrendous in life. Regarding this Charles Milligan° writes: "It makes the shift from metatechnology—trying to get something by means of religion—to God 'coming of age'* and mysticism,† where an underlying motive is a sense of beatitude grounded in gratitude."‡

*See Chapter 8.
†See pages 272–275.
‡From the personal correspondence of Charles Milligan.

Milligan places great stress on this dimension of religion, especially where college students are concerned. He writes:

> I would stress this precisely because many college students are (or should be) making that transition from rather self-centered orientation to the realization that their lives are graced with unearned nurture and gifts. Many people would be surprised to learn that that is one of the things that religion is about, and that the cultivation of thanksgiving is a basic technique of mature religion as a resource for confronting and transcending the nonmanipulable, horrendous, tragic and finiteness of existence.*

Before your birth, actually before your conception, the number of genetic possibilities was astronomical. The odds were something like 400 million to one that the male sperm with a chromosome complement that could become you would really be the one that reached and fertilized the ovum that did become you. That you were born instead of one of those other 400 million possible infants is fantastic to contemplate. For such a "gift of life" one might sometimes rejoice in exploding gratitude to whatever creative mystery made it happen that way. You are alive. What a gift!

And as if the gift of life itself were not enough there is the gift of the whole world spread out before us to see and touch, even as Bliss Carman° did one day when he

> . . . took a day to search for God,
> And found Him not. But as I trod
>   By rocky ledge, through woods untamed,
>   Just where one scarlet lily flamed,
> I saw His footprint in the sod.
>
> Then suddenly, all unaware,
> Far off in the deep shadows, where
>   A solitary hermit thrush
>   Sang through the holy twilight hush—
> I heard His voice upon the air.
>
> And even as I marveled how
> God gives us Heaven here and now
>   In a stir of wind that hardly shook
>   The poplar leaves beside the brook—
> His hand was light upon my brow.
>
> At last with evening as I turned
> Homeward, and thought what I had learned
>   And all that there was still to probe—
>   I caught the glory of His robe
> Where the last fires of sunset burned.[6]

. . . .

*Ibid.

TOTAL COMMITMENT — Both Cognitive and Affective

Another observation to be made about religious behavior concerns the affective and/or intellectual involvement in the religious commitment. Religious behavior, when genuine, is total behavior. It is affective and intellectual behavior. Religion is not an intellectual exercise, on the one hand, or a noncognitive emotional binge, on the other. It is an amalgam of both. Edna St. Vincent Millay,° in her poem "Interim," tells us that it is faith that keeps the world alive, not truth. The poem goes on to declare that birds fly because they have "unconscious faith," and fishes swim, and the world follows its orderly way because all things basically give themselves in trust. They believe, and the believing is more than just an intellectual nod. It is a complete persuasion. "I not only *know* that this is so, but *feel* it to the marrow of my bones." It involves a believing that is both of reason and of passion. Religious faith is an emotional commitment, a passionate giving of oneself. But it is not just passion. It is passion surrounding a proposition, or a whole system of propositions, that make it, also, an affair of knowledge, of intellect, of truth. It is to certain "truths" that the believer is tenaciously loyal and emotionally committed.

Just as science and philosophy are concerned with the facts of existence and with true understandings, so is religion. But religion is not only concerned with the controlling facts of science and the clear understanding of philosophy; it is also concerned with establishing the whole person in dynamic, saving relation with the power or powers believed to determine life and destiny—with the God or the Gods. Keenly aware of the frustrations of finitude, or horrendous nonmanipulables, people turn not just their hands and heads to the basic problems of life, but their hearts as well. And in this fact (that the heart is involved) religion, at least theoretically, differs sharply from both science and philosophy. Religion is an engagement with life, an existential engagement; science and philosophy try not to be. Science and philosophy are "objective" in their approach to facts and truth and human welfare. The scientist and philosopher try to remove themselves, their prejudices, passions, biases, from the experiments and critical examinations. Presumably all is cold and calculated and cautiously reasonable. But religion is not like that. Rather it is willfully emotional and personal. It is concerned not only to know the truth but also, in the very act of knowing, to be engaged totally, committed completely, and saved utterly.

Apropros of this pretense of objectivity in science (to say nothing of philosophy), Pierre Teilhard de Chardin° has this to say:

In its early naive stage, science, perhaps inevitably, would imagine that we could observe things in themselves, as they would behave in our absence. Instinctively physicists and naturalists went to work as though they could look down from a great height upon a world which their consciousness could penetrate without being submitted to it or changing it. They are now beginning to realize that even the most objective of their observations are steeped in the conventions they adopt at the outset and by forms or habits of thought developed in the course of their research; so that, when they reach the end of their analysis they cannot tell with any certainty whether the structure they have made is the essence of the matter they are studying, or the reflection of their own thought. And at the same time they realize that because of the return shock of their discoveries, they are committed body and soul to the network of relationships they thought to cast upon things from the outside: In fact, they are caught in their own net.[7]

SALVATION

Some people deal with life's finitudes by living in the expectation of, and even the experience of, salvation. To be saved utterly, this is the destination of the transcending hope and the total commitment of religion. Salvation, also called by other names such as *moksha* in Hinduism and *satori*° in Zen Buddhism, is the ultimate religious answer given to the human condition. It represents the final conquest of finitude.

Many times salvation is associated with a place such as Heaven, and it is often anticipated as something yet to come. But a close scrutiny of the existential nature of salvation indicates that it is not essentially identifiable with a place and is not necessarily futuristic. Rather it is a condition of being, a kind of consciousness, which may happen in Heaven or some similar place, later on, but may also happen here and now. In Zen Buddhism, it (satori) apparently happens abruptly here and now. Gautama's "enlightenment" also was a "here and now" happening.* And the divine possessions reported by shamans (as we shall see in some detail later) happen in the present, wherever the shaman happens to be.

Salvation appears to be an experience in which the "old man" is reborn as a "new man," and the transformation is complete; the whole nature is changed. If this account is accurate, it follows that salvation is not simply a meta-psychological affair, in which one self-consciously or subconsciously achieves a new spiritual morale for the facing of horrendous and non-manipulable circumstances. Rather, salvation seems to be not a limited modi-fication in one's normal psychological responses but a major transformation of one's basic psychic set, that is, of the essential depth structure of one's psychic system. The one who experiences salvation apparently does not become a rearranged person, but a radically re-formed person. St. Paul describes how it was with him. In his letter to the Galatians he states boldy: "I

*See pages 000–000.

have been crucified with Christ; it is no longer I who live, but Christ who lives in me'' (Galatians 2:20 RSV). Similarly Gautama, after his moment of enlightenment, was simply not the same man. As we shall see later when we investigate the religious experience in Chapter 15, primitive religions often claim that the shaman's "helper spirit" actually takes over the body and soul of the entranced shaman, who thereby becomes literally what the possessing spirit is.

In the salvation process a new person is created. "The old psychic set is transcended and transformed into something as radically (qualitatively) different from its old form as a Brillo box is from a Warhol painting.''[8] Jones is still Jones. He still eats and sleeps, catches colds, works, loves, weeps, laughs, suffers, dies. But there is a difference. He seems to have gone through religious need to the other side and to have found liberation. He is no longer the anxious slave of finite frustration, but seems to have come to a point of view that accepts finite limitation as somehow a minor dimension in the total scheme of things. Ordinary life may be as precious to him as to anyone, and as threatened, but for him it seems not to be the whole of it, or the truly important part of it. He has gotten hold of something and in getting hold of it has been made different by it.

Simply to say that someone was saved (saved from the Devil, saved from drowning, saved from anything) implies that that person was saved *from* something, saved *to* something, and saved *by* something. Thus far we have been saying what, in religious salvation, one is saved to; namely to a new condition of being. One is saved *from* the anxiety (*angst*) of the self-conscious human condition, from the trauma resident in one's vivid awareness of finitude. Finitude is the core of the problem. Humans want infinity but possess on their own only finiteness. In the contradiction between mankind's projection of itself toward infinity and the fact of human finitude (as demonstrated horrendously by death), we see the paradox of human life—a paradox that makes of the meaning of life, as Albert Camus° puts it, an utter absurdity. The meaning of human life demands infinity; the fact of life offers finitude; therefore, for humans all is finally absurd. It should be noted that Camus is not lashing out against "things" that are wrong. His absurdity of life does not arise because of an especially absurd age, or because of pain, or poverty, or disease, or war, or any other pernicious thing or combination of things. These things are but symptoms of the deeper malady, which is, as we observed earlier, a natural condition of human estrangement, which arises from the nonprogrammed (therefore, self-conscious, disturbingly imaginative) nature of the human beings. It arises because humans "know" that their only significant meaning is to be like God. The human project, as Sartre puts it, is God. But humans are not God. They are not infinite.

Thus Camus concludes that all is absurd. But it is absurd only for a genuine atheist like Camus, who does not subscribe to the final transcending hope of any religion. With others, the reach for infinity, the project God, is possible, as evidenced in the gigantic doctrines of apocalyptic resurrection of Christianity; of Karma, reincarnation, and Nirvana in Hinduism and Buddhism; of the cycle of rebirth in the religion of the Trobrianders; of the day of Yahweh in Judaism.

To come to total commitment is finally to come to what one believes can effect transcendence from the life-negating traumas of human existence, can overcome finitude. The commitment is to divine power—to God.

NOTES

[1] Bronislaw Malinowski, *Magic, Science and Religion* (Glencoe, Ill.: Free Press, 1948), pp. 165–166.

[2] William Bernhardt, *A Functional Philosophy of Religion* (Denver, Colo.: Criterion Press, 1958), p. 157.

[3] William James, "The Moral Philosopher and The Moral Life," in *Essays in Pragmatism*, ed. Alburey Castell (New York: Hafner Library of Classics, 1951), p. 86.

[4] Alfred North Whitehead, *Religion in the Making* (Cleveland: World, Meridian Books, second edition, 1969), p. 16.

[5] Alfred North Whitehead, *Science and the Modern World* (New York: Macmillan, 1944), p. 275.

[6] Bliss Carman, "Vestigia," in *The World's Great Religious Poetry*, ed. Caroline Hill (New York: Macmillan, 1942), pp. 32–33.

[7] Pierre Teilhard de Chardin, *The Phenomenon of Man*, tran. Bernard Wall (New York: Harper & Row, Torchbooks, 1965), p. 32.

[8] William C. Tremmel, "The Converting Choice," *Journal for the Scientific Study of Religion* (Spring 1971): 17–25.

PART TWO

God—Bright and Dark

And God stepped out on space
And he looked around and said:
I'm lonely—
I'll make me a man.

James Weldon Johnson°1

I am the Lord your God. . . . You shall
have no other gods before me.

Deuteronomy 5:6a−7

II.   Doing so from the conviction that there is at the center of human experience, and even of all reality, a being, or beings, or process (a divine reality) in which and through which a person (or community of persons) can transcend the life-negating traumas of human existence, can overcome the sense of finitude. [See page 7.]

Chapter 6

GOD

"Beware the Jabberwock, my son!"
Lewis Carroll°

'Twas brillig, and the slithy toves
    Did gyre and gimble in the wabe:
All mimsy were the borogoves,
    And the mome raths outgrabe.

So begins Lewis Carroll's "Jabberwocky," in good English, but what does it mean? And why quote it to introduce a chapter on God? We quote it because the first problem with Carroll's "Jabberwocky" is meaning. What does it mean, if anything? And this is also, according to some modern critics,* the first problem in theology. According to modern analytic philosophy, the first question in talking about God (doing God-talk) is the word "god" itself. Initially the question should not be, "Does God exist?" but "Does the word 'god' itself have a matter-of-fact meaning or is it just a 'Jabberwock' noise, an expression of emotion?" Although it appears to be meaningful, does the word "god" really make any informative statement about anything at all?

Instead of attacking the question of God from the erudite heights of metaphysics° and epistemology,° this attack begins with the "lowly" examination of common language, from which originate such seemingly simple questions as what is an ordinary word? sentence? concept? definition? But high or low modern philosophical analysis is the kind of operation that God-talkers have been embroiled in during the last twenty-five years and a controversy with which those of us who seek to discover *religion: what is it?* should have at least a passing acquaintance.

GOD AND THE QUESTION OF VERIFICATION

Analyzing God-talk—The Attack from Below This attack is not against the "truths" of a theology or the adequacy of a method, but against the "mean-

---

*Analytic philosophers, also called modern language philosophers.

ingfulness" of talking about God at all. This attack "from below" asserts that
God-talk perhaps sounds like real talk (talk about factual things), but it is, in
fact, nonsense talk, or at best only emotional utterances.

A proposition that purports to be informative (such as "God exists," or
"there is a tiger in the bedroom") must be empirically verifiable or falsifiable,
at least in principle—so say certain modern analytic (language) philosophers.
They also often say that many religious propositions (such as God exists) are
not of this character, but are propositions where seeming meaningfulness
disappears in a retreat of endless qualifications. For example, there is nothing
that a theist will admit is truly falsifying of the proposition "God exists" or the
proposition "God is good" or any other basically important theological
proposition. Every time one raises a negating item, the "true believer"
disqualifies the negative item by another item of unverifiable dimension.

If, for example, someone tells us, "There is a tiger in the bedroom," we
have before us a *meaningful* statement. It may not be true, but at least it is
meaningful. It is meaningful because it is "verifiable in fact" here and now,
even though analytic philosophers tell us "verifiable in principle" (whatever
that means) would suffice. The tiger-in-the-bedroom proposition can be verified or falsified by simply examining the bedroom. There is, indeed, a tiger
there; or I see no tiger. So we look into the bedroom and see no tiger. We go in
and look under the bed, behind the drapes, in the closet. Still no tiger. We
declare the meaningful proposition to have been false, and we report, "You
are wrong. There is no tiger in the bedroom."

But at this point our tiger-claimer says, "Oh, yes, there is a tiger here. You
just can't see it. It is an invisible tiger."

Our suspicions tell us that we are being kidded, so we say, "You're
kidding."

"No, not kidding. It's an invisible tiger."

"If it's an invisible tiger, and it's here, why can't I hear it growling."

"It's not a growling tiger."

"I can't smell it either."

"It has no odor."

"Well, what does it have so I can tell (and you also) whether or not it is
here?"

"It is an absolutely inexperienceable tiger in any empirical way. It is a
transcendent tiger. But it is real, and it is here."

At this point we, the skeptics, decide the game has gone far enough. It is
senseless to engage in such a conversation.

As the tiger affords no evidence of itself, it cannot be verified or falsified.
Discussion of its presence is, therefore, both a waste of breath and an
improper *philosophical* exercise.

The tiger story we invented, but it is parallel to the kinds of "parables"
various modern language philosophers have invented to elucidate their skep-

ticism of engaging in God-talk. One parable in particular, told first by John Wisdom,° launched a debate called the University Discussion[2] among professors and clergymen in England in the 1950s. Indeed, both sides of the debate—those who declared religious propositions about God meaningless, and those who declared them meaningful—invented and employed modern parables.

In an article entitled "Gods"[3] in 1940, John Wisdom created a parable in which he pointed out *"how it is that an explanatory hypothesis, such as the existence of God, may start by being experimental and gradually become something quite different. . . ."*[4] He told a story about two men who return to a long neglected garden and are surprised to find among the weeds a number of garden plants growing vigorously. One of the men exclaims, "Surely someone has been coming here and caring for these plants." "No," replies the other man, "if anyone had been coming here to care for this garden, he would surely have pulled these weeds." They checked with the neighbors, but no one had seen a gardener there. "Perhaps he comes at night." "No, someone would have heard him." The first man was not about to give up. He said, "Look at the arrangement of these plants. There is purpose here, and beauty. This cannot be happenstance. I believe that someone not visible to the human eye comes here, is here; and the more we look for evidence the more convinced we shall be of the existence of the invisible gardener."

The men go on examining. They find some reasons to believe the invisible gardener hypothesis and more evidence to disbelieve it. They even speculate on what happens to gardens if they are truly untended.

Each man knows everything the other knows about this garden mystery. So when one says, "I still believe the gardener comes" and the other says "I don't," their different opinions are not based on facts. Their examination of the situation has ceased to be experimental. One says that a gardener comes unseen and is manifested in his works that are before us. The other declares that there is no gardener, as anyone should be able to recognize in the lack of works that are before us. Their decisions for or against are simply decisions of feeling toward the garden.

John Wisdom concluded that the claims of these two men are not expressions of belief based on matters of fact. The facts (the bewildering, beautiful garden world) are the same for both of them. Their conclusions are opposites. They are not speaking with empirical meaning.

> The one says "A gardener comes unseen and unheard. He is manifested only in his works with which we are all familiar." The other says "There is no gardener" and with this difference in what they say about that gardener goes a difference in how they feel towards the garden, in spite of the fact that neither expects anything of it which the other does not expect.[5]

Antony Flew,° referring to the parable told by John Wisdom in his "haunting and revelatory" article "Gods," points out that (as with our tiger) the invisible gardener (God) is reduced to meaninglessness by endless denials of falsification evidence, until at last "the skeptic despairs, 'But what remains of your original assertion [there is a gardener who tends the garden]? Just how does what you call an invisible, intangible, eternally elusive gardener differ from an imaginary gardener or even no gardener at all?'"[6] Flew assailed religious (theological/metaphysical) talk as being (1) without any real meaning because (2) it is unverifiable and/or unfalsifiable. Naturally the opposition fought back.

With regard to item (1), *the purported absence of meaning,* R. B. Braithwaite° asserts that the evidence for the meaningfulness of religious belief is to be seen in the willingness of people to embrace such beliefs and to *commit themselves* morally to them. He said:

> The view which I put forward . . . is that the intention of a Christian [or believer in some other faith] to follow a Christian [or other religious] way of life is not the only criterion for the sincerity of his belief in the assertions of Christianity [or any other faith system]; it is the criterion for the meaningfulness of his assertions. Just as the meaning of a moral assertion is given by its use in expressing the asserter's intention to act, so far as in him lies, in accordance with the moral principle involved, so the meaning of a religious assertion is given by its use in expressing the asserter's intention to follow a specified policy of behavior.[7]

The word "god," then, and other religious terms as well, have meaning as people accept what they purport to define and then commit themselves to the attitudes and actions entailed in the definition, description, and expectation of the theology involved.

Concerning item (2), *the verifiability and/or falsifiability of religious beliefs and assertion,* John Hick° in his "Theology and Verification" presents his own persuasive opposition parable.

> Two men are travelling together along a road. One of them believes that it leads to a Celestial City, the other that it leads nowhere; but since this is the only road there is, both must travel it. Neither has been this way before, and therefore neither is able to say what they will find around each next corner. During their journey they meet both with moments of refreshment and delight, and with moments of hardship and danger. All the time one of them thinks of his journey as a pilgrimage to the Celestial City and interprets the pleasant parts as encouragements and the obstacles as trials of his purpose and lessons in endurance, prepared by the king of that city and designed to make of him a worthy citizen of the place when at last he arrives there. The other, however, believes none of this and sees his journey as an unavoidable and aimless ramble. Since he has no choice in the matter, he enjoys the good and endures the bad. But for him there is no Celestial City to be reached, no all-encompassing purpose ordaining their journey; only the road itself and the luck of the road in good weather and in bad.[8]

Hick points out that his parable demonstrates that during their journey the two men do not expect different details with regard to the road itself. They are on, and they see, the same road in the same way. Their different expectations are only in the ultimate destiny. "And yet when they do turn the last corner it will be apparent that one of them has been right all the time and the other wrong."[9] So, although the issue between them has not been an experiential difference, it has been a real, meaningful issue. One man sees the totality of the universe as fundamentally different from what the other sees. But the difference is not a difference within the ordinary events of the universe. The two men do not expect (or need to expect) different events to occur in the temporal process, but one (the affirmer of God) does expect what the other (the denier) does not expect—an end-state that fulfills a special purpose: the creation of the kingdom of God. Their opposed interpretations of the road constitute genuinely rival assertions, and these assertions have the "peculiar characteristic of being guaranteed retrospectively by a future crux."[10]

Hick proposes, then, that statements about God are finally verifiable— eschatologically° verifiable. If there is life after death, verification will occur. If there is no life after death, falsification, strictly speaking, will not be accomplished for there will remain no experience from which to draw the empirical evidence; but this circumstance might be regarded, although Hick does not suggest it, as verification *by default.**

As our own parable for meaningfulness in God-words we shall borrow again from Lewis Carroll, this time from "Humpty Dumpty." Alice and Humpty Dumpty are having an interesting conversation about un-birthdays. Humpty has told Alice that the King and Queen have given him a fine cravat as an un-birthday present. Humpty then tries to explain to Alice about un-birthdays: 365 minus 1 = 364 un-birthdays when you might get un-birthday presents.

> "Certainly," said Alice.
> "And only one for birthday presents, you know. There's glory for you!" said Humpty.
> "I don't know what you mean by 'glory,'" Alice said.
> Humpty Dumpty smiled contemptuously. "Of course you don't—till I tell you. I meant 'there's a nice knock-down argument for you!'"
> "But 'glory' doesn't mean 'a nice knock-down argument,'" Alice objected.
> "When *I* use a word," Humpty Dumpty said, in rather a scornful tone, "it means just what I choose it to mean—neither more nor less."

In our dealing with the God-word (and other metaphysical dimensions in theology) we are taking a position in the general neighborhoods of Braithwaite and Hick; that is, religious propositions are meaningful in that: (1) people take

---

*This sort of philosophical game was carried on in a deceptively whimsical fashion in the University Discussion. The parables and arguments of Wisdom, Flew, Hick, and others, were delightfully attractive "letter-bombs." These philosophers were, in fact, deadly serious. Other persons got in the debate and the whole series is worth reading.

them with serious commitment, and (2) they make a difference in basic human expectation. More precisely, like Humpty Dumpty, our own position is that words "mean" what people say they mean. We would not go as far as Humpty Dumpty. We would more modestly propose that words and propositions mean what communities of persons agree that they mean for the purpose of common conversation. Physicists agree on what they mean by their scientific jargon, economists by their economic jargon, football fans by football jargon, and theologians by theological jargon. If, for example, people use the word "god" to stand for what it is they believe originally and basically causes things to be, and to be the way they are, that is what the word, in their discourse of religion, properly means. If they want to add qualifiers to their terms and say, for example, that by "god" they also mean a loving person, no one should stop them by declaring that such a qualifier is without meaning. An argument may legitimately ensue as to whether the qualifier is an accurate description of the power that causes things to be, but truth or falsity is a different matter from meaningful propositions, and not "truth" but "meaningfulness" was the issue at hand in the University Discussion and other essays by analytical philosophers.

THE GOD-WORD

Some Jewish scholars believe that God's name Yahweh (יהוה) derived from the Hebrew verb *hayah* (היה; to be), and means basically "He who causes beings."* If this is so, the word "Yahweh" has the distinction of being not only God's proper Hebrew name but also the proper denotation for the entire class of God. For the God-word is commonly used to designate what it is, or what is believed to be, that which *causes*. God is that which causes things to be, and to be as they are. The God-word is our usual answer to Heidegger's question, "Why are there beings rather than nothing?" The God-word functions essentially as an explanatory principle in God-talk, in theology; and as an operational principle in religious behavior, in rituals and religious morality. This means that the God-word is used to explain why things are as they are, especially things that are horrendous and nonmanipulable; and how one is to operate (perform ritualistically and morally) to deal with the horrendous and nonmanipulable aspects of God's existence.

As people rationalize themselves and their world, as they do theology, the concept of determinative power emerges in their thinking. In terms of this (discovered and/or invented) determinative power, or powers, human life is explained and arranged if people are going to deal adequately with their religious needs. God is the answer given by religion to the problems of the human condition, to the threat of nonbeing, to the awareness of human

---

*"I cause to be what I cause to be" (or what occurs).

finitude. Religion offers the option of believing (against the horrendousness of an unrationalized phenomenon of birth-life-death) *that there is at the center of human existence a being or process, a divine reality, in which and through which a person, or community of persons, can transcend, or even overcome all the life-negating facts of human existence.* *

GOD CLASS

The notion and fact of determinative power constitutes the class of God. This is what people mean, at the bottom of it, when they use the God-word, or some functional equivalent of the God-word, such as demons, mana, Brahman, father, or even mother nature and evolution. The God class is constituted of all the concepts and terms that identify or explain what is the *cause* of beings, and the cause of the destiny of beings. God is that which causes and directs the destinies of worlds and people. We arrive at this classification, not completely arbitrarily, but by articulating what seems to be the common practice of religious people everywhere. When people do religion, especially when they do mythology and theology, they normally employ the God-word (or a functional equivalent) to designate what they believe to be the cause of themselves and their world; what they believe is dominating and directing, at least in general ways, the world in which they immediately find themselves. A primitive person who speaks of spirits, demons, black magic, mana-power, or The-Old-Man-in-the-Sky-Far-Away is referring to the power that causes, so he believes, things to be, and to be the way they are at the moment, and might be different at a later time. When Christians speak of God, they mean pretty much the same thing. For all the fine remarks that Christians make *about* God (calling "Him" omnipotent,° omniscient,° omnipresent, "that than which nothing greater can be conceived"), they are basically referring to the Father, Son, and Spirit who causes, and causes to be this way and not that. Similarly, Brahman is the causative source of all reality, and Allah created the world and directs all individual fates. To identify God so closely with the cause and destiny of things is not to say that all God concepts are fatalism concepts, that is, beliefs that all things and lives are rigidly predetermined and predestined. It is, rather, to say that all God ideas are intimately involved in "fates." God is importantly involved in the determination of destinies, and it is the amount of God's involvement in human fates, or possible involvement, that gives the God-word its dimension of destiny determination.

It is important at this point to make an observation about one of the consummate religions that seems not to possess a concept of God, much less a concept of God as a determinative power. That religion is the conservative

*See page 7.

form of Buddhism, called Theravada or Hinayana. This great religion of Southeast Asia tries to take a literalist position with regard to the teachings of the Buddha. The Buddha, it is claimed, did not speculate on ultimate reality; therefore, the Theravadist monks avoid such speculation also. In the sacred writings called *Majjhima Nikaya,* Gautama (in Pali, Gotama) is reported to have instructed his followers to remember what he had talked about and what he had not talked about. He had not said that there is an eternal world. He had not said that there is no eternal world. He had not said that the world is finite. He had not said that it was infinite. He had not said that the holy man who has accomplished enlightenment will exist after death. He had not said the opposite. In short, he had refused to discuss metaphysical things. He had talked only about the psychology of salvation. He reportedly said:

> What have I elucidated? Misery have I elucidated: the origins of misery have I elucidated; the cessation of misery have I elucidated. And why have I elucidated this? Because this does profit, has to do with the fundamentals of religion, and tends to absence of passion, to knowledge, supreme wisdom and Nirvana.[11]

Commenting on this, Daniel Bassuk° stated that the Theravadists declare the experience of enlightenment to be divine nature, but beyond this they make no declarations or even speculations. Whatever God is, or even if God is, is of no major concern. The purpose of religion is to free humans from the dislocations of living that are attendant upon human desire and craving. Whatever the causative and determinative power is, it is not the means to religious liberation. The power to save is a human power.

The Theravadists hold that Buddha did not go beyond this point in religious doctrine; therefore, they do not go beyond it. Nevertheless, underlying the concept that humans are situated in dislocation (are in life, out of joint) is the inference that there is power that causes that dislocation—causes things to be, and to be as they are, which is what the God-word fundamentally denotes.[12]

DIMENSIONS OF THE GOD CLASS

The Universal Dimension   In defining God as ''that which causes,'' it becomes apparent that the God-word has two related dimensions. First, there is what can be called the universal dimension. The God-word stands for the power (or powers) responsible for the existence of all things, events, and beings. This is the All-Cause. This is the primitive's High God, who once long ago created the world, and the tribe, and established the customs and the rules; this is the Judeo-Christian ''Creator of Heaven and Earth''; this is the Hindu's issuer of the kalpa;° this is the Theravada Buddhist's unspeculated framework of reality. In this dimension the God-word refers to the power that is causative of all things. In this quintessential dimension the word stands for the power that causes mountains and rivers and rainbows and universes—everything—and thus the cause of many things that may or may not have much religious significance to a given worshipper or a particular theology. The heavens may "declare the glory of God," and the earth "showeth his handiwork," but one may hardly notice the fact, and may find such things as the moons of Saturn, or the planet Mercury, or the galaxy of Andromeda of no practical religious significance at all. Even the Hebrews, who often sang God's praises as the God of nature, did not really base their faith on any kind of nature worship. They acknowledged God as the God of creation (the author of nature), but it was as the God of history that they engaged him religiously. Which brings us to the point of saying that besides the universal dimension of the God class, there is also a religious dimension.

The Religious Dimension The God-word is used not only as a word to identify universal creation, but also to designate the dynamic cause *of what concerns humans ultimately,* that is, humankind's ultimate values. By ultimate values in this context we mean anything held to be of critical value to the welfare of an individual person, or to the welfare of a community of persons, or even to all mankind, especially when the thing so valued is in jeopardy. It is in the context of circumstances that are horrendous and nonmanipulable that the God of religion (and not simply creation) comes into his own. When finitude crushes down upon a person, it is not the God of starry heavens or wondrous earth that is called upon, but the God of threatening power, terrifying portent, shattering anxiety. The God of religion is the God that stands astride the human issues of life and death, devastation and joy, estrangement and reconciliation. This is the God to whom, in moments of finite nudity, people turn to find meaning in their rock and succor in their helplessness, the God in whom or through whom rescue from finitude is believed possible. "God," writes William Bernhardt, "is the religious name for the dominant phase or controlling power in reality as a whole, the power to which we must submit ourselves in our search for [and preservation of] religious values."[13]

THE NAMED GOD

In dealing with God as a central aspect in religion, people are inclined to do more than simply respond in awe and wonder or fear and trembling. They are also inclined, one might say almost impelled, to specify God, to discern or assign the attributes of God and discern or assign God's name. God is particularized; given "sectarian" images.

Apropos of this was the answer given by a professor when one of his students asked: "Did God create man, or man create God?" The professor said, "Yes." Being urged to elucidate, the professor pointed out that it is an obvious fact, corroborated by science, that once there were no people on earth, but now there are people. This must mean that there was a being or a process that created or caused them to become. Whether this was accomplished by divine fiat, or as an emanation from a divine source, or out of a process of evolution does not alter the fact that the human was a created creature. Therefore, there was a God-who-created-mankind reality some place in the world; ergo, God created humans. But beyond this, once created, or sometime thereafter, humans, being creatures of reason and imagination with a passion for words, turned back upon the God that created them to describe, if they could, the nature of their creator. In doing so, they created (and yet create) concepts of what God was like. They assigned attributes to God; defined God; named God; gave God various kinds of qualities, such as life, love, intelligence, personality, and so on. And this God-talk then became an important dimension in the life of the "human creator," because this talk was then taken to be true. God was really like that. In this sense, at least, mankind creates God. The professor's answer remains, yes.

In this illustration the professor dealt first with the simple affirmation that something caused humans to be. But people do not settle for saying simply that there was a "something" that caused them to be. They name it. They describe it. They discover or invent its characteristics. They particularize God. There are a few people in the world (for example, the holy men of India, the sannyasins) who simply meditate upon God undescribed (Nirguna Brahman), but most people, for religious reasons, must "see" God somehow and somewhere. They particularize God in order to get God into some kind of meaningful and manageable form. They name God so that God can be thought about religiously and ritualized meaningfully. To deal with God religiously, to secure religious values, people use words to describe God and God's relationship to the world and to people.

THE CATEGORIES OF PARTICULARIZATION

God is described in innumerable ways, but generally in the East and in the West the innumerable descriptions fall into two categories of description: (1) a living being, and (2) a creative principle, or ground of being. We shall look at these two categories and also at the category of those who eventually despair of describing God: the category of ineffability.

God as a Living Being In primitive religions, as we have observed, people believe that the world is populated with spirits and souls (animism). The spirits and souls are not simply free-flowing powers; they are living powers. Spirits and souls have "personalities." They have minds, feelings, wills. They respond in personlike fashion: lovingly, angrily, moodily, happily.

Many of the spirits of both primitive and ancient people have nonhuman forms, but not all of them. Many appear in the forms of men and women. There was the Old One, far away and long ago, who made everything. He was "a man." There was the primordial Yahweh who walked in the Garden of Eden in the cool of the day, looking for his man Adam and his woman Eve. Such Gods were more than merely alive; they were manlike (anthropomorphic).

The Greek philosopher Xenophanes° once observed that if an ox had a God, the God would be as a great Ox. So with men; their God was often a man "twelve feet tall." For example, the Greeks (especially with Homer and Hesiod) particularized their Gods anthropomorphically. Mercury, the God of speed, was a young man-God with winged feet. Aphrodite was a beautiful woman-Goddess of delightfully erotic propensities. Zeus, king of the Gods, was a handsome, bearded patriarch. The Jews, also, particularized their God in this fashion. God was for them a grand, solitary, personal being, awful and frightening, yet, paradoxically, the God of a people whom he loved with infinite tenderness. Yahweh was lord of their lives, their immediate protector, their daily companion. In contemporary times (in response to some who said that God had died, which implies, of course, that God was once alive), little jokes were made that were exceedingly anthropomorphic in their implications. Some student wrote on a lavatory wall at Harvard: "God is not dead. He just doesn't want to get involved," and here and there one saw bumper stickers that read, "God is not dead. He is alive and well in Argentina." It all adds up to the same particularization: God is the great manlike one. The inverse of God creating man in his image, in Genesis chapter 1, is that God is also in man's image.

God as Principle of Creativity or Ground of Being   As we have seen, God in "his" most primitive form was probably neither animistic nor anthropomorphic. The first particularization of God was probably simply power: mana, as Bishop Codrington's Melanesians named it. Mana is invisible power that causes things to be special. It is not itself pictured, but is identified according to what it does. It is not unlike the way we think of electricity, except that mana is involved in all sorts of things and situations: in a stone that sparkles more than others or is harder, in a stronger wind, or a swifter river, or a more terrible thunderclap. It is seen in trees that grow taller than others, in birds that fly faster or higher, in animals that are more powerful or ferocious. It is in the warrior who wins battles, the artist who paints beautiful pictures, in the shaman who not only has mana but who knows how to manipulate and even make mana. Mana is simply multifarious, localized extranatural or supernatural power. It is not good or bad, moral or immoral. It is just powerful, and it is not animallike or humanlike.

Something distantly similar to mana is to be seen in the Hindu's God

Brahman and the Chinese God Tao. They are not humanlike either. The consensus of the Hindu Upanishads is that God, whether material or spiritual, is THAT (not he or she) which is the cause of all worlds. God is simply all-inclusive, unitary, spiritual energy. It is the ultimate "substance," infinite in essence and self-sufficient. It is not a person, or personlike. It is, rather, sheer creative power. The Tao, also, is the Way of Heaven and Earth, not a personal creator and ruler of heaven and earth.*

In the religions of the West (Judaism, Christianity, and Islam) God is the "person" who created the world and is to be regarded as different from it. The world is natural, God is supernatural. God stands above all things as their creator and as the willful power that determines their destinies. This kind of God-talk tends to take God out of nature, and even out of the world, and make God the wonder of all wonders. God has created the world; the world vaguely reflects his "image," but he is not truly in the world. This, however, is not the direction in which the maturing Eastern religions went. They developed in the opposite direction, and God became not something out of this world, but something in it. God became the soul of the world (Brahman), or the creative process and direction of the world (Yang/Yin and Tao). Here God is imma-nent. Of this position William Bernhardt writes:

> God, no matter how conceived, is believed to be within the cosmic totality . . . the term God . . . symbolizes some phase, character, structure or behavior pattern of the Environing Medium. . . . [As G. T. W. Patrick, in his *The World and Its Meaning* put it] God is "the soul of the world, an indwelling spiritual presence, a creative, organizing and perfecting power, the source of our moral, religious and aesthetic ideals.[14]

God as Ineffable (a God Unknown)   In both East and West, sensitive reli-gionists became leery of all of the things they were saying about God. They began to suspect their God-talk as imperfectly describing what God was really

---

*This particular form of Hinduism is called Vedanta° and was developed initially and primarily by a man named Sankara (A.D. 788–820). Sankara's system may be called "nondualism" because it holds that the world of nature, and the souls of humans, and the power of being (Brahman) are fundamentally the same reality. We should note, however, that this nonpersonalistic monism was not the only concept of God held by Hindus. Hinduism developed personalistic theologies also. One Vedanta philosopher, Ramanuja (1040?–1137), held that God was a supreme person. Relying especially on the *Bhagavad Gita* (see pages 198–199), he concluded that the physical world, individual souls, and ultimate reality are each real, but nondivisible, the first two making up the body of the supreme being. This supreme being is a personal God whose name is Vishnu. In other words, Vishnu, a personal being, is Brahman. A third form of Vedanta, developed in the fourteenth century by the philosopher Madhva, is clearly a theology of monotheism. God and the world are not the same. This is a metaphysics of dualism. Vishnu is the supreme, personal, supernatural God. Madhva held that human salvation comes through the son of God Vishnu—Vaya, the wind-God. This form of Vedanta Hinduism was apparently seriously influenced by Christianity or Islam, or both; each known in India in the thirteenth and fourteenth centuries.

like. For example, as the Jews moved more and more toward their consummate religion, some of them became uncomfortable with so much particularization of God Yahweh. They felt, at times quite keenly, that God was not like anything they were saying about him; that he was, in fact, beyond any true description. In Hebrew thought and practice God's name became too sacred to be used regularly. They began to address God with circumlocutions such as My Lord (*Adonai*), or as The Name of the Lord (*Ha-shem*), or as Creator (*Boray*), or as Our Father Who Is In Heaven (*Avenu She-ba Shamayim*).* They began to avoid using God's name Yahweh. God's name was not spoken, except once each year by the high priest in the innermost part of the Temple, the Holy of Holies.

In the Middle Ages, theologians in Judaism, Christianity, and Islam proposed speaking of God's attributes only negatively. Thus, to say "the living God" would mean not that God had life as a person had life, but only that God was not dead. To attribute knowledge to God would not mean that God knows as humans know, but only that God was not ignorant. The oneness of God did not mean that God was as the concept one, but only that God was not plural.

This uneasiness of talking about God (particularizing God) in the Near Eastern religions, was the modus vivendi of certain theologies in India and China. To discerning Hindus, Brahman was experienceable but unutterable. Those who had experienced Brahman literally had nothing to say. The Chinese Taoist Lao-tzu° put the ineffability of God in these words:

> The Tao that can be expressed
> is not the eternal Tao;
> The name that can be defined
> is not the unchanging name . . .†

From this point of view, to speak of God (whether God be called mana-power, spirit, ox, tall man, principle, oblong blur, or even to call God he, or to say that God is one or good or exists) is to commit an error. One might call it "the fallacy of false naming," or the "fallacy of the pseudonym." If God is ineffable, then to particularize God is to commit an error, if not a sacrilege. Such particularization, however, has a very practical function. It gets the God-word, the God experience, into some kind of manageable dimension so that one can conceive of *him*, or worship *him*, or understand *him*, all for religious purposes; namely, to deal metatechnologically and/or metapsychologically, or mythologically, or theologically, or ritualistically, or morally, with him.

---

*Other epithets for God were *Ha-Makom*—The Place, the Omnipresent; *Ha-Gibor*—The Power; *She'chinah*—The Divine Presence; *Rachamah*—The Compassionate; *Ha-Kadosh Baruch Hu*—The Holy One Blessed Be He; *El* or *Elohim*—God.
†These are the opening lines of the Tao Te Ching ascribed traditionally to the sage Lao-tzu.

The question might be put to such theologies: if one cannot define God in any adequate way, why not give up the attempt? Why not disband theology? The answer to such a challenge could be given on both psychological grounds and pragmatic grounds. People cannot stop talking about ultimate things as long as people are people. They must deal with religious needs. They must interpret their existence to themselves in terms of their ultimate values, and in terms of that which they believe creates, sustains, and finally destroys those values. People will talk about God simply because people are talkers. They are the linguistic animals. They have a veritable lust for words. People talk, for not to talk is not to be human. To be human is to search for meaningful life and the key to meaningful life for humans (unlike the instinct-guided other animals) is to search for the meaning of life as it arises in the divine encounter. So people always search with words to express God's nature, and will continue to do so as long as they are human. And although their nets of words (according to the notion that God is ineffable) have never captured God, and never will, the nets have become increasingly better meshed and finer and richer, and people, if not God, have been greatly edified. The admonition, then, would appear to be not to stop engaging in the fallacy of false naming, but only to recognize that the pseudonym is a pseudonym.

God and the Demonic We have mentioned, in several places, belief in demons and devils. A little, dangling question might be: Where in God-talk, where in theology, does the Devil, by whatever name he is called, belong? The answer is that demons and devils belong to the class of God quite as much as Yahweh and Tao belong there. The God class, as the ultimate power structure, confronts humans both positively and negatively. It creates and supports them and their values, and it also assaults and destroys them and their values. In both instances they are confronted with the power that causes things to be and to be as they are. They may call the one good and the other bad, but in fact they both belong to the same class, and calling them this or that is simply a particularization, primarily for religious reasons.

For analytic purposes we could dispense with the demonic in this brief fashion, but because the Devil and his ilk have become so popular in recent times, it behooves us to return to the Devil in a later chapter and, as they say, "give him his due."

God and Atheism We are also now in a position to deal with another little, dangling question, namely, What exactly is atheism? Who is an atheist? We have observed that when doing theology, people refer to God on two levels of meaning: the universal level, which refers to God as the creator or source of all beings and events, and the religious (particularizing) level, which describes what God is like. To be a genuine atheist one would have to deny the reality of God on both levels. Besides all sectarian Gods, one would have to deny that there is any being or process that causes and directs things and events. Such a person would deny that there is any meaning or value any place in the universe, except the small amount of meaning and value that people themselves create. There are few atheists of this genuine stature. Jean-Paul Sartre and Albert Camus would qualify, but Karl Marx would not qualify. Marx believed in the inevitable, meaningful, redemptive, perfecting process of history. He called it dialectical materialism, which is to say that at the heart of human history there is a dynamic that propels mankind toward a final destiny, toward a utopian order. In other words, there is a power resident in the social order itself that compels and determines the lives of humans.

But, one might question, how can you say that Marx was not an atheist, except by splitting hairs, or reading the term into an abstraction that nobody ever uses? After all, are not atheists simply people who call themselves atheists, who deny the reality of God, and then, perhaps, call religion an opiate of the people, to boot? And the answer could be: If that is what one means by the word atheist, then call Marx an atheist and anybody else an atheist who denies some particularization of God. But then, of course everybody becomes an atheist from somebody's point of view, for we all reject somebody's God as unreal. The fact is that few people deny that there is a dynamic determinant affecting their ultimate values—a metaphysical reality in terms of which they must relate to achieve adequate courage to live with zest not simply because of, but in spite of, the lives they experience. Most often where people "commit atheism" where they deny God, is at the point of particularization, at the point of a God made up in some sectarian theology. They reject somebody's idea about what God is like. This surely amounts to what could more properly be called pseudoatheism. The true atheist, the genuine atheist, must be that rare soul who has struggled through to the end of theological and philosophical speculation and has been forced to conclude, in anguish, that there really is nothing there in which and through which all the life-negating facts of human condition can be transcended. Such a person deserves to wear the epithet "atheist." That person has earned it in agony and despair; that person is not some sophomore who is simply rebelling against the family's Baptist God.

THEODICIES

Some people regard theodicy as a scandalous/sacrilegious term. *Theo*, as we know, means God. *Dikē* (Greek) means judgment. *Theodikē* is a judgment made about God regarding the evil in the world God created. Theodicy is people putting God on trial because of the evil so obvious in the world God created. How do we judge God? Have we learned nothing from Job!*

Actually I am overdramatizing here. Theodicies are vindications of divine

*See "Job" in Chapter 10, page 167.

justice in the face of the existence of evil.† They are efforts to give reasons for the fact of, and enormous amount of, suffering that characterizes life, human and otherwise. God's very existence is challenged, some people believe, because of the suffering rampant in this world. And if not God's existence, at least God's omnipotence and/or omniscience are to be questioned. Put simply and directly: If an omnipotent and omniscient God created the world, why is it so flawed? Did God not know what "he" was doing? Or couldn't God stop things from going wrong? Or did God simply not care?

Humans and animals not only die, but they sometimes suffer excruciatingly. In the Nazi Holocaust six million Jews died, as well as millions of other "undesirables." And they not only died, they died in mental and spiritual and physical agony. Where was God during Auschwitz? But, of course, it wasn't God who killed the Jews. It was the Nazis and their madman leader. But someone asks, "Had God no power over Nazis? Was God unaware of what was going on? Did God not care?" "Or," asks another, "is it perhaps the case that there is no God to be powerful, knowledgeable, or caring? Perhaps God is just a wish that people invented to make life appear as if it were not 'solitary, wolfish, brutish, and nasty'!"†

In Dostoevsky's° *The Brothers Karamazov*, brother Ivan challenges his brother Alyosha:

> "[T]ell me," said Ivan earnestly, "I challenge you—answer. Imagine that you are creating a fabric of human destiny with the object of making men happy in the end, giving them peace and rest at last, but that it was essential and inevitable to torture to death only one tiny creature—a baby . . . for instance . . . would you consent to be the architect on those conditions? Tell me, and tell the truth."
>
> "No, I wouldn't consent," said Alyosha softly.[15]

Taking a similar posture to that of Ivan, Antony Flew pointed out the suffering of children to discredit the claim that God loves humans as a parent loves a child. Flew writes:

> Someone tells us that God loves us as a father loves his children. We are reassured. But then we see a child dying of inoperable cancer of the throat. His earthly father is driven frantic in his efforts to help, but his Heavenly Father reveals no obvious sign of concern.[16]

The amount of sheer physical suffering in the world at any moment is staggering to contemplate. This is a problem for everyone, but it is a special

---

*Gottfried Wilhelm von Leibniz° (1646–1716) coined the term for the title of his book *Theodicy* (1710) in which he argued that evil has no reality because everything that happens in this life happens for the best in what is the best of all possible worlds.

†Thomas Hobbes° (1588–1679), English philosopher who wrote the *Leviathan,* an impressive treatise on the philosophy of politics, saw the nature of "God's world" as one of constant warfare in which, he remarked, the human condition is "solitary, wolfish, brutish, and nasty."

kind of problem for those who believe the world is ruled by a God of power, omniscience, and goodness, and who reputedly loves humans as a father loves his children. If one is an unbeliever he has no need to explain evil *in God's world*. But for a believer it is difficult not to consider evil *in God's world*. Even the most unphilosophic believer, when confronted with the enormity of suffering and evil in this world, recognizes a dilemma: Either God wills to remove evil and is not able to do so, or God does not will to remove it. One who accepts the first horn of this dilemma is admitting that there are other powers equal to God, or even superior to God.* The other side of the dilemma is even worse, for if God can stop evil but will not, God is not worthy of love and trust. On this "horn" God is seen as morally inferior to some of his creatures. What father or mother would not go to any ends to stop the suffering of his or her child, if stopping it was in any way possible.

The point should be made by now: There is a "problem of evil" in this world, and it is a religious problem. It is both horrendous and nonmanipulable. And it raises serious questions about the nature and even the existence of God.

In the world there seem to be two types of evil—natural evil (suffering from such natural causes as disease, earthquake, famine, tornado, volcano), and moral evil (that is, evil caused by human sin). The question is how can any of this evil exist in a world that God created?†

To deal with this problem has been a major concern of Western philosophers and theologians (as well as ordinary people). The following are seven more or less successful answers given to the dilemma of suffering and evil in a world created by a purportedly omniscient, omnipotent, and good God.

Answer 1   It is not a question to be asked. As Job discovered, one is not to ask for an explanation of evil. We are simply supposed to accept suffering and evil assuming that God knows what God is doing. Ours is to be the attitude of reverent agnosticism.‡ Indeed, to ask such a question, to question God, is itself evil.

But if this is so, one might ask, "Why did God give humans a mind capable

---

*One way of arguing in this regard is to say, as David Hume° did, that, perhaps, God is incompetent. Perhaps the world was built by an amateur. "This world, for all [we know], is very faulty and imperfect, compared to a superior standard; and was only the first rude essay of some infant deity, who afterwards abandoned it. . . ." David Hume, *Dialogues Concerning Natural Religion* (Oxford: Clarendon Press, 1976), Pt. V., p. 194.
†This problem is more severe in those religions that ascribe personhood to God; and especially in those religions that ascribe omnipotence and omniscience to God—Judaism, Christianity, Islam. If when God created the world, God had the omniscience to know what would happen, and the omnipotence to control it, why didn't he?
‡See "Reverent agnosticism," pages 164–167.

of such questions, and a passion for asking them?'' To say Jobian fashion, ''This, too, is too wonderful for us to know,'' is not satisfactory. Indeed, the whole Jobian mode is a ''cop-out'' that critics will not permit us easily to take.

Answer 2   Earlier than Job's answer, Hebrews had offered an equally unsuccessful answer by saying that suffering was a direct result of sin and a recompense for it. (This was the theory of Job's friends as they ''commiserated'' with him in his difficulties.) It was also the notion that lay behind the often repeated biblical explanation that Israel's troubles were caused by Israel's sinful behavior.

> And the people of Israel did what was evil in the sight of the Lord and served the Baals; and they forsook the Lord, the God of their fathers, who had brought them out of the land of Egypt; they went after other gods, from among the gods of the peoples who were round about them, and bowed down to them; and they provoked the Lord to anger . . . and he gave them over to the plunderers, who plundered them and he sold them into the power of their enemies round about, so that they could no longer withstand their enemies. Whenever they marched out, the hand of the Lord was against them for evil, as the Lord had warned, and as the Lord had sworn to them; and they were in sore straits.   *Judges 2:11–15, RSV.*

One might accept such a notion—a nation suffers for its sins. The notion might even be extended to individual adult humans. We often, even in this life, reap what we sow. The face we have at twenty (someone once told me) is the face God gave us, but the face we have at fifty is the one that we deserve.

But what of children? A child dies of leukemia—because of having sinned!? To get around this sort of question the ancient Hebrews lamely proposed that the sin, the ''iniquity,'' had been committed before the child was born.

> I the Lord thy God am a jealous God, visiting the iniquity of the fathers upon the children unto the third and fourth generation of them that hate me.[17]

And what of the suffering of animals? Does that count for nothing?

Answer 3   Another idea that Hebrews began to propose sometime after 300 B.C.E.° (alongside the Jobian answer) was the idea of metaphysical dualism— the Satan answer. This Satan answer, although thoroughly amalgamated into Hebraism, was initially a foreign idea. It was not so much Israelite as ancient Iranian—the Persian religion called Zoroastrianism.*

Founded by Zarathustra,° the Zoroastrian religion appeared first sometime during the seventh century B.C., and it declared, among other things, that the world was created by not one omnipotent-omniscient God, but by two opposing Gods: the God of light and goodness (Ahura Mazda), and the God of darkness and evil (Angra Mainyu, also called Ahriman and Satan).

*See pages 130–131.

According to Zoroastrian doctrine Ahura Mazda is not all powerful, but is powerful enough to overpower eventually, in the end of time, his metaphysical adversary, Ahriman/Satan, after which the kingdom of righteousness will come into being. In this eternal kingdom of God, Ahura Mazda will dwell with his angels and archangels, and with all those humans who at the final resurrection and judgment are found worthy. Ahriman and his demons and dark angels will be destroyed, along with all the resurrected humans found unworthy. In the meantime the world, because of Ahriman/Satan, is oppressed by suffering and evil.

In this dualism we can, of course, see the Judeo-Christian concept of Satan, which should not surprise us for that is its source. However, and this is a critical "however," the Jews and Christians never let Satan even approach the status of God Yahweh/Jehovah.° Indeed in Jewish-Christian mythology, Satan was one of the creatures of God and always under the control of God. So to call Satan the source of evil in this world is to stop short of the basic issue, which becomes in this case: "Why a Satan in God's world?" God created Satan. Did God not know what Satan would do? Could God not stop Satan once Satan got started?

Answer 4   Some people have tried to vindicate God by denying the reality of evil. Evil is not a thing of God. It is not a thing at all. It is (1) an illusion, or (2) simply the absence of good.

The "illusion" hypothesis is popularly represented in the theology of the Church of Christ, Scientist (Christian Science) as developed by Mary Baker Eddy.° It is also a central theological concept in Hinduism. Basic to Hindu thought is the claim that all reality is God Brahman. All things exist in the unity of God. God is all: All is God. The everyday world that we encounter is the world as it appears, not the world as it really is. If we could just see the real world, the underlying world, the God-world, we would see that evil has no status in reality. It is metaphysically nonexistent. Suffering and evil are the illusions of erroneous thinking, of mistaking appearance for reality. When one comes to understand completely that he and God are the same reality (as the Hindus say it, *tat tvam asi* "that thou art") even the appearance of evil disappears. Ignorance (Hindu *avidya*) is overcome. God is exonerated. One knows that it was not God but man who was the cause of the "evil" that, in fact, never did at any time truly exist. It was all a mistake.

This is a position tenable in a religion that does not believe God to be a personal being, knowing and caring for human beings. God Brahman, for example, in Hindu thought, is not a self-conscious, all-powerful, omniscient being. God Brahman does not do good, or do evil. God Brahman simply is. God Brahman is the ground of being, not the architect of the universe. Such a God cannot be held morally accountable. But with a personal, omniscient and omnipotent God, as in Judaism, Christianity (including Christian Science), and Islam, the story is quite different. Such a God is accountable—if not for *real evil* in this case, at least for the *appearance of evil*. Even if evil is only an appearance, does not this appearance itself continue the problem of "how" and "why" God let it originate with all the suffering it entails? Surely the "illusion of pain" is as painful as "real pain." Is not illusion itself an evil unworthy of a God who reputedly loves us? When our child cries out in the night, do we not go immediately to reassure him or her that it is only a dream, nothing real, it will not hurt? Would a loving God do less?

L. P. Jacks° once asked, "How shall we think of evil?" and then answered his own question, "We shall think ill of it." However, he went on:

> For my own part, I would rather live in a world which contained real evils which all men recognized than in another where all men were such imbeciles as to believe in the existence of evil which has no existence at all.[18]

Jacks may be a little rough in his comment, but he may also have a legitimate point to make.

Some people justify God and evil by saying that all of God's creation was good. He looked on everything he had made and called it good.[19] But some of that good creation was subsequently corrupted by the choices of some of the free beings God created—both angels and humans. Evil is not something; it is the absence of something; namely, the absence of good.

St. Augustine° (354−430) held that each thing in God's world, whether of exalted or lowly order, was good. Nothing in itself, in its appropriate form, was evil. A worm was not evil because it was lower than a human; a human was not evil because it was lower than an angel. Each order had its appropriate nature (goodness). Evil, then, was not a fact of existence, but a lack of existence—a loss, a failure. Augustine called it *privatio boni* (removal or deprivation of good). The next question, then, must be "Why?"—why this lack, this loss, this failure, this deprivation? If all of God's creation is good, from whence does evil come? It comes, Augustine held, whenever anything willful violates its proper goodness, its true nature, by becoming something less than its proper God-intended self. Evil occurs only when willful corruption enters and a thing (or order of things) stops being true to its own nature and starts functioning with a lower nature. How a worm might do this is hard to comprehend. Perhaps there are no evil worms, except, perhaps, the worm/snake Satan. But how angels or people might do it is easy to see. Angels were corrupted, so the ancient myth informs us, when they chose not to be angels anymore, but to be God's enemies when under Lucifer/Satan's leadership they revolted. They renounced their proper place in the divine scheme of things and ceased to be what God intended them to be. This same thing happened, according to another ancient faith story, in the fall of humankind's first parents. God had created a perfect world and had placed a perfect man and woman in it, but those two (like the angels before them) had the capacity to corrupt themselves because God had given them (as he had given the angels) free wills. Their proper will was to will what God wanted them to be—will to be perfect man and perfect woman, living in fellowship with God. But the man and the woman began to do their own willing, and their own willing led them to *privatio boni*.

Answer 5 Evil is useful. Without evil as a contrast and stimulus, perfection would never be attempted, much less accomplished.

The German philosopher and mathematician Gottfried von Leibniz argued extensively against those who propose that God might have made things better than he did. Such persons propose that God was a faulty architect. This Leibniz rejected. He argued that any created world must have within itself imperfection. Only God is absolutely perfect. But this is the best of all possible worlds. Its imperfections are minimal. Furthermore, the imperfections of this world are not pure negations. They contribute to the masterful architecture of the whole. Imperfection, evil if you will, can be seen as making a positive contribution in that it stands as a contrast highlighting the goodness and beauty of the whole creation, just as in a painting dark strokes and smudges are helpful in giving perspective to the whole.

The next step beyond this Leibnizian conception, taken by a number of eighteenth-century theologians, is the proposal that evil was not simply an accident necessary in finite creation, but a part of God's plan. There had to be evil in the *part* that the *whole* might be good. Evil is a necessary concomitant° to the existence of goodness. Evil is necessary in high moral endeavor because a world without evil for persons to resist would not present the situations for those moral decisions necessary to develop moral strength. Although suffering sometimes crushes the sufferer, it also often results in a spiritual maturity in the sufferer, or those who witness the suffering, that could not otherwise be accomplished. To expect victory where there is no real antagonist is to expect the impossible—no pain, no joy; no sin, no salvation. One who experiences the pain of a toothache can surely appreciate more fully the pleasure of not having a toothache. But why does it have to be such a bad toothache? Some evil, perhaps, but why so much evil? Could not the glory of the whole be accomplished, the fulfillment of individual selfhood achieved, with something less than the death of six million Jews or even the death of one child?

Answer 6 Some people employ as their theodicy the contention that God is not unlimited in power or, perhaps, in knowledge. There is evil in the world not because God does not care, but because God could not in the beginning avoid its coming into existence, or afterwards destroy it, or even always control it.

The idea that God is limited has a long philosophical heritage going back as far as Plato.° In his dialogue titled *Timaeus*, Plato depicted God not as an omnipotent creator, but as a cosmic artisan (*demiurgos*). God knowing the "forms" of existence, took undifferentiated matter (formless matter) and used it to "form-up" the world. God wanted to build a perfect world—a perfect duplicate of the perfect world of forms and ideas—but matter resisted. For all his shaping and reshaping, God's world (the world we live in) was always (is always) only an imperfect copy of the ideal world in God's vision, or in God's mind.

In more recent times religious thinkers have updated the ancient Athenian notion of divine limitation. William James,° E. S. Brightman,° W. P. Montague,° and Peter Bertocci,° all proposed in one way or another that the problem of God and evil demands the hypothesis of limitation. One must hold as inviolable the goodwill of God (the loving character of God) and recognize that God could not always avoid or overcome the fact of evil in human life. He may not have always known how newly created things would finally work out or have had the power to stop them once they got started. God is like people. As Peter Bertocci puts it:

> In basic structure, God's experience does not differ from ours. There is form and content in God's mind, and there is challenge, enjoyment and struggle in his life.[20]

Answer 7   Thomas Aquinas° once said, "Nothing which implies contradiction falls under the omnipotence of God."[21] This means that God can do anything that can be done, but God cannot do what cannot be done, for example, create a round-square, a black-white, a finite-infinite.

That "epitomizer" of modern religious clarity, C. S. Lewis,° in his excellent little book *The Problem of Pain*, presents this same notion. The major difficulty people have in attempting to rationalize God and evil arises in the contention that God is omnipotent. If God is omnipotent, God should have the capacity (the power) to do anything. And God can do anything—*that can be done*.

At this point language may mislead us. With language we can ask what appears to be a reasonable question, "Can God create a round-square (or a finite-infinite)?" The answer is, "no," but not because God lacks some capacity, but because the question is Jabberwocky-talk. Round-square (finite-infinite) is contradiction talk, meaningless talk. Although it sounds as if something is being asked, this is illusion. It is of the same character as a "squik-diddle."°

What Lewis (and Aquinas) recognized is that the term "omnipotent" is equivocal. "God is omnipotent" seems to be a straightforward proposition—simply what it says, "God can do *anything*." But it is actually a truncated proposition. It implies an "if." "With God all things are possible,"[22] *if*. If what? If they are not self-contradictory. God's omnipotence, says Lewis,

> means power to do all that is intrinsically possible, not to do the intrinsically impossible. You may attribute miracles to him, but not nonsense. This is no limit to

his power. . . . It remains that all *things* are possible with God: the intrinsic impossibilities are not things but nonentities.[23]

Peter Bertocci, concurring with Lewis, put illustrations to the concept. He wrote:

> We simply cannot have water which will quench thirst and yet not drown people, fire which will warm homes and not scorch flesh, minds which are sensitive but not capable of becoming insane.[24]

How does this conception of God's power affect God's relationship to evil? It explains, at least partly, how evil can exist in the world of an omnipotent, omniscient God, who is also concerned with the welfare of mankind. For example, it could be that before God created the world he made a choice. He chose a world where freedom of choice and genuine morality are truly possible. He could have chosen differently, but he did not. Having made this decision God proceeded to create a world in which things could happen that would surprise him—things he did not foreknow. If humans were to have freedom of choice and moral responsibility, they must have true freedom—freedom unpredictable even by God. Not even God could have it both ways: a free-unfree man and woman. Indeed, free-unfree, like a square-circle, is nonsense. It is a nonentity. It is one of those contradictions that Aquinas pointed out does not fall under the omnipotence of God. When God chose to permit genuine freedom and true morality, he necessarily chose to permit misuse of freedom. His free beings, be they angels or humans, could choose against him.

With this the door was open to one of the two kinds of evil found in this world—moral evil, sin; the evil that mankind inflicts. With reference to that other form—natural evil—the principle of noncontradiction can again be employed. If only God is perfect, then anything else created must be less than perfect. Not even God can create a perfect-imperfect, a finite-infinite. Being less than perfect establishes the ground for natural catastrophes—a landslide just as a saint walks by; a bit of chemical misformulation in the lymph gland of a child. The question said David Elton Trueblood,° "is not whether this is the *best* of possible worlds, but whether it may be the *only* possible world."[25] And is it a physical world in which God slants at least some natural events in favor of mankind? Concerning this Peter Bertocci writes:

> God governs our human lives through the minimum laws of physical, biological, and mental nature. There are some things which . . . are done for us whether we know about them or enjoy them or not. Were the laws of physics, the reflexes of the body, or the associative and logical capacities of the mind to vary with individual preference, there could be no established, dependable order in the world. The impersonality of these laws reflects, therefore, not lack of divine concern for man but the most intelligent kind of purpose if there is to be any corporate life and existence. The underlying and persistent expression of God's intelligent good will, then, is to be found in the permanencies without which human beings could not exist.[26]

Under any condition human freedom and natural law seem bound for conflict. Volcanoes erupt because of internal pressures; if people live nearby they may get hurt. Everyone knows of the San Andreas Fault, yet millions of people still choose to live in California. On March 23, 1981, in Italy, an earthquake killed 3,000 people. Today San Angelo De Lambardi, the site of the catastrophe, is functioning as before, as a town in which people live as before. We might try to imagine a world where God would protect us from such catastrophes and not let an earthquake happen when people were around, or a volcano erupt. But such imagining would answer no pertinent questions, for that is not the way things are, or apparently ever were, or probably ever will be.

It appears that natural evil is more difficult to explain in a proper theodicy than is moral evil. One can see that to expect the development of high moral character is to expect something that may come at a high price. The freedom essential to moral character can damage as well as perfect. This helps, perhaps, explain a concentration camp, but it will not explain the suffering caused by an earthquake in Italy or a volcano in the state of Washington. We can see, perhaps, that God needed to give costly freedom in order to make real persons, but did he need volcanoes, earthquakes—and leukemia? Or is it that God cannot control volcanoes, earthquakes, leukemia; or, God forbid!—does not care?

NOTES

[1] James Weldon Johnson, *God's Trombones* (New York: Viking Press, 1965), p. 17.
[2] The Wisdom parable started what came to be known as the University Discussion, which included other British professors speaking for and against the idea of the meaningfulness of religious talk (theology). This symposium (part of which was originally carried by the BBC) included the following prominent English professors— Antony Flew, R. M. Hare, Basil Mitchell, and Ian M. Crombie. Others have at various times continued the debate, including Robert L. Calhoun, J. J. C. Smart, John Baillie, John Hick, and R. B. Braithwaite. The University Discussion was published as *New Essays in Philosophical Theology*, ed. Antony Flew and Alastair MacIntyre (New York: Macmillan, 1955).
[3] John Wisdom's article "Gods" is to be found in the *Proceedings of the Aristotelian Society*, new series, 45 (1944–1945): 185–206. It appears also in John Wisdom, *Philosophy and Psycho-Analysis* (Oxford: Basil Blackwell & Mott, 1953), pp. 149–159. It is also available in a number of collected writings, including: *Issues in Christian Thought*, ed. John B. Harrington (New York: McGraw-Hill, 1968), pp. 309–326.
[4] *Issues in Christian Thought*, ed. John B. Harrington, p. 314.
[5] Ibid., p. 315.
[6] From the University Discussion, available in *New Essays in Philosophical Theology*, ed. Antony Flew and Alastair MacIntyre (London: S.C.M. Press, 1955), p. 95; and in *Issues in Christian Thought*, ed. J. B. Harrington, p. 327.

[7]R. B. Braithwaite, *An Empiricist's View of the Nature of Religious Belief* (Cambridge: Cambridge University Press, 1955), pp. 11–26. Excerpts found also in various readings collections, e.g., *Philosophy of Religion, A Book of Readings*, ed. George L. Abernethy and Thomas A. Langford (New York: Macmillan, 1962), pp. 349–357. Quote here is cited from Abernethy, p. 376.

[8]John Hick, "Theology and Verification," *Theology Today*, (April, 1960); quoted in *Issues in Christian Thought*, ed. John B. Harrington, pp. 342–343.

[9]*Issues in Christian Thought*, p. 343.

[10]Ibid.

[11]Henry Clarke Warren, *Buddhism in Translation* (Cambridge: Harvard University Press, 1922), p. 122.

[12]For further consideration of Gautama, Buddhism, and God, see Charles Hartshorne and William Reese, *Philosophers Speak of God* (Chicago: University of Chicago Press, second edition 1963), pp. 411–415.

[13]William Bernhardt, "The Meaning of God in Religious Thinking," *Iliff Review* (Winter 1946): 25.

[14]Ibid., pp. 28–29.

[15]Fyodor Dostoevsky, *The Brothers Karamazov*, tran. Constance Garnett (New York: Dell), p. 180.

[16]*New Essays in Philosophical Theology*, ed. Antony Flew and Alastair MacIntyre (London: S.C.M. Press, 1955), p. 108.

[17]Exodus 20:5.

[18]L. P. Jacks, *Religious Foundations*, ed. Rufus Jones (New York: Macmillan, 1923), p. 105.

[19]Genesis chapter 1.

[20]Peter A. Bertocci, *Introduction to the Philosophy of Religion* (New York: Prentice-Hall, 1951), p. 443.

[21]Thomas Aquinas, *Summa Theologica*, IaQ XXV. Art. 4.

[22]Mark 10:27; Matthew 19:26.

[23]C. S. Lewis, *The Problem of Pain* (New York: Macmillan, 1948), pp. 15–16.

[24]Bertocci, *Introduction to the Philosophy of Religion*, p. 414.

[25]David Elton Trueblood, *Philosophy of Religion* (New York: Harpers, 1957), p. 253.

[26]Bertocci, *Introduction to the Philosophy of Religion*, pp. 474–475.

Chapter 7

THE DEVIL'S DUE

*May you be a long time in Heaven before the
Devil knows you're gone.*

Anonymous

Not since the witch burnings in Salem in 1692 has the Devil seemed to have
gotten as much attention as he has been getting in recent times. As if by
popular demand, he appears to be doing a repeat performance, replete with
demons, witches, satanism, and witchcraft. And the word ''exorcism,''
which a decade ago was a term little known, is now about as common as
''plastics'' or ''astronaut.'' Not that the Devil has not been around the whole
time in this religion or that one. He just has not been around so obviously.
Ernest Jones,° in his *On the Nightmare,* tells us

> the idea of evil supernatural powers, although perhaps not absolutely universal, is
> exceedingly widely spread among ruder peoples, and was so with civilized peoples
> of antiquity. On investigating specific instances more closely, however, it is
> striking to note how very rarely these powers were purely evil in nature. With
> almost the sole exception of the Persian Ahriman . . . one may say that before
> the advent of Christianity there was no definite conception of a supernatural being
> professionally devoted to evil.[1]

Jones makes two points that we should pursue somewhat further: (1) the
notion that most devils are not totally evil, and (2) that the Persian Ahriman
and the Christian Satan are exceptions. They are totally evil.

Semidemonic Gods   In Hinduism the great God Shiva is a demonic God who
is, in fact, only half-fiendish. In ancient Hinduism there was a God named
Rudra. Rudra was Shiva's predecessor, and he was the fierce author of the
devastating storms that swept down from the Himalayas. He destroyed
people. He was held in fear and awe, but he was, also, appealed to in prayer as
if he might listen and be kind. Furthermore, was not Rudra the one who ruled
the mountain passes where the medical plant grew? Surely he was not entirely
malevolent, for sometimes the winds from the mountains were gentle winds,
and the medicine was good.

Later Rudra was called Shiva, which means ''auspicious,'' and his title
was *Mahadeva,* which means ''the Great God.'' The Great God destroyed,
but not simply for the love of destruction; he killed, but not simply for the love

of killing. He did so to make room for new creation. Shiva was in the fall of the leaf, but if the leaf did not fall, the spring could not come. Shiva was demonic, but not totally so. The same cannot be said for the Zoroastrian-Christian devil God, Satan.

The Professionally Demonic Gods   Jones simply referred to Ahriman (also called Angra Mainyu)* as another totally evil supernatural power in addition to the Christian "supernatural being professionally devoted to evil." But Ahriman was more than just another devil. Ahriman was an important predecessor of the Christian Satan.

The Satan of Christian doctrine is not as ancient as is usually surmised. There are, in the Jewish Bible (the Old Testament), other supernatural powers besides God Yahweh, but they are not given much stature. They never stand against God as archenemies, but are, rather, powers tolerated by him and even used by him for his own purposes. The serpent of Eden, for example, is not Satan in disguise but one of God Yahweh's creatures who is cursed only after he tempts the woman. Again, the Satan who appears in Job is not at all like the later figure called the Devil. Rather, Job's Satan appears to be a part of God Yahweh's court playing the role of dialectical adversary in God Yahweh's department of justice. Indications of a power systematically opposing God in Hebrew thought do not appear until the Book of First Chronicles, written in the late fifth century B.C. Earlier, around the eighth century B.C., in the Book of Second Samuel, chapter 24, one reads that the "Lord tempted" David to carry out a census of the people, and then when David did this, punished him for doing so by sending a plague to reduce the numbers of Hebrews, after which the Lord "repented him of the evil." This same story is told again in First Chronicles Chapter 21, many centuries later, only this time it is not God Yahweh but Satan who tempts David. Between the eighth century and the late fifth century something had happened. The Hebrews had become acquainted with the religion of the Persians (Zoroastrianism) which did conceive of a supernatural force of evil constantly opposing a supernatural force of good: the Devil Ahriman (Angra Mainyu) against God Ormazd (Ahura Mazda).

After the Babylonian Captivity, and especially in a period of two centuries before and a century after the birth of Christ, an extensive extrabiblical literature emerged in which there was a fully developed demonology headed by a first-class Devil. This Devil was not simply an angel dialectically opposing God or tempting God's children, but a Devil who was God's archenemy, a Satan of apocalyptic dimensions, the Fiend of Hell, who would eventually be identified as Lucifer,† an angel who had instigated a revolt, had been defeated, and had been, with his diabolical host, driven from Heaven.

*See pages 130−132.
†The identification of Lucifer with Satan was a contribution of the Church Fathers. It was the result of a wrongly interpreted biblical passage: Isaiah 14:12. The Prophet Isaiah had compared

THE SATAN IDEA IN JEWISH NONBIBLICAL LITERATURE

To find the "real Satan" in Hebrew literature one must go not to the Bible but to what is now called the pseudepigrapha°—a body of literature developed in Israel from about 200 B.C. to A.D. 100. These writings were falsely ascribed to such great Hebrew personages as Enoch,° Baruch,° Moses, Abraham, and the twelve sons of Jacob.° They reveal the *Zeitgeist°* of religious life and belief in Israel (or at least an important segment in Israel) two centuries before and one century after the birth of Christ, and were read by Jews and Christians. It is in this literature that the Semitic origins of the "real" Satan are to be found. However, the Satan popular in Christian tradition (the Satan of the New Testament) that began in the pseudepigrapha (and even earlier in the religion of Zarathustra) was finally a Christian product.

Three books of the pseudepigrapha give three accounts of how evil entered the world and of Satan's part in the coming of that evil:* (1) In *First Enoch* we are told that evil entered the world when certain angels seeing earth women desired them and entered into carnal relations with them. (2) In *The Books of Adam and Eve* the story is that evil entered the world (500 years earlier than the angel-woman story has it) when Eve, enticed by the serpent, who was either Satan or an agent of Satan, ate the forbidden fruit, and then got Adam to join her in the disobedience. (3) The third account of the "invention" of evil, as told in *Second Enoch*, declares that evil occurred before the fall of Adam and Eve when Satan dared to assail God and promote himself as potentially God's equal—the revolt in Heaven on the second day of Creation.

THE STORY IN FIRST ENOCH

In the sixth chapter of *First Enoch* (also called Ethiopic Enoch), as in the sixth chapter of Genesis,† heavenly beings look down from Heaven and see the beauty of earthly women. They lust after these women and desire to descend

---

the king of Babylon, surrounded as he was with wordly splendor, before his death, with Lucifer, which is the Latin equivalent of the Hebrew word *helēl*, bright star, son of the dawn; that is, the planet Venus when it appears above the Eastern horizon just before daybreak. Just as the brilliance of Lucifer/Venus surpassed that of all other stars, so the splendor of the king of Babylon surpassed that of all other monarchs. And just as Venus quickly disappeared from the sky, so did the king of Babylon quickly disappear. Several leaders of the early Christian church (e.g., Origen°) misunderstood Isaiah's passage: "How art thou fallen from heaven, O Lucifer, son of the morning, how art thou cut down to the ground which didst weaken the nations" (Isaiah 14:12, AV), as referring to the fall of a rebel angel. The result of this mistake was that the name Lucifer was subsequently used as a synonym for Satan. The two names, however, were not generally so identified until the time of St. Anselm, archbishop of Canterbury (A.D. 1033−1109), who, in his *Dialogue de causa Diaboli*, considerably elaborated on the story of the fall of Lucifer/Satan from heaven.

*In the pseudepigrapha Satan goes by several names: Semjaza, Azazel, Mastema, Beliar, Sammael, Satanail.

to earth and mate with them. According to *First Enoch* one of the leaders of this company of 200 angels, an angel named Semjaza (a Satan figure), did not want them dashing off without a serious commitment to his project. He was afraid that after getting to earth his companions might repent their disobedience and leave him, their leader, to suffer the major punishment. All 200 of the Watchers,[2] as they were called because they were a class of angels who never slept and probably functioned as guardians, took an oath and descended to earth in the days of the great-great-great grandson of Adam named Jared, which means descend. Thus, according to this story, 500 years after the creation of the world these angels alighted on earth and took for themselves human wives. This was a disobedience and a violation of their natures. This was evil. And this evil became evident in the issue of these unions. The offspring were monsters, demons called Nephilim (giants) who soon began to devastate the earth, destroying both animals and humans.

THE STORY IN *THE BOOKS OF ADAM AND EVE*

As years went by the idea that evil entered the world because of the mating of angels with women began to give way to the idea that evil entered the world when Adam and Eve disobeyed God and ate of the fruit of the knowledge of good and evil.[3] According to *The Books of Adam and Eve*, this occurred when the Devil with the assistance of the serpent seduced Eve into eating the forbidden fruit. But why did the Devil do this tempting? According to this story, Satan finally told Eve why he did it. He told her that it all started on the sixth day of Creation when God created Adam and Eve. Having created them in his own image, God ordered all the angels to bow before Adam. The archangel Michael immediately obeyed, but Satan refused, saying:

"I have no (need) to worship Adam. . . . I am his senior in Creation; before he was made was I already made. It is his duty to worship me.

"When the angels, who were under me, heard this, they refused to worship him. And Michael saith, 'Worship the image of God, but if thou wilt not worship him, the Lord will be wrath with thee.' And I said, 'If He be wrath with me, I will set my seat above the stars of heaven and will be like the Highest.'

"And God the Lord was wrath with me and banished me and my angels from our glory; and on this account were we expelled from our abodes into this world and hurled on the earth." *Vita Adae et Evae 14:1 – 16:1*[4]

---

†Genesis 6:1 – 4, this passage tells how the sons of God took the daughters of men as wives and produced progeny of mighty men. Originally this passage was probably a popular legend about giants, but in later Jewish and Christian thought it became a means of explaining how evil spirits and demons got into the world. In the book called First Enoch we are informed that the giants bred offspring who were invisible and incorporeal and who were dedicated to doing evil. Furthermore, these spirits and demons were under the command of the chief of fallen angels who was sometimes called Mastema, sometimes Belial, and sometimes Satan.

This story moves the coming of evil into the world back 500 years from the days of Jared (the angel and woman story) to the sixth day of Creation. And it was not lust for women that did Satan in, but jealousy and pride. He was jealous of the favor shown Adam and Eve, and too proud to bow before them even though they were in the image of God.*

THE STORY OF SECOND ENOCH[5]

In later pseudepigrapha writings there are many indications that the Jews came to believe that Satan's revolt occurred before the sixth day of Creation. It occurred before mankind was created and was a revolt intended to usurp the place of God.

In *Second Enoch*, the story is that Enoch visited the seventh heavens. While in the fifth heaven he learned about the fall of the angels. He discovered that on the second day of Creation, God created ten companies of angels of different orders. One of the companies was led by Satanail (Satan) who "conceived an impossible thought, to place his throne higher than the clouds above the earth, that he might become equal in rank to my [that is, God's] power."[6] For this affront God threw Satanail and his angels out of Heaven (the height), and left him and them "flying in the air continuously above the bottomless."[7] In this account Satanail and his angels fell while still in Heaven. They revolted against God. The fall came when Satan, in inordinate pride, conceived himself as being potentially equal to God. He fell, as Christian theology would later hold, because of the sin of pride. He thought he was good enough to be God. Apparently Satan just got it into his head to be God—to take over, which was a theory that later became fairly standard Christian belief.

In the pseudepigrapha can be seen a Satan composed of both Old Testament story elements and Zoroastrian story elements. We can see a Satan of mature dimensions here. He began as a high order angel; he fell from that lofty position through his own willful pride; he became master of fallen angels and demons; he was involved in the temptation of Adam and Eve; he is the evil

---

*In the seventeenth century, in John Milton's *Paradise Lost,* it is reported that Satan's jealousy was directed not against Adam and Eve, but against Christ. Before the fall of Adam and Eve, the angel Raphael came warning them not to let Satan lead them astray. The angel told them that God had made them perfect, but not immutable: "[G]ood he made thee, but to preserve/He left it in thy power." (*Paradise Lost* 5.525–526). Disobedience was the dangerous prerogative of free beings. They might be tempted to disobey. Indeed, Raphael reported that disobedience had already happened once before—in Heaven. He told them that before their world was formed, or even planned, God called all the hosts of Heaven and told them that he had given primacy to his "only Son," and that "to him shall bow/All knees in Heaven, and [all] shall confess him Lord" (5.603–609). God further said that whoever disobeyed the Son would be cast out "from God and blessed vision, would fall/Into utter darkness, deep engulfed . . . /Ordained without redemption, without end" (5.613–615). Satan, filled with jealous rage, refused to obey God; refused to acknowledge the primacy of Christ. With that literally "all Hell broke loose."

prince of this world—tempting, enticing, leading astray all those who are not wary.

In the New Testament Satan's name appears twenty-nine times and the term "Devil" more than forty times, but such basic questions as: What is the Devil's metaphysical status? Where did Satan come from? How did he come into power? Where did he find his horde of demonic assistants? are never asked, much less answered. Apparently by the time of the writing of the New Testament a full-blown Satan concept was common belief. The New Testament writers simply appropriated it. They did not explain Satan; they simply endorsed Satan. They accepted the common belief. Besides, they were telling the Jesus story, not the Satan story.

A century after the New Testament writers (c. 50–125), the philosopher-theologian Origen° of Alexandria (185?–224?) did speculate on the origins of Satan. He was, apparently, the first church leader to identify Satan as Lucifer. He also argued that the fall of Lucifer-Satan was due to inordinate pride. Giovanni Papini, in his book *The Devil,* states that Origen not only believed that Satan was Lucifer, but that "Lucifer, once a heavenly spirit, had fallen into the pit for having wished to make himself equal to God. . . ." Papini then goes on to say that among the Church Fathers "it is only with Origen that the idea dominant today appears and is sustained, i.e., the theory of pride. . . ."[8] Satan fell because of the sin of pride.

Satan's pride would be restated and reelaborated in the centuries to come, but the issue was fundamentally settled: Lucifer-Satan, the most beautiful of the angels, in a willful moment, fell from all his pristine glory, never again to be restored, because he was proud enough to think he could be God.

The New Testament writers and early church leaders all believed that Satan held a vital role in the economy of salvation. He was a separate power from God. He presented theologically a genuine metaphysical dualism. Satan was really a separate power opposed to God. But it was a dualism kept under control. Neither Jews nor Christians (unlike Zoroastrians) ever conceived of Satan as being equal to God. Satan existed only by God's sufferance, and in the end would be destroyed. The impetus for the concept of Satan may have come originally from Zoroastrianism, but Satan in the Judeo-Christian tradition never made it all the way to Ahriman.

In the literature of Jews and Christians, both before and after the beginning of the common era, the figure of Satan has been pictured in several dimensions. There was the pale Satan arguing with God about the righteousness of Job. There was the pesky Satan tempting David to take a census. There was the confusing, variously depicted, demon of the pseudepigrapha writings. There was the figure of the diabolical fiend of the book of Revelation, who greatly resembled the demonic Devil Ahriman of the Zoroastrian religion. Later in secular literature there was the figure of Satan most dramatically portrayed in Milton's *Paradise Lost:* a figure of tragic majesty—a rebel whose cause was permanently shattered; a rebel puzzled and remorseful, trying to understand his own behavior; a rebel who was realist enough to know that he was forever lost and could blame no one but himself; a rebel eternally committed to promoting sin and death, but who also had a conscience.

After the stature attained in Revelation and *Paradise Lost,* the figure of Satan was sadly degraded into the mockery one sees in the Satan of witches and witchcraft—the Satan with horns and hooves and a tail, copulating with drug crazed witches on Walpurgis Night, which is a far cry from the giant figures of the Persian Ahriman, or the Fiend of Revelation, or the Lucifer of *Paradise Lost.* Eventually the giant of the apocalypse became a parody, a travesty, a joke.

Jakob Grimm, in 1835, in his *Deutsche Mythologie,* observed that the devil idea was a composite of various figures. "He is at once of Jewish, Christian, heathen, elfish, gigantic and spectral stock." But mostly he was Persian.

In the Middle Ages this Persian, Jewish, Christian, heathen, elfish, gigantic, spectral Satan became the God of an inverted religion known as witchcraft, or, at least, so we have been told.

WITCHCRAFT

In common usage, witchcraft is a vague term often used to stand for sorcery, magic, necromancy, voodoo, or almost any other trafficking with spirits or demons. One hears of black witches and white witches and gray witches, and little witches out for tricks or treats on Halloween. But real witchcraft is something else. There have been witches and sorcerers and magicians back beyond when "the mind of man runneth not to the contrary," but, following most modern scholars on the subject, we shall contend that "witchcraft does not antedate 1350 and many authorities would declare this as a century too soon."[9] Witchcraft was a cult movement that purportedly developed in the Christian Middle Ages when God was replaced by Satan as the object of worship and as the source to which people turned to deal with horrendous and nonmanipulable aspects of their miserable existences.

Theories on the Origins of Witchcraft.   There are a number of speculations on the origin of witchcraft. We shall look at four of them: (1) It was a cult created by the Devil from ancient times—the "orthodox view." (2) It was a surviving primitive cult in the midst of Christendom. (3) It was a perverted response of people to their conditions of misery and hopelessness. (4) It was a fantasy created inadvertently by a kind of heresy-mania that infected the Catholic Church during the Middle Ages.

First, the "orthodox theory" goes something like this: In the beginning there was only God, magnificent and alone, omnipotent, omniscient, omnipresent, the absolutely perfect, "than which nothing greater can be conceived." But there was one thing wrong. There was no one except God to appreciate his absolute perfection. Indeed, one might almost suspect that God was lonely. He had no companions, no community, no communication. This problem was solved by an act of creation. God created the heavenly host—angels and archangels—to see and adore him. Now, God could have created automatons to sing his praises: good beings who could only be good, beings who loved and adored him because they were completely programmed to do so. But even greater would be the adoration not of robots but of free beings—beings who could choose to adore God or not to adore him. That kind of adoration was superior, and that kind of being God created. But there was a danger, and the danger became manifest in one of the most powerful and beautiful of all of the angels: the one named Lucifer. Lucifer fell under the sin of covetousness. He wanted to be God. Desire stirred in him. Avarice swelled in him. Deceit spoke to him. He became a subversive, seducing other angels to help him fulfill his ambition. His power grew. The time came. He rose in revolt. War erupted, with Lucifer and his cohorts on one side and God and his loyal angels on the other. Under the logistical competence of God's general, Michael, Lucifer was defeated and cast from Heaven into the outer darkness, along with his corrupted angels, now hideous and demonic.

By this revolt, the choirs of Heaven were somewhat depleted. To rectify this, God set up a kind of experiment. He would create a new world and put on it free beings (mankind) and let them prove themselves before admitting them to take the vacant seats in Heaven. So the physical world was created, and a man and woman placed on it. They were innocent and free, unrestricted except by one commandment: They were not to eat of the Tree of Knowledge of Good and Evil. And so, for a time, Adam and Eve dwelt in Paradise. But out there, in the outer darkness, there was Lucifer-Satan, angry and vicious, still desiring to thwart God in any way he could. So he came in the guise of a serpent and told the woman that if she and her husband ate of the forbidden fruit, they would not die, but would know what God knew, and would in that way become Gods. She ate of the fruit and gave some to her husband. The experiment failed, so God drove the man and his woman from the garden and turned his back on them. Satan moved in and took over, and Adam and Eve began begetting the generations of ''fallen men.'' Some time later God tried again, using Noah as his starting point. But this too failed. Time went by and God tried a third time, this time with a Chosen People.

Through the history of these Chosen People, God wrought, by hard learning, a firm realization in humans that they could not be God, or even create a perfect world. When enough of the Hebrew people came truly to believe this, and to wait for the coming of the promised Savior, God made his final and magnificent move. He sent his Son, his very being, into the world to suffer and die for the redemption and perfection of those persons who would cleave only to Christ and forever renounce the Prince of Darkness, Ruler of the Earth, the Devil.

With the coming of Christ, Satan went into a frenzy. At first he tried to tempt Christ to join him. When this failed, he loosed his wrath upon Christ's church, and through the power of Imperial Rome tried to wipe it out. When this too failed, Satan went underground, and through stealth and dark, nighttime action, secured as many men and women to worship him as he could seduce, giving them power and pleasure in exchange for their souls. Against God's church he arrayed not only himself and his demons but thousands and millions of human witches: depraved creatures who performed black magic, devoured babies, worshipped at an evil mass, engaged in sexual orgies, and bedeviled and corrupted as many priests, nuns, virgins, Christian matrons, and honest God-fearing men as possible.*

In this view Satan has ontological and apocalyptic status. He is a structure out of God's own being, that is, out of God's original loneliness or desire for community and is the major negative force in history, to be finally thwarted only at the end of time. And witchcraft is one of the major devices that Satan employs to thwart God's desire to have the souls of men and women with him in Heaven.

Second, a more modern theory of the origin of witchcraft is proposed by Margaret Alice Murray.° She holds that anyone who examines the records of medieval witchcraft is actually dealing with the remains of a pagan religion, which predated Christianity in Europe and which stubbornly resisted the invasion of Christianity, even to the death. As Christianity became more firmly established, the "Old Religion" retreated to the less frequented parts of the countryside and was practiced by the more ignorant members of the European community. Murray is proposing that there existed a well-defined religion coexisting with medieval Christianity. This religion was later interpreted as Devil worship by the Christian authorities. The witch trials, which spanned three centuries, marked the effort of the Christian church to extirpate its rival.

Murray's reconstruction of the Old Religion includes the existence of covens dedicated to the worship of a horned God, which was a nature deity going back to neolithic times. She further argues that witchcraft was a well-organized belief system that made appeal not only to ruder folk, but even to such superior souls as Thomas à Becket° and Joan of Arc.° Also, Murray includes in the Old Religion King Rufus of England, and Gilles de Rais,° soldier, knight protector, and important champion of the French king Charles VII.[10]

After Murray's thesis became popular, and after the last of the English laws condemning witchcraft were removed from English statutes, several persons came forward to claim and demonstrate that Murray's witch cult survived even into the twentieth century. Gerald B. Gardner wrote *Witchcraft Today,* with an introduction by Margaret Murray. Sybil Leek° surfaced and exposed

---

*This is a statement of the "orthodox" or generally endorsed view as it developed. It actually took on its major dimensions in the late Middle Ages. As Robert Linder,° in private correspondence, states, "The linkage of Satan to witchcraft is strictly medieval and represents a change from earlier teaching."

her own coven in the New Forest, in Hampshire, England. Alex Sanders, self-styled king of the witches, set out on a well-publicized effort to recruit witches into the Old Religion.

This is all quite fascinating: There was an Old Religion; it got a bad name and was driven underground by the avidity of conquering Christianity; but it survived and is alive and well today in places like New Forest, Miami, and San Francisco. But, Murray's thesis is not everywhere highly regarded and many competent scholars do not accept it. They acknowledge her as a good Egyptologist, but with witchcraft she seems to have let her desires and her imagination run away with the facts. Some authorities hold that she was just plain sloppy in her work on witchcraft.[11] However, "many scholars accept her general thesis that witchcraft is really an old pagan religion, vestiges of which have lingered to the present day,"* and her thesis and whole set of arguments are highly regarded by nearly all modern practitioners of witchcraft.

A third thesis on the origin of witchcraft is that it was a perverted response induced by the misery, the squalor, and the frustrations of medieval life. Witchcraft, thus identified, existed as a rebellion against the restrictions of the medieval church and the impotence of the Christian God to deal with the misery and privation in which the masses of Western people lived between the decline of the Carolingian Empire and the coming of the Modern World. Ernest Jones comments on the impotence of the Christian God by observing that the church increasingly identified the miseries of life with the activities of Satan. Pestilence, war, famine, and oppression were all caused by Satan, and no amount of appealing to the Christian God seemed to improve the people's plight. Thus many of the peasants of Europe

> in despair at the obvious failure of God and the Church to relieve their misery, greedily absorbed the doctrines of the wonderful powers of the Devil, so that not a few took refuge with him. . . . The extent of the belief in the Devil's influence on even the most trivial everyday happening was so colossal that one cannot read the records of the time without thinking that Europe was being visited by a mass of psychoneurosis of an unusually malign type.[12]

The miserable masses of Europe were not finding adequate solace in the teachings and practices of the church. Some of them turned elsewhere. In turning elsewhere, to what did they turn? To the religion that ancient Lucifer established? To Murray's Old Religion of pagan origins? Or possibly to something else: to the simple sorcery and magic and conjuring carried on by independent witches and magicians; to some explorations into demon worship; to the kinds of superstitions and practices engaged in by some people in the backwoods places of Europe and America even today? Small groups may have been organized around a witch or wizard. Secret meetings may have been held. Spells cast. Drugs taken. Orgies performed. But nothing like the

---

*Robert D. Linder, from private correspondence.

vast and highly organized underground religion envisioned by the heresy-hunting inquisitors of the church, or Margaret Murray's Old Religion.

A fourth thesis on the origin of witchcraft is the "fantasy theory." The medieval records describing the nature and extent of witchcraft must have been extravagantly overstated by the church's heresy-hunting inquisitors. In reading them one has ample reason for suspecting that they include quite as much fantasy as fact.

In 1967, when Evans-Pritchard° retired from his Chair of Anthropology at Oxford, the association of Social Anthropologists of the Commonwealth decided to hold a conference in his honor. Because of Evans-Pritchard's interest in witchcraft (he had published in 1937 an extremely influential book on the subject), it was decided to make witchcraft the theme of the conference.

Among the persons who read papers at that conference was Norman Cohn.° He titled his paper "The Myth of Satan and His Human Servants" and he opened it with this statement:

> This paper is concerned with a fantasy and the part it played in European history. The fantasy is that there exists a category of human beings that is pledged to the service of Satan; a sect that worships Satan in secret conventicles and, on Satan's behalf, wages relentless war against Christendom and against individual Christians. At one time in the Middle Ages this fantasy became attached to certain heretical sects, and helped to legitimate and intensify their persecution. A couple of centuries later it gave the traditional witchcraft beliefs in Europe a twist which turned them into something new and strange—something quite different from, and vastly more lethal than, the witchcraft beliefs that anthropologists find and study in primitive societies today. And the fantasy has also frequently been attached to the Jews—and not only in far off times but in the late nineteenth and early twentieth centuries when it helped to prepare the way for the secular demonology of the Nazis. It is a long story but a perfectly coherent one, and it is excellently documented.[13]

In his paper Cohn examines the long and often grisly witchcraft story. Satan, identified as the heart of the fantasy, is traced back to Christian, Jewish, and Persian origins. It is pointed out that the Fathers of the Church regarded the deities of the pagan religions as demons who served Satan's purposes. Thus the church took a dim view of any kind of trafficking in the sorcery and magic of the pagan cults. In this attitude the early church prepared the ground for the great demonization of human beings, which was to take place centuries later in Western Europe.

In spite of the church's rejection of paganism, the observances of pagans were not always ruthlessly suppressed, and many became incorporated into the practices of the church. But in the early years of the twelfth century things began to change radically. Up to that time there had been few heretical sects in Western Christendom, but from that time on they began to appear and proliferate, especially in the urban centers of northern Italy, France, and in the Rhine Valley. These sects were often supported by nobility, clergy, merchants, and artisans. They were, thus, to be taken seriously by both ecclesiastical and secular authorities, who became increasingly intolerant of any deviations regarding matters of faith. Heretics were systematically ferreted out, imprisoned, and even burned at the stake. Cohn informs us that "It was in the context of this struggle against heresy that, for the first time in Western Europe, groups of human beings were described as Satan-worshippers."

In 1022 several canons of the Cathedral of Orléans were condemned as guilty of heresy and burned at the stake. Their heresy consisted primarily of rejecting the Catholic concepts of Eucharist, baptism, and the efficacy of invoking the intercession of saints. They advocated, rather, the coming of the Holy Spirit through the laying-on of hands, and the receiving of "heavenly food." This receiving of heavenly food set imaginations running among the opposition. A contemporary chronicler, Adhemar de Chabannes, reported that these "heretics" had been bound into a Devil sect by eating the ashes of murdered children. In this abominable rite, Satan appeared to them, sometimes as a Negro and sometimes in the guise of an angel of light, and commanded them to reject Christ, even while pretending publicly to be true followers of Christ. They were also commanded to abandon themselves to every sort of perverted vice. Some eighty years later Paul, Monk of Chartres, with similar imaginative freedom, reporting on the Orléans incident said:

> They came together by night, each carrying a light. The demons were invoked with particular formulae, and appeared in the guise of animals. Thereupon the lights were extinguished, and fornication and incest followed. The children born as a result of this were burned and their ashes were treasured like holy relics. These ashes had such diabolic power that anyone who tasted even the smallest bit of them was irrevocably bound to the sect.[14]

That the heretics not only associated with demons but actually worshipped Satan was "demonstrated" by the English chronicler Walter Map (or Mapes), who lived in France at the end of the twelfth century. He described meetings that took place in Aquitaine and Burgundy in which Satan appeared as a black cat and was adored by the satanists. In 1233 Pope Gregory IX issued a bull describing how, at heretical assemblies in Germany, Satan appeared as a black cat, or as a frog or toad, or as a furry man, and how the company would give him the obeisance kiss and then embark on perverted orgies. But it took yet another seventy years before such accusations became part of an actual trial for witchcraft, and then the trial was not against real heretics, but against the Knights Templars of France. The Knights Templars were an order of warrior monks who for two centuries had protected the conquests achieved by the crusaders in the Near East. The order had become enormously wealthy, even to the point of becoming an international banker with whom kings and popes did business. In 1307 Philip IV, king of France, who had already despoiled the Jews and the Lombard bankers, turned covetous eyes toward the Templars' wealth. The Templars were accused of defiling Christ by trafficking with and worshipping the Devil, in the form of a black cat, or as an idol called Baphomet. They were accused of doing all the things that witches do—black magic, sex orgies, Devil worship. The Templars were arrested and tortured so severely that some died under the torture, and others "confessed."

Quite supportive of Cohn's "fantasy theory," we might observe that most of what we know about witches was told us by witches under torture. So many witches "confessed" to the crime of witchcraft and then told all that we have information to burn. The only trouble with this information is that most of it was obtained just that way—with burnings and other sorts of equally effective persuasions. The accused witch faced a tough set of inquirers (even professional inquisitors), as Julian Franklyn° tells us:

> To be engaged in supporting Satan against God was an act of major treason for which the punishment was death. Since no one could be expected to admit guilt unless forced to do so, it was reasonable to use force to extract confession. . . .
>
> Every witch brought to trial on the Continent of Europe went through the torture-chamber. Notwithstanding that there was sufficient evidence against the accused to burn her, to which she added her voluntary confession, torture was applied to ensure that the confession was genuine, and complete: the agony inflicted would invariably extract desired additions.[15]

Under torture anyone accused of trafficking with Satan sooner or later "confessed" to everything the tormentors wanted to hear. Did you participate in a Mass of desecration? When the screws were turned sufficiently, the eyelids cut off, the hands doused with oil and set on fire, the "witch" said, yes. Did you have carnal relations with Satan? Yes. Did you fly to the sabbat on a broom? Yes. Did you curse the miller's wife and cause her to die? Curse the farmer's cow and cause it to go dry? What else did you do? And what the witch confessed to—orgastic cavortings, and naked dances, and murderous cursings—got widely publicized at the trials, and was duly noted and recorded in various learned books, such as *Treatise on Heretics and Witches*[16] and *Handbook on Witchcraft,*[17] and in court records as widely separated as Toulouse, France; London, England; and Salem, Massachusetts. The odds are that the vast majority of people executed for witchcraft were not witches, or even magicians or sorcerers, but that their confessions added enormously to the store of misinformation about witchcraft, which today confuses both laypeople and scholars.

Out of overzealousness the inquisitors created the typical stereotype of witchcraft, with its witches and warlocks meeting in secret covens and at sabbat assemblies that were presided over by Satan and where the cannibalizing of infants and sexual orgies were performed.

> In this way the inquisitors built up a fantasy of a mysterious sect, endowed with supernatural powers, which at Satan's bidding was waging incessant war on Christians and Christendom.

This sect was wholly imaginary. Whereas heretical sects did at least exist, there was no sect of witches.[18]

The early inquisitors created a witchcraft mania that was to sweep large areas of Western Europe long after the Inquisition° had ceased to function there. The persecutions that began in the fourteenth century came into full swing in the sixteenth and seventeenth centuries. In these latter centuries they were carried out mostly by secular authorities, some Catholic, some Lutheran, some Calvinist. It cannot be determined exactly how many people were executed for witchcraft in those two centuries, but estimates place the figure from fifty thousand upward to a million.* And for what? According to Norman Cohn, for a fantasy. A fantasy for murdering that did not end in the seventeenth century but only went dormant, to revive again in pogroms against the Jews in the nineteenth century and in the Nazi Holocaust in the twentieth century.

Witchcraft and the Jews   Cohn sees the Nazi destruction of European Jewry as a direct result of the "fantasy of witchcraft." By the eighteenth century the witchhunt mania in Europe had played out. There were still a few people hunted down and killed in backward areas, accused of practicing sorcery, but the idea of a satanic cult of witches had lost its appeal. This, however, was not the case with the idea that there were still servants of Satan in the world. In the nineteenth century the idea revived in the myth of Jewish world conspiracy under the auspices of Satan.

(A caveat is in order here. Cohn has many critics, especially regarding his highly conjectural theory that the "fantasy of witchcraft" is the root of the Holocaust destruction of European Jews by the Nazis.)

During the early years of the medieval period there had been little serious conflict between Christians and Jews. But when, in the twelfth century, heretics came to be regarded as servants of Satan, a similar fate befell the Jews. For the first time they were accused of such things as ritual murder of Christian children, of defiling the consecrated wafer of the Holy Eucharist, and of practicing black magic and worshipping Satan. From the twelfth to the eighteenth centuries, Jews suffered privations and restrictions and martyrdom such as they had never known from Christians before.

With the French Revolution came an emancipation for the Jews, which spread from one country to another during the nineteenth century. But with emancipation there came, also, a wave of panic among the non-Jewish people, stimulated partly by the fact that once freed many Jews quickly achieved

---

*After extensive examination, Robert Linder has concluded that "the correct number was something like 100,000, but nobody knows for certain. In general, the figures given in the past have been rather inflated. The demographic information we have about Europe in that period simply will not support such high numbers as 500,000 or a million." From private correspondence with Linder. Also see Jeffrey B. Russell, *A History of Witchcraft, Sorcerers, Heretics and Pagans* (New York: Thames and Hudson, 1980), pp. 11–12.

influence (in banking, journalism, radical politics) quite out of proportion to their numbers. But Cohn insists the roots of the panic lay much deeper, and he refers to the book of Gougenot des Mousseaux, *Le Juif, le judaisme et le judaistion des peuples chrétiens* (The Jew, Judaism, and the Judaizing of the Christian People), published in 1896, which not only condemned the Jews as diabolical conspirators, but also became, Cohn holds, the source book for modern, political anti-Semitism. Des Mousseaux was convinced that the world was in the grip of a mysterious body of Satan worshippers, whom he called Kabbalistic Jews. He said that there was a secret demonic religion that had been established by the Devil at the very beginning of time. The grand masters of the cult were Jews. The cult centered in the worship of Satan, and its ritual consisted of orgies, interspersed with episodes when Jews murdered Christian children to use their blood for magical purposes. The book claimed to unmask a Jewish plot to dominate the whole world through the control of banks, the press, and political parties.

Out of similar fantasizing there emerged in Russia, in 1905, a widely popular document identifying the Jews again as being satanic world conspirators. The book was called the *Protocols of the Elders of Zion* and has had a long history of unwarranted attention. In the 1920s it was published in an American version entitled *The International Jew: The World's Foremost Problem.* Half a million copies were sold. By the time Adolf Hitler became Chancellor of Germany the *Protocols* was in its thirty-third German edition. According to reliable reports, Hitler read the *Protocols* and took it seriously. Indeed, he not only identified the Jews as major enemies, but elected to utilize the trickery proposed in the *Protocols* to his own Nazi ends. As reported in the *Protocols*, some of the trickery proposed by the Jewish elders to be used against the gentiles included: corrupting the young by subverting good education, taking control of people by playing on their vices, destroying family life, undermining respect for religion, encouraging excessive luxury to distort good thinking, poisoning the human spirit by introducing destructive theories, weakening the human body by microbe inoculations, fostering international hatred, concentrating the world's gold in Jewish hands and then precipitating world bankruptcy.

In summarizing his proposal that Hitler's obsession against the Jews was of the same character as earlier attacks on Satan worshippers, Cohn states:

> At the heart of Hitler's anti-Semitism is the fantasy that, for thousands of years, all Jews, everywhere, have been united in a ceaseless endeavor to undermine, ruin, and dominate the rest of humanity. And although in Hitler's mind and in Nazi ideology this fantasy is dressed up in the pseudo-scientific garb of racism, the fantasy itself stems from quite another source.[19]

That source was the fantasy of witchcraft, the fantasy that the Devil was alive and well and had thousands and thousands of secret human servants who were endowed with uncanny and infinitely sinister powers. Through such beliefs enormous amounts of hatred and fantastic devices for murdering without qualms of conscience could be achieved, and most horribly were achieved in the extermination of perhaps a million witches in medieval Europe and six million European Jews in our own time.

EXORCISM

In Chapters 1 and 5, we proposed that one might analyze religion in a dual-polar fashion: (1) as an effort to exorcise the demonic elements of life (life's threatening finitude aspects), and (2) as an effort to experience the divine elements of life (the transcendence of finitude). Religion is thus seen as an affair of exorcism and ecstasy.

To use exorcism in this way is to define the term with a very broad stroke— religion tries to correct, eliminate, exorcise the horrendous-nonmanipulable aspects of human existence. The term "exorcism" as we shall now view it (and as it is more popularly conceived) is much more narrowly targeted. It is intended to identify only those religious rites that are intended to eliminate malignant spiritual beings (demons) from persons, places, and things. Especially exorcism is used to cure people who seem to be affected with "possession-diseases," that is, people who have been diagnosed as suffering from demonic possession. There is very little of this in the Jewish Bible (the Old Testament). Except perhaps for Saul's seizures suffered when Yahweh° sent an evil spirit to torment him,[20] there is no suggestion of disease caused by evil spirits. Demon possession is much more widely acknowledged in the New Testament, and this increased recognition must have been seriously affected by intertestament experience and writing.

According to intertestament writing,* the first demons were the offspring of the fallen angels, and they caused so much trouble to humans and animals that God ordered them to be banished from the earth. But when, according to the Book of Jubilees, the Nephilim (demons) were finally rounded up to be banished from the world, Mastema-Satan, called "chief of spirits," came before God and requested that

> some of them [the demons] remain . . . and harken to my voice, and do all that I shall say unto them; for if some are not left to me, I shall not be able to execute the power of my will on the sons of men; for these are for the corruption and leading astray. . . ." And He [God] said, "Let the tenth part of them remain before him. . . ."[21]

Thus Mastema-Satan got an army of demons for the tempting of humans and the punishment of sinners.

In the New Testament, reports of demonic diseases (possessions) are restricted to the Synoptic° authors—Mark, Matthew, Luke. John's Gospel has no example of demonic possession. Occasionally in this Gospel the charge

---

*See the discussion of pseudepigrapha earlier in this chapter, pages 102–106, and in the Glossary, page 343.

of "having a demon" is made against Jesus,[22] but this was probably simply a way of questioning his sanity.

In the Synoptics some maladies are simply organic,* others are said to be caused by unclean spirits or demons. These demons seem to be ruled by Satan. In Mark, for example, the scribes proposed that Jesus could exorcise demons because, they said, he was himself "possessed by Beelzebub,° and by the prince of demons he cast out the demons."[23] From Jesus' answer we know that Beelzebub and Satan were considered the same being.[24] According to the Synoptic Gospels, Jesus was an exorcist and gave his disciples the power to exorcise demons.[25]

Belief in demons and the practice of exorcising demons in New Testament times continued in Christian history through the days of the early church fathers (Tertullian, Minucius Felix, Cyprian, Origen) when it became organized and institutionalized. By the middle of the third century, Pope Correlius, in a letter preserved by Eusebius,° reported that exorcists were one of the orders of the clergy.[26]

During the years of witchcraft mania in Europe, England, and America (from the middle of the fourteenth century through the seventeenth century), Christian exorcism was a common practice. Witches were often accused of inflicting disease and injury upon people and animals† through demon assistants, and exorcisms were employed to cure the human victims. The animals were, apparently, on their own; except at times when they were diagnosed as demon possessed and were destroyed.

During the Protestant Reformation (beginning in Germany in the sixteenth century), Protestant dissatisfaction with exorcism arose. First the Lutherans questioned the Catholic practice of exorcising material elements; for example, the water used in the baptism rite. Yet, the Lutherans did for awhile, retain certain other exorcism practices in baptism, and practiced exorcism to dispel demons from persons. But by the end of the sixteenth century many Protestants were discarding all exorcism as superstition. The Calvinists held that exorcism had worked in the early church, but no more. In England Reginald Scott,° in his *Discovery of Witchcraft* (1584), ridiculed popish claims, curses, and exorcisms. He denied all diabolical possession. A century later Thomas Hobbes,° in the fourth book of *Leviathan* denied the existence of demons.

But belief in demons and exorcism rites continued in the Roman Catholic Church, and continues to this day.‡ In Catholic literature there is a book

---

*For example, leprosy (Mark 1:40–42; Luke 5:12–16), paralysis (Mark 2:1–12; Matthew 9:1–8; Luke 5:17–26), blindness (Mark 8:22–25; 10:46–52; Matthew 20:29–34; Luke 18:35–43).

†The earliest account of animals being possessed by demons recorded in Christian history is the story told in the Synoptic Gospels of the man or men (one man in the Mark and Luke account, two men in Matthew) possessed by a "herd" of demons. Jesus exorcised the demons from the man/ men. The demons then entered a herd of pigs, which promptly rushed down a cliff into a lake and were drowned. See Mark 5:1–20; Matthew 8:27–32; Luke 8:26–39.

called the *Roman Ritual,* which dates mostly from the early sixteenth century. It was originally in Latin and is still utilized in that language, but copies are also available in English and other modern languages.[27] This is a handbook of ceremonies and rites used by Roman Catholic priests, and it includes rites for exorcising demons. Demons may be exorcised from persons, places, and things—wherever they have taken up "residence." Exorcising demons from persons was and still is taken most seriously; from places, less seriously; from things more or less routinely.

First we should observe that the Roman Catholic Church, although it still sanctions belief in demon possession and exorcism of demons, has become increasingly cautious about admitting demon possession. Indeed, as early as 1614, in the *Roman Ritual* published under Pope Paul V, the following rule was stated:

> First of all he [the exorcist] should not easily believe that anyone is possessed by a demon, but let him know the signs whereby a possessed person can be distinguished from those [who suffer from some disease, especially those caused by psychic factors. Now the signs of a possessing demon can be] the speaking of many words or the understanding of a speaker in an unknown tongue; the revealing of distant and occult things; the manifestation of powers beyond the nature of one's age or condition; and other things of this sort, which when several occur together are all the more decisive indications.[28]

In 1917 a Vatican rule again promulgated a caution:

> No one who has the power of exorcism can legitimately exercise it upon the possessed unless he has obtained the special and explicit permission of his ordinary.°
>
> This permission will be granted by the ordinary only to a priest endowed with piety and prudence, and of upright life; he is not to proceed with the exorcism until a diligent and prudent investigation reveals that the person to be exorcised is really possessed by a demon.[29]

These rules (and others promulgated by diocesan° and provincial synods°) greatly reduced the number of diagnosed possessions and subsequent exorcisms, but the concept still remains. For example, Karl Rahner,° a contemporary Catholic theologian of renown, proposes that all the "natural evils" of this life are influenced by diabolic powers, but that at times genuine cases of diabolical possession can be diagnosed.

> From the religious point of view, it is neither possible, nor particularly desirable to draw a *sharp* distinction between possession and natural sickness, especially as

---

‡Other contemporary church denominations also take exorcism seriously—for example, the Anglican Communion (Church of England, Episcopal Church), and "Charismatic Christians of all denominations practice the rite today, many of them without benefit of the guidance of a fairly cautious document like the *Roman Ritual.*" Quote is from private correspondence with Robert D. Linder.

the latter may be a symptom as well as an occasion of possession. . . . Even where a phenomenon is to be deemed possession in the stricter sense, it will be the manifestation of that fundamental diabolical dominion that becomes tangible for us only through the circumstances "permitted" precisely in this case; but which also merely reveals what is always present in the world and therefore does not eliminate natural causes but uses them for its own purposes. To distinguish adequately between diabolical influence on the one hand and the intellectual and imaginative world of a person or a period, dispositions, possible illnesses, even parapsychological faculties on the other, is neither necessary nor possible.[30]

Rahner does not specify how one can diagnose demonic possession in the strict sense. Indeed, he dances about the subject in a way that might suggest he would prefer to have the whole idea go quietly away. But when his say is said the fact remains that this highly regarded Catholic theologian admits that genuine demonic possession does exist.

TWO EXORCISM RITES FROM CATHOLIC RITUAL

First, in the baptism rite for adults, an exorcising of the demon of original sin; an exorcising of evil from a material substance (salt); and three exorcising commands leveled against the Devil Satan.

In the rite of baptism for adults,[31] used until recently in the Roman Catholic Church, Satan and two other evil spirits or evil elements are exorcised no fewer than six different times. The first of the six exorcisms occurs at the church door. The catechumen (the one to be baptized) stands outside. In responsive questions and answers, the priest asks who he is and what he wants. The catechumen declares his desire for faith and eternal life. The priest then asks the catechumen to renounce Satan, which the catechumen does. The priest questions the catechumen's understanding of faith. Then "the priest blows three times upon the catechumen's face and says once: Depart from him (her), unclean spirit, and give place to the Holy Spirit, the Consoler." Thus the first demon (the demon of Adam's transgression, the demon of "original sin") is exorcised.

Still at the church door, the ritual continues with appropriate blessings and prayers, until the rite arrives at the "Blessing of Salt." Salt symbolizes preservation, but the salt must be purified and blessed. It is purified by exorcising the demonic element it contains. The priest says, among other things: "O salt, creature of God, I exorcise you in the name of God the Father almighty and in the love of our Lord Jesus Christ and in the strength of the Holy Spirit. . . ."

The ritual then continues with the placing of some of the "dedemonized" salt in the catechumen's mouth as "a symbol of wisdom" and "life everlasting."

Then, still at the church door, in three separate successive ritual steps, Satan, himself, is exorcised with powerful statements, such as:

. . . accursed devil, acknowledge your condemnation . . . and depart from this servant of God . . .

. . . accursed Satan, I adjure you by the name of the eternal God and of our Savior Jesus Christ, depart. . . .

I exorcise you, unclean spirit . . . depart from this servant of God . . .[32]

Second, an exorcism of evil spirits (demons) from persons, and from places.

In the *Roman Ritual* we find "The Roman Ritual of Exorcism" presented in three chapters. Chapter 1 presents the rules governing the performance of exorcisms. They declare that:

1. The exorcist must have "explicit permission of his Bishop." He must also be a person of "piety, prudence and personal integrity."
2. The exorcist must prepare himself for the ordeal by acquainting himself "with the many practical writings of approved authors on the subject of Exorcism."
3. He should be skeptical in his diagnosis. He "must not easily believe that someone is possessed by Evil Spirit. He must be thoroughly acquainted with those signs by which he can distinguish the possessed person from those who suffer from a physical illness."
4. The exorcist should be wary of "the tricks and deceits which evil spirits use in order to lead him astray."
5. The exorcism can be performed "in a church or in some other religious and appropriate place apart from the public eye."
6. The "possessed should be encouraged to pray to God, to fast, to get spiritual strength from the Sacraments of Confession and Holy Communion. . . ."
7. The possessed person should have religious symbols before him/her, such as a crucifix, relics of the saints.
8. In performing the exorcism, "the exorcist should use the words of the Bible rather than his own or somebody else's."
9. If the exorcism is successful, the person freed from possession "should be advised to be diligent in avoiding sinful actions and thoughts" or "he may give Evil Spirit a fresh occasion for returning and possessing him" again. "In that case, he would be in much worse condition than before."

Chapter 2 presents ritual for exorcising persons possessed by Evil Spirit. First the priest appointed by a bishop to perform the exorcism should "make a good Confession."* Then appropriately dressed in clerical garb, the exorcist should stand before the possessed person and invoke protection on that person, on himself, and on his assistants, "by making the Sign of the Cross

---

*Engage in the Sacrament of Confession.

and sprinkling Holy Water.''* The ritual then begins with an invocation, and a response by the assistants, and a prayer, part of which reads:

> Holy Lord! All-powerful Father! Eternal God! Father of Our Lord Jesus Christ! . . . snatch from damnation and from the Devil . . . this man (this woman) who was created in your image and likeness. Throw your terror, Lord, over the Beast who is destroying what belongs to you. Give faith to your servants against this most Evil Serpent, to fight most bravely. . . . Let your powerful strength force the Serpent to let go of your servant, so that it no longer possesses him (her) . . .

Second, the exorcist addresses the evil spirit with such words as:

> Unclean Spirit! Whoever you are, and all your companions who possess this servant of God. By the mysteries of the incarnation, the Suffering and Death, the Resurrection, and the Ascension of Our Lord Jesus Christ; by the sending of the Holy Spirit; and by the Coming of Our Lord into Last Judgment, I command you: . . . Do no damage to this creature (the possessed), or to my assistants, or to any of their goods.

Third, Gospel passages (John 1:1–12; Mark 16:15–18; Luke 10:17–20) are read.

Fourth, prayers and exorcism commands are presented, such as:

> I exorcise you!
> Retire, therefore, in the name of the Father, and of the Son, and of the Holy Spirit.
>
> I enjoin you under penalty, Ancient Serpent! In the name of the Judge of the Living and the Dead! . . . In the name of the creator of the world! In the name of him who has the power to send you into Hell! Depart from this servant of God who has had recourse to the Church . . .

The exorcism concludes with the presentation of a profession of faith (from an early church father, St. Athanasius), and a reading of eight Old Testament psalms, and a concluding prayer, part of which reads:

> We pray you, all-powerful God, that Evil Spirit has no more power over this servant of yours, but that it flee and not come back. Let the goodness and the peace of our Lord Jesus Christ enter him (her) at your bidding Lord . . .

Chapter 3 presents ritual for exorcising places possessed by evil spirits. First, appropriately enough, the "most glorious Prince of the Heavenly Army, Holy Michael the Archangel" (who, as the story has it, defeated Satan long ago on the battlefields of Heaven) is supplicated to do battle again "against the princes and powers and rulers of darkness in this world, against the spiritual iniquities of those former angels . . . and make captive . . . that Ancient Serpent . . . and reduce it to everlasting nothingness, so that it no longer seduces the nations."

Second, the rite continues with scripture selections (Psalm 67), prayers, and finally a long exorcism that invokes against Satan:

---

*Throughout the rite the exorcist is instructed to make the Sign of the Cross repeatedly. This is regarded as a very powerful force.

The Lord Jesus Christ;
God the Father,
The "Sacrament of the Cross."

. . . Go Satan! Inventor and master of all falsehood! Enemy of human salvation!
Give way to Christ . . .

Third, the rite closes with a prayer that ends as follows:

We humbly supplicate you in your majesty and glory: Liberate us, through your
power, from all the power of Evil Spirit, from its traps, deceptions, and treachery;
and deign to keep us safely. Through Christ Our Lord. Amen.

The place of exorcism is then blessed by the sprinkling of holy water.

BLACK MASS EXORCISM

Usually in exorcisms Satan or some agent or element of Satan is banished in
the name of Christ. But in the San Francisco based Church of Satan* the
tables are turned, the exorcism stood on its head—Christ is exorcised! This is
done in a ritual called *La Messe Noire* (The Black Mass).

One of the purported features of medieval witchcraft was the desecration of
the Catholic sacrament of the Eucharist in a ritual called the Black Mass.
According to various accounts a parody of the Catholic Mass was enacted at
each sabbat gathering. Consecrated hosts were either stolen from Catholic
churches or consecrated on the spot by apostate priests. Some accounts state
that a slice of blackened turnip was used as the host in the Black Mass.
However it was done in past times, there is available for examination a
published ritual of the Black Mass as it has been performed in current times by
the Church of Satan.[33] In this ritual a priest, assisted by several other persons,
including a woman who lies naked on the altar, performs a Mass to the glory of
Satan. At a high point in the service, Christ is banished into oblivion—Christ
is exorcised.

First, Christ is condemned for heinous crimes. He is a liar and a fraud,
promising to redeem mankind, to return in glory, but doing neither; preaching
deception, "hope, be patient, angels will serve thee, heaven open," but he
knows better. He knows the angels, disgusted by his indifference, his inert-
ness, have abandoned him. He is an impostor! a fraud! et cetera, et cetera.

After being extendedly condemned, Christ is exorcised. Satan, "the Infer-
nal Majesty," is called upon to "condemn him to the Pit, evermore to suffer in

---

*According to Robert D. Linder, the Church of Satan, headed by Anton LaVey, is only one
branch of modern Satanism. LaVey claims to have 100,000 members worldwide. His church is an
official denomination recognized by the Internal Revenue Service (IRS) for tax purposes. This
makes the Church of Satan in San Francisco an expression of establishment Satanism. Most
satanists do not operate in an open manner with IRS recognition. Thus they would be classified as
nonestablishment. For more information on Satanism today see Arthur Lyons, *The Second
Coming: Satanism in America* (New York: Dodd, Mead, 1970).

perpetual anguish.'' Satan is petitioned to bring down the gates of heaven "that the murders of our ancestors may be avenged!''

> Vanish into nothingness, thou fool of fools, thou vile and abhorrent pretender to the majesty of Satan! Vanish into the void of thy empty Heaven, for thou wert never nor shall thou ever be.[34]

This is, indeed, a parody, for these Satanists, unlike the Catholics, do not really believe in Satan. In his *Satanic Bible,* Anton Szandor LaVey,° founder of the Church of Satan, states:

> Most Satanists do not accept Satan as an anthropomorphic being with cloven hooves, a barbed tail, and horns. He merely represents a force of nature—the powers of darkness which have been named just that because no religion has taken these forces *out* of the darkness.[35]

The flailing against Christ appears to be more an angry response to Christianity than to any belief that Christ is real or is being banished.

Whether or not LaVey's *Messe Noire*[36] is in format anything like the Black Mass of medieval witchcraft (if there was such a thing), it seems to strike the same angry note of rebellion suggested by Ernest Jones: ''. . . in despair at the obvious failure of God and the Church to relieve their misery''* suffering humans turned to the Devil. God had failed. Christ had failed. Let the mass be black. Let Satan in.

Again, whether or not there is such an absolutely evil being as Satan, or whether or not there is a host of demonic imps and black angels fouling the life of man, satanism and demonism have been violent beliefs in Christianity, and remain, if not so violent as before, fixed and tantalizing aspects of the Western Christian scene, as is abundantly evidenced by the voluminous amounts of popular writings on witchcraft and satanism devoured by Western readers, as well as the fantastic popularity of William Peter Blatty's spine-chilling demon-chasing novel called *The Exorcist.*† If 6.3 million copies were sold before the movie itself started setting attendance records, one may safely surmise that there must be a few people left who have an inordinate interest in a very old and macabre way of thinking.

---

*See page 109.

†This book was published by Harper & Row in May, 1971, and released as a film in December 1973. It was supposed to be based on a real exorcism performed in Washington, D.C., in 1949, for a fourteen-year-old boy. For an account of this exorcism see Henry A. Kelly's *The Devil, Demonology and Witchcraft,* rev. ed. (Garden City, N.Y.: Doubleday, 1974), pp. 94–102. Concerning Blatty's book, Kelly states: "First, the documentary aspect of the story is highly exaggerated. Secondly, the facts of the 1949 case of alleged possession . . . have been greatly distorted. And thirdly, the possession that supposedly occurred in 1949 seems to have been a pseudo-possession induced by the rite of exorcism itself.''

NOTES

[1] Ernest Jones, *On the Nightmare* (New York: Liveright, 1951), pp. 156–157.

[2] References to angels as Watchers in *First Enoch:* 10:7; 10:15; 12:2–3; 14:1,4; 15:2; 15:9; and 16:1,2.

[3] Genesis, chapter 3.

[4] *The Apocrypha and Pseudepigrapha of the Old Testament in English,* ed. R. H. Charles (Oxford: Clarendon Press, 1963), vol. 2, p. 137. All references and quotes from the pseudepigrapha writings are taken from the Charles work.

[5] Also called The Book of the Secrets of Enoch; also called Slavonic Enoch, vol. 2, p. 137.

[6] *Second Enoch*, 29:1–5.

[7] Ibid, 29:5.

[8] Giovanni Papini, *The Devil*, tran. Adrienne Foulke (New York: E. P. Dutton & Company, 1954), pp. 31, 36. Papini here refers to Origen's *De Principiis*, XII, 4.

[9] Julian Franklyn, *Death By Enchantment* (New York: Putnam's, 1971), p. 9.

[10] For a more extended study of Margaret Murray's theory on witchcraft and the Old Religion, see her *The God of the Witches* (Oxford: Oxford University Press, fourth edition, 1979).

[11] For example, Henry Ansgar Kelly° points out that Murray, in her article on "Witchcraft" in the *Encyclopaedia Britannica*, is, first, willing to use Lord Coke, an early-seventeenth-century jurist, as her definer of the term "witch": "a person who hath conference with the Devil to consult with him or to do some act." That sort of thing one might pass over as unimportant, but when she actually makes a scholarly attempt to define "devil" and misses, that is a different matter. She states: "The word 'devil' is a diminutive from the root from which we also get the word 'divine.' It merely means god." Kelly points out that if Murray had simply read the *Britannica* article "Devil," she would have been properly informed that the true derivation of the word comes from the Greek translation of the Hebrew word "satan." The *de* element corresponds to the prepositional prefix *dia*, which means "through," and the *vil* element to *ballein*, which means "to throw." Again, Murray blithely states that "it is a well-known fact that when a new religion is established in any country, the god or gods of the old religion become the devils of the new." This is not only not a well-known fact, but it is, in fact, seldom the fact. See H. A. Kelly, *The Devil, Demonology and Witchcraft,* rev. ed. (Garden City, N.Y.: Doubleday, 1974), pp. 55–56.

[12] Jones, *On the Nightmare*, p. 164.

[13] Norman Cohn, "The Myth of Satan and His Human Servants," in *Witchcraft Confessions and Accusations,* ed. Mary Douglas (London: Tavistock Publications, 1970), pp. 3–16.

[14] "Paul, Monk of Chartres, Liber Aganonis," *Cartulaire de l'Abbaye de Saint-Père de Chartres*, ed. M. Guerard, Tom. I. Paris, 1840, p. 112. Quoted by Cohn, p. 9.

[15] Franklyn, *Death By Enchantment*, pp. 72–73.

[16] Paulus Grillandus, published c. 1525.

[17] Francesco Maria Guazzo, published in 1608.

[18] Cohn, "The Myth of Satan," p. 11.

[19] Ibid., p. 15.

[20] I Samuel 16:14.

[21] Book of Jubilees 10:7–10.

[22] John 7:20; 8:48.

[23] Mark 3:22 (AV). See also Matthew 12:22–32 and Luke 11:14–23. Also spelled Beelzebul.

[24] Ibid.

[25] Luke 10:17; Mark 1:21–28; Luke 4:31–37; Mark 3:22–26; Matthew 12:22–32; Luke 11:14–23; 12:10 (Beelzebul); 9:14–28; Matthew 17:14–21; Luke 9:37–43a.

[26] Eusebius, *Ecclesiastical History* 6, 43, 11 GCS 9, 618.

[27] *Rituale romanum* (Boston: Benziger Brothers, Inc., 1953).

[28] *Rituale romanum* 12, 1, 3. The words in brackets were placed in the rule in 1952, replacing "who suffer from black bile or some disease."

[29] *Cordex iuris canonic* 1151, ed. P. Gasparri (Vatican City: Vatican, 1963) pp. 385–386.

[30] K. Rahner and H. Vorgrimler, "Possession," in *Theological Dictionary*, ed. C. Ernse, tran. R. Strachan (New York, 1965), p. 365. Cited also in Henry Ansgar Kelly, *The Devil, Demonology and Witchcraft* rev. ed. (Garden City, New York: Doubleday, 1974), p. 91.

[31] See *Collectio rituum* (Vatican City, Vatican, 1964).

[32] This ritual for adult baptism in its entirety is to be found in *Collectio rituum*, 1964. In 1969, the rite for the baptism of infants and children was revised, deleting all the former exorcism aspects.

[33] See Anton Szandor LaVey, *The Satanic Rituals* (New York: Avon, 1972).

[34] The above quotations are from LaVey, *The Satanic Rituals*, pp. 49–51.

[35] Anton S. LaVey, *The Satanic Bible* (New York: Avon, 1969), p. 62.

[36] LaVey, *The Satanic Rituals*, pp. 37–53.

Chapter 8

GOD COMING OF AGE

I am the Lord your God . . .
You shall have no other Gods before me.
Deuteronomy 5:6 –7

Religion goes back a long way. A million years ago man-who-stands-upright (*Homo erectus*) may or may not have been religious. We know that these prehistoric humans used stone tools. We know, also, that at times they crouched in terror before mysterious threatening elements in their harsh world, as all animals occasionally do, and at times they must have stood awestruck by some magnificence in that same world—which means that the basic elements of religion (terror and awe) were surely present in their lives. But whether they had enough self-consciousness and imagination (enough intelligence) to be religious, we have no way of knowing and doubt we ever will have.

Beginning 100,000 years ago we have a different story to tell. By then man-who-is-wise (*Homo sapiens*) was coming on the scene and was religious. There is artifact° evidence to support this claim. In 1856, in the Neanderthal, a valley near Düsseldorf in West Germany, the remains of humans going back to this Middle Stone Age° (Mesolithic Age) were identified. Those people not only used tools, but also performed religious services. We know this because grave site evidence shows that they buried their dead ceremonially, in special graves, supplied with tools, and food, and weapons. It seems reasonable to assume that they must have thought the dead would need such things, which means they thought the dead went on to another life, a spirit life. Or possibly they thought that the dead person's possessions were charged with some special supernatural potency because of the death. In this case they again would be operating with ideas we would call religious. Also, those people, apparently, conducted some kind of religious service in relation to the bear they hunted for food. They placed bears' heads and long bones on stone slabs or in wall niches in special caves. From this sort of evidence, we might reasonably guess that they were performing religious services to propitiate° the bear-spirit, or to assure themselves of hunting success in the future, or

125

perhaps, to make an offering to some superior God. Whatever they were doing, it was religion.

Later in the Middle Stone Age, sometime about 20,000 years ago, a people of more advanced culture than the Neanderthals came on the scene. Those people are today referred to as the Cro-Magnons.° They too lived in Europe, but farther south, in present-day France and Spain. Like the Neanderthals the Cro-Magnons were true humans (*Homo sapiens*), but they were a more advanced race of humans. Indeed, they were not only taller and more rugged than their Neanderthal predecessors, but also generally taller and more rugged than humans today. Like the Neanderthals, the Cro-Magnons were nomads traveling the hunting trails for food; but during the colder months of the year they lived in caves or lean-to shelters built under protecting cliffs.

In a way similar to the Neanderthals, the Cro-Magnons buried their dead in special graves and supplied the dead with tools and food and weapons. In addition, they painted the bodies of their dead with red ochre.* They also painted other things. Indeed painting and sculpting became advanced arts among these people. They painted remarkable murals on the walls of their caves and molded and sculpted figures in clay and on bone and antler. Their sculpting was usually of animals, but not always. Sometimes they carved small figures of female humans, little "Venus" statues, usually about four to six inches tall. The faces were indescript or actually blank, but the breasts and the bellies and the hips were voluptuously full. They were probably used as mother figures in fertility rites,° and there probably developed early in human history a mother goddess cult.

Also, the cave murals done by the Cro-Magnons were apparently religious in meaning. They were painted on the walls far back in the caves where it was too dark to see them except when illuminated by torch light. They were obviously not painted for the pleasure of everyday viewing. Why then? The likelihood is that they were part of religious rituals. This notion is supported by, for example, a vivid mural painted in the cave of Trois Frères in Ariege, France. It is of a masked man with a long beard and human feet, wearing wolf's or bear's ears, lion's claws, stag antlers, and a horse's tail. This picture probably portrays a most important religious personage in primitive religious life—a person still important in contemporary primitive cultures: the shaman.°† Other cave paintings depict hunting scenes, for example, the bison hunt painting in the Cavern of Montespan. And some of the paintings were magnificently done, as, for example, the bison painting in a cave in Altamira, Spain, executed with the talent of a genius. These murals were probably

---

*The Neanderthal people had also used red ochre in relation to the dead. In Bavaria a collection of skulls of Neanderthalers was discovered that had been immersed in red ochre. The color red probably symbolized blood, which meant life and life after death, as it has so signified to later primitive peoples.

†Also called medicine men and witch doctors.

elements in rituals of hunting magic. Usually the animals portrayed were of the kind hunted and eaten and were often painted with spears and arrows piercing their sides.

Also, the Cro-Magnons painted scenes that probably represented fertility rites. For example, a mural in the rock shelter at Cogul, Spain, depicts nine women surrounding a naked man who seems to be either the subject of an initiatory rite, or the male figure in a fertility ritual, or possibly a male god.

During the Middle Stone Age, in its later years, primitive cultures changed dramatically. The old nomadic hunting families were gradually replaced by stationary tribes who now survived not only on the meat of the hunt, but also on the fruit of the land. They ate berries, grains, fruits, and vegetables gathered by the women and children. They also caught fish using hooks and fiber nets, and invented boats (mostly dugout canoes) for better fishing. And for better hunting they domesticated dogs to assist them.

Life continued, life changed. Berry picking gave way to more sedentary agriculture—tilling and planting. Also, animals were domesticated, and hunting was replaced by the tending of herds and flocks. Primitive people moved into a new age—the New Stone Age, the Neolithic period from about 7000 B.C. to about 3000 B.C., and not only did the economics of their lives become more elaborate, but so also did their religious practices.

Artifacts from this period indicate an extensive increase in the importance and complexity of burial rites. Funerals were conducted with elaborate ceremony in which animals were sometimes sacrificed, and sometimes, apparently, even human beings. Burials were under gigantic boulders, or in stone vaults, often constructed with incredible effort out of huge stones. It was during this time, too, that megalithic monuments were erected: menhirs (single stones standing on end), dolmens (two upright stones topped by a capstone), and cromlechs (stones in a circle, like Stonehenge°). What these monuments symbolized and how they were used remains a mystery, but they were certainly in some way connected with religion.

All of this is simply to say that religion is very old—apparently as old as mankind. It is also as new as next year. With the rise of civilization, after the ages of flint tools gave way to bronze and iron, religion continued apace as a central concern in Egypt, Iran, Palestine, India, and China, and, in spite of sometime woeful cries to the contrary, religion is alive and well in the world today. It is safe to say that where you find humans, you find religion, both in the past, now, and always.

Primitive religions appear to be sufficiently different from "civilized" religions as to be unrelated to them. They are so preoccupied with attempts to introduce extranatural, supernatural powers into natural processes (with metatechnology) as to seem to be of a different class entirely from modern religions. And certainly (at least at first glance) there appears to be little affinity between a God class composed of mana, spirits, souls, demons, and a

God class dominated by a Yahweh or a Brahman or a Tao. Yet we know for a fact that modern world religions also employ metatechnology, and in doing so they generally endorse, as do primitives, a dual natural-supernatural reality. Also we know that the lesser Gods of primitives fulfill the same function in primitive religions as the greater Gods of civilized religions. In each case, the Gods represent the power or the powers to which religious people try to relate in their efforts to transcend, or even overcome, the life-negating facts of their human existences. The function is the same. It is the degree of sophistication that is different. Primitive people see God through primitive eyes. Civilized people see God through civilized eyes. Indeed, civilized people are seeing the primitive Gods "come of age." The various Gods of the dozen or so major religions in the world today are all Gods that emerged in the metamorphoses of very ancient and primitive forms of religion. All the great world religions go back either directly or indirectly to primitive beginnings and to primitive-type Gods.

We shall now examine briefly the metamorphoses and maturing of God concepts in several of the world religions. It should be recognized that this will be done only in broad outline. Neither time nor space is available for anything approaching a complete examination of this subject. The metamorphosis and maturation of any God concept in any major religion is extremely compli- cated, with almost endless intercultural connections and nuances. Neverthe- less, it is important to try to get a sense of the emergence of the idea of a universal God. The concern here, then, is to give only the broad outlines of the coming of age of God in Iran, Palestine, India, and China. But before going directly to those ancient times and places, we shall establish several terms to assist the analysis: primordial religion, consummate religion, and kairotic episode.

Primordial Religion   By primordial religions we shall mean those religions with a God class composed of many supernatural powers and beings; those religions that do not conceptualize a universal power but conceive of super- natural power as being multifarious and localized. The Gods are many and the God powers are limited to various locations in the world or to specific situations in the world, or to both. For example, the Trobrianders of the South Pacific live in a world they believe is populated by a multitude of spirits and souls,* each and all of which are limited in what they do and where they do it. Again, the Yahweh° of ancient Hebraism was the protector and war leader of the Hebrews (that was his job), and he was where they were. At the same time, there were other Gods in Palestine: the Baals, which were agricultural

---

*We should draw a distinction between spirits and souls. Spirits are supernatural powers and beings of nonhuman origins such as Gods, Goddesses, angels, devils, demons, and similar divinities. Souls are supernatural powers and beings of human origin, the ghosts and souls of ancestors.

Gods, each having a specific fertility power for a particular plot of ground. And outside of Palestine, and away from the Hebrew tribes, there were all sorts of Gods, of other people, doing other jobs, in other places.

The God class of primitive and ancient people, generally speaking, was (1) multifarious—composed of many spirits and souls, and (2) localized—the spirits and souls had specific powers and places. Consummate religions resulted when these two factors were each inverted.

Consummate Religion   A consummate religion is one in which the concept of universe has been accomplished, and God is no longer attached to a specific place, or limited power. People think of themselves as living in a universe, and God has become for them a universal power; indeed, God has become *the* universal power. For example, unlike the primordial Yahweh of the wilderness experience who was a God in Palestine and a private Hebrew God, the Yahweh of the post-Babylonian Exile, was a God of all people everywhere—a God of absolute and universal power.

Over the millennia, as certain primitive people advanced out of the Stone Age and a nomadic existence into the use of metals, stable agriculture, and urbanization, a new step was taken in God-talk. People began to say that the multitude of destiny-determining powers in the world was essentially a unity of some kind, that behind the spirits and souls there was an ordering power. The notion of universal order emerged. The ultimate source of determinative power (God) became focalized; seen as one, or two, or perhaps a few, but no longer innumerably multiple. Instead of the primordial notion of localized power there developed the notion of universal power. God power was seen as operating universally. There might be spirits (lesser Gods, Goddesses, divinities, demons), but they were themselves agents of one ultimate power (or of a few ultimate powers). They were all dominated by a great God and were empowered by that God. The world became a universe.

The Kairotic Episode   The third central term for our analysis is kairotic episode. A kairos is a special time, and in our use of it we shall mean those special times and episodes in which and through which the Gods of the great world religions of today grew into maturity. This coming of age took place between about 800 B.C. and 500 B.C. in Iran, Palestine, India, and China. The consummate religion of Iran (Zoroastrianism) particularized the universal power as dualistic and personalistic; there were two ultimate Gods who were anthropomorphic in character. In Palestine the consummate God was conceived as monotheistic and personalistic—there was only one God and he was at least somewhat manlike in character. In India (in Hinduism) the ultimate power was a monistic, all-pervading, nonpersonal power. More needs to be said at this point, for Hinduism was a transcendent monistic, nonpersonal pantheism. What it transcended was the phenomenal world, the world that people normally know and live in. Religion functioned to guide them out of this phenomenal world. In Taoism,° which was also monistic, nonpersonal, and pantheistic, the negations of Hinduism were reversed. In Taoism religion functioned to guide people into the way of the world, the true way: the Tao.

We shall now take time to look in broad outline at the God-word as it came of age in the classical theologies in Iran, in Palestine, in India, and in China.

FROM PRIMORDIAL TO CONSUMMATE RELIGION IN IRAN

The ancient Iranians came to the semiarid plateau of Iran from Central Asia. Although information about their religion at the time of their migration is scanty, it appears to have been what we are calling primordial; that is, a religion in which the God class was composed of multifarious and localized spirits and souls. The spirits (*mainyu*) were divided into good spirits (*ahura*) and evil spirits (*daevas*), with some of the spirits important enough to be called Gods. In addition to supernatural beings of nonhuman origin, the Iranians also believed in the existence of the souls of deceased persons—the Fravishis, or Fathers (ancestors).*

In the seventh century B.C. a revolution in religious ideas occurred in Iran (ancient Persia) when the prophet Zarathustra° began to preach. Before he finished preaching he had not only founded a great new religion (Zoroastrianism), but had also brought that religion to a consummate form. He had "invented" the metaphysics and theodicy of dualism. He had initiated a double movement of thought both away from primordial polytheism toward monotheism and away from monotheism toward radical dualism. In the *Gathas,* ancient Zoroastrian hymns presumed to have been composed by Zarathustra, three superior spirits are identified: Wise Lord (Ahura Mazda), Holy Spirit (Spenta Mainyu), and Bad Spirit (Angra Mainyu). Of these three Wise Lord was declared supreme above all other Gods and spirits. The old Gods and spirits of Iran were generally nature powers—sun, moon, stars, fire, water, winds. Also the Aryan folk gave special prominence to a God named Mithras, the God of the sky, the sun God, who was a God of war, of loyalty, of light. Zarathustra subsumed all of these Gods and spirits, including Mithras, under Wise Lord. Thus he organized a primordial system into a consummate system. The ancient Gods and spirits might yet exist, but they were all under Wise Lord.

---

*Fravishis, apparently, were initially ancestral souls, who if properly worshipped, guarded the family. Later the concept expanded to make them ideal selves, who were also guardian genies for both Gods and humans. Each person was thought to have a genie. Fravishis, which started as primordial ancestor souls, became finally spiritual or immortal elements of living personalities. They preceded human birth and continued after death. Prayer and sacrifice were offered to the Fravishis in return for their efforts in assisting humans achieve salvation.

At the same time that Zarathustra was making this move towards monotheism and universalism, he was also setting the stage for a later dualistic metaphysics. In one of his hymns he wrote:

> Now the two primal Spirits, who revealed themselves in vision as Twins, are the Better and the Bad in thought and word and action. And when these twin Spirits came together in the beginning they established Life and Not-Life.[1]

These "twin spirits" (at least according to several modern interpreters)[2] were the twin sons of Wise Lord (Ahura Mazda): Holy Spirit (Spenta Mainyu), and Bad Spirit (Angra Mainyu). These two were begotten as identical twins, but because they both possessed free will one could choose to become a righteous force in the world, the other to become an evil force. Through their freedom, one son advanced the goodness of his father; the other countered that goodness with evil. Thus we see that Wise Lord's goodness was supreme but not unopposed. Against the goodness of God there was the evil of Bad Spirit, who would later be called Ahriman, Shaitan, Satan.

Apparently Zarathustra himself held to the supremacy of Wise Lord, but held also that the two sons were responsible for all created things—both good things and bad things. In this way Zarathustra held a monotheistic posture with reference to the supreme God, but also accounted for the obvious dualism of good and evil in the world.

If this idea of a Father God and Twin Sons was actually Zarathustra's position (the evidence is unclear at this point), it was soon modified by his followers. Soon after Zarathustra's death there was apparently a melding of Wise Lord and Holy Spirit. The father and son became identical and was henceforth simply called Wise Lord (Ahura Mazda), who was regarded as the brother and opponent of Bad Spirit (Angra Mainyu). With this Zarathustra's original monotheism-dualism disappeared into a radical or absolute dualism. In both cases, however, primordial religion has been transformed into consummate religion.

Not only were the spirits, good and bad, unified under Wise Lord and Bad Spirit but the generic distinction between spirits and souls disappeared, and human souls were also unified in this one universal spirituality. Zoroastrianism identified the souls of living people as battlegrounds where Wise Lord and Bad Spirit waged war. The spiritual destiny of each person was determined by the side that person chose in this battle. A person who chose for Wise Lord would, in life after death, join Wise Lord in Heaven. One who chose for Bad Spirit would, at death, join Bad Spirit in the torments of Hell.

Personal Gods   The two consummate Gods of the mature Iranian religion were personalistic Gods. To say that a God is personalistic is to say that the God possesses the characteristics of a human being (male or female). The God is anthropomorphic. The God possesses at least what humans possess in the way of self-consciousness, intelligence, and will. The God may be a great deal more than a human, but he is not less than human. Both of the Zoroastrian Gods were particularized so. Wise Lord was a personlike being who was the source and power of all the good things humans enjoyed. Bad Spirit was a personlike being who was the source and power of all the evil things that hurt people.

(God Yahweh of the Hebrew religion was also personalistic, but God Brahman in India and God Tao in China were not personlike. They were both nonpersonal Gods, as we shall see.)

FROM PRIMORDIAL TO CONSUMMATE RELIGION IN PALESTINE

The ancient Hebrews were a tribal people, speaking a Semitic language, and living in the arid areas of the Near East. Before the Hebrews, as a people, were heard from in history, similar people had filtered out of the Arabian desert into Mesopotamia and Egypt. The Hebrews, thus, once they arrived on the scene, were just one of many Semitic people in that part of the world, struggling to establish and maintain themselves. According to tradition, the Hebrews originated as a separate people through the leadership of the clansman Abraham and his kinsmen, who migrated from Mesopotamia into the Palestinian area (also called Canaan). Hebrew identity was furthered by the leadership of Moses when he effected the escape from Egypt of at least some of the Hebrew people who had migrated that far south, had settled and lived there, and had finally become enslaved and oppressed there. The Hebrew identity as a nation of people was finally established a thousand years before the common era, B.C.E. (that is, before the Christian era) when the various Hebrew tribes, better to effect their invasion of Canaan/Palestine, united their tribes under the kingship and military leadership of Saul.

When the Hebrews began their push to establish themselves in Palestine, about 1200 B.C.E., they found themselves opposed by other Semitic people who had arrived ahead of them: Phoenicians, Aramaeans, Moabites, Edomites, and others, as well as a non-Semitic people, originally from Crete, known as Philistines. They also found an array of Semitic Gods and divinities. Of special importance and influence in subsequent Hebrew religious thought and practice were the Baalim° or Baals, who were believed to be the localized Gods, the lords of the land. They were the Gods credited with producing crops in Canaan. On many of the hilltops of Palestine and in many of the groves, the local Baalim were duly recognized by those who depended on the crops of those particular pieces of land. Each plot of land had its own Baal, or rather, each plot of land was "owned" by a particular Baal. These Baalim already in Palestine were taken over by the Hebrews as they became established on the land because the Hebrew God, Yahweh, acquired somewhere in the Sinai

Peninsula, was not a farmer God but a nomadic God, a war God, and particularly a God of history, not of nature.

The multifarious and localized character of the ancient Hebrew religion was further seen in the Hebrew's veneration of stones and pillars. Apparently these stones and pillars were originally believed to be alive, to be supernatural in and of themselves. Later they were regarded as the dwelling places of demons or minor Gods. Also, as would be expected among a desert people, wells and springs and streams had a special sacred character. Trees, especially evergreens, were believed to be full of spirit energy. Groves became holy places. John B. Noss° informs us that

> serpents were universally feared (and as universally revered) for being demon-ically sly and cunning, if not indeed possessed by fiery spirits (known to the later Hebrews as *seraphim*, "burning ones"). Goats were regarded as incarnations of "hairy ones" (Hebrew *seirim*). As for untamable wild things of the desert—panthers, leopards, hyenas, wolves, and foxes—they were the savage flock of demon gods of the wasteland.[3]

The Hebrews believed in spirits of human shape also (like the *jinn* of later Arabia), and even in seductive female night-demons, like Lilith who, in Hebrew tradition, led Adam astray. All of these various spirits and divinities, both good and bad, were given a name current among Semitic people: *el,* or in the plural *elim* or *elohim,* a word with the general meaning of superhuman or divinity. As we have it, the name of Abraham's God was El Shaddai, "God of the Mountain." As in other primordial religions, the ancient Hebrews identi-fied the various superhuman divinities as either spirits of nonhuman origin (*ruach*), or as human souls (*nephresh*).

For all the multifariousness and localization of their divinities, the Hebrews after Moses had one God in particular. This was the God who, according to tradition, spoke to Moses from the burning bush, effected the escape of the tribe from Egypt, established a covenant at Mount Sinai, and guided and protected the Hebrews for forty years in the wilderness. This was, also, the God that later tradition would like us to believe, was to the ancient Hebrews the one and only God of the universe. But the facts were otherwise. Whatever may have been Moses' posture, the Hebrew people who left Mount Sinai were not monotheists. At best they were henotheists, holding to one God in particular, their own God, in a world populated by numerous Gods. Moses may have been a monotheist, even an Egyptian monotheist of the Ikhnaton° (Aton)° variety, as Freud suggested, but his people, or the Hebrew people he led out of Egypt, never accepted his monotheism. Not for another 800 years did they do so, even though in the eighth and seventh centuries the great Prophets of Israel and Judah tried to persuade them, and one king, Josiah, literally drove the "false gods" and their "false priests" out of Jerusalem. Apparently not even the great King David (c. 1000 B.C.E.), one of Yahweh's true champions, saw his God as more than the God of a people, a history, and a place. In I Samuel 26:18–20 we are told that while David was fleeing from the wrath of King Saul, who surely intended to destroy the man he feared would usurp his throne, David made his plea:

> Why must your majesty pursue me? What have I done? What mischief am I plotting? Listen, my lord, to what I have to say. If it is the Lord who has set you against me, may an offering be acceptable to him; but if it is men, a curse on them in the Lord's name; for they have ousted me today from my share in the Lord's inheritance and have banished me *to serve other gods!*[4]

The real religious position of the Hebrew people before the Babylonian Exile has been succinctly summarized in the final, fifth-century edition of their history. In the second chapter of the Book of Judges we are told that they forsook their own God and went after other Gods, Gods of the races among whom they lived, such Gods as Baal and Ashtoreth.*

The numerous Baalim (and their consorts, Baalaths) each had a place of worship on some hilltop or elevated ground, or in a grove. Canaanite° priests conducted services at these shrines. Sacrifices were made there and nature worship was performed. Also there were special festivals, in spring, early summer, and fall, in which a fertility Goddess was given special prominence. Astarte (the Hebrew Ashtoreth) was by far the most important of such divinities. She was usually represented as naked and not always gentle or kind. She was, when aroused, a very primitive and powerful force: primordial sexuality. It was chiefly in connection with her worship that the Canaanites practiced temple prostitution. In the divine marriage between Astarte and the Baal of Heaven,[5] which the Canaanites celebrated in the autumn, Astarte was the earth become woman, and the Baal of Heaven was the husband who fertilized her.

The Hebrews, turned farmer in Palestine, found it convenient to adopt most of the Canaanite agricultural worship. Yahweh was a nomad's God, the God of a people, a God of history, not a farm God. He was still *their* God, but the more agricultural they became, the more need they found for the meta-technological assistance of the Baalim and the Baalaths, the Baal of Heaven and Astarte, and others. Without deserting their faith in Yahweh as the God who presided over the nation and guided them in war, the Hebrew farmers became worshippers also at the shrines of the resident agricultural Gods.

As time passed at least some Hebrews must have become convinced that Yahweh was not just the God of Hebrew history and religious life but was the power behind the agricultural divinities; he was, in fact, the God of nature. Evidence of this was in the Yahweh shrine at Shiloh, which in the days of the Judges held only the Ark of the Covenant, but in later times the shrines at Bethel and Dan contained bull-images, that is, nature symbols. Apparently

---

*Ashtaroth is the plural of Ashtoreth (the Phoenician and Canaanite Goddess Astarte; and the Babylonian Ishtar), Goddess of fertility, reproduction, and sexual love.

the God who had led the Israelites through the wilderness was becoming identified as the God who also provided fertility to field and flock. The exalted, austere God of Moses was in danger of devolving into a local nature power.

In the ninth century B.C.E., serious protests against all forms of Baalism began to be raised, and with these protests the first theological steps were taken by the Hebrews away from their primordial Gods toward their consummate one God. With Elijah the prophetic protest began in earnest. Appearing in Israel when King Ahab, under pressure from his foreign wife Jezebel, was moving to make the Tyrian form of Baalism dominant in Palestine, Elijah made his dramatic stand in defense of Yahwism. He tried to demonstrate that Yahweh was the most powerful God, and the only God for Hebrews. Elijah's successor, Elisha, carried on this battle to a sweeping political and religious revolution, but, even though Baalism received a hard blow, it continued and recovered. One thing, however, was accomplished for Yahweh. His supremacy over any and all Baalim was established. Baalism would be practiced henceforth only as a secondary and peripheral cult.

In the eighth century B.C.E., the greatest of the protestors for Yahweh began to appear in Israel and Judah: Amos, Hosea, Isaiah, Micah, Jeremiah, Ezekiel, Deutero-Isaiah.° They said: (1) There is only one God, creator and father of the whole universe and all mankind; (2) he is a God who wants from humans not "lambs of a year old," or "first fruits," or "rivers of oil," but justice and mercy; (3) and, from his bride Israel, he wants fidelity and love. "On that day she shall call me 'my husband' and shall call me no more 'my Baal'; and I will wipe from her lips the very names of the Baalim; never again shall their names be heard."[6] These magnificent champions for Yahweh stumped the land both north and south, and they got a hearing, but often only a hearing. The people were reluctant to give up the fertility worship of the Baalim. They must have feared to do so because of possible ill effects that might result if they gave up a form of worship and metatechnology that had served them so long. Besides, the sternly ethical religion of the Prophets must have appeared to them as bare and cold when compared to the sensuality of a fertility religion.

Nevertheless, the Prophets' reform did get a serious and dramatic hearing from King Josiah[7] of the seventh century B.C.E. The problem in Jerusalem in Josiah's day was not Baalism but imported Assyrian Gods. This invasion of foreign Gods had occurred as part of Judah's attempt to curry favor with the great, threatening national power of Assyria. Josiah's grandfather, Manasseh, had gone so far as to build shrines, even within the courts of the Jerusalem Temple, to the Gods of both Babylon and Nineveh. He also set up an asherah to Ishtar and even sacrificed one of his own sons to the child-devouring God Moloch.° It was against such abominations that Josiah, in the eighteenth year of his reign, inspired to do so by the "discovery" of the Book in the Temple—and, one may surmise, by the urging of Hilkiah, the High

Priest—launched his Yahweh reform. It all began in 621 B.C.E., and it swept clean all the idolatrous religious practices condemned in the Book.* Josiah did not stop with Jerusalem, but ranged throughout Judah as far as Bethel, destroying the worship places of all false Gods, both foreign and domestic.

But the reform, begun with such energy, was not completely successful. Josiah was killed at the Battle of Megiddo, and some of the drive went out of the reforms. The people lacked Josiah's enthusiasm. The fact was that besides being too severe (for example, all worship was to take place only in the Temple in Jerusalem), the people were still not convinced. They had not really acquired the mentality of a consummate religion. They were still semiprimitive/primordial. Yahweh remained for them one of many, and Baalism, even though outlawed by the new law, continued. Something more was needed to transform the old Hebrew (primordial) religion as practiced by the people into a new (consummate) religion.

That something, that kairotic episode, came in the form of a national catastrophe: the destruction of Judah by Babylon and the subsequent years of captivity and exile (586–538 B.C.) in a foreign land. In Babylonia, on the banks of the River Chebar, Baal worship was no longer an issue. The Baals were back in Palestine, no longer a concern to the Jews.[8] The critical question now was what would happen to Yahweh. Was it over with Yahwism too? Would these Hebrews from Judah become lost and Yahweh forgotten, as had been the case with the Hebrews from Israel when that nation fell to Assyria 135 years before? The happy fact was that neither the Hebrew "nation" nor its special God was lost. Indeed, the God, as conceived and preached by the great Prophets, finally came into his own; became finally transformed from a primordial (one-among-many localized) status to a consummate (one-only-and-universal) status. Since the days of Josiah, the Hebrews had believed that Yahweh could be worshipped only in his Temple in Jerusalem, but now the Temple was no more and the Jews were far from Jerusalem. So now what the great Prophets had said made pragmatic sense (just as worshipping the Baals formerly in Palestine had made pragmatic sense): Yahweh, the Prophets had proclaimed, was everywhere. Amos had said it plainly enough:

> Are not you Israelites like Cushites for Me?
>   says the Lord.
> Did I not bring Israel up from Egypt,
>   the Philistines from Caphtor, the Aramaeans
>   from Kir?[9]

Yahweh was God of all nations. The God of everywhere. With further help from two exile Prophets (Ezekiel and Deutero-Isaiah) Yahweh became, once and for all, for the Sons of the Covenant, the only God anywhere, whose

---

*The Book, so called in II Kings, chapter 22, is now identified as having been actually the book now called Deuteronomy. See also Chapter 11, page 193.

sphere of activity was the whole world. "Before me was no God formed, and after me there shall be none" (Isaiah 43:10).

The time had come when the Shema would become the irrevocable center of all Jewish religious thought and action: *Shema Yisroel, Adonai Elohanu, Adonai Echod* (Hear, O Israel, the Lord our God, the Lord is one).

God had come into his majority in Israel, and the ancient Hebrew religion had finally arrived fully as a mature, consummate religion. There might still be divinities besides Yahweh, but all of them (even the latter-day Satan) would receive their creaturehood and power from the one and only God, creator and moral ruler of the entire universe: He who causes beings.

FROM PRIMORDIAL TO CONSUMMATE RELIGION IN INDIA

Before 2000 B.C., India was inhabited by a dark-skinned people called Dravidians. Then at some time in the middle of the second millennium there came pouring over the passes of the Hindu Kush Mountains in the northwest, a tall, light-skinned Indo-European stock, who called themselves Aryans. They drove the Dravidians southward. Later these Aryans would push their way into Southern India and the Dravidians would be reduced to serfdom. Once settled in northwest India, the Aryans began to establish a new religious tradition for themselves. Their first sacred writings, called Vedas, were developed. One of the Vedas, the *Rig-Veda*, was an anthology of religious poetry in ten books, containing over a thousand hymns. The hymns were prayers addressed to various divine beings. Three of these divine beings probably came with the Aryans into India. They were Gods shared with other Indo-European peoples. There was Sky Father (Dyas Pitar), and there was Earth Mother (Prithivi Mater), and there was Mitra, God of loyalty and morality. These three Gods were rather vaguely depicted in the Vedic poems. Much more prominent in the *Rig-Veda* were those deities that were representative of the environment of northwest India. Prominent among these were blustering Indra, a storm God, a war God, and the patron God of Aryans; Rudra (later Shiva), a fierce and dreaded God who caused the destructive storms that swept down from the high, snow-covered Himalayas;[10] Vishnu, a God not prominent in the Rig-Veda, but destined to become one of the major deities of later Hinduism. The *Rig-Veda* expounded many other nature divinities also: *Vayu,* the wind; Ushas, the dawn; Yama, the first man to die who then became a God and ruled the afterworld; Varuna, God of moral law; Rita, God of orderliness. The ancient Hindus[11] also had ritual-type Gods: for example, Agni, God of fire, especially the sacred altar fire; Soma, God of the ecstatic intoxication of the soma plant (possibly a hallucinogenic mushroom); and Brahmanaspati, the deified power of sacred prayer. Brahmanaspati was especially important in later Hinduism because this impersonal power inherent in prayer was the embryo concept that was destined to advance into the great God Brahman of consummate Hinduism. The Aryans of India in the second millennium B.C. possessed a primordial religion, which was composed of numerous supernatural beings, each of which had a local and special function.

Then, around 800 B.C., in the later Vedic writings, some theological speculations began pointing in the direction of a consummate religion. The Hindu religion was beginning its kairotic move. There were beginning speculations that suggested that the powers of the universe were somehow unified in a system. In the late hymns of the *Rig-Veda* three grand figures, which were more than localized nature Gods, suddenly appear. One was Vishvakarman, whose name means "He Whose Work is the Universe"; another was called Prajapati, which means "Lord of Creation"; a third was Purusha, the "Soul of the World." Also, Hymn 129 of the Tenth Book of the *Rig-Veda* was addressed to "That One Thing," which apparently was a causative principle that existed even before there was a universe and must have been the ground from which the universe came forth.

The ritualistic God Brahmanaspati also began to change. Earlier in the *Rig-Veda*, Brahmanaspati was the power inherent in the sacred prayers. Now this prayer-power began to take on larger and larger dimensions of power. It was about this time, in the seventh century B.C., that the Aryans began moving down from northwest India into the Ganges Valley, where they overran the territory and made serfs of the Dravidians they found there. In taking the southern part of India, the Aryan nobility (the Kshatriyas) were kept busy fighting and governing, so it fell more and more to the priests (the Brahmins) to develop and administer religious affairs. In doing so they naturally began to emphasize the importance of the priestly function. The concept of holy power inherent in sacred prayers was greatly expanded. It was finally claimed that the sacred prayer formula, once uttered, was so powerful that not only nature and humans, but even the Gods had to obey it. In other words, the old Aryan Gods were beginning to fall under a unifying power: the power of ritual. Ritual became increasingly important, and a new literature began to appear. This literature was called the Brahmanas. Primarily it was for priests, intended to instruct them on how to perform their sacred prayers and rituals, but mingled with these instructions were statements that indicated a growing notion that there was something unifying the powers of this world: a principle or a power of creativity and unity. Apparently it was occurring to some Brahmin priests that the holy power of prayer (Brahmanaspati), which could alter cosmic events and force obedience from both men and Gods, must be some kind of ultimate power. Was it, perhaps, the central power of the universe?

Between 700 and 300 B.C., the Hindus engaged in one of the greatest speculative periods in the history of religions. Another new literature was produced. It was called the Upanishads.° This literature was profoundly concerned with the nature of ultimate reality; and although no final, single doctrine of ultimate reality was established in the Upanishads, they generally concluded that the true reality—the ground of being, the high and final God, whether material or spiritual—was "an all-inclusive unitary reality, beyond sense-sufficient; it [was] the only really existing entity. This reality [was] most commonly called *Brahman*." [12] By this time the word "Brahman" no longer meant the power of prayer. It now meant the power of being. Brahman had become the impersonal matrix from which the whole world had issued forth and to which it would eventually return. "Verily, this whole world is Brahma[n]. Tranquil let one worship *IT* as that from which he came forth, as that in which he will be dissolved." [13]

The religion had arrived at its consummate form. All power was united in the universal Brahman. All the phenomenal world had arisen from Brahman. Whatever was real was God Brahman, and this was especially true of human souls. Not only were all Gods and nature a manifestation of Brahman, but humans, too, were a manifestation. The human soul (*atman*) and Brahman were identical. To think of humans as separate, individual selves was to be in spiritual ignorance and outside Hindu salvation. The human soul and the world-soul (*paramatman*) were the same. Also, although Hinduism still had its personal Gods, they were all simply particularizations of Brahman.

In a long and profoundly intellectual kairotic period of time in India, the God-word had passed from a primordial (multifarious, localized) status to a consummate status in which a single, nonpersonal power unified all things and made them one. Hinduism had arrived at a nonpersonal, monistic pantheism: a truly consummate religion.*

The consummate religion of India was not only nonpersonalistic, monistic, and pantheistic; it was also "negating." What it negated was the world as it appears to be. The religion of the early Aryans had been robust, optimistic, and direct. It took the world straight, as it appeared to be, and did religion accordingly. But in the later Hindu thought all of this changed. It changed from a religion in which the world was simply affirmed to be as it appeared to be into a religion that profoundly denied that the world was as it appeared to be. The function of religion was not to deal directly with the immediate

---

*Later, especially in the philosophical theology of Ramanuja (1034?–1137), a form of Hindu theology developed that declared the ultimate God Brahman, the God come of age in the philosophies of the Upanishads, to be not an impersonal power, but a supreme person. Ramanuja took his clues for this doctrine from certain passages in the Upanishads (for example, from the Brihadaranyaka Upanishad, 3.7.3, where Brahman is declared to be the "inner Controller" of the universe) and from the *Bhagavad Gita* (see pages 198–199), which not only stresses the unity of all things in Brahman, but also proclaims the supreme Brahman to be not impersonal, but personal, namely, God Vishnu.

To the followers of Ramanuja's theology (and later, in the fourteenth century, in the theology of Madhva), God Brahman is not the abstract Brahman of earlier Hindu thought, but a specific person, omnipotent, omniscient, omnipresent, and also merciful and loving. In other words, Brahman is Vishnu.

appearance of things but with the subtle and hidden reality of things. It was not to save people in "this world" but to guide them beyond these appearances into the "real world."

At least three conditions conspired to transform Hinduism from world-affirming to world-denying. These conditions were the caste system, the Law of Karma, and the doctrine of reincarnation or transmigration of souls.

First, the Caste System   A rigid social stratification of society developed in Hinduism when, about the seventh century B.C., the Aryans moved from northwest India down into the Ganges Valley. They conquered the Dravidian natives and immediately made them into a serf class (the Shudra). The three other large classes of Hindu society were the nobles (Kshatriyas), the priests (Brahmins), and the commoners (Vaisyas). These castes became increasingly rigid to the point where not only were intermarriages forbidden, but even friendly social intercourse was forbidden. Besides these castes there was a growing number of people who were "outcastes," those who for one reason or another had been expelled from caste. They were the miserable dregs of society, impoverished, untouchable, hopeless. By 500 B.C. the castes had divided into hundreds of subcastes with added social restrictions. The whole structure was becoming oppressive. People were being shut off in every direction. And this restrictiveness was given a moral and religious justification by identifying caste as effected by Karma and reincarnation.

Second, the Law of Karma and the Doctrine of Reincarnation   Quite early, possibly from the Dravidian natives, the Hindus came to believe that life was repeated. People were reborn, and the status of their rebirth was determined by their thoughts, words, and deeds in a previous life. Karma was the law of just desserts. People received or became in the next life what they deserved. As the *Chandogya Upanishad* puts it, "Those who are of pleasant conduct here . . . will enter a pleasant womb, either the womb of a Brahman, or the womb of a Kshatriya, or the womb of a Vaisya. But those who are of stinking conduct here . . . will enter the womb of a dog, or the womb of a swine, or the womb of an outcaste.[14]

In Hindu thought one was doomed to return to this world with all the suffering and pain, with all its anguish of finitude, again and again, unless and until through a life of religious devotion or altruistic works or spiritual insight, or a combination, one's soul attained sufficient moral and spiritual purity to make possible its escape from the Wheel of Rebirth, and its return and reunion with God Brahman. Hinduism, in its most exalted form, was mysticism. Rejecting this world of falseness, it directed people finally to seek escape by entering Nirvana, by becoming completely identified, not with oneself and one's world, but with the God behind the world, with the reality beneath all phenomenon, with Brahman.

The final maturity of God in India led to world rejection. In one sense, the idea that "all is God-Brahman" declared that all was right because everything was basically divine. But in another more practical sense this notion became world negating and pessimistic, for it denied any true individuality to persons, depriving the independent person of all significance. It crushed one with a sense of unreality and made this worldly life a helpless, hopeless existence in which a pessimistic world withdrawal was the only way out of the human condition and the anguish of finitude. In India the multifarious supernatural powers became unified in one basic power. The localized supernatural powers became unified in a universal power. An early primordial world optimism became pessimistic and world renouncing. As God Brahman became all, the world and individual people became nothing, or worse than nothing—they became delusions.

FROM PRIMORDIAL TO CONSUMMATE RELIGION IN CHINA

At about the same time that monistic theology was developing in India and being recorded in the Upanishads, there was a movement in China to order the spirits, to establish a universal theology.

The religious practice of the early Chinese was typical of primordial cultures. It was a mixture of nature worship and reverence for ancestors. The Chinese believed in a multitude of spirits and demons, seen primarily in agricultural models. They were especially devoted to earth Gods called *she,* and symbolized by earth mounds located in each Chinese village. The mounds were the center of an agricultural cult.

As time passed the worship of earth was extended upward, apparently, to include the heavens. During the Shang° (eastern) dynasty (1766−1122 B.C.), the Chinese began to address Heaven as a God, *Ti* or *Shang Ti. Shang* means "upper" and *Ti* means basically "ruler." This God, however, was a sort of ancestral figure located in the upper regions of the sky; it was far from being an almighty God ruler of the universe. During the Chou (western) dynasty (1122−255 B.C.) another name came into use as the home of the Sky God— *T'ien* (Heaven). Eventually T'ien came to be regarded as the superior power of supernatural forces, and the ultimate determiner of human destiny.*

But earlier than both Shang Ti and T'ien, and continuing in Chinese history to modern times, were spirits and demons by the millions. Many of them were good spirits, beneficial friendly spirits, but more were demonic. From earliest times the Chinese had something close to paranoia concerning devils and

---

*Guide to pronouncing Chinese words according to what is called the Wade-Giles System: consonants or pairs of consonants followed by an apostrophe should be pronounced as in English, but when not followed by an apostrophe t = d, ts = dz, ch = j, ih and ju = r, hs = sh (or h as in hard); e.g., *Tao* is "dao," *Shang Ti* is "shang de," *Fu Hsi* is "foo she," *P'an Ku* is "pan goo."

demons. They believed that devils and demons thronged around every human dwelling, haunted lonely places, infested roadways, especially at night, lurked in forests and mountains. There were demons in the water, in the air, in the ground. There were animal demons, bird demons, fish demons, and snake demons; and human-eating demons, vampires, ghouls, by the hundreds and thousands. Probably never was there a people more afraid of devils and demons than the Chinese, or a people who ever did more to protect themselves from bad spirits, on the one hand, and get assistance from good spirits, on the other hand.

In Chinese mythology, there were, besides the Sky-God, many other spirits of sufficient importance to be regarded as Gods. There were Yu Ch'ao, who taught men to build houses; Sui Jen, who taught men to make fire; Fu Hsi, who taught men to domesticate animals, use iron, fish with nets, write, forecast with eight trigrams, make music; Shen Nung, who taught the arts of agriculture and medicine; Huang Ti, who invented bricks, vessels of clay, the calendar, and money. But even before these great personages there had been the first man, P'an Ku, who had become a God after he had, with hammer and chisel, during a period of 18,000 years, separated Heaven from earth, hewed out the places of the celestial bodies, dug out the valleys, and piled up the mountains on earth. When he died various parts of his body became the five sacred mountains of China: T'ai Mountain in the east, Sung Mountain in the center, the Heng Mountains of the north and south, and Hua Mountain in the west. His breath became the wind, his voice the thunder, his flesh the fields, his sweat the rain and, finally, the insects on his body became people.

Of all people, the Chinese were, also, the most solicitous of the dead. The cult of ancestor worship was exceedingly old and important in Chinese history. The purpose of the cult was to ensure prosperity and to avoid adverse influence from the powerful souls of departed family members. Indeed, the dead were regarded as full-fledged living members of the family capable of advancing the welfare of the family, or, if offended, afflicting it with punishment. The ancestors were to be honored, respected, eulogized, remembered with prayers and sacrifices, and consulted in all matters of family planning and fortune.

The kairotic movement away from multifarious and localized spirits and souls toward a single, universal God-power began sometime after 1000 B.C., when Chinese philosophical speculation moved to invent or discover two concepts of central importance. One was called Yang/Yin. The other was called Tao. Chinese philosophers and theologians became increasingly observant of the flowing polarity in all things, both in the heavens and on the earth.

They observed light and darkness (day and night) flowing into and out of each other; hot and cold, each a condition of the other; male and female each separate, yet not alien, not really completely different; each was a little of the other. Yang/Yin might be symbolized by the banks of a river. There was the sunny bank and there was the shady bank, yet both were banks of the same stream. Unlike the Zoroastrian divine aliens (Wise Lord and Bad Spirit), the Chinese Yang/Yin blended into each other, both parts of the same whole. The Yang principle, although containing elements of Yin, was the dominant mode: male, bright, dry, active, warm. The Yin, on the other hand, was female, dark, moist, cold, passive. All things in the world got their nature or character from the dominance of one or the other of these two energy principles. Indeed, the universe itself was an activity of Yang and Yin. Heaven was full of Yang. Earth was mostly Yin.

With Yang/Yin the Chinese arrived at a universal energy system, but they were not content simply to have a theory for the becoming, being, and passing away of things and events. They looked deeper and discovered or invented the harmony and order of nature as a whole. They concluded that there was a character and a direction to all the Yang/Yin activity in the universe. The world was ordered, directed, controlled by the Way, by the Tao. They drew a distinction between the mechanism of the universe (the Yang/Yin process) and the powerful *Way* in which, as by an inner necessity, the mechanism ran. This Way was conceived to have been before all else, before the earth, before the heavens, and even before the principles Yang and Yin. First, there was the plan, the "way to go" (which is what Tao means), and then there was the going. The Way was preestablished—a way of harmony, integration, cooperation. Thus, it was the basic way of nature to move toward peace, prosperity, fulfillment. Indeed, if it were not for the perversity of humans and the wickedness of devils and demons all would be well in this world, for to be well is the way of the High God; the single, universal nonpersonal ultimate power—Tao.

Tao is as much the ground of beings in Chinese thought as Brahman is in Hindu thought, but the Tao is immanent in a way that Brahman is not, for Tao affirms the world in its natural course. Tao is the glory of *this* world, seen in the flight of a bird, the blooming of a flower, the birth of a child, the flowing of a river, the changing of the seasons. Unlike Brahman, Tao does not direct one out of the world but into it. The Western benediction "Go with God," is an even more proper wish for those who follow the way of the Way than for those who follow the way of the Nazarene, for to go with God Tao unresistingly, unaggressively, flowingly is to live *wu-wei,* which means to live and act in such a way that there occurs no interference with the natural way, with the way things should go.

Although the two native religions of China (Confucianism and Taoism) differ greatly in their interpretation of the true way of the Tao, they both affirm the Tao as the definitive power behind all spirits and souls, and all things and events. The Confucians say that the Tao (called by them Heaven) gives the proper rules for the way a father and son should relate to each other; an elder and a younger brother should relate to each other; a husband and wife to each other; elders and juniors to each other; rulers and subjects to each other. There is a Way. If it is followed, good life, happiness, tranquility, prosperity flow forth naturally. So say the Confucians, but the Taoists, unhappy with codes and restrictions, say "No, not by Heaven's rule, but by Nature's way." Flow with nature. Reject the mind's rebelliousness. Suppress the aggressive attitude. Feel the wind and go with it. See the sunset and become enchanted by it, merge into it. Taste the honey and be delighted. Do not try to create order; surrender to it as it moves Yang/Yin in all natural things and events.

The fact is that Confucianism is a consummate religion arising from the practice of ancestor worship so ancient in Chinese life, whereas Taoism, also a consummate religion, flows from the strain of nature worship which was equally ancient in Chinese life. Both affirm the Tao, the single, universal nonpersonal, ultimate power of the universe, but each does so from only one part of the ancient Chinese religion tradition. It is probably because of the different emphasis made by Confucianism, on the one hand, and Taoism, on the other, that these two great religions have been able to exist side by side with little conflict over the centuries, and how it is that so many Chinese are both Confucian and Taoist at the same time.

As "God came of age" so also did religion come of age. This is to say that the primary emphasis in religious activity shifted from metatechnology to encounter and gratitude—from attempts to use the Gods for mundane purposes, to attempts to live harmoniously with God (be it Yahweh, Christ, Allah, Brahman, Tao), seeking divine encounter, spiritual health, moral integrity, wholeness of life; and voicing in words and attitudes, in ritual and reverence, a joy of gifts not earned.

NOTES

[1] Yasna 30.3–5, tran. James Hope Moulton in *Early Zoroastrianism* (London: Constable and Co. for Hibbert Trust, 1913), p. 349.

[2] See R. C. Zaehner, *The Dawn and Twilight of Zoroastrianism* (New York: G. P. Putnam's Sons, 1961) and Jeffrey B. Russell, *The Devil* (Ithaca, New York: Cornell University, 1977) pp. 42–43.

[3] J. B. Noss, *Man's Religions* (New York: Macmillan, third edition, 1963), p. 496.

[4] The New English Bible (New York: Cambridge University Press, 1971); author's italics.

[5] Besides the multitude of local Baalim there was the Baal of Heaven, a storm God and chief among the lesser Baalim.

[6] Hosea 2:15b–17, The New English Bible (NEB).

[7] For an account of this see II Kings, chapter 22:1–23:30.

[8]During the exile the name Jew came into use, and from that, Judaism.

[9]Amos, 9:7 (NEB). *The New English Bible* (New York: Cambridge University Press, 1971).

[10]Rudra was an early form of the later important Hindu God Shiva, the destroyer.

[11]The Persian word for India was *Hind,* thus the inhabitants of India became known as Hindus.

[12]J. B. Noss, *Man's Religions* (New York: Macmillan, 1956), pp. 139–140.

[13]*Chandogya Upanishad*, 3.14.1, tran. R. E. Hume, *The Thirteen Principal Upanishads* (London: Oxford University Press, 1934), p. 209.

[14]Ibid., 5.10.7, p. 233.

PART THREE

The Techniques of Religion

What does the Lord require of you,
But to do justly, and to love mercy,
And walk humbly with your God?
Micah 6:8

III   And doing so by the employment of various religious techniques: (a) a belief system (myths, doctrines, and theologies); (b) a ritual system (reverent behavior and dramatic performances); (c) a moral system (ethical doctrines and rules). See page 7.

Chapter 9

THEOLOGY: ONE TECHNIQUE IN RELIGION

Brothers and sisters, this morning—I intend to explain the unexplainable—find out the undefinable—ponder over the imponderable—and unscrew the inscrutable.

James Weldon Johnson°

Our observations have informed us that to deal with certain kinds of problems (horrendous, nonmanipulable problems), humans employ religion. We need now to observe how they do this. We shall examine the techniques of religion. By technique we mean simply any systematic procedure by which a complex task is accomplished. In religion this means what people do in order to be religious and accomplish the benefits of religion.

One thing they do, and it is important to do, is think about religion and talk about religion. They think and talk because in religion it is extremely important to know and understand the beliefs (the story) of a particular religion if one is to embrace that faith and enjoy its benefits. Said differently, if one wants to please God, one must know God and know what God expects. One must be concerned with God-talk, which is what the word theology literally means—*theos,* ''God''; *logos,* ''talk'' or ''speech.'' Theology is one of the techniques employed in doing religion. Besides theology there are also, as we shall observe in Chapters 12 and 13, the technique of myth/ritual and the technique of religious morality.

THEOLOGY

The ''logy'' of theology does not mean only ''words'' and ''speech,'' as suggested above. It also means ''reason,'' as in thinking about and knowing. It is a technique employed to explain and make reasonable, from a religious perspective, the hidden forces that control the destinies of mankind and the ultimate meaning of human life. Theology tries to explain humans to themselves in their world. It functions to deterrorize the horrendous nonmanipulables of life and to offer proper ways of dealing with them. "In the night imagining some fear/How easy is a bush supposed a bear!"[1] To overcome the paralysis that accompanies any undefined, terrifying experience, we name it; we explain it; and then, in terms of the name, we get a basis for action. Once the name is given and the explanation is available, we are prepared to act in some reasonable way: to run if we name it "bear," to offer sacrifice or prayer if we name it God. Subsequently, it may be beneficial to get the right name, but initially we need get only *a* name. Theology gives names (descriptions and explanations) to the life of humankind, especially in the face of the horrendous, nonmanipulable issues of human existence.

THEOLOGICAL TYPES/STYLES

Hermeneutical and Creedal Theology   The word "hermeneutics" comes from Greek *hermeneutikos,* which means "interpret." Hermeneutical theology is the interpretation of the basic items of a given faith system: interpretation of such things as scripture, dogma, doctrine, myth, practice. When, for example, Jews read in the Bible, "Thou shalt not kill," they need a rabbinical interpretation. Kill no one? Not even invading enemies? Not even in self-defense? How should this Sixth Commandment be interpreted? And when Jesus said, "Simon, I shall call you Peter (the rock), and on this rock I shall build my church," Christian hermeneutists on both sides of the issue, both Catholic and Protestant, rush in to interpret.

Hermeneutical theology can be as brief as a sentence: *Shema Yisroel, Adonai Elohanu, Adonai Echod*—Hear, O Israel, the Lord our God, the Lord is one; or again, *la ilaha illa Allah*—"(There is) no god but Allah." These two sentences are two of the most powerful theological statements in two great world religions—Judaism and Islam. In Hinduism the one line theology *tat tvam asi* (That art thou!) is also a powerful theology. It declares the central Hindu belief that the human soul (*atman*) and the soul of the universe (Brahman) are the same soul—atman and Brahman, person and God, are the same reality.

These theological proclamations are obviously succinct summary statements of belief. More extended summary statements are also common in religion. They are often called creeds from the Latin word *credo,* "I believe." A creed is a formal, authoritative statement of religious belief; sometimes called a "confession of faith." Creeds usually arise out of theological controversies and are intended to act as devices for assuring persons that they are truly of orthodox belief and for identifying those who are not truly of orthodox belief. For example, early in Christian history there arose a controversy over the nature of Jesus Christ; namely, how Christ was related to God. Some said he was a man who had been, at his baptism, adopted by God (a position taken by Paul of Samosata, bishop of Antioch, c. 260–272). Some said that Jesus was similar (*homoiousion*) to God, but not the same as God (a position taken by Arius, a scholarly presbyter who lived in Alexandria in the early fourth century). Some said that he was the same as God (*homoousion*), of the same essence as God (a position taken by Athanasius,° a fourth-century church leader and bishop of Alexandria, who was Arius's archopponent).*

The controversy, especially between Arius and Athanasius, resulted in a church council called by Constantine,° the first Christian Roman emperor. The council met in the city of Nicea in 325, and there (and in a later council in Constantinople called by Emperor Theodosius in 381) a creed now called the Nicene Creed was hammered out and made official theology.

The Nicene Creed

We believe
  In one God, Father Almighty, maker of all things visible and invisible;
  And in one Lord Jesus Christ, the Son of God, begotten of his Father, only begotten, that is of the substance of the Father, God of God, Light of Light, true God of true God; begotten, not made, of one substance with the Father, by whom all things were made, both things in heaven and things in earth;
  Who for us men and our salvation, came down from heaven and was made flesh and was made man; suffered and rose again on the third day, ascended into the heavens and comes to judge the living and the dead.

  The Nicene Creed embodies the theology of Athanasius, who was at the time of the Council of Nicea a scholarly deacon of the church at Alexandria. Later he was made bishop of Alexandria and remained bishop there for more than forty years.

Beginning in the second century, but not emerging in finished form until the fifth century, was formulated the familiar Apostle's Creed. This creed, despite its name, did not come directly from the Apostles. It was, rather, a church created, authorized, summary of the teachings of Christ as purportedly transmitted by the Apostles, and as preserved by the churches.

I believe in God, the Father Almighty, Maker of heaven and earth; and in Jesus Christ, His only Son our Lord; who was conceived by the Holy Spirit, born of the Virgin Mary, suffered under Pontius Pilate, was crucified, dead, and buried; the

*In the struggle between the theology of Arius and that of Athanasius on the nature of Christ it was the Athanasian position that finally triumphed and became for Roman Catholicism the official theology.

third day He rose from the dead; He ascended into heaven, and sitteth at the right hand of God the Father Almighty; from thence He shall come to judge the quick and the dead. I believe in the Holy Spirit; the holy Catholic Church, the communion of saints; the forgiveness of sins; the resurrection of the body, and life everlasting. Amen.[2]

Systematic Theology and Philosophical Theology   It is not surprising, of course, to find the theologians doing theology in systematic and philosophical fashion. They do it inductively, deductively, phenomenalistically—a posteriori,° a priori,° existential. We shall consider three pieces of philosophical theology concerned with rationalizing the central symbol of religion; namely, God. These theologians are Christians, and they have in mind the Christian God, but their arguments have universal significance. What they have to say about God (which is actually nothing especially Christian) applies everywhere, and if their theological arguments are valid and incontrovertible, they are as valid in Tokyo as in Rome. The first two philosophical theologies are proofs for the existence of God: one by St. Anselm° of Canterbury in the eleventh century, and the other by St. Thomas Aquinas° in the thirteenth century. Anselm makes his theology on strictly "rational" grounds; Thomas makes his several arguments on "empirical" grounds. We shall start with Thomas.

Empirical Grounds (A Posteriori Reasoning)   Empirical theology is the kind of religious knowledge that is grounded in shareable sense experience. It is religious "truth" established and guaranteed by systematic observations of the world around us.

The great thirteenth-century theologian Thomas Aquinas attempted to reason empirically in order to prove the existence of God. Looking at the world, Thomas was convinced that he saw it as contingent—depending on God in a number of ways for its existence. In trying to demonstrate this dependence and therefore the necessary existence of God, Thomas performed what amounts to the classical attempt to reason from the world to God. Thomas believed that people could practice "natural theology." They could arrive at certain religious truths by thinking about the world as they experienced it. To be sure, there were certain religious truths that humans did not have the capacity to discover by their own reasoning: for example, that Jesus Christ was both God and man; that Father, Son, and Spirit constituted a single Godhead. Such truths God had to deliver to humans through divine revelation. But there were some religious truths that people could discover on their own. One of those truths was the truth of God's existence.

Thomas offered five arguments for God's existence. In each one he argued that we could not have the kind of world we all experience unless there was a sufficient reason for this world and for this kind of world; namely, a world that is here and a world that demonstrates purposeful activity and accomplishes values. Each of Thomas's arguments was empirically based and contained at least one premise known by experience to be true of the world we live in. (1) From the obvious fact that things move, he argued to a necessary source of all motion—an unmoved mover. (2) From the obvious fact that things are caused, he moved to the necessary source of all causation—a first cause. (3) From the obvious fact of change, he moved to the unchanging necessity that must underlie all change—necessary being. (4) From the obvious fact of gradation in things (some things are better, more perfect than others), he moved to something "which is to all beings the cause of their being, goodness, and every other perfection." (5) From the obvious intelligible processes of nature, he moved to the need for an ultimate, intelligent planner of all the world's teleological activity.

Probably the most persuasive of Thomas's arguments is the third argument—the one from possibility and necessity, or from the contingency of the world.

> The third way is taken from possibility and necessity and runs thus. We find in nature things which are possible to be and not to be, since they are found to be generated, and to be corrupted. . . . But it is impossible for these always to exist, for that which can not-be at some time is not. Therefore, if everything can not-be, then at one time there was nothing in existence, because that which does not exist begins to exist only through something already existing. Therefore, if at one time nothing was in existence, it would have been impossible for anything to have begun to exist; and thus even now nothing would be in existence—which is absurd. Therefore, not all things are merely possible, but there must be something the existence of which is necessary. . . . This all men speak of as God.[3]

Thomas was saying that (1) we experience the world, but (2) we do not experience anything which is absolutely necessary. Everything we experience comes into being and goes out of being. But (3) if this were all there were to it, there would be no world to experience, because there would have been a time when none of these contingent things existed. If there had been such a time, there would be nothing existing now, because "something" (what we experience now) could not come from nothing. This is a substantial argument because it basically argues that we experience the world in such a way as to demand a reason for its being. We ask Heidegger's° famous question, "Why are there things rather than nothing?" and the only answer seems to be: There must be something not contingent, something essential. There must be, to use Tillich's postulate, a *ground of being*, which is the source of all the beings we see and taste and touch and smell—even the whole cosmos.*

---

*Thomas was not talking simply about a ground of being. He was talking about a specific kind of God: the personalistic God of theism; a God who both knows and plans, and who causes the world to be, and to be as it is. Yet Thomas's arguments do not necessarily lead to that conclusion. The sum of his five arguments actually supplies us with several possible conclusions about the ultimate reality. First, we can conclude, with Thomas, that there is a God out there, intelligent and creative, who is the cause, necessity, and teleological director of the world. But, second, we

Rational Grounds (A Priori Reasoning)   Besides knowledge from sense experience, there is knowledge established directly from the operation of deductive reasoning: rational knowledge. Reason itself, proceeding formally from established premises, can establish conclusions that cannot be invalid. Unlike empirical reasoning, which may be persuasive but seldom absolute, this formal logical operation appears to be indubitable. To build theology out of this kind of logical operation would be, it would seem, highly desirable.

The classic example of this kind of theology is an argument made to prove the existence of God by St. Anselm (1033–1109), a Benedictine monk and Archbishop of Canterbury. He presented in rigid rational form what has become known as the Ontological Argument—the argument from the nature of God's perfect being. Although Anselm was a true believer who needed no further proof for God's existence than his own faith, he yet desired, so he stated, to establish a "single argument which would require no other for its proof than itself alone: and alone would suffice to demonstrate that God truly exists."[4] Anselm tells us that he struggled desperately to discover this argument, but could not find it, and finally desired only to forget that he had ever sought it. But by that time the problem had become an obsession he could not escape, until "one day, when I was exceedingly weary with resisting its importunity, in the very conflict of my thoughts, the proof of which I had despaired offered itself, so that I eagerly embraced the thought which I was strenuously repelling."[5]

The argument he conceived, he worked out in two forms. The first began with a capsulizing of the Christian concept of God into a formula: God is "a being than which nothing greater can be conceived." By "greater" Anselm meant more perfect. God is the most perfect being that can be conceived. If such a being is to be conceived, then the existence of such a being must also be conceived, for existence would be one of the attributes of absolute perfection.

---

could equally well conclude that the entire series of natural events itself could be the necessary ground of its own being. One does not have to go out of the natural realm to explain motion, or cause, or ground of being. All one has to do is shift the presuppositions from Aristotelian theology to modern physics, astronomy, and biology, in which can be found all the motion, causation, and ground necessary for the entire universe. It is possible to conceive that the entire series of natural events is totally self-sufficient. In an energy-based, oscillating universe, one seems to have all the motion and causation one needs, and as far as intelligent (that is, intelligible) process is concerned, one need not say it is imposed from the outside. Intelligent process may be nothing more than the way we read the orderliness with which an oscillating universe oscillates and the way that biological life, under evolution's mandates, sustains itself.

To be for God or for nature in this circumstance seems to come down finally to one's metaphysical overview. If we are theists to begin with, we are persuaded, with Thomas, that the experienced world is from a supernatural source. If we are atheists, we believe that the experienced world is from itself. And if we are pantheists or immanentalists, we agree with both, partially: The world is its own source and that creative source is what God is—not just an energy system oscillating, but a ground of being of infinite spiritual capacity and worth.

Think of it this way: A person says, "I conceive of a being that contains absolute perfection. This being is the ultimate in perfection. There can be no greater being." A second person asks, "Does the perfect being you conceive have actual existence outside your mind?" The first person replies, "No. This is purely a conceptual being." The second person can then reply, "You have not conceived of a being than which nothing can be greater (more perfect), for I have conceived of a greater being than yours. My being has all the perfections of your being and has also the added perfection of *perfect objective existence*." Anselm said it this way:

> if that, than which nothing greater can be conceived, exists in the understanding alone, the very being, than which nothing greater can be conceived, is one, than which a greater can be conceived. But obviously this is impossible. Hence, there is no doubt that there exists a being, than which nothing greater can be conceived, and it exists both in the understanding and in reality.[6]

Anselm formulated his argument a second time, this time directing his argument not simply to the existence of God but to God's uniquely necessary existence. Here he defined God in such a way that it was impossible to conceive of God as not existing. To say that the most perfect being is conceivable and at the same time can be conceived as not existing is to deny and affirm something at the same time; namely, that God both is and is not "that than which nothing greater can be conceived." In his own words, Anselm states:

> If that, than which nothing greater can be conceived, can be conceived not to exist, it is not then that than which nothing greater can be conceived. But this is an irreconcilable contradiction. There is, then, so truly a being than which nothing greater can be conceived to exist, that it cannot be conceived not to exist.[7]

To say that one can conceive of a being that has necessary existence but does not exist is to say a contradiction.

René Descartes° reformulated the ontological argument (Anselm's first form above) in the seventeenth century and attracted wide attention to it. He insisted that existence must be included among the predicates of God just as surely as 180 degrees must be included among the predicates of a triangle. A triangle with internal angles that did not equal two right angles would not be a triangle. Even so, God without the predicate of existence would not be God. Descartes stated:

I find it manifest that we can no more separate the existence of God from his essence than we can separate from the essence of a rectilinear triangle the fact that the size of its three angles equal two right angles, or from the idea mountain the idea of a valley. Thus it is no less self-contradictory to conceive of God, a supremely perfect Being,

> who lacks existence—that is, who lacks some perfection—than it is to conceive of a mountain for which there is no valley.
>
> From the fact alone that I cannot conceive of God except as existing, it follows that existence is inseparable from him, and consequently he does, in truth, exist.[8]

With all of this we should not forget that Anselm did not rest his faith on this argument or any other argument. He was a "true believer" because of assurance, an assurance that came from an inner esoteric knowing. His Ontological Argument was more an act of reverence than a basis of faith. As Anselm put it:

> I do not endeavor, O Lord, to penetrate thy sublimity, for in no wise do I compare my understanding with that; but I long to understand in some degree thy truth, which my heart believes and loves. For I do not seek to understand that I may believe, but I believe in order to understand.[9]

On The Existence of God in Modern Philosophical Theology: à la Paul Tillich   Like Thomas and Anselm, Paul Tillich° was also a philosophical theologian, but his theology is not like the Aristotelianism of St. Thomas, nor does it take the ontological stance of St. Anselm. Rather, Tillich came at theology from the dimension of modern existentialism° and phenomenology.° Whereas both Thomas and Anselm were concerned with establishing proof for the existence of God, Tillich argued that such philosophizing misses the crucial point that for God to have existence means that God is just like other "things." A God with existence would simply be another being, albeit, perhaps, the most perfect being. But God is not a being, Tillich argued— rather "God as God is being-itself." In the first volume of his *Systematic Theology*, Tillich writes:

> The being of God cannot be understood as the existence of a being alongside of others or above others. If God is *a* being, he is subject to the categories of finitude, especially to space and substance. When applied to God, superlatives become diminutives. . . .
>
> [T]he question of the existence of God can be neither asked nor answered. . . . It is as atheistic to affirm the existence of God as it is to deny it. God is being-itself, not *a* being. . . . Being-itself is beyond finitude and infinity; otherwise it would be conditioned by something other than itself, and the real power of being would lie beyond both it and that which conditioned it. Being-itself infinitely transcends every finite being. There is no proportion or gradation between the finite and the infinite. There is an absolute break, an infinite "jump." On the other hand everything finite participates in being-itself and in its infinity. Otherwise it would not have the power of being. It would be swallowed by nonbeing, or it never would have emerged from nonbeing. This double relation of all beings to being-itself gives being-itself a double characteristic. In calling it creative, we point to the fact that everything participates in the infinite power of being. In calling it abysmal, we

point to the fact that everything participates in the infinite power of being in a finite way, that all beings are infinitely transcended by their creative ground.[10]

"Popular" Theology: Preaching and Storytelling   Not all theology is as formal as creed builders and systematic theologians make it. Indeed, much more often it is loose in structure, even poetical in form, and it covers the whole range of religious life. There is, for example, theology for popular consumption regularly presented in the form of preaching: *sermonic theology.*

James Weldon Johnson wrote a book called *God's Trombones.* In it he presented in poetic form seven sermons like those he had, as a boy, heard preached by black preachers. In these "sermons" we find marvelous preaching replete with theological interpretations. Theological interpretation was, apparently, what such preaching was all about, as Johnson indicates in the preface of his book. He tells about one old preacher "who after reading a rather cryptic passage took off his spectacles, closed the Bible with a bang and by way of preface said, 'Brothers and sisters, this morning—I intend to explain the unexplainable—find out the undefinable—ponder over the imponderable—and unscrew the inscrutable.'"[11]

In his poem called "The Creation," Johnson hits a fine stride in depicting both preaching and theologizing. The poem begins:

And God stepped out on space,
And he looked around and said:
I'm lonely—
I'll make me a world.

God looked out onto the darkness of nowhere, "Blacker than a hundred nights down in a cypress swamp"; and then he smiled and it all began—the light, the sun, the stars, the moon; the earth, the valleys, the seas; the green grass sprouting, and the flowers, and the pine tree pointing "his finger to the sky"; and the rivers running down to the sea; and there was a rainbow too. "Then God raised his arm and waved his hand" and fishes, and birds, and beasts roamed the forests and the woods; "And God said: That's good!"

Then God walked around,
And God looked around
On all that he had made.
He looked at his sun,
And he looked at his moon,
And he looked at his little stars;
He looked on his world
With all its living things,
And God said: I'm lonely still.

Then God sat down—
On the side of a hill where he could think;
....

And God thought and thought,
Till he thought: I'll make me a man![12]

One should read the whole poem to hear all the excellent preaching, but we have here made at least the theological point about which the preaching was basically concerned. There is here one very large piece of new, creative theology that does not appear in the scripture from which the sermon came. The preacher tells us that all this creation took place because God was *lonely*.

Story Theology   Not dissimilar to sermon theology is the somewhat different style of doing theology, which may be called story theology. A story is told that may be *the* story, or it may be a story that illuminates *the* story—*the* story being, of course, the God story, the mythos. This kind of theology is especially important to those religions such as Judaism and Christianity that explain themselves by reporting unique and remembered events of the ancient past: an Exodus, a Crucifixion, a spectacular birth, a convenant at Mount Sinai.

Elie Wiesel,° once said that "God created man because he loves stories." There is a neat dangling phrase here, a marvelous ambiguity: which "he" loves stories—God or man? Or, is it both "he's" love stories. Well, we don't know about God, but there is no question that people love stories, and some of their best stories are story-theologies.

Robert McAfee Brown,° in a paper delivered at the annual conference of the American Academy of Religion in 1974, told of his growing friendship, during the Vietnam War years, with Rabbi Abraham Heschel,° and of how he began to notice that every time he asked the rabbi a theological question "he would reply, 'My friend, let me tell you a story.'" This Jewish propensity to make a religious point by telling a story is traditional not only in Heschel's Judaism but also in Brown's Christianity. Jesus told stories. He seldom made points with rational arguments, even, apparently, when invited to do so. For example, we are told that a lawyer once engaged him in a conversation. "What must one do to inherit eternal life?" the lawyer asked. Jesus gave a quick formal answer which should have fit comfortably into a lawyer's way of thinking. "Keep the law," he said. "Love God, as the law commands, and love your neighbor." But when the lawyer persisted and asked, "Who is my neighbor?" Jesus moved immediately into a theology of storytelling: Once upon a time, "a man went down from Jerusalem to Jericho. . . ." He told a story.

Jesus, among other things, is justifiably famous for his parables. In principle a parable is used to interpret abstract teachings by the use of concrete analogies. A parable is a popular way of teaching rather than a scholarly way of teaching. More than two dozen of Jesus' parables were preserved in the Synoptic Gospels. They vary in length from a sentence to a short story. The following is a list of Jesus' parables as they appear in the Synoptic Gospels:

The Sower, Mark 4:1–9; Matthew 13:1–9; Luke 8:4–8.
The Growing Seed, Mark 4:26–29.
The Mustard Seed, Mark 4:30–32; Matthew 13:31–32, 34; Luke 13:18–19.
The Weeds, Matthew 13:24–30.
The Yeast, Matthew 13:33; Luke 13:20–21.
The Hidden Treasure, Matthew 13:44.
The Pearl, Matthew 13:45.
The Net, Matthew 13:47.
The Lost Sheep, Matthew 18:10–14; Luke 15:3–7.
Unforgiving Servant, Matthew 18:21–35.
Workers in the Vineyard, Matthew 20:1–16.
The Two Sons, Matthew 21:28–32.
The Tenants in the Vineyard, Matthew 21:33–44; Mark 12:1–12; Luke 20:9–19.
Wedding Feast, Matthew 22:1–14; Luke 14:15–24.
The Ten Girls, Matthew 25:1–13.
The Three Servants, Matthew 25:14–30; Luke 19:11–27.
The Good Samaritan, Luke 10:25–37.
The Rich Fool, Luke 12:13–21.
The Unfruitful Fig Tree, Luke 13:6–9.
The Lost Coin, Luke 15:8–9.
The Lost Son (The Prodigal Son), Luke 15:11–32.
The Shrewd Manager, Luke 16:1–13.
The Rich Man and Lazarus, Luke 16:19–31.
The Widow and the Judge, Luke 18:1–8.
The Pharisee and the Tax Collector, Luke 18:9–14.
The Rich Man, Luke 18:18–30; Matthew 19:16–30; Mark 10:17–31.

The Christian church, in its earliest years, followed Jesus' example. One may be sure that when a missionary went out from Antioch to "circuit-ride" the newly formed churches in Asia Minor, he was not asked to read a paper on the nature of the Divine Being or even read from the Bible. He was asked to tell them the stories of Jesus. And a little later, when Mark, for example, wanted to make theological statements about Jesus (that he was, among other things, the Messiah) he did so in a story called the Good News.

The Christian Gospels are especially good examples of story theology. These documents, with author's names ascribed to them accurately or not, are literally stories in which theology is made. Matthew, Mark, Luke, and John all use items from the life of Jesus to present what they individually regarded as essential theologies. At first glance these Good News stories appear to be histories of Jesus, but at second glance (or upon more systematic examination) it appears the authors were simply using history to make theology. It was not history that they were concerned with presenting. It was theology. To make this point we might observe that one does not write history or biography by telling something about the hero's birth, what the hero did at the age of twelve, and then concentrate exclusively on the last year (or three years in John's Gospel) of the hero's life. No. The writers of the Gospels were all writer-editors with theological intentions. They were all theologians presenting the events in the life of Jesus with special theological emphases. Matthew, for example, was interested in presenting Jesus as the promised one of Hebrew prophecy, as well as a rabbi and lawgiver. So Matthew marshaled his source materials, edited them, and rewrote them to make his theological points as effectively as possible.*

The double talent of writer and theologian can be seen in the Gospel of Mark, especially in what has come to be called the "messianic secret." Mark told his story about Jesus as the unfolding of a secret: the secret of who Jesus really was—the Messiah. Of course everyone in Mark's "congregation" knew that already; and they knew it from Mark's introduction (1:1–13) in which they were informed that Isaiah had prophesied it, John the Baptist had announced it, and God's voice had confirmed it—all in the first dozen verses of the Good News. But the people *in the story* did not know who Jesus was. The story characters did not know, and they only gradually discovered who he was as the story unfolded. In the beginning no one knew who Jesus really was. In the end all those who had "eyes to see" knew who he was, even the pagan centurion standing before the cross.

The story opens with Jesus being told privately by the voice from heaven that he is the one chosen of God to be God's son. No one there, not even John the Baptist, hears the heavenly voice. Jesus goes from his baptism, his real identity unknown.

The story develops. Jesus gathers disciples and goes about performing miracles. He is recognized as an amazing man, but no one identifies him as the Son of Man and the Son of God, except the demons whom he occasionally exorcises. Being supernatural creatures they know who he really is and they cry out, but Jesus silences them (1:25, 34; 3:12).†

The unveiling of the secret comes in a series of climactic scenes: first, on the road to Caesarea Philippi, Jesus asks his disciples, "Who do you think I am?" and Peter answered, "You are Messiah-Christ" (8:27). Second, on the Mount of Transfiguration, Jesus' real identity becomes obvious to the inner circle of disciples—to Peter, James, and John (9:2–8). On each of these occasions Jesus orders the disciples not to tell what they now know. The time for the world announcement has not yet come. That time would come finally and only when the Son of Man had risen from the dead (9:9). The third scene of

---

*See William Calloley Tremmel, *The Twenty-Seven Books That Changed the World* (New York: Holt, Rinehart and Winston, 1981), p. 138.

†Other indications of the messianic secret motif are seen in other instances when Jesus enjoined silence: (1) after performing mighty works (1:44; 5:43; 7:36; 8:26); (2) after Peter's confession, Jesus charged his disciples not to tell anyone (8:30; 9:9); (3) Jesus gave his disciples private instructions (4:10–12; 7:17–23; 9:30–49); (4) Jesus traveled through Galilee incognito (7:24; 9:30).

unveiling comes in two instances on the day of Jesus' death. In a midnight session the Jewish high priest asks Jesus if he is the Christ, and Jesus replies, "I am . . ." (14:61–62). Later that same day, when Christ dies, the centurion looks up at his body and says, "Truly this man was the son of God!" (15:39). The final and conclusive unveiling comes, of course, with the announcement that he had risen from the dead (16:1–8).

If nothing else, the employment of the messianic secret as a story line made the Mark Gospel a good story—a mystery story. Everybody who read the Gospel (all the Christians anyway) knew all the time who Christ was; but what an interest catcher to see the story traced out among the people who did not know who he was—the people who were actually there!

But that was not all there was to it, at least according to Norman Perrin,° a New Testament scholar. The theological theme of the "messianic secret" was not simply that Jesus was the Messiah, but that he was a special kind of Messiah. Perrin proposed that the messiahship was kept secret in order to ensure that Jesus' title would be properly understood; that is, no one was to call him Messiah and think only of a miracle-working Son of God. Perrin saw the secret as the device whereby not just Jesus' messianic status was presented, but also a special kind of messianic status was presented—a messiah who was not only the "Son of God" but also the "Son of Man"—one who must suffer. The secret, according to Perrin, was an "open secret." The demons let it be known to anyone who heard them, and Jesus' miracles proclaimed to anyone who saw them that he was a man who had come in the power of God. But the true nature of the power was not comprehended by anyone around Jesus, including the disciples. Perrin held that Jesus' miracles identified him in the common Hellenistic tradition of a "divine man." Then Mark introduced the motif of secrecy to this divine-man image (3:12; 5:43; 7:36), and eventually the motif of the necessity of suffering (8:31–34; 9:30–31; 10:32–34). According to Perrin, Peter in his confession that Jesus was the Christ would have understood fully if he had identified "Christ" with "Son of Man" *and Son of Man with "must suffer."* Mark's full christological intentions (the complete revelation of the messianic secret) was brought to a climax when the high priest asked, "Are you Christ, [the title which has been identified with the suffering Son of Man] the Son of the Blessed?" (namely, the Son of God), and Jesus accepted the titles by answering "I am," (that is, by using the ancient formula identifying God—see Exodus 3:14–15). The secret of who Jesus really was was thereby revealed. He was both Son of Man and Son of God: As Son of Man he would suffer and die; as Son of God he would be resurrected.*

---

*These comments on the messianic secret have been taken from *The Twenty-Seven Books That Changed the World,* William Calloley Tremmel (New York: Holt, Rinehart and Winston, 1981), pp. 146–147. For Norman Perrin's discussion of the messianic secret see his *The New Testament* (New York: Harcourt Brace Jovanovich, Inc., 1974), pp. 152, 153, 154, 157, 160.

Although an oversimplification, the theological claims of the various Gospel writers can be stated so: Mark presented Jesus dramatically as the Messiah, a secret revealed only gradually in the Mark story. Matthew, supporting the messianic claim, wanted to say in addition that Jesus was also Teacher, Lawgiver, a second Moses, and even more than Moses, he was the new Abraham, the fulfillment of Israel. Luke wanted to present him more widely as the savior of mankind. And John, finally, presented him as not just Messiah, or Lawgiver, or Savior, but as the Word of God, the Logos, even God himself.

In the beginning was the Word, and the Word was with God, and the Word was God. He was in the beginning with God; all things were made through him, and without him was not anything made that was made. In him was life, and the life was the light of men. The light shines in the darkness and the darkness has not overcome it.

.....

And the Word became flesh and dwelt among us, full of grace and truth; we have beheld his glory, glory as of the only Son from the Father.   *John 1:1–4 (RSV)*

Though he was in the form of God,
  he did not deem equality with God
  something to be grasped at.

Rather, he emptied himself
  and took the form of a slave,
  being born in the likeness of men.
Philippians, 2:6–7 (NAB)

In the theology of storytelling, the stories are first told, then retold, and retold again, and collected, and arranged, and reflected upon, and rearranged, and gradually systematized, and given official sanction, and declared scriptural, as we shall see in Chapter 11.

Mythological Theology   We are observing, then, that not only council delegates and philosophical theologians make theology, but so also storytellers make story-theology. And some of these story-theologies come from so long ago that no one remembers the author's name, except perhaps it was "mankind." Such theology can be called mythological theology. One rather charming example of such mythology is found among the writings of the ancient Hebrews, the story of the creation of Eve. Somewhat paraphrased it goes like this:

In the beginning, after God had created his world, he created mankind. He took dirt and molded it, and breathed into it the breath of life, and Adam was "born."

God placed Adam in the Garden of Eden to live there and tend the garden. But there was something wrong. Adam never stopped to hear a bird sing. He never heard the plop of a jumping fish or saw the water rings where it had been. He never saw a coyote slip quietly away, looking back. And although he did not know it, had no word for it, Adam was lonely because he was the only animal on earth. God decided it was not good for Adam to be alone—lonely, so God created other animals, one after another, and brought them to Adam who thereupon admired and named them. But, perhaps, not knowing when he was well off, Adam was still not satisfied. So God caused him to fall into a deep sleep, and took one of his ribs, and created Eve. And when Adam opened his eyes and saw her he knew that she was the answer—what he had had in mind the whole time.[12]

Theology reinterprets life from a religious perspective. It looks at life "solitary, wolfish, brutish and nasty,"[14] and gives voice to a richer meaning and promise to a better way. It offers salvation here or hereafter.

NOTES

[1] William Shakespeare, *A Midsummer Night's Dream*, act V, scene 1, lines 21–22.
[2] The Apostles Creed is thought to have emerged in its initial form around 140 in Rome, possibly as a baptism affirmation. It arose out of an intense disagreement in the church over the origins of the world and the nature of Jesus Christ. In what came to be called Docetism and Marcionism, the world was held to be not the creation of the Christian God, who was too perfect for such a vile creation; and Christ was held to be not truly a person born of a woman with a real body, who suffered, died, descended into hades or sheol. It was not unusual in the ancient world to have stories of miraculous births, as from a virgin. The divinity of Jesus was not under debate among Christians, but the humanity and physicality were. The classic work on this is Arthur Cushman McGiffert's *The Apostle's Creed* (New York: Scribner's 1902).
[3] *Summa Theologica*, Question 2, Article 3.
[4] Anselm, *Proslogium*, tran. Sidney Norton Deane, in *Readings in the Philosophy of Religion*, John A. Mourant (New York: Thomas Y. Crowell, 1969), p. 9.
[5] Ibid., p. 10.
[6] Ibid., p. 11.
[7] Ibid., p. 11.
[8] René Descartes, "Fifth Meditation," *Meditations on First Philosophy* (Indianapolis: Bobbs-Merrill, 1960), pp. 63–64.
[9] Anselm, *Proslogium*, p. 10.
[10] Paul Tillich, *Systematic Theology*, (Chicago: University of Chicago, 1951), vol. 1, pp. 235–237. Also see Chapter 1, pages 3–10.
[11] James Weldon Johnson, *God's Trombones* (New York: Viking Press, 1965), pp. 4–5.
[12] James Weldon Johnson, *God's Trombones* (New York: Viking Press, 1965), pp. 17, 19–20.
[13] Genesis 2:4–25.
[14] Thomas Hobbes, *Leviathan*. (New York: E. P. Dutton, 1950).

Chapter 10

SALVATION THEOLOGY

Some night when early
winter's in the air I'll hear
an owl call my name.
W.C.T.

Eternal nothingness is O.K. if you're dressed
for it.
Woody Allen[1]

Theology is an attempt to interpret the faith stories and doctrines of a particular religious system. A theologian stands inside a particular faith circle and tries to make religious sense for that circle. The faith circle itself is a community of people who have generally accepted (usually been born into) a salvation theology: a theology that offers a plan for salvation—a way to transcend, in some fashion, the horrendous, nonmanipulable aspects of human existence. In the last analysis, all theology is salvation theology.

Pursuing theology further, we shall pick up the proposal at the end of Chapter 5 and observe several ways in which the question of ''being saved'' is handled in several different religions. What are people to do? What are they to believe as they face major life problems, horrendous, nonmanipulable circumstances, the human condition, their finitude? We shall consider several proposals: (1) that people resign themselves to the tragedies of life by assuming a kind of reverent, Jobian agnosticism; (2) that all will be made right in a life after death; (3) that one can escape finitude by losing (that is, finding) oneself in union with God. Also, (4) that one might assume a quasi-religious, hopefully philosophical attitude of indifference. We shall now look at these proposals in some detail.

Resignation or Reverent Agnosticism   "It was God's will." In this statement is contained a religious resignation of tremendous metapsychological potency and of far-reaching theological significance. It can mean, as in the Turkish *kismet,* that one's fate is allotted and only a fool kicks against the briars. One can push against the shove, but it is wisdom to know when the pushing is futile and then simply to accept the shove resignedly. This "fatalism" becomes a theology when one is told (or simply learns) to accept finitude and to trust that God will finally make right a human condition that to all appearances is unhappily wrong. *Let God's will be done.* Whatever it is, one is encouraged to resign oneself to it as *somehow* a meaningful part of God's inscrutable plan. This is a tremendously potent bit of religious conviction. In the face of a really bad event (for example, the tragic, premature, seemingly meaningless death of a loved one) many people accomplish an amazing amount of assurance and spiritual serenity by saying, "I do not know why, but God must know. It is God's will." Shifting the "blame" trustingly to God puts the dimension of infinity into a tragically finite circumstance and, apparently, empowers the true believer to "walk and not faint."

This theme is played out in grand style in the ancient theological drama-poem Job.* The story line of Job is simple, and apparently much older than the finished dramatic portrayal we currently possess. The basic story is told in Job 1, 2, 42:7–17. It is a brief tale of a shepherd prince named Job who is a man of excellent character and great wealth. God himself is proud of his servant Job, but Satan, who is pictured here not as the fiend of Hell, but as a member of God's advisory cabinet,[2] suggests that Job is loyal to God only because he is so well treated by God's gracious providence. Let Job suffer enough and he too will turn against God. At Satan's urging, God permits Job to be put to the test. His wealth and family are wiped out. His good health is destroyed. He is reduced to poverty and misery. But, according to the ancient tale, Job remains patient and loyal, and finally, the test completed, is restored by God to his former condition of prosperity and happiness.

An unknown poet-dramatist-theologian, probably in the sixth century B.C., took the ancient tale and developed it into a theological treatise on human suffering and what should be a person's religious response to suffering. This new author kept the story line of the original author. Here, too, at the behest of Satan, Job was tested to determine his loyalty to God. But now the story was expanded into an assault on the older Hebrew notion that human suffering was to be understood as punishment for breaking God's laws, an explanation of suffering that the author apparently felt was inadequate. Job suffered in spite of being a loyal keeper of the law. He was a righteous man. He did not deserve to be punished, but he was punished horribly and shatteringly, and no reason was ever given to him to justify his suffering.

In this expanded account, Job carried on a series of arguments with several men who came ostensibly to commiserate with him, but who were, in fact, spokesmen for the "old broken covenant" answer to human suffering. They

*Technically the Book of Job is a theodicy (an explanation of evil in the world God created), but asic effect is to give a salvation posture in which one is to trust God no matter what. One is to oe reverently agnostic.

argued with Job accusing him of some hidden wickedness that justified his punishment at the hands of God. Job, however, staunchly denied that he deserved such punishment. He further pointed out that the world was full of wicked people who were never punished. In fact, they often prospered. In this "second edition" of Job, the new author turned the patient Job of the first edition into an impatient, angry rebel, who did not accept his lot complacently, but finally railed against it, even to the point of demanding an answer from God himself.

And finally God did answer Job. He answered Job, symbolically enough, out of a whirlwind, and the answer given was a theology of resignation or reverent agnosticism.° The author did not simply have God tell Job directly that he should be resigned in the face of things he could not possibly comprehend; namely, why God does what he does to humans. Rather, the author had God squelch Job with tremendous speeches that clearly place Job, as well as all mankind, in his proper place.

Then the Lord answered Job out of the whirlwind:

Who is this whose ignorant words cloud my design in darkness?
Brace yourself and stand up like a man;
I will ask questions, and you shall answer.
Where were you when I laid the earth's foundation?
Tell me, if you know the answer.
Who settled its dimensions? Surely you should know.
Who stretched his measuring-line over it?
On what do its supporting pillars rest?
Who watched over the birth of the sea, when it burst in flood from the womb—
when I wrapped it in a blanket of clouds and cradled it in fog,
when I established its bounds, fixing its doors and bars in place
and said, "Thus far shall you come and no further,
and here your surging waves shall halt."
In all your life have you ever called up the dawn or shown the morning star its
place?
Have you taught it to grasp the fringes of earth and shake the Dog-star from its
place;
to bring up the horizon in relief as clay under a seal,
until all things stand out like the folds of a cloak,
when the light of the Dog-star is dimmed and the stars of the Navigator's Line
go out one by one?
Have you descended to the springs of the sea or walked in the unfathomable
deep?
Have the gates of death been revealed to you?
Have your ever seen the door-keepers of the palace of darkness?
Have you comprehended the vast expanse of the world?
Come, tell me all this, if you know.   *Job 38:1–18*³

The essential theological point of the tremendous speeches of God was that the problem of suffering was too great for Job's finite mind. He was asking to know what he could not know and had no business to know. Human knowledge of finite things was slight; how, then, could Job expect to know the meaning of infinite plans and infinite meanings? Job had asked to know the impossible; he had asked to know as God knows and to know what God knows. He had, in fact, made league with the cardinal vice and stumbled at exactly the spot of Adam's transgression. Job, like Adam before him, had reached for the fruit of the ultimate knowledge that he might be like God, knowing good and evil.

The truth of his condition struck Job like a physical blow, and once in the midst of God's tirade he cried out:

> What reply can I give thee, I who carry no weight?
> I put my finger to my lips.
> I have spoken once and now will not answer again; twice have I spoken, and I
>   will do so no more.[4]

And then when God's speech was finished, Job spoke in humility and resignation.

> I know that thou canst do all things and that no purpose is beyond thee.
> But I have spoken of great things which I have not understood,
> things too wonderful for me to know.
> I knew of thee then only by report, but now I see thee with my own eyes.
> Therefore, I melt away; I repent in dust and ashes.[5]

Now Job realized both his own weakness and God's capacity; his own need and God's concern, and no other knowing was necessary. He did not understand, but he believed. He was sincerely and reverently resigned in his agnosticism. In trust he was saved.

Thus we see that one possible theological answer to suffering and death is the posture of reverent agnosticism. A person cannot know why some things happen, but can believe that God knows, and that God knows best, and that in the end, in this life or in another life, the person who clings to faith in God and God's goodness will, as Job in the end, be compensated a hundredfold.

Life After Death—Reincarnation   Of contemporary philosophers, Martin Heidegger° is the one who most emphatically defines human existence as a condition determined by the anticipation of death. "Life," he tells us, "is being-unto-death." Because it is a universal, horrendous nonmanipulable of condition, and the major dilemma confronting human salvation, death gets high priority in all theologies. It gets answered, and the answer most often given is in the form of a reincarnation theology. We quickly associate reincarnation doctrine (or transmigration of souls) with the great Eastern religions (Hinduism and Buddhism), but there are many other religions that deal with the problem of death and life after death in this fashion. Indeed, somewhere Arnold Toynbee° has stated that for all our Western skepticism about reincarnation, Christianity is one of the "peculiar religions" that does not teach this doctrine.

To see this kind of theology at work, we shall examine a simple form of reincarnation theory; the form found in the theology of the inhabitants of the Island of Kiriwina, which is one of the islands of the Trobriand chain, a group of islands east of New Guinea. Our information about these people comes from the work of anthropologist Bronislaw Malinowski.° The people of Kiriwina believe that all people have souls, which they call "baloma." At death the soul, which is apparently an ethereal duplicate of the human being, that is, a ghost, detaches itself from the body and soon travels to a special island (Tuma) where it enters a spiritual life much like its former physical life. It eats, drinks, socializes, falls in love, gets married. Malinowski's informants told him that the spirit women of Tuma were very beautiful and seductive, and they took special pains to distract the newly arrived male ghost from remembering his earthly wife. They usually succeeded. The ghost-man forgets his former wife and settles down with a new spirit wife. However, Malinowski reports:

> a man may wait for his widow to join him in Tuma, but my informants did not seem inclined to think that many would do this. . . . The spirit, in any case, settles down to a happy existence in Tuma, where he spends another lifetime until he dies again. But this death is . . . not complete annihilation.[6]

At its "death" on Tuma, the baloma is reborn in a human form back on the island of its former life.*

The baloma in its life on Tuma grows old. Its eyes dim, its teeth fall out, its strength fails, until in the last stage the baloma goes down to the sea and sloughs off its skin, much as a snake does. What is left is the *waiwaia*, that is, the embryo of a new to-be-born child. This embryo is picked up by a baloma woman and carried back to the island of its former habitation and secretly implanted in the womb of a woman, which has been opened by former copulation. Or it may be (a different explanation) that the baloma goes to sea, where it is transformed into the waiwaia. Then it either washes ashore, where it is found by a baloma woman, or it drifts to the island of former habitation and seeks on its own an open vaginal passage in one of the girls or women bathing in the sea. Thus life begins over. There is a cycle of life on earth, then the passage over to the cycle of spirit life, and finally the passage back to the cycle of reborn human life: reincarnation.

---

*Kiriwinians have some interesting ideas about pregnancy and how it relates to the preexisting baloma. They believe that the only function of the male in conception is to open the woman so that the baloma embryo (waiwaia) can have passage into the woman's womb. The waiwaia is a metamorphic stage in the reincarnation process. It is the baloma-ghost prepared to return to life as a human.

With this brief account of Trobriander reincarnation doctrine we can see that primitives can and do have elaborate theological systems. And although much of what they believe may appear to us as theologically naive and scientifically inaccurate, it is not without religious profundity. These people have looked at the succession of life and death and have declared that it constitutes a meaningful order. They have looked at death (at being dead) and have declared that it is neither terrifying nor meaningless. They have transcended finitude, have dealt adequately with the horrendous nonmanipulable of death, and have accomplished a viable salvation theology.

The idea of reincarnation in Trobriand theology differs in one major respect from the more elaborate reincarnation theologies of Hinduism and Buddhism. In the South Pacific theology there is no element of reward and punishment involved in the cycle of death and rebirth. This is not the case in Eastern theologies. In the East, reincarnation means rebirth in accordance with the Law of Karma. Karma is the law that governs rebirth according to the worthiness of the preceding life. Good people, because of the Karma principle, are rewarded with a better life next time than last time. A bad person gets a worse life. Each passage through life is determined by the character of the person's life in the last passage, until eventually, when perfection has been accomplished and the perfect life lived, no more rebirths are demanded by the Law of Karma, and the soul may pass into Nirvana and become united with God Brahman.

Life After Death—Immortality and Resurrection Although the terms "immortality" and "resurrection" refer to life after death, they are not identical; in fact, according to some theologians, they are radically different. One is a Greek concept; the other is Hebrew. Greek (Platonic) philosophy argues that the soul is by its own nature without beginning and indestructible; Judeo-Christian theology denies this, holding that souls are created by God and could be destroyed by God. Furthermore, the destiny of the soul in Platonic thought is to escape the entrapment of the body and be free. In Jewish and Christian thought its proper destiny is to be reunited with the body (resurrected) that it might once again have a full life. We shall first look at the radical difference between immortality theology and resurrection theology, and then look at how some of the church fathers modified Greek thought and dressed immortality in Christian garb.

In the Ingersoll Lectures of 1955, Oscar Cullmann read a paper that drew the radical difference between immortality and resurrection. This difference he dramatically portrayed by presenting as contrasting illustrations the death scenes of Socrates of Athens and Jesus of Nazareth.

In Plato's dialogue entitled *Phaedo* we have an account of the serene and noble death of Socrates. That ugly-bodied, most beautiful of men had been condemned to die by an angry and vindictive city. The charges brought against him had been vague but adequately deadly: association with traitorous people, corruption of the youth, denial of the Gods, radicalism. Tried and convicted, he had been in prison for two months awaiting execution. Then the time came.

Phaedo tells his friend Echecrates how it was. Throughout the day a number of Socrates' friends, including Phaedo, had been with him in the cell. The old man had wanted to talk about death and immortality, and so his young friends and disciples had once again followed with fascination the marvelous thinking of the great teacher. He had led them to understand that death was a friend, a great liberator, for it freed the soul from the confines and restrictions of the body. The soul was indestructible—immortal. With such "theology" to support him, Socrates welcomed the coming of the end of the day and with it the end of his days.

Phaedo told Echecrates how as the sunset hour arrived, the jailer came in and tearfully apologized to Socrates for the act that he had to perform and how Socrates was so impressed by the man's distress and commented upon what a kind and friendly man he was. Throughout the day, Phaedo said, they had all managed to hide their distress at what was happening there, but seeing the jailer and hearing Socrates praise the man, and knowing that the time could not be put off much longer, they began to break down. Phaedo confessed that he found himself weeping openly, until Socrates reprimanded them, telling them that he had sent the women away to avoid such a scene, for he believed that a man should die in peace. Socrates then said they should get on with it. But Crito, who was also there, begged him to wait a while for it really was not late and that many condemned people put it off to the very last minute. Socrates said that he could understand how others might want to put it off as long as possible, but it would not be right for him to put it off, for "I do not think that I should gain anything by drinking the poison a little later; I should be sparing and saving a life which is already gone; I could only laugh at myself for this. Please then do as I say, and not refuse me." So Crito called for the jailer to return with the poison, and Socrates drank it. He went on talking for a while, until the poison began to take effect. Then he lay down and covered his face for a while. Toward the end he uncovered his face and said, "Crito, I owe a cock to Asclepius, will you remember to pay the debt?" "The debt shall be paid," said Crito; "is there anything else?" There was no answer. . . . "Such was the end . . . of our friend, whom I may truly call the wisest and justest and best of all men whom I have ever known."[7]

So died the sage of Athens, quietly, serenely, securely, supported by a philosophical-theological conviction that the human soul is indestructible, is literally and absolutely immortal. Because it is not a material substance as in the body, it is, by its own nature, imperishable. The very simplicity (noncompoundedness) of the soul makes it necessarily permanent. Furthermore, the soul (the pure reason of humans) has no real affinity with the body that encases it. The body is its prison. Only with the death of the body can this prison be opened and the immortal soul be freed. So believing, Socrates went to his death not wanting to avoid it, or even put it off a little longer.

Not so with Jesus. When death came to him it seemed more like a fiend from Hell. Alone in the Garden of Gethsemane he faced it as a terrifying catastrophe. The records tell us that "he sweat blood." Why? Why the difference? Surely Jesus was as courageous a man as Socrates. He, like Socrates, deliberately chose the path that led to his own execution. He was not afraid of the men who would kill him. He had faced dangerous men many times. Surely it was not just the thought of the pain that would come. He could have fled from the garden, escaped into the Judean hills, avoided the agony of crucifixion. No, it must have been something else that he feared. *It was death itself that he feared.* Death was not his friend, not his liberator. Death did not come blessedly to free his immortal soul. Death came to annihilate him. Death was his enemy, because death was God's enemy.

In his Ingersoll Lectures, Cullmann put these two death scenes side by side to indicate how differently two distinct theological positions present the concept of life after death. Cullmann asserts:

I have put the death of Socrates and the death of Jesus side by side. For nothing shows better the radical difference between the Greek doctrine of the immortality of the soul and the Christian doctrine of the resurrection. Because Jesus underwent death in all its horror, not only in his body, but also in his soul . . . and as he is regarded by the first Christians as the mediator of salvation, he must indeed be the very one who in his death conquers death itself. He cannot obtain the victory by simply living on as an immortal soul, by fundamentally *not* dying. He can conquer death only by actually dying, by betaking himself of the sphere of "nothingness," of abandonment by God. When one wishes to overcome someone else, one must enter his territory. . . .

Furthermore, if life is to issue out of so genuine a death as this, a new divine act of creation is necessary. And this act of creation calls back to life not just a part of the man, but the whole man—all that God has created and death has annihilated. For Socrates and Plato no act of creation is necessary. For the body is indeed bad and should not live. And that part which is to live on, the soul, does not die at all.

If we want to understand the Christian faith in the resurrection, we must completely disregard the Greek thought that the material, the bodily, the corporeal is bad and *must* be destroyed, so that the death of the body could not be in any sense a destruction of the true life. For Christian (and Jewish) thinking, the death of the body is *also* destruction of the God-created life. No distinction is made: even the life of our body is true life; death is the destruction of *all* life created by God. Therefore, it is death and not the body which must be conquered by the resurrection.[8]

According to Cullman, Christians (and Jews), when acting out of their own religious tradition and not out of Platonic philosophy, reject the immortality doctrine in favor of the more radical doctrine of re-creation or resurrection. A person who is dead is dead! Totally. Only as God re-creates that person does he or she live again. To die is to be annihilated. To live again is to be resurrected, and, according to John's Revelation, resurrected only at the end of time.

Cullmann's comparison is highly illustrative of the "philosophical" difference between the concept of immortality and the concept of resurrection. It may also be an accurate description of Jesus' own theological position and the theological position of the very first Christians. It is for a fact an accurate observation of biblical theology on the subject. But for all this, it is unquestionable that traditional Christian theology does endorse a doctrine of immortality, as well as a doctrine of resurrection. Quite early the influence of Socrates' student Plato was felt, and Christian theologians made accommodations for immortality as well as resurrection in Christian belief. To them, in the interval between death and resurrection, the soul had an independent life of its own—an "immortality." But in their theories of immortality, the early Christian theologians departed from Platonic theory in one important aspect. They did not endorse the idea that the soul was immortal by its own indestructible nature. Whatever immortality the soul possessed, it possessed as a gift from God. God created it, and he could destroy it. Justin Martyr, Irenaeus, Tatian, Theophilus, Arnobus, Lactanius—all held that the soul lived because God willed it so, and would cease to live if that became God's pleasure. Even Augustine, who used Platonic arguments to prove the soul's immortal nature, nevertheless stated that although

> the soul of man is, according to a peculiar sense of its own *(secundum quendam modum suum)*, immortal, it is not absolutely immortal as God is.[9]

The theologians had ample philosophical support in Greek philosophy for the doctrine of immortality, but they found little support for resurrection theology in Greek philosophy, except as they could interpret transmigration of souls as analogous to resurrection theology. Resurrection was not a Greek idea. In Christian theology it comes from Judaism.

Apparently neither resurrection nor any other serious theology of life after death was a part of the religious tradition of the early Hebrews. Early biblical literature was so silent on the subject that some scholars have held that the idea of life after death was not a part of early Hebrew beliefs. This, however, was probably not the case. Probably, as did other Semitic people, the early Hebrews believed that the soul *(nephesh)* or spirit *(ruach)* survived physical death. The place of this survival was called Sheol. In Sheol the shade or ghost of the departed person existed probably in a state resembling sleep. As some Hebrews picturesquely put it: The soul of the departed slumbered on the bosom of Abraham. Sheol was clearly not a place of reward or punishment. In neither the writings ascribed to Moses nor the writings of the Prophets was Sheol presented as similar in any way to the later ideas of Heaven or Hell. Nor did the idea of resurrection have an important place in early Hebrew thought. In fact, Hebraism was predominantly concerned with this life and especially the prosperity and future of God's Chosen People—the nation of Israel. Those ancient people seemed to have been perfectly satisfied simply to assign the dead to "Abraham's bosom."

At the same time, as early as the eighth-century Prophets, there were in ancient Hebrew thought the seeds of the eschatologies that were to be elaborated by later Pharisees and early Christians. First, there was the idea of the Day of Yahweh. The Hebrews came to believe that there would come a day when God would come and rescue his nation from its enemies and punish those enemies—the oppressive Gentile nations. The idea was eventually modified (beginning especially with the Prophet Amos) to include a punishment for all of God's enemies, wicked Hebrews as well as the Gentile oppressors. Amos prophesied that the Day of Yahweh would be a terrible day of judgment for all wicked people. Second, there was in ancient Hebrew thought the idea of rehabilitation of the Hebrew nation, that is, a kind of national "resurrection," at the end of time. If the nation was to be reconstructed, would not one expect Abraham to be there, and Isaac and Jacob, and Moses? Was it not reasonable to expect that some of the righteous dead in Sheol, the heroes of the past, would also be reconstructed; would be resurrected in new bodies? And if heroes, why not all good people, even everybody?

These ideas developed rapidly and impressively after the time of the Babylonian Captivity. In 586 B.C. the Hebrews (Southern Judean Hebrews) were overrun by Nebuchadnezzar of Babylon, and the major Hebrew families were carried into slavery. In Babylon they lived first under Babylonian rule and then, after Cyrus of Persia conquered the lands of the Babylonians, under Persian rule. The contact with Persia was especially important to Hebrew thought. In Babylon the Jews (a term that came to be applied to the Hebrews during the captivity) were apparently influenced by (1) the idea of God struggling with a great supernatural enemy (including and especially the Zoroastrian Bad Spirit, Angra Mainyu, also called Satan), and (2) the idea of a place under the earth where evil souls were punished as they deserved because of the wickedness of their lives on earth.

At this time, or shortly thereafter, a new type of literature began to emerge in Jewish culture: the apocalypse, of which Daniel in the Old Testament and later Revelation in the New Testament are fine examples. Concerning this type of literature, Martin Rist informs us that:

> Apocalypticism is the belief that this present evil and corrupt world, now under the control of Satan, will soon be ended and destroyed, along with Satan and his demonic and human agents, by the direct intervention of God, heretofore tran-

scendent; who thereupon will establish a new and perfect age and a new and perfect world, both under his immediate control, in which the righteous from among the living and the resurrected dead will enjoy a blessed, righteous existence without end.[10]

As we can see from this analysis, an apocalypse is an eschatology, that is, an account of the end of time. In both post-captivity Judaism and early Christianity the end of time would involve: (1) a resurrection of all the dead, (2) a universal judgment, (3) destruction or punishment for all the wicked, and (4) blessed, eternal existence for the righteous.

The idea of Hell for the wicked dead appeared in late Palestinian Judaism and early Christianity. Apparently the idea of a place of flaming punishment came from the Hebrew Gehenna. Gehenna was a valley west of Jerusalem where the Hebrews burned the refuse of the city and also the bodies of executed criminals. It was a place where in earlier times the Assyrian God Moloch had been worshipped and where human sacrifices had been thrown to the flames of Moloch. In eschatology, Gehenna became a place of punishment for sinners and was located, not in the Jerusalem garbage dump, but under the earth.

Although the Jews eventually developed a theology of life after death, this concept never became a central theme of Judaism. Judaism remained (and remains) true to its early biblical emphasis. It was a religion of God and God's Chosen People. It was a religion not of life-after-death salvation, but of moral righteousness and of national salvation. Jews may or may not believe in their own personal survival after death, but to the degree that they are Jews they hold firmly to the keeping of God's holy law and to the ultimate triumph and fulfillment of Israel as the kingdom of God.

It was Christianity that took personal resurrection and immortality into the center of its religion and made life after death the great goal and expectation of religion. In Christianity the human soul, through repentance of sin, faith, and the grace of God made possible in the redemptive action of Christ's death on the Cross, could be translated from its separate (fallen) condition into a supernatural condition wherein it would enjoy immortal life resurrected in a spiritual body, and living eternally with God. All of the Hebrew nationalistic elements had been expunged. The kingdom of God for Christians was "not of this world" (John 18:36). The Christian concern and expectation were not to live in a righteous kingdom but to live in the unutterable joy that would be known when one lived in the direct and immediate presence of God in Heaven: when one lived in the Beatific Vision.

Identity or Union with God (That Is, with the Infinite)   In this kind of theology people are to overcome their finiteness by being or becoming infinite. It is held that the nature of mankind (or its potential nature) is such that it is possible for a human soul to become identified with the infinite reality of God; for a person to become, more or less, what God is. We shall examine two forms of this kind of theology—one from ancient Egypt, the other from modern India.

Five thousand years ago in Egypt people strove to become God Osiris. Osiris was a soter God, a savior God. He was a Man-God who was killed and resurrected and who after his resurrection left the human world and went to the world of the immortals (to Khenti-Amenti), where he became judge of the dead and ruler of the blessed immortals. Human beings could go to the world of the immortals if they had in this life become like the God—if they had, in fact, become Osiris. This was not easy to do. To become Osiris, a man or woman must first be initiated into the cult of the God and must be clean of hand and pure of heart. The essence of such a person must have been transmuted into the divinity of Osiris by eating and drinking the sacred eucharist (the bread and wine that were the body and blood of Osiris). There were other prerequisites also, such as a proper funeral including embalming and proper prayers said by official priests, but the point of importance for our consideration was that the person became the God. Person and infinity were united.

In more extreme forms (namely, true mysticism) participants believe that they can solve the problem of finitude either by having their souls absorbed into the Godhead or by discovering (becoming absolutely convinced) that their souls are already infinite, in fact, that their souls are already what God is.

In certain forms of Vedanta° Hinduism,* salvation is also conceived of as a human-divine unity, but here humans do not become divine; they are already divine, even from the beginning. The problem is they are ignorant of this fact. They believe themselves to be separate, distinct persons living among other separate, distinct persons—things among things. But this is illusion; this is error. There is only one reality, God Brahman, and salvation comes to people when they know this finally, even in the very marrow of their bones.

Although Hinduism is finally a world-transcending system, it is not characterized by gloom or pessimism. It does not condemn a joyous living in this world, but only, finally, proclaims that ultimate joyousness is in something other than the things people usually pursue. With patient wisdom, Hinduism recognizes that humans naturally and, therefore, legitimately seek a number of goals in life. They seek pleasure (kama), and power (artha), and moral integrity (dharma), and eventually in the course of many rebirths, salvation (moksha). No religion is more sensitive to natural human needs and desires or more generous in endorsing satisfaction of human needs and desires. It recognizes that people naturally want pleasure, and this is not decried. Instead, it is identified as one of the four proper goals of living. People should seek pleasure. Of course, hedonism, like anything else, demands good sense.

*See footnote, page 86.

People cannot just "eat, drink, and be merry"—or tomorrow they may wish they had died. But as long as the basic rules of intelligent indulgence and proper morality are followed, people are free in Hinduism to seek all manner of pleasure. If pleasure is what people desire, let them not suppress the desire. Hinduism promotes pleasure, and then waits. It waits for that time when the pleasure seeker will recognize that pleasure, no matter how extensive, is not the final answer to a fulfilled and joyous life.

One who begins to recognize this fact is instructed by the Hindu religious philosophers (and all Hindu philosophers are religious philosophers) to try a second proper goal of life. Let that person try for success. Success in the form of wealth, fame, and power is endorsed as perfectly natural and worthy of serious concern. There have been many wealthy people who were good. Be both wealthy and good at the same time; there is nothing wrong with that. But, as with pleasure, the wealthy and the powerful will eventually lament, "Surely there is more to life than just this."

At this point, Hinduism will suggest that one try a new approach. Instead of pursuing selfish pleasure and power and wealth, turn outward altruistically toward others. Turn from self-centered living and begin to live for the welfare of others. Get married. Become a parent and responsible householder. Become concerned with the community life and the needs of humankind. Such a life can be good, rich, rewarding, perhaps good enough to satisfy one to the end of one's days—this time around.

But, alas, even this kind of living is not truly enough, and this fact will become apparent either in this life or in some future reincarnation. It does bring praise from peers and self-respect, but in the end it does not satisfy the deepest and most demanding human desire: to be part of what is infinite and unchanging, and eternally beatific and beautiful. There comes a time when nothing in the world, as the world appears to us phenomenally, is enough. It is not that the world is necessarily bad. Indeed, much of it is good, exciting, wonderful; but eventually the question will be asked: "Is this really all there is to it?"

And this is the moment that religion, especially the Hindu religion, awaits. This is the moment it has been coaxing since it first proposed that there were proper goals in life. Now at last Hinduism can speak its piece: "No, this is not all there is to it, for beyond pleasure and success and even duty there is a *beyond* that is not out in the world somewhere, but in the depths of your own being. For within you there is a self, a soul, the *atman,* which is the very stuff of God. It is infinite, absolute, complete. Center your life in this atman, and you will never again seek to satisfy a need, for all needs will be satisfied automatically. All finite things will cease to distress you, or even interest you, for you will know that you are not finite, not limited, not restrained. You are free. You are complete. You are God. Your soul, your spirit, is not different from or separated from the soul and spirit of God Brahman. In essential nature, you and God are one.

This is the message of the final goal: union with God. But between the message and the accomplishment of union, there is an arduous discipline. Hinduism, which is a family of religions rather than a single theological system, offers three orthodox disciplines toward the ultimate union with God, which is called Nirvana. The discipline chosen will be largely determined by the kind of person (intellectually, psychologically, emotionally) the searcher is. We shall look at the discipline called the way of knowledge *(Jnana Marga)* because it illustrates the point we are trying to make: namely salvation through identification with God.*

For persons of strong intellectual powers, Hinduism offers a path to God through diligently acquired knowledge. Here the proposition is that salvation (the fourth and final goal of life) comes through a complete aesthe-noetic° (through the senses and the mind) identification with the ground of being, God Brahman. This is accomplished through a rigorous discipline of philosophical investigation and introspection. What is sought is the ability truly to see the difference between the surface self (the personality), which stands in the forefront of our being, and the basic and real self (the atman), which lies at the base of both personality and the physical self.

The searcher after final truth must (1) become acquainted with the philosophy that argues that unknown to the surface self there is at the center of the human being a spirit or soul that is actually the source of being itself—which is what Brahman is. The proposal is that the real person (the atman) and God (the Brahman) are not different beings but the same being. This hypothesis must be thoroughly examined in a critical, philosophical manner; and then (2) it must be thought about in prolonged and intensive reflection until the hypothesis is transformed from a mere concept in the mind to a momentous reality in the convictions. Thoroughly understood, it is, finally, thoroughly endorsed. The end sought is an overwhelming awareness that whereas "I" seem to live in "my" personality, there is a deeper, more basic self, which is actually the source of personality. Personality is really only the actor's mask through which the deeper spirit speaks. To the degree that one thinks of "myself" as a personality, separate and independent, that person is mistaking the mask for the actor. The task of religious meditation is to correct this error.

---

*The other two ways are the way of works *(Karma Marga)* and the way of devotion *(Bhakti Marga)*. The former is primarily a way of ritual, especially domestic ritual. It is followed by the majority of Hindus who carry out rites and ceremonies and religious duties in order to advance themselves in merit. Many hope that they can gain sufficient merit to pass at death into one of the heavens of afterlife, or to be reborn on a higher spiritual and intellectual plane that they might in the next reincarnation achieve union with God Brahman through the higher religious way—the way of knowledge *(Jnana Marga)*. Many other Hindus, also not capable of the intellectual demands of the way of knowledge, concentrate their religious life in devotion to one or another of the multitude of Gods and Goddesses in the Hindu pantheon, from whom they expect to get aid and comfort in the trials of life. Neither of these ways compares in prestige or importance or finality with the Way of Knowledge *(Jnana Marga)*, which offers final and complete salvation: unity with God Brahman.

As Huston Smith° points out, "Turning his awareness inward [the yogi] must pierce and dissolve the innumerable layers of the manifest personality until, all strata of the mask at length cut through, he arrives finally at the autonomous and strangely unconcerned actor who stands beneath."[11]

The searcher who can eventually establish a lively awareness of the true self underlying all personal values, all phenomenal personality, will be ready for the next (3) step: the shifting of self-identity from the phenomenal, passing, personality level of being to the deep, permanent, spiritual level. Doing this requires meditating in prolonged and intense concentration on the proposition that the atman, which is now known, is the true identity. This will not be easy; it is an exacting art, because people are almost wholly self-identified in their own body and personality. The searcher must dissolve that identity and see himself or herself in a completely different dimension of reality; as *in* but not *of* one's own body and phenomenal self; as being what God is and separated from God's total being only as a drop of sea spray may be separated from the sea itself in the brief time between the wave striking the rock and the droplet falling back into the water. The believer who, in referring to God, can say of himself or herself, *"tat tvam asi"* ("that·thou art"), has become the *true* believer, the emancipated believer. That person is at one with God. That person is saved.*

Before leaving this consideration of salvation theology as union with God, we should make one more observation. It is different from the theologies of

---

*In each of the ways of religion the word *"Yoga"* appears. Yoga means union: union with God through works or devotion or knowledge. Yoga is also a discipline of behavior that fosters union with divine reality. It is especially important as one of the physical disciplines in the Way of Knowledge. Yoga is a technique of meditation and concentration that assists in the final accomplishment of the experience of release from error, liberation from ignorance, and absorption into Brahman *(samadhi)*, which is the ultimate salvation in Hinduism. The technique became highly refined in the hands of Patanjali, a yogi of the second century A.D. The Raja Yoga of Patanjali has eight steps:

1. *Yama:* the five desire-killing vows. Here one vows to abstain from harming living things, from deceit, stealing, unchastity, and from acquisitiveness.
2. *Niyama:* observance of self-disciplinary rules of cleanliness, calm, mortification, study, and prayer.
3. *Asana:* proper posture, especially the lotus posture.
4. *Pranayama:* regulation of breathing, whereby one gradually comes to control all of the rhythmic processes of one's physical being.
5. *Pratyahara:* control of all physical sensation through which the outside world is shut out of consciousness.
6. *Dharana:* concentration in which the mind focalizes on one single object of thought until all other consciousness disappears.
7. *Dhyana:* meditation in which all of the above disciplines are in full operation.
8. *Samadhi:* the last step in which the mind, emptied of all content and no longer aware of either object or subject, is absorbed into the divine reality—into God.

reincarnation, resurrection, and immortality in that it does not propose that one must wait for death for salvation to occur. Salvation is promised immediately. It is not only a beatific vision, the direct knowledge of God, later, but the beatific vision now. Salvation for Osirians and Hindu mystics and others is not simply a future reward but an immediate experience.

Studied Philosophical Indifference   Many people attempt to have a sort of nontheology of death and salvation (to be indifferent) by trying never to talk about or even think about such things—a good trick if you can do it. A different attempt is to try to establish, by talking and thinking, a philosophy of indifference, which is also a good trick if you can do it.

Epicurus° of Samos and Athens, who in the fourth century B.C. founded a school of philosophy that became known as Epicureanism, made this move. Epicurus wanted people to be happy, to live untroubled lives. He observed that some of the things that upset people and filled them with unease, and even dread, were fear of God (that he would punish) and fear of death (when the punishment would happen). In his letter to Menoeceus, he tried to allay both of these fears. God, he said, was not concerned with punishing humans. God was blessed and attended to his own blessedness. From that quarter people had nothing to fear, and they had nothing to fear from death either. One need not fear death, not because death was blessed, but because death was nothing and could not cause harm. In his letter Epicurus counseled:

> Become accustomed to the belief that death is nothing to us. For all good and evil consist in sensations, but death is the deprivation of sensation. And therefore a right understanding that death is nothing to us makes the mortality of life enjoyable, not because it adds to it an infinite span of time, but because it takes away the craving for immortality. For there is nothing terrible in life for the man who has truly comprehended that there is nothing terrible in not living. . . . So death, the most terrible of ills, is nothing to us, since so long as we exist death is not with us; but when death comes, then we do not exist. It does not concern either the living or the dead, since for the former it is not, and the latter are no more.[12]

We will never know whether Menoeceus found Epicurus's theology of indifference adequate. If he did, he was among the few who accomplished the feat. Many more of us, it would appear, are incapable of such studied indifference. We are more like Hamlet—unable to avoid wrestling with:

> . . . the dread of something after death—
> the undiscovered country, from whose bourn
> No traveler returns—puzzles the will,
> And makes us rather bear those ills we know
> Than fly to others that we know not of?
> Thus conscience does make cowards of us all,
> And thus the native hue of resolution
> Is sicklied o'er with the pale cast of thought . . .[13]

THE PROBLEM OF DEATH

Suffering and death are two central problems with which theology must deal, but they do not raise the same questions. With suffering the question is especially: How can so much suffering exist in a world where there is a God who cares? Suffering challenges the existence and nature of God. With death, on the other hand, the question is: Since death is inevitable, what is the meaning of life?* Reinhold Niebuhr,° in his *Nature and Destiny of Man*, states, "When life is 'cut' off. . . the very meaningfulness of life is called into question."[14] It is this meaningfulness of life we shall now examine, having examined the question of God and suffering in an earlier chapter.†

An answer to the question of death (What happens after we die?) sets the conditions for answering, Where do we come from? and Why are we here? If, for example, we are told that when people die they go either to Heaven or Hell, the implications are that we originally came from God as part of God's salvation scheme and that we are, while here, to pursue that salvation scheme according to God's will. Of course, if we do not do this we are slated for the Hell side of the salvation equation.

On the other hand, we may be told that when people die they are not annihilated or consigned either to Heaven or Hell, but return to this life again and again until with great spiritual effort, after almost endless reincarnations, they achieve union with God—Nirvana. For this we may infer that people come into this life from the endlessly spinning wheel of returning life and that they are to live this life, and each succeeding life, so that their goodness will eventually and finally overcome their *karma* sufficiently for them to escape the "wheel" and enter into impersonal and eternal bliss.

But what if, as another example, we are told that this is it—all of it—that death is truly the end of the line for us? From such an announcement perhaps we cannot theologically explain where we came from or why, but the meaning of life is nonetheless implied. If this is all there is, we had better make it count. Live each day as if it were a whole lifetime. Live now! Do not waste any of it. This time is not only the "only time around," it is the only time. Such comments are also "a theology," albeit a negative one. They, too, are intended to give "meaning to life" because of death.

As it imposes the question of the meaning of life, death is a human problem. It is a fact, of course, that all living things die, but, so far as we know, only humans know this horrendous fact. One of the prices we pay for being human is the inescapable knowledge that each one of us is appointed once to die.

To be sure, as much as possible, we try to smother this awareness, this

---

*In the face of death God's existence is not to be doubted so much as eagerly affirmed. The need is to answer the questions: Where do we come from? Why are we here? Where are we going? An affirmation of God's existence is a big help in making positive, hopeful theology.
†See Chapter 6, pages 91–98.

knowledge, by avoiding the thought: Other things die, even people, even those we love. This we can think, but not ourselves. As Emily Dickinson° once said, "I can't imagine . . . my own death scene." Yet Dickinson knew and we know that die we shall on "some fair or stormy day." John Donne° said it as well as anybody. He observed that when the church bell tolls you need not "send to know for whom" it tolls—"it tolls for thee." The bell tolls for us. And in that tolling at least two kinds of fear can be heard: first, the fear of annihilation, of nonbeing. Death, when looked at bleakly, is the end of the world. With death, *my* world ends. And I also end. But such a thought is incomprehensible. I simply cannot imagine my not being. And when I let myself feel in the direction of that impossible thought, I shiver.

> No man is an island, entire of itself; every man is a piece of the continent, a part of the main. If a clod be washed away by the sea, Europe is the less, as well as if a promontory were, ... Any man's death diminishes me because I am involved in mankind, and therefore never send to know for whom the bell tolls; it tolls for thee. *John Donne*[15]

That when we are annihilated our world annihilates with us is a thought that, in spite of Epicurus's gainsaying and Nirvana's negative promise, or the Tao's gentle indifference, is enough to give us pause. It is weird. And the weirdness of this scene is caused to some degree, as Ludwig Wittgenstein° observed, by the fact that death is not an experienceable event. Different from a birthday that can be celebrated and remembered, death is the end of all celebration and remembering. "At death," said Wittgenstein, "the world does not alter, but comes to an end."[16]

Second, paradoxically, death threatens not only with the prospect of annihilation, but also with the possibility of life after death. But is that not good? Life after death? Perhaps, "yes" but also perhaps, "no." Death may be neither a glorious experience nor a dreamless sleep. It may be, as Hamlet worried, a horrible nightmare.

> To die, to sleep;
> To sleep: perchance to dream: ay, there's the rub;
> For in that sleep of death what dreams may come,
> When we have shuffled off this mortal coil,
> Must give us pause . . .
> . . . the dread of something after death . . .[17]

People fear the prospect of "nothingness" so much that they dismiss the thought, and then, as often as not, replace it with a threat of judgment and damnation. According to Reinhold Niebhur, "Nothing expresses the insecurity and anxiety of human existence more profoundly than the fact that the fear of extinction and the fear of judgment are compounded in the fear of death."[18]

Nevertheless, in the final analysis, theology solves the problem of death on a more positive note. Life may end, but that end is not, or need not be, the end of "you." There is more to it. Indeed, in the various theologies available, there are all sorts of "more to it," and most of them are prosperous, or can be.

ANSWERS TO THE PROBLEM OF DEATH

Immortality of Influence   One way to try to put meaning into death is to say that life transcends death in the continuing influence of a person's accomplishments. The Greek poets Homer° and Hesiod,° for example, presented ancient Greek heroes in this fashion. Believing that only the Gods were immortal, it was believed that such heroes as Odysseus,° Achilles,° and Hector° lived on at least in the telling of their stories. They continued to live in their "living legends." As long as their names were uttered and their stories told, they went on living.

In the Christian world the greatest giant of influence was, of course, Jesus of Nazareth. His influence can be immediately observed in the dating of time. Once Jesus lived and because he lived the world redefined the telling of time— B.C., "before Christ" and A.D., "in the year of the Lord" (anno Domini), that is, after Christ. If considered only in his secular influence (all Christian commitment aside), Jesus lives today more profoundly than he ever did in his own day. Once only a few people in a funny little place, a kind of "nowhereville," knew him—but today! The same thing is true, more subtly perhaps but just as true, of Plato and Aristotle, of St. Paul and St. Augustine, of Isaac Newton, Thomas Edison. They live on in our lives every day.

To a greater or lesser degree, this is true of all persons. People we have known, the ones who made a difference, live on in us.

Immortality of Progeny   Another way to "cheat death" is in children. The Hebrew patriarch Abraham (also known as Abram) was not promised any life after death, any eternal bliss by his God, but he was offered children.

> When Abram was ninety-nine years old the Lord appeared to Abram, and said to him, "I am God Almighty, walk before me and be blameless. And I will make my covenant between me and you, and will multiply you exceedingly . . . you shall be the father of a multitude of nations." (Genesis 17:1−4)

And just to prove his good faith, God made it possible for Sarah (also called Sarai), despite her advanced age, to conceive and bear Abraham the first in his promised immortality: a son named Isaac. And to this very day (more than

3,500 years after Abraham died and disappeared) his children live and love, work and play, and speak his name reverently.

Immortality of Devotion   Abraham can also serve as our example of the immortality of devotion. He and the other patriarchs and the Prophets of Israel (such as Isaac, Jacob, David, Amos, Isaiah, Jeremiah) did not expect to be rewarded in an afterlife. Their salvation was a "now" salvation. It came in the keeping of God's law. Obedience to that law itself rewarded the obedient person. But most important of all was the privilege of participating in the continuing existence of God's Chosen People.

Life After Death   Immortality of influence and of progeny may be all right, but for some people it is not enough. Woody Allen, in the Los Angeles *Times*, October 4, 1975, confessed: "I don't want to achieve immortality through my work. I want to achieve it by not dying." In the history of theologies it is obvious that a great many people agree with Allen.

As we have observed, multitudes of people (the major religions of the world today) deal with the problem of death by affirming not only a life after death, but a prosperous one. To be sure, death is fraught with dangers, but with a proper theology, properly applied, the dangers can be skirted and (with Plato, for example) the immortal reason-soul can return to the realm of pure mind— to a place of eternal, ideal forms. The atman (in Hinduism) can, with proper theology, properly applied, slip the wheel of reincarnation and enter Nirvana. People can also, so we are told, with proper theology properly applied, assure themselves that one day beyond death they will be re-created body and spirit to live forever in God's presence. Each of these theologies (immortality, reincarnation/Nirvana, resurrection) that seem so different is basically promising the same thing. They all promise beatitude. They promise the ineffable experience of living with "God."

Jesus is reported to have sermonized one day regarding the eschatological° beatitude. Although that ultimate bliss cannot be spoken in any definitive way, he spoke of it in a finite, human fashion:

> Blessed are the poor in spirit, for theirs is the kingdom of heaven.
> Blessed are those who mourn, for they shall be comforted.
> Blessed are the meek, for they shall inherit the earth.
> Blessed are those who hunger and thirst after righteousness, for they shall be satisfied.
> Blessed are the merciful, for they shall obtain mercy.
> Blessed are the pure in heart, for they shall see God . . .   *(Matthew, 5:3–8)*

However they define God, major religions all declare as the culmination of salvation, as their final theological promise, that we shall "see God"—shall live in Blessed Presence, shall know indescribable joy.

Whether it be a promised ecstasy or a poignant loss, death splashes life with vivid thought.

> I remember
> Two brown eyes
> And a little elfin grin
> And how I held him in my arms
> And how I thought we'd win.
>
> I remember saying:
> "Hey guy,"
> And firmly proper: "John,"
> But mostly, always
> In my heart
> It was: "The Little One."
>
> How long ago it seems today;
> Yet not so long at all —
> I swung him up to shoulder high
> To make him "Daddy-tall."

Fierce, fierce and sweet
I held him then.

Defying God.
Defying men.
It would not happen to my son!
I'd drive it back,
Nor let it come —
That darkness
To the little one.

> I remember two brown eyes;
> A little elfin grin,
> And how I thought;
> Yes, how I thought —
> How I thought we'd win.

W.C.T.

Of course, we have been functioning in this discourse on the assumption that if God created something, it must have a meaning, must have a purpose. Kurt Vonnegut,° in his *Cat's Cradle*, wondered about this. Adam and God were talking:

Man blinked, "What is the purpose of all this," he asked politely.
"Everything must have a purpose?" asked God.
"Certainly," said man.
"Then I leave it to you to think of one for all this," said God and went away.[19]

SUMMARY VIEWS ON THE NATURE OF THE AFTERLIFE

Judaism   Judaism maintains that every person has a God-given soul. It also maintains that there is a world to come *(Olam Haba)*. This world to come will not be the same time as the time of the Messiah or the Resurrection. It will be, rather, a living forever with God, close to his divine glory. But, as Maimonides° taught, one should not attempt to formulate a picture of this place or experience. Just as we do not know God in any definitive way, so we do not know what God has in store for us. It should be observed that although Judaism affirms life after death, it does not devote excessive thought to the subject. Judaism is primarily a religion of this life—a religion dedicated to the keeping of God's way as described in the Holy Law. Do this and "salvation" will care for itself. Also, Judaism affirms that not Jews only, but all righteous people will share in the world to come.

Many Jews today reject the notion of afterlife. Like the Patriarchs and the Prophets of old, they believe that this life is adequate for the salvific encounter with God. Such thinking is not regarded as heretical in Judaism for Judaism does not stress doctrinal agreement over such questions. Rather it stresses responsible moral life now.

Christianity   Unlike Judaism, Christianity takes life after death most seriously. Whereas Judaism is a morality-centered religion, Christianity in its long tradition has emphasized a "world-to-come" centered religion.* Death according to the Christian gospel is both the penalty of sin and the doorway to afterlife. With sin came estrangement from God. The overcoming of such estrangement was made possible through the death of Christ, the second Adam. As in Adam's fall (however interpreted)† all humankind fell from innocence; in Christ's sacrifice, all humankind can know redemption.

---

*There are many Christians who, in a more liberal trend in modern Christianity, downplay life after death and put an extra emphasis on life now—especially a morally disciplined life now; and often a life of social responsibility (for example, the social responsibilities proposed by the "liberation theologies" currently popular in South America). But in both the past and present majority Christianity has been and is future life directed. What one does "now" in the way of religious commitment is done with an eye to the "forever after."

†According to ancient Christian tradition, Adam's disobedience corrupted all subsequent mankind. Many still believe this. But not all present-day Christians interpret the Fall in this way. One could argue, for example, that the Fall is really no more than a symbol for the maturing of humans beyond the innocence of childhood. Children are not born morally corrupt. They are just born children. But if they survive and grow to the age of reason, knowing right from wrong, they will fall from innocence as surely as night follows day. They will of their own volition, become Adam-like and need redemption; not that they can again be childlike, but that they can be a new person—Christ-like. Paul Tillich° holds that "the Fall" is a symbol for the "created" character of human existence. In essence human nature is perfect, but, in its "createdness" it is less than perfect by the fact of finitude. Only God is perfect in both essence and "fact." Tillich writes, "Theology must clearly and unambiguously represent 'the Fall' as a symbol for the human situation universally, not as the story of an event that happened 'once upon a time.'" See Paul Tillich, *Systematic Theology* (Chicago: University of Chicago Press, 1957), vol. 2, p. 29.

In Christian theology the crucified Son of God has drawn the sting of death—sin; but the follower of Christ must still undergo the "second death," the final, permanent estrangement from God. The saved person lives even now in a newness of life and has, in this new life, learned how to die.

Hinduism　This present life, according to Hinduism, is the result of the Law of Karma and reincarnation. That is what Hindus call *samsara*. Samsara is based in the inexorable law of moral cause and effect. What people do in this present life, they will be in the next life. If he is a poor man, gentle and kind, worshipping the Gods, performing all his proper duties, next time around he may be a rich man. As a rich man he may also be gentle and kind, worshipping the Gods, performing all his proper duties; then in the next reincarnation he may be given the intellect and sensitivity to be a holy man (truly on his way to Nirvana). But both the poor man and the rich man can fail in their proper duties, and in that case, the next time around each will receive "his just desserts" and be reincarnated in a lower form of existence. This is an *almost* endless cycle of birth, growth, decay, death; but not absolutely endless, for one can break the "wheel" in an experience called *moksha*—release from samsara. When that happens, when finally one has by his bootstraps risen to the existence of "most holy man," he enters into "godness" immediately, and at death he enjoys complete release into Nirvana. He merges into the indescribable joy of God.

Taoism°　Because mankind is one aspect of Tao (God), death is but another incident in the eternal, harmonious motion of nature. Just as fall merges into winter, and winter into spring, and spring into summer, so does human life arise, flow, and return to the order of all things, which is what God is. To grieve over death is to show oneself ignorant of Tao. In Tao (original philosophical Tao)[20] there is no positive view of life after death, but only the idea of motion from one form of flowing nature to another.

The Theological Accomplishment　Theology tries to give us assurance that what we want to believe and need to believe is true. If people are to work out their salvation from something, by something, to something, they need to know the "truth" about the *from*, the *by*, and the *to*. For faith to function adequately, or even be accepted, it must be true, or at least be believed to be true. If the statements, the dogmas, of the faith are not believed, they lose all their force. David Elton Trueblood° once speculated on how effective the Covenant of Mount Sinai would have been if the Hebrews had been told, or had come to believe; that God did not really give those Commandments to Moses; Moses just made them up. They would have been the same Commandments, but how "commanding" would they have been? That religious truths are difficult to understand, or are hidden, or are even irrational, may not violate the religious consciousness, but to be told that the religious truths are not true and that this is not important is unacceptable in the extreme. It is difficult to see how people could accept what they knew to be fallacious religious doctrines just because they found that those doctrines were religiously helpful. They might support pragmatic truths for someone else, saying, for example: "The Trobrianders' religion is a fine religion for Trobrianders. Of couse, it isn't true, but it works for them." But would anyone embrance the Trobriander religion for himself or for herself so long as he or she believed it was only operationally true, but not "really" true? Religion is not simply a pragmatic affair. Beliefs are not held just because they work. They are held because they work and *because they are true*. Much of the business of theology is to say so, and to say how so.

NOTES

[1] Woody Allen, *Getting Even* (New York: Waren, 1972), p. 31.

[2] In recent considerations of the figure of Satan in the Old Testament, some scholars suggest that the Satan of Job is really a personification of the Hebrew God Yahweh. Satan is actually the dark side of God: God's alter ego, in this instance, God's own doubt about Job. See Rivkah S. Kluger, *Satan in the Old Testament,* tran. Hildegaard Nagel (Evanston, Ill.: Northwestern University Press, 1967).

[3] The New English Bible (New York: Cambridge University Press, 1971).

[4] NEB, Job 40:3−5.

[5] NEB, Job 42:1−6.

[6] Malinowski, *Magic, Science and Religion* (Boston: Beacon Press, 1948), p. 135.

[7] "Phaedo, The Death of Socrates," in *The Republic* and Other Works by Plato, tran. B. Jowett (Garden City, N.Y.: Doubleday, 1960), pp. 551−552.

[8] Oscar Cullmann, "Immortality of the Soul or Resurrection of the Dead," in *Immortality and Resurrection,* ed. Krister Stendahl (New York: Macmillan, 1965), pp. 18−19.

[9] *Epistolae.*

[10] Martin Rist, *Daniel and Revelation* (Nashville, Tenn.: Abingdon, 1947), p. 3.

[11] Huston Smith, *The Religions of Man* (New York: Harper & Row, Perennial Library, 1965), p. 37.

[12] Epicurus, "Epicurus to Menoeceus," in *Ethics,* ed. Oliver A. Johnson (New York: Holt, Rinehart and Winston, 1974), p. 78.

[13] William Shakespeare, *Hamlet,* act 3, scene 1, lines 78−85.

[14] Reinhold Niebuhr, *The Nature and Destiny of Man* (New York: Scribner's, 1943), vol. 2, p. 293.

[15] John Donne, "Meditation XVII," in *The Norton Anthology of English Literature,* ed. M. H. Abrams (New York: W. W. Norton & Co., 1968), p. 528.

[16] Ludwig Wittgenstein, *Tractatus Logico-Philosophicus,* tran. D. F. Pears and B. F. McGuinnes (New York: Humanistic Press, 1963), p. 147.

[17] William Shakespeare, *Hamlet,* act 3, scene 1, lines 64−68, 78.

[18] Reinhold Niebuhr, *The Nature and Destiny of Man,* vol. 2, p. 293.

[19] Kurt Vonnegut, *Cat's Cradle* (New York: Dell, 1965), p. 215.

[20] Actually Taoism includes many traditions besides this Tao of philosophical quietism.

Besides quietism, which encourages the peaceful acceptance of death, there is another form (prominent during the Han Dynasty, 206 B.C.—A.D. 221) that sought for immortality in this life. That form sought to postpone death indefinitely. Some Taoists concentrated all their efforts on overcoming harmful physical habits that wasted life force or impeded its free circulation. For them unity with Tao was not resignation to fate but a call to action intended to restore one's primordial conditions, believed to be long life, even as much as a thousand years. This activity involved all kinds of things: diet, breathing, exercise, drugs, various forms of "beneficial" sexual intercourse. In popular thought the Chinese did endorse the belief in life after death as is evidenced in their elaborate and extensive ancestor worship, and their belief in numerous paradises, such as, the island mountain P'eng-lai and the Pure Lands of Maitreya and Amitabha, two great and compassionate Buddhist Gods.

Chapter 11

REVELATION AND SCRIPTURE

The words of Jeremiah . . . to whom the word
of the Lord came in the days of Josiah . . . in
the 13th year of his reign.

Jeremiah 1:1

In Chapter 9 theology was defined as systematic statements about God and God's relationship to the world and mankind. Three types of theology were identified: (1) hermeneutical/creedal theology, (2) systematic theology, and (3) mythological theology. The first two are interpretations of the third. Since both hermeneutical/creedal and systematic theology use the faith story for their interpretations, it is obvious that mythology comes first. But where does mythology come from? Where do theologians get "the truths" they are interpreting? From faith itself, from revelation.

Our quotation from Anselm in Chapter 9 ("I do not seek to understand that I may believe, but I believe in order to understand") suggests that theology does not begin from zero and start explaining God and religious things, but rather begins with some kind of revealed knowledge. As Paul Tillich points out in the first pages of volume 1 of *Systematic Theology,* there is a theological circle in which the theologian stands to do his theology. His work is rooted in and circumscribed by a "mystical a priori." A theologian works from, and within, a fund of "revealed" knowledge. Theological speculations may in sophistication become universal in application, as did the ontological and cosmological arguments of Anselm and Thomas, but the work begins in a given revelation and does not intentionally desert or violate that revelation. We shall now look at two forms of revealed religious knowledge that may be classified as general revelation and special revelation.

GENERAL REVELATION

We have already noted that Thomas Aquinas believed that knowledge of God and religious things was disclosed partly from nature itself when people employ their human reason to discover such knowledge. John Calvin, in the sixteenth century, similarly declared that God had conspired "so to manifest his perfections in the whole structure of the universe, and daily place himself in our view, that we cannot open our eyes without being compelled to behold him."[1] The Hebrew writer of Psalm 19 announced that: "The heavens declare the glory of God; and the firmament showeth his handiwork." William Carruth° was saying the same thing in his "Each In His Own Tongue."

> A haze on the far horizon,
>   The infinite tender sky,
> The rich ripe tint of the corn-fields,
>   The wild geese sailing high.
> And all over the upland and lowland
>   The charm of the golden rod,
> Some of us call it autumn,
>   Others call it God.[2]

This form of revelation is called general revelation or natural theology. The endorsers of this position believe that people have the ability to discover religious knowledge on their own. To do this would appear to be a highly respectable and beneficial pursuit, but it is not, for all that, universally endorsed.

Rejection   General revelation was emphatically rejected by the important Hindu philosopher Sankara° (A.D. 788–820). Grounding his thought in such Upanishadic statements as the following:

> Now, one should know that Nature is illusion
> And that Mighty Lord is the illusion-maker.

Sankara argued his case from a nondualistic world view. In final reality he held there was only God Brahman. The world did not have a separate existence. People did not have separate existences. They just seemed to. They lived in illusion *(maya)*. By illusion, Sankara meant, in a sense, what the great Western philosopher Immanuel Kant° meant when he called the world we experience an "appearance." Kant's position was that people do not experience or conceptualize the world as it really is, but only as it appears to be. The "thing-in-itself," he held, was beyond thought. This opposition between Kant's phenomenal and noumenal world was matched by Sankara's world of maya and world of God Brahman. Sankara insisted that people who relied on their senses for knowledge were doomed to live in ignorance *(avidya,* "nonknowledge"). To live in ignorance was to exist only in a low form of "pragmatic truth," and be unsaved. Only when people broke out of maya, and in deep insight attained the revelation that their separate self was not really separate but the same as the divine self, did they attain true knowledge and with it salvation.

Some early Christians also rejected general revelation, not because the world was an illusion, but because it was utterly evil. Early in Christian history the Gnostic° Christians, in their acceptance of a radical dualism between spirit and flesh, earth and heaven, nature and the supernatural, rejected out of hand any thought that God could be discerned any place in the natural world. Not even Christ could be viewed as a natural man. He only *looked* like a natural man. He was, they claimed, God incognito, who only appeared to be born and appeared to live and appeared to suffer and appeared to die.*

This attitude of rejection is still to be found in some Christian theology. Those modern Christians who emphasize the "Fall of Man" often mean by it that there is a vast abyss separating finite, feeble humans from the infinite, absolute God. God can be known only as he discloses himself in some form of special revelation.

SPECIAL REVELATION

Besides general revelation there is a much narrower idea about how one can get God-words and God-talk. It is special revelation: revelation in which, through special religious means, God and ultimate truths are made known. God speaks, either in a literal or metaphorical sense, and the one who hears God informs others of what God has said or what message God wants conveyed. Some people become convinced by hearing a voice or by having an "enlightenment" occur within their consciousness that they are in special communication with divine reality. God, reportedly, spoke literally to Moses, but to Gautama Buddha, apparently, the revelation of ultimate truth came as a sudden insight. However it comes, the prophet seems always constrained to share the revelation. Prophets speak out to their communities, even when, as is often the case, the communities would prefer not to hear. But they are heard and sooner or later taken seriously by a constituency. Sometimes the constituency begins very small, even only one person as with Muhammad's wife Khadija, who believed the Prophet's revelations even before he was really sure himself. Eventually the constituency grows, and the members not only listen to the prophet, but tell others about the message that the prophet has gotten from the Divine. In due course the prophet's words are written down and become scripture.

REVELATION AND SCRIPTURE

Scripture is not the revelation itself; it is the reporting of the revelation and a reporting that has received the authority not simply of the prophet, but also of

*This is called docetism from the Greek word *dokein*, "to seem, to appear."

a community. It is a written document that has been accepted by some religious body as a document that reveals truths about God and/or what God has done or plans to do for mankind and/or what God expects mankind to do for itself. By first preserving and then stamping with its official endorsement, the believing community establishes a scripture. For example, the Jewish Bible is not simply the words of prophets, but is a set of special prophetic statements and a written account of God's mighty acts in the history of Israel, and a collection of wise sayings and celebration hymns and revered stories, *that were preserved* by the Jewish community and eventually *given official, canonical status* by a council of rabbis who met in the town of Jamnia about A.D. 90. Revelation is born in a moment of divine human encounter, but scripture is made more laboriously by savants and true believers.

New Scripture and the Scripture Idea   Some of the sacred scriptures of the world's living religions are very old. Parts of the Hebrew Bible go back 3,000 years, and some of the Hindu Vedas go back probably 4,000 years. But not all sacred scripture is ancient. For example, in Iran, in 1844, a certain Mirza Ali Muhammad began to call himself Bab-ud-Din (Gate of Faith) and to proclaim that his mission was to prepare the way for one who would come to complete God's work of perfection on earth. Bab-ud-Din declared that his writings were revelations equal to the Qur'an. This put him afoul of the Muslim authorities, and he was executed as a heretic and disturber of the peace. But his religious movement did not end. His followers were called after him Babis, and the religion he fostered became known as Baha'i. One of Bab-ud-Din's youthful followers took the name Baha'u'llah (Glory of God) and ten years later announced that he was the one who was to come. His writings too became regarded as sacred scripture; among them is the *Kitâb-i-Iguàn* (*The Book of Certitude*), which was revealed to Baha'u'llah in 1862, in two days and nights.

A few years earlier, in 1832, a revelation occurred in the United States. Joseph Smith of Ontario County, New York, reportedly found in a stone box on a hillside the record of some ancient people (c. 600 B.C. – A.D. 421) who had lived in the Americas. They too, as people of Palestine, were witnesses "that Jesus is the Christ, the Eternal God." The record Joseph Smith found was engraved on gold plates. He was permitted "by the gift and power of God" to translate and copy what came to be known as The Book of Mormon, which in the Church of the Latter-Day Saints is accepted, along with the Christian Old and New Testaments, as a divine revelation and holy scripture.

There is nothing to foreclose the writing of new sacred scripture, for a sacred scripture is, after all, simply a document that has been accepted by some religious body as a writing that contains truths about God and about God's concern for mankind.

A sacred scripture is, first of all, an idea. The word "scripture" in its universal meaning denotes, first, not a set of documents, but an idea about the character of certain documents. It denotes the idea that the word of God, divine truth, ultimate reality, is to be discerned in certain written documents; that religious truth has been, one way or another, transcribed into written form. This is the Bible Idea, or more correctly, the *scripture idea*.

In the religions of the Near Eastern world,[3] the scripture idea appears to have developed first in the early decades of the seventh century B.C. In 2 Kings, in the Hebrew Bible, we are told that in the eighteenth year of the reign of King Josiah a book was discovered in the Temple that declared in written form the relationship between God and Israel and the will of God for the Hebrew people. With this book, now identified as the Book of Deuteronomy, the Hebrews came to a new conception of how one could discern the way and the will of God for mankind. Before that time they had relied on living voices (prophets and prophetesses), or on various forms of divination, to get God's word on any matter. Now they had a "God's book," and with it the idea that would expand their one book into a whole library of God's books: *ta biblia* (the books), the Bible.

SCRIPTURE: EAST AND WEST

All of the great religions of the world have their own sacred writings. And they are all considered as being somehow inspired. They are believed to contain revelations of ultimate reality. But, in general, Eastern scriptures are different from Western scriptures in that they arise in, and inform, in different conceptions, the way of the world. The Western religions are often referred to as "historical religions." In this reference "historical" means seeing the world in time, moving from a specific beginning to a definite ending. The world is seen as beginning in the innocence of Eden and moving toward its final fulfillment in a Divine Kingdom. Eastern religions, instead of being historical in this sense, are cyclical. Their world does not begin and move forward to a perfect fulfillment, but returns upon itself again and again, forever. For example, in Hinduism, developing after the Hindus had established themselves in the Ganges Valley and between 700 and 300 B.C., and recorded especially in their holy writings called Upanishads, there developed the doctrine of a cyclic destruction and re-creation of the world. At the end of every *kalpa* (period of created being) the world dissolves.* All the souls in the universe depart from their bodies and enter a state of slumbering suspension. After a period of "nothingness," called *pralaya*, the world comes into being again and the quiescent souls take up new embodiments in plants, animals, humans, Gods, and demons. The holy Vedas (primal scriptures) are recomposed and another kalpa proceeds to its inevitable end.

---

*A single *kalpa* lasts 4,320,000 years.

Against this kind of world view the Hindus see their lives, religion, and scriptures differently from those who see the world as beginning, moving forward through time, and finally ending permanently in a utopian condition. Westerners have a God of history: a God involved in and concerned with history, a providential God. Easterners, although their Gods often involved themselves in the lives of humans, do not conceive of the world as an "historical event" under the providential aegis of the great High God. Yahweh watches and responds, but not Brahman, or Tao, or Heaven. Brahman, undisturbed, receives into its own being for the remainder of the kalpa any soul who finds the secret of salvation. Tao lends strength and fullness to any person who discerns the true way. Heaven's harmony reigns upon people and nations when propriety is maintained. None of these great Gods is like the Westerner's Yahweh who broods and agonizes when his people turn away from his laws and ordinances, and who rejoices with all his angels when even one sinner repents.

Against such metaphysical differences, one might expect that the attitudes of Easterners toward scripture would be different from the attitudes of Westerners and that the scriptures themselves would be quite different; in general, this is how it is. Perhaps the best way to characterize the differences of both attitudes and writings is to say that the attitudes and scriptures of Eastern religions are more meditative and philosophical, whereas the attitudes and scriptures of Western religions are more matter of fact and historical. There is, to be sure, vision literature in the Western scriptures—for example, Ezekiel, Daniel, Revelation—but it is markedly concerned with the history and destiny of people in a perfect world to come. And there is poetry, and there are passages suitable to meditation, but not anything like, for example, the ten books of 1,028 hymns to be found in the Hindu *Rig-Veda*. Perhaps the most obvious difference between the character of Eastern and Western scripture is to be seen in their concerns for philosophical speculation. The fact is that there is little philosophical speculation in the Western scriptures. It is surprising to discover that nowhere in the Hebrew-Christian scriptures are there any philosophical discussions on either the existence of God or God's ultimate nature. God is simply accepted as some kind of powerful, supreme, personal being, and the scriptures go on from there. Not so in the East. Throughout the voluminous 200 books called Upanishads in Hinduism there is an almost endless search for the existence of, and nature of, Divine Being. Farther East in China, the basic scripture of the Taoist faith, the *Tao Te Ching*, is a subtly written philosophical search for the place and meaning of God in the realm of actuality or being, or both.

The differences are real between East and West, and one might almost agree with Rudyard Kipling° that never the twain shall meet; but actually, East and West do meet. In both Eastern and Western religions, theology is rooted in a fund of "revealed" knowledge. In China, the Taoist philosophers begin with the subtle philosophy of the *Tao Te Ching*. It is from there that they explain their world and themselves and derive their principles for salvation and morality and even for doing their art. In India, the Hindu theologians (even those who wrote the Upanishads) went back to the basic fund of original revelation, to the primal Vedic scriptures, even as Western theologians, who are as widely different as Maimonides° and Richard Rubenstein° or Anselm° and Thomas Altizer,° go back to their revelation sources before attempting their flights of theology.

LIVING SCRIPTURE WORLDWIDE

Jewish Scriptures   The Bible of the Jews is composed of thirty-nine books or writings, generally known as the Old Testament by Christians, but to Jews, properly and simply, the Bible. These books are usually divided by Jews into three groups:

1. *The Torah or Law:* Genesis, Exodus, Leviticus, Numbers, and Deuteronomy.
2. *Nebiim or The Prophets:* Joshua, Judges, 1 Samuel, 2 Samuel, 1 Kings, 2 Kings, Isaiah, Jeremiah, Ezekiel, Hosea, Joel, Amos, Obadiah, Jonah, Micah, Nahum, Habakkuk, Zephaniah, Haggai, Zachariah, Malachi.
3. *Kethubim or Sacred Writings:* Psalms, Proverbs, Job, Song of Solomon, Ruth, Lamentations, Ecclesiastes, Esther, Daniel, Ezra, Nehemiah, 1 Chronicles, 2 Chronicles.

Most of these books were originally composed in Hebrew. Approximately half of Daniel, parts of Ezra, and a verse in Jeremiah were written in Aramaic.

The Talmud is also read by the Jews and is held to be of special religious value, which at least approximates scripture. Between A.D. 70 and the end of the fifth century, Jewish scholars in Jamnia (Jabneh), Galilee, and Babylonia compiled and organized a tremendous mass of rabbinical teachings. First the *Mishna* (instruction), which was largely rabbinical interpretations of Torah (the law), and, second, the *Gemara* (completion), which was largely commentary on the *Mishna*. These two works taken together are called Talmud (teachings). They are a record of the rabbis' teachings about the law *(Halakah)* and the rabbis' teachings about historical matters, moral rules, and general religious instructions *(Haggadah)*. The Talmud is divided into thirty-six books, or tractates, containing some two and a half million words.

Besides the Bible and the later Talmud there are several writings that were considered scriptures by some Jews, especially in Alexandria. These writings are today called Apocrypha (hidden writings). The Apocrypha consists of fifteen writings: some of which are whole books, some additions to existing biblical books. The earliest, *Tobit*, a short novel teaching Jewish morality, was written about 200 B.C. The latest, *Baruch*, a composite book attributed to the secretary of Jeremiah and combining prophetic statements and wise sayings, was written about 100 B.C. The apocryphal writings were included in many early Hebrew Bible collections, but many rabbis doubted that they should be.

A decision concerning which books of the many books available belonged properly in the Bible was made by the rabbis in the Council of Jamnia about A.D. 90. The canon of the Bible for Orthodox Judaism was declared to be the thirty-nine books mentioned above. The additional apocryphal writings were excluded. This canon of biblical books is today called the Masoretic° Text, but it did not everywhere replace the more expanded text that included the apocryphal writings. This was especially the case with the Greek translation of the Hebrew Bible, called the Septuagint.

The Septuagint   Beginning in the third century B.C. the Jews of Alexandria in Egypt made a translation of the Hebrew Bible into the Greek language. That translation included most of the writings that are now called the Apocrypha. The translation was called the Septuagint for the seventy (or seventy-two) scholars to whom legend attributed the translation. In the middle years of the first century A.D., this was the Bible that was most available (and usable because it was in Greek) to the Gentiles who began to join the reform movement that was destined to become the Christian Church.

In the fifth century A.D., when St. Jerome° translated the Bible into Latin, he included in it several of the apocryphal writings found in the Septuagint. The remainder of these apocryphal writings came into the official Catholic Bible (the Vulgate) from other old Latin translations. They remain in the Catholic Old Testament to this day.

But in the sixteenth century, the Protestant reformers chose to restrict the Old Testament to the Hebrew canon established at the Council of Jamnia. With some exceptions, the Protestants continued to regard the remaining books of the Septuagint as worthy to be read and included them in a separate portion of the Bible, either between the Testaments or at the end of the Bible, calling them the Apocrypha, which was a name first given to these books by St. Jerome.

The New Testament   Originally the Bible Idea among Christians was limited to the Greek Septuagint translation of the Jewish Bible. Christian writings were produced, but they were not identified as scripture. Then in A.D. 140 a Gnostic Christian, Marcion° of Sinope, desiring to divorce Christianity from its theological connections with Judaism, proposed setting aside the Jewish Bible as a spurious scripture and putting in its place some Christian writings, namely, the Gospel of Luke and the Letters of Paul.

Marcion's gnostic theology and rejection of the Jewish Bible was unacceptable to the orthodox Christians, but apparently his idea of a new Christian scripture was acceptable. Within a short time the authorities of the orthodox church were busy identifying the writings that were to be regarded as new scripture for the Christians.

By the end of the century the idea of collecting Christian writings and identifying them as scripture had spread throughout the church. Irenaeus of Lyons, Theophilus of Antioch, Tertullian of North Africa, Clement and Origen of Alexandria—all moved to select and promote Christian scripture. The various authorities did not always see eye to eye on all the books to be included in the canon, or excluded from it, but they all agreed that the Gospels Mark, Matthew, Luke, and John, and Paul's letters should be included. And apparently the title New Testament had arisen as the name for the collection. Melito, Bishop of Sardis (c. 180), wrote a letter (preserved by Eusebius°) that made specific reference to the "books of the Old Testament." This would imply recognition of a New Testament.

Thanks to Marcion's heretical efforts, the Bible Idea had been established for a Christian scripture. Now all that remained was the church's final decision on what belonged in that scripture. This took some doing. However, gradually, over the years, agreement was reached, and in his famous Festal Letter, Athanasius° of Alexandria, in the latter half of the fourth century, listed as New Testament exactly the twenty-seven books now accepted, and about them he remarked: "These are the springs of salvation so that the thirsty may be filled with the utterance within them. In these alone is proclaimed the good news of the teaching of true religion. Let no one add to them or remove aught from them." In 397 the Third Council of Carthage ordered that only canonical writings were to be read in church under the title of divine scripture. A New Testament had been finally, securely established.

Islamic Scripture   Islam also endorses both the Jewish scripture and the Christian New Testament as sacred. These scriptures represent earlier prophetic revelations from God to mankind. However, Muhammad° was God's Prophet, and the last of the Prophets, sent to correct distortions in the earlier prophesies and to give the world one final and magnificent scripture: the Qur'an, or Koran. The Qur'an is to all true Muslims a book of absolute truth, because it is the word of God himself. It is the last and final revelation from God, revealed completely and perfectly to Muhammad.

Shortly after the death of Muhammad, A.D. 632, Abū Bakr,° who took command of the movement, supervised the collecting and writing of the revelations that had come to Muhammad. A dozen years later, Othman, third caliph, made an additional study of the revelations and prepared an authentic version. The Qur'an as it was finally arranged consists of 114 suras, or chapters. The first sura is a short prayer. The remaining 113 chapters are arranged in the order of their length. The first has 286 verses, and the last has only 3 verses.

Zoroastrian Scriptures   Another living religion of Near Eastern (Persian/ Iranian) origin is Zoroastrianism. The religion founded by Zarathustra (Zoroaster) in the seventh century B.C. survives today largely in India among a people called Parsees (Persians). There are about 125,000 Parsees, most of them in Bombay and the surrounding area.

Many of the ideas found both in Judaism and Christianity stem directly from Zoroastrianism, although the religion itself is not mentioned anywhere in the Hebrew-Christian scriptures. Many of the kings of Persia mentioned in the Old Testament were Zoroastrians; for example, Cyrus, Artaxerxes, Ahasuerus, Darius. The Magi, wise men from the East who came to the birth of Jesus, were Zoroastrian priests. Satan, as described in the pseudepigrapha writings of the Hebrews and in the New Testament, was a concept that first appeared in Zoroastrian thought, as was the elaborate scheme of angels and demons, the idea of a savior, the doctrine of resurrection and final judgment, and the conception of a future life to be lived in Paradise. These ideas and others taught by Zarathustra and his followers became incorporated into the sacred scriptures of Zoroastrians called *Avesta* or Knowledge.

The *Avesta* consists of four main groups of writings. The Yasna deals with worship and sacrifice and contains the seventeen *Gathas* or Psalms, and is composed largely of prayers, confessions, invocations, exhortations, and praise, combined in many literary forms. The *Visperat* is a collection of invocations to all the Gods. The *Vendidad* is a priestly code that deals with various religious, ritualistic, and civil matters. The *Yashts* is a collection of religious poetry and hymns. Another book, the *Khorda-Avesta*, or Little Avesta, is sometimes included as part of the Avesta. The *Khorda-Avesta* is a handbook of litanies and prayers for daily worship and prayer.

Hindu Scriptures   The Vedas or Books of Knowledge had their origin sometime between 2000 B.C. and 1000 B.C. and form the basis of all Hinduism. There are four Vedas: the Rig Veda, or Veda of verses; the Yajur Veda, or Veda of sacred formulas; the Sama Veda, or Veda of chants; and the Atharva Veda, or Veda of charms. During the next 750 years after the writing of these scriptures, Hinduism underwent several major changes. Each change produced a new scripture based on the original Vedas, but different from them. Between 1000 B.C. and 800 B.C. a strong priestly organization developed in Hinduism. Scriptures called the Brahmanas developed from this period. Following the priestly period, between 800 B.C. and 600 B.C., from a period of extensive philosophical interest came the Upanishads, or books of philosophic discussion. A strong legal emphasis in Hinduism about 250 B.C. produced the *Laws of Manu*, or code of Hindu law.

At the beginning of the common/Christian era a dramatic poem of great beauty and high moral precepts emerged from the Hindu religion: the *Bhagavad Gita*, Song of the Blessed Lord. The *Bhagavad Gita* makes an attempt to synthesize the three classical paths to salvation in Hinduism—the way of knowledge, the way of action (or good works), and the way to devotion. But in fact, the Gita opts for devotion as the superior way. The point is made dramatically. Krishna is the charioteer of Prince Arjuna of the family of Pandavas at a time when the Pandavas are at war with their kinsmen, the Kurus. Just as the battle is about to begin, Arjuna is stricken by the horrible thought of relatives killing relatives. He turns to Krishna for counsel. The charioteer reminds him of his duty as a warrior and prince, and that death is, after all, simply an illusion. Life is not destroyed by death. Only the body dies. The soul lives on. Krishna then continues his counsel by reminding Arjuna of the several ways to reach the goal of spiritual liberation, which is what salvation is in Hinduism. There is the way of knowledge that comes from meditation (Jnana Marga), and the way of action (Karma Marga). Both lead to final peace. But there is an even grander way—that of devotion (Bhakti Marga). Krishna begins to recite:

> I am the Sacrifice! I am the prayer . . .
> I am—of all this boundless Universe—
> The Father, Mother, Ancestor and Guard!
> The end of learning! That which purifies
> In lustral water! I am OM! I am . . .
> The Way, the Fosterer, the Lord, the Judge.
> . . . .
> Death am I, and Immortal Life I am . . .
> . . . Visible life
> And Life invisible.[4]

Krishna then reveals himself in the divine form of Vishnu, the eternal Brahman in God-form. The display is so astonishing that Arjuna not only expresses his adoration, but begs that the too sublime vision be removed and that the God return again in the form of Krishna. This happens and Krishna, now revealed as an avatar (a God-Man), delivers the heart of the Gita's message—a demand for utter surrender in complete devotion to God Vishnu.

This dramatic poem is one of the great classics in religious literature. It is a magnificent writing, even in English translation. When I once asked a devotee of Hinduism if he really thought there was once a Prince Arjuna, who had a charioteer named Krishna, who was in fact Vishnu, I got an oblique, but worthy reply. "How," he asked, "could anything as perfect as the *Bhagavad Gita* be less than true?" So be it.

Buddhist Scriptures   Another religion that developed in India, but was destined to have its lasting strength not in India but in China, Japan, and Southeast Asia, was Buddhism. Buddhism was founded by Gautama who lived from 563 B.C. to 483 B.C. The scriptures of this first great international religion are the Tripitaka, or Three Baskets. The first Basket is the *Vinaya Pitaka*, or monastic rules. It contains the many rules imposed on those who enter the orders of high-class Buddhists. The second Basket is the *Sutta Pitaka*, or discourses. This scripture is of special importance because the principal voice heard in it is that of the Buddha himself. Also in it is contained the very important moral treatise, the *Dhammapada*, or verses on the law. The third

Basket is the *Abhidharama Pitaka*, or the metaphysical basket. It is a detailed explanation of Buddhist doctrines and of Buddhist psychology.

Two other scriptures that developed in India were (1) the *Agamas*, or precepts of the Jainist religion, which was founded in India by Mahavira, who lived from 599 B.C. to 527 B.C. and (2) the *Granth*, which is the sacred scripture of Sikhism, a religion founded in the fifteenth century A.D. in the province of Punjab by Nanak.

Far Eastern Scripture   In the Far East, in China, there are scriptures for the two indigenous religions: for Taoism and for Confucianism. The scripture of the Taoists is the Tao Te Ching, or treatise of the Tao and its power. This scripture was traditionally credited to the founder of the Taoist religion, Lao Tzu,° who lived between 604 B.C. and 531 B.C., but as it stands today the Tao Te Ching is hardly the product of one mind, although it may be basically so. Interpolations and repeated editings have altered the original form. Most of the present version comes from the fourth century B.C. It is a book, difficult to translate, of about five thousand Chinese characters. It is concerned with the nature of God Tao (the Way of Reality) and with the ethics of quietism, nonaggression, and nonmeddlesome action that are appropriate to the Tao.

The scripture of the other indigenous Chinese religion, Confucianism, consists of the Five Classics and the Four Books. Included in the Classics are the *Books of History* (*Shu Ching*), the *Book of Poetry* (*Shih Ching*, the *Book of Changes* (*I Ching*), the *Book of Rites* (*Li Chi*), and the *Annals of Spring and Autumn* (*Ch'un Ch'iu*). Some authorities add a sixth book to the Classics, the *Book of Filial Piety* (*Hsiao Ching*). The Four Books are the *Great Learning* (*Ta Hsüen*), the *Doctrine of the Mean* (*Chung Yung*), the *Anelects* (*Lun Yu*) the Works of Mencius (*Meng-Tze*).

In Japan two of the sacred scriptures of the Shinto religion are *Records of Ancient Matters* (*Kojiki*), and the *Chronicles of Japan* (Nihongi). The *Records* tells the story of the age of the Gods before people existed on earth. The Chronicles tells of the creation of Japan and the rule of the emperors. There is a third sacred document of Shinto called the *Institutes of the Period of Yengi* (*Yengishiki*). This book dates from about the tenth century A.D., and is a collection of prayers. A fourth scripture of Shinto is *Collection of Ten Thousand Leaves* (*Manyoshu*). It is an anthology of 4,496 poems dating from the fifth to eighth centuries A.D.

READING SCRIPTURE—ATTITUDES AND EXPECTATIONS

A small boy came home from Sunday School and when asked what he had learned, told this story: "We learned about Moses." "*And what did you learn about Moses?*" "Moses was a Hebrew who led a guerrilla army in Egypt, and the Egyptian army got them trapped down by the Red Sea. Moses saw they were in trouble so he had his engineers build a pontoon-bridge out across the sea and the Hebrews went across it and got to the other side. Then Moses looked back and saw the Egyptians were following them across on the pontoon-bridge, so he called in an air strike and bombed the bridge and the Egyptians were all drowned." A startled parent then asked, "Johnny, is that the way the Sunday School teacher told that story?" And Johnny said, "No, but if I told it her way, you'd never believe it."

Sometimes we are confused by what scripture is really supposed to be. Some people call it "God's Word," and seem to imply that it should be taken literally. Others say that scripture, because it was written in ancient, prescientific times, should be demythologized to free its true meaning—its deep spiritual insights. Still others seem to read scripture primarily with a reverence that amounts to a mystical devotion. It appears, then, that people tend to approach the reading of scripture with at least three kinds of attitudes and expectations: (1) to get the "Word of God" in a stenographic manner; (2) to get meaningful insights concerning God and human life; or (3) to effect an experience of divine presence.

People in all literate religions (religions with sacred scriptures) read their holy writings in all three of these attitudes and expectations, but the "Word of God" approach is a special concern of Orthodox Jews, conservative and fundamentalist Christians, and Sunni° and Shiite° Muslims. The "insight" approach is a special concern of liberal Christians and liberal (Reform) Jews, and some Hindu and Buddhist philosophers. The "divine presence" approach is a special concern of Hasidic° Jews, Sufi° Muslims, and in Bhakti Marga (way of devotion) Hindus.

Word of God   Many people see scripture as a literal message from God. It is believed that, one way or another, God communicated special information to a human "stenographer," who in turn faithfully transcribed the words of God into languages of mankind. In the Book of Exodus, for example, we read that God delivered to Moses to be set before the Hebrew people all of his commandments and ordinances. God spoke to Moses, and dutifully, exactly, Moses repeated God's words to the Hebrew people. Again, at the beginning of Isaiah's ministry we read that the Prophet cried out: "Hear, O heavens, and give ear, O earth, for Yahweh hath spoken." The writer of the Book of Revelation leaves no doubt about the source and character of his message. In the beginning paragraph he defines his book as

[the] revelation of Jesus Christ, which God gave him to show to his servants what must soon take place; and he made it known by sending his angel to his servant John, who bore witness to the word of God and the testimony of Jesus Christ, even to all that he saw. *Rev. 1:1–2, (RSV).*

In this kind of revelation God is seen as using a human agent to write what God is literally thinking or saying or showing to his chosen vessel of transmission. This kind of claim is not, of course, limited to the Hebrew-Christian scriptures. The same claim is made for Joseph Smith and the Book of Mormon, for Muhammad and the Qur'an, and for others.

The strength of this position is that the beliefs and creeds of one's religious sect can be quickly and effectively evaluated against an established criteria; namely the criteria of what the scripture says. For example, the Jews' claim to be the Chosen People can be readily evaluated and defended by referring to appropriate passages of scripture. The Christians' claim that Jesus was born of a virgin and arose from the dead can be "proved" by referring to those scripture passages that claim so. The Muslims have a precise criteria for their claim that Muhammad was the Prophet of God Allah. The Qur'an says so. What the scripture says is the strength of this position.

Interestingly, it is also one of the weaknesses of the position, because what the scriptures say is not always all that clear and distinct. For example, the account of Jesus' last Passover meal and the institution of the Lord's Supper is sufficiently imprecise for Catholics to claim absolutely one thing (the bread and wine used are actually the body and blood of Christ) and most Protestants to claim absolutely the opposite. Again, to Roman Catholics there is no proposition in the Bible more clear and distinct than Jesus' endorsement of Peter (in Matthew 16:18), and therewith of all the bishops of Rome as heads of Christ's Church on earth. There are very few Protestants, if any, who are not unalterably sure that Jesus' conversation with Peter that day meant nothing of the kind.

Another weakness is to be seen not in how biblical propositions are interpreted, but in what they state in one place that seems to be contradicted by what they say elsewhere in the same scripture. For example, in the Gospel of Matthew the Holy Family flees from Palestine to Egypt on the night of Jesus' birth, so it would appear; but in the Gospel of Luke they remain in Palestine, and forty days later Joseph and Mary present Jesus in the Jerusalem Temple. There are two different accounts of the death of Judas Iscariot (in Matthew 17:5 and Acts 1:18), and four different accounts of what happened at the tomb on Resurrection Day: Who saw what, when, under what circumstances? Again, how did the animals go into the Ark? two by two, or seven by two? What is the order of creation of the world, especially man, animals, woman, as stated in Genesis chapter 1 and in Genesis chapter 2?

Insight Approach   A second approach to the reading of scripture holds that scripture is not a literal message from God to mankind, but a set of documents that contains deep insights concerning the relationship of humans to God, and God to humans. In the Judeo-Christian tradition, for example, the scriptures are seen as a witnessing of a people (the ancient Hebrews) who had a special genius for religion, much as the Greeks had a genius for philosophy, the Romans for practical politics, and modern Westerners for scientific technology. The scripture is not a stenographic, propositional self-disclosure of God to mankind, but is a fallible interpretation of God's disclosure as seen and recorded by certain ancient people. As this is the case, the scripture contains both profound religious insights and a great deal of ancient, mythological nonsense. The problem that confronts the modern reader is to separate the true religious insights from the mythology in which these insights are presented.

Most scripture was written for a different age, a prescientific age; for a world where miracles were expected and accepted as common occurrences in daily life; a world where Heaven was straight up and Hell straight down (that is, a simple three-storied world); where evil demons invaded human bodies causing illness, and were exorcised by faith healers and miracle workers. It was a world where people believed that all sorts of supernatural things could happen at any time, and so (or so it seemed) all sorts of supernatural things happened. The Hebrew-Christian Bible was written in that world and in that fashion. Its language was prescientific. To deal with this situation, Rudolf Bultmann° and others, propose that this mythological style be deleted. They say the Bible must be "demythologized," not to get rid of the scripture, not to demean or deny the biblical revelation, but to make it meaningful in a modern, scientifically oriented world.

The following is an example of interpreting a biblical text not literally, but insightfully. In the second chapter of the Book of Genesis there is a marvelous story of the creation of Eve. God had placed Adam in the Garden of Eden to live there and tend the garden. But Eden proved to be a lonely place for Adam because he was the only living animal there. To deal with Adam's loneliness, God created the other animals, bringing each one to Adam that he might name it. But, as the scripture has it, "there was not found a helper fit for him" (2:20b RSV), until God, causing a deep sleep to fall on the man, took one of Adam's ribs and with it made a woman.

This is an intriguing story, but how is it to be dealt with seriously, especially if it cannot be accepted as a literal account of woman's first appearance on earth, to say nothing of the apparent implication that she is just a helper for man—an animated male-rib? Of course, one could dismiss the story as simply erroneous mythology. But one might also look at it asking not what important scientific thing is being said here, but what important religious thing. Doing this one might see that the author of this story, himself, discerned an insight from the story. He closed the story saying, "Therefore a man leaves his father and his mother and cleaves to his wife, and they become one flesh. . . ." The point of the story is not the genesis of woman so much as the meaning of mating. And a little more looking may reveal further insights, such as: the mating of a man and a woman is not just something between the man and the woman. It is not even just something between the man and the woman and their two families, or the community at large. It is something of God! Something instituted by God since the beginning of human time. Something sacred. Something, as the marriage vows state it, "not to be entered into unadvisedly, but reverently, discreetly, and in the fear of God."*

*From the marriage ritual of the United Methodist Church.

A non-Western example of scripture understood as a non-literal presentation of fundamental religious insights is to be seen by some devotees in the Hindu scripture called *Bhagavad Gita (Song of the Blessed Lord)*. As we saw above, this is a dramatic poem that deals with the conflict between two Aryan clans, the Kuru princes and their relatives the Pandavas (sons of Pandu), and the place of God-Krishna in these exploits. A central theological insight is present in one scene in which Arjuna, the great warrior of the family of Pandavas, hesitates just as he is about to lead his brothers and their allies into battle against the Kuru princes, sons of his uncle, the blind Dhritirashtra. Krishna, who is there acting as Arjuna's chariot driver, tries to stir the reluctant warrior to action, but Arjuna continues to hesitate, saying, among other things: "What rich spoils/Could profit; what rule recompense; what span/Of life seems sweet, bought with such blood?" He asks Krishna for counsel, which he receives in a long dialogue that first affirms the duties of caste. Arjuna is a Kshatriya (a nobleman-warrior). In a just war it is his duty to fight whether it means killing his relatives or not. Furthermore, he is to remember the fundamental (Hindu) truth that the souls of the fallen kinsmen will not be slain, only their bodies. Krishna proclaims:

> "Thou grievest where no grief should be! thou speak'st
> Words lacking in wisdom! for the wise in heart
> Mourn not for those that live, nor those that die.
> Nor I, nor thou, nor any of these,
> Ever was not, nor ever will not be.
> All that doth live, lives always! . . .
>   . . . Indestructible,
> Learn thou! the Life is, spreading life through all . . .
> But for these fleeting frames which it informs
> With spirit deathless, endless, infinite,
> They perish. Let them perish, Prince! and fight!
> He who shall say, 'Lo! I have slain a man!'
> He who shall think, 'Lo! I am slain!' those both
> Know naught! Life cannot slay. Life is not slain."[5]

Some Hindus take the *Bhagavad Gita* as a literal account of God Vishnu's incarnation as Arjuna's charioteer, Krishna. But other Hindus see it as a sacred story in which profound religious insights concerning, among other things, the responsibilities of humans and the continuing, "indestructible," character of life.

Scripture should not be confused with science. A scripture is not a book of scientific facts about the natural world. Generally the writers of scripture were persons devoid of anything that even approaches our modern scientific information—astronomical, biological, medical, social, psychological—but what they did know, or have, was a religious message for mankind, a revelation of God's truths.

Opponents of this insight position say that it imposes a criterion upon the scripture that is not proper. Science and modern thought are taken as correctives for the Bible. The Bible is treated as if it were just another ancient manuscript. But, they claim, it is not just another ancient book, and one does not have a right to delete from it anything that does not fit into modern "mythology." Either take the Bible for what it purports to be (the Word of God) or reject it, but do not mutilate it. Again, this position is criticized in the fact that what the kerygma (the true message) behind the myth is said to be is often, if not always, just what the "liberal" theologian has been looking for.

Existential Encounter   A third point of view in special revelation is that of existential encounter. It is possible not to take the scriptures in a literal sense, yet not regard them as simply human insight into the nature of Divine Being. One can take the scriptures to be meditation documents for encounters with God. They are writings, but they can become more than just writings. As writings they can be seen as the product of fallible people who have witnessed to their own encounter with God. On this literal level, the scriptures are fascinating and inspiring in that they show how passionately certain ancient people believed in and recorded their encounters with God. On another level, the level of scriptural criticism, the scientific level, it is important to know everything that can be known about the text—who wrote its various parts, for what purpose, at what place, at what time, according to what conceptions of the natural world. Such information will help keep one from falling into the superstitions of credulous people who believe that everything in the scriptures was divinely revealed and faithfully recorded, including, maybe, even the punctuation. But having said this much, it can still be insisted that nothing basic has been said about true religion or the true purpose of the scriptures. True religion is not a set of propositions, or even a supply of insights, but a living engagement. The scriptures are instruments, not *in which* the self-disclosure of God is to be found, but *through which* the self-disclosure of God occurs. God does not speak in his scriptures to the heads of people but through his scriptures to the hearts of people.

From this point of view, revelation is not regarded as practical information about God for the purpose of "saving souls." Nor, as in the insight theory, is it handled in a way intended to make it adaptable and relevant to the twentieth century. Rather, from the position of existential encounter, revelation is an experience in which a person encounters the mystery of God, and finds it to be energizing, cleansing, renewing, authenticating. The mystery of God is not unraveled, but it is unveiled. The *I Am* of God is directly experienced, and although the experience is ineffable, it is nonetheless convincing.

Realizing that one can approach scripture with various attitudes and expectations should encourage a student not to be turned off from scripture reading because of a single unacceptable notion as to what scripture is all about.

Certainly many people read the scriptures believing they are reading truly the words of God. Such people undoubtedly find great rewards in their approach to the scriptures. But one who cannot be a literalist need not therefore relegate scripture to the back shelf of antiquated curiosities. One may assume other attitudes and expectations. Scripture can be read to discover the authority-base of a religion, or to discern spiritual insights, or for meditative and devotional purposes, or, for that matter, just out of curiosity. Whatever one's reasons, the effort is rewarding.

NOTES

[1] John Calvin, *Institutes of the Christian Religion* (Grand Rapids, Mich.: Eerdmans, 1953), vol. 1, p. 51.
[2] William Carruth, *Each in His Own Tongue and Other Poems* (New York: G. P. Putnam's Sons, 1909).
[3] Judaism, Christianity, and Islam.
[4] Sir Edwin Arnold, *The Bhagavad Gita: The Song Celestial,* 9:16–19.
[5] *Ibid.*, 2:11–20.

Chapter 12

MYTH AND RITUAL

Ritual is the language of religion.
Morris Adler[1]

In doing religion, people reinterpret their world so that its devastating aspects are seen in a more meaningful and hopeful light. They establish a religious view of the world. In keeping with this view they proceed to act appropriately so that they may be correctly related to the power or powers that control their lives and destinies. One form of appropriate behavior is called ritual. Ritual is dramatic portrayal of the "truths" of religion—of a particular religion—and is often done as the reenactment of a special event in the past when God (or the Gods) acted in behalf of mankind. The Catholic Mass, for example, is the reenactment of Christ's sacrificial death on the Cross. Passover° is a dramatic reliving of the story of the Hebrew Exodus from ancient Egypt, a sojourn that each year each Jewish family makes with Moses.

Ritual, then, is sacred drama, and the *sacred*, as we observed with Rudolf Otto, is an awareness of the mysterious, powerful, fascinating, numinous "out there" toward which all people must, for their own good, be cautiously respectful. No one, and especially no primitive person, deals with this power casually or carelessly. Sacred places are off limits (taboo°) to the uninitiated or otherwise unqualified person. Moses, we are told, took off his shoes because the ground whereon he stood was holy ground (Exodus 3:5). The voice from the throne in John's Revelation (19:5) instructed all people who feared God to praise him. In the presence of sacredness there is anxiety. In this anxiety there is need to act and to act properly: to appease the holy, or to praise it, or at least to acknowledge it. Upon entering a Catholic church, people cross themselves with holy water. On the door of a little Protestant church at the foot of the mountains of Colorado there is a sign that reads: "Compose yourself. No one entering a house ignores him who dwells in it. This is the house of God." In each case, one does something appropriate lest the sacred be profaned.

Rituals, of course, are not performed only by individual persons as they cross themselves or compose themselves. Rituals are also performed by communities of persons for the purpose of community acknowledgment of the sacred, for community benefits expected from the sacred by such recognition, and to remind the community of the basis and authority for its spiritual and moral life. In many religions there are special rites[2] to bring prosperity and good health to the community, to make the soil productive, the cattle fertile, the fishing successful. There are other rites performed regularly to celebrate God (or the Gods), ancient heroes, saints, seasons, a kairotic moment in history (see pages 129–130), or to make sacrificial offerings to the divine being. Other rites celebrate special events in community life: the birth of a child, the maturing of the child (rites of passage from childhood to adulthood), the marriage of two who are no longer children, and the burial of a person who departs the community in death.

MYTH

Closely associated with ritual is the narration that accompanies the ritual—the myth.[3] In today's world, to call something a myth usually means that it is a false or fictitious belief. This meaning has a long history going back at least as far as the Greek philosopher Xenophanes (c. 565–470 B.C.), who criticized the stories (myths) of the Greek Gods as told by the poets Homer° and Hesiod.° Xenophanes said these myths were stories that could not possibly be true. After Xenophanes, the Greeks continued the process of emptying mythos of all religious and metaphysical value. This carried down finally to the contemporary notion that any untrue statement people believe and organize their behavior around is a "a myth."

But modern religious studies scholars use the term differently. They use it to refer to basic, original faith stories, and they refrain from making value judgments about these stories. The truth or falsity of myths as actual ancient events is another matter. Mircea Eliadé,° a contemporary history of religions scholar, calls them "sacred hisstories": "Myth narrates a sacred history; it relates an event that took place in primordial Time, the fabled time of the 'beginnings.' In other words, myth tells how through the deeds of Supernatural Beings, a reality came into existence, be it the whole of reality, the Cosmos, or only a fragment of reality—an island, a species of plants, a particular kind of human behavior, an institution. Myth, then, is always an account of 'creation'; it relates how something was produced, began to *be*."[4]

Eliadé's limiting myth to "primordial time" and "creation episodes" is too restricted for our purposes. We shall also observe myths that explain how alienation from God (or the supernatual) came about and myths that tell how the whole world story will finally end.

KINDS OF MYTHS

Myths are faith stories that deal with cosmic-size events. Some myths are about primal origins, telling how the world and life began. Others tell how an original rapport between God and humankind became alienated. Still others are prophesies of "end time," telling how the end of the world will come and what the new world (in historical religions) or the new beginning (in eternal return religions) will be like. The stories are often fantastic accounts, but they are not to be taken as fantasies. They are held to be statements of sacred truth and are to be taken as true accounts of how things were or how they will be.

Myths of Origin   Some myths are about primordial time. They tell how the world got here. The following two stories are myths of origins; one is from the Hopi Indians, the other is from the ancient Norsemen.

According to the Hopis, this is how it all began. At first there was only the creator, Taiowa. All else was endless space, without beginning, without end, shapeless, timeless, lifeless. Then Taiowa in his mind conceived the world and first created Sótuknang to be his primary agent in creation. He said to Sótuknang, "I have created you as a person to carry out my plan for life. I am your Uncle. You are my Nephew. Go now and create, laying out the universes so they will function harmoniously according to my plan."

So Nephew Sótuknang began the creation. He made water, wind, and world. And Taiowa was pleased. He said, "This is good, but your work is not yet finished. You must create life." Following Taiowa's instructions, Sótuknang went to the First World (Tokpela) and out of it created Spider Woman (Kókyangwúti). She was to dwell on earth and make it live—fill it with joyful movement and joyful sound. To do this she was given the knowledge and love necessary to create all living things. So she created from the earth, trees, plants, flowers, grasses, bushes, and also birds and fish and other animals.

Sótuknang was pleased by what Spider Woman had done. It was all so beautiful. He called Taiowa to come and see what had been accomplished. And Taiowa pronounced it good. Then he said, "Now we are ready for the final thing to complete my plan. We are ready for the creation of human life."

So Spider Woman gathered soil of four colors, black, white, yellow, and red. She wetted the soil with her spit, molded it into four figures, covered the figures with the white cape of creation wisdom, and sang the creation song. When Spider Woman lifted the wisdom cape, the forms were human beings in the image of Sótuknang. Then she created four other beings after her own form. They were the *wuti*—the female partners of the four male beings. As they were uncovered, the forms came to life. This was the early time, the dream time, the time of first purple light, the dawn time.

Here we have an interesting story, but it is not just a story. It is a story that tells about God, and the actions of God, and the things of God. It is "theos-logos"—God-talk.*

---

*For this story in more detail, and for much more in the way of mythological theology, see Frank Waters, *Book of the Hopi* (New York: Ballantine Books, 1971).

In the Elder Edda, a source book of Norse mythology, we find another creation story. In the Edda we are told that

> Of old there was nothing,
> Nor sand, nor sea, nor cool waves.
> No earth, no heaven above,
> Only the yawning chasm.
> The sun knew not her dwelling,
> Nor the moon his realm.
> The stars had not their places.

But, in fact, there was more than the "yawning chasm." There was also the place of cold and death in the north (Niflheim) and the place of fire (Muspelheim) in the south. From the north flowed twelve rivers into the chasm, and gradually freezing, filled it with ice. At the same time warm clouds flowed up from the south causing mist to rise. This mist formed the frost maidens and Ymir, the first giant. Ymir's son was the father of Odin, the premier God of Norsemen. Odin's mother was the frost maidens.

Odin and two of his brothers killed Ymir, and from him they created the world—the earth from his body, the heavens from his skull, the sea around the earth from his blood. Then they took fire-sparks from the south and placed them in the sky as sun, moon, and stars. Using Ymir's eyebrows, they built a wall around the place where humans were to live. It was called Midgard. In Midgard the first man and woman were created—the man from an ash tree, the woman from an elm. These two were the parents of mankind. Also dwarfs were created. They were ugly creatures who lived under the earth, but were masterful artisans. Also elves were created. They were lovely little creatures who tended flowers and streams.

Thus was the world created. But it is a world that is endlessly threatened by Frost Giants and Mountain Giants who are the enemies of people, Gods, and all that is good, and who will eventually, despite the efforts of both Gods and humans, annihilate everything—the earth where humans live, Valhalla where the slain (*Val* means "slain") heroes are, and even Asgard where the Gods dwell. The Olympian Gods might have been immortal and invincible, but not the Gods of the Norsemen. Finally even they will be destroyed. The glory of this life is to live for what is good and to die for it, if necessary, but not to expect any kind of eternal reward.

The mythology of the Norsemen was, apparently, truly heroic. However, there is in the Elder Edda one brief prophesy that holds out a glimmer of hope. It is suggested that after all has been destroyed a new heaven and a new earth might be created by One who is even higher than Odin and beyond the reach of evil—

> A greater than all
> But I dare not even speak his name,

And there are few who can see beyond
The moment when Odin falls.

Myths of Alienation   Some myths tell how God and mankind, early on, became alienated. They tell how an original "paradise" was lost, or why the God who was with his people in the beginning withdrew to another place.

In contemporary Western religions, the best-known myth of alienation is, of course, the story of Adam and Eve's eating the forbidden fruit. With that disobedience, the close face-to-face relationship between God and mankind ended. Adam and Eve were driven from Paradise, they and all their generations.

Other cultures have other accounts of how life with the God was lost, or more paradisiacal existence was lost. In Ashanti° mythology, for example, God Onyankopon originally lived on earth, but he became so irritated by the behavior of one old woman that he went away to live in the sky. The people tried to follow Onyankopon by building a tower to heaven. They built it level on level, higher and higher, until they were almost to the sky. But then, just short of their goal, they ran out of bricks and mortar. On the advice of the same old woman, they took off the bottom layer of the tower to use it on the top. The result that should have been predicted was, at least in retrospect, discovered. And so Onyankopon lives in heaven. The Ashanti do not.

The Navajo have a similar twist in one of their myths—one that explains not the withdrawal of the God, but the loss of earthly life. Coyote, who was often depicted as a deceptive, tricky character in Indian mythology, observed one winter that the food supply was running low. He proposed that the old people should be given to Death. He argued that this would be only a temporary condition because the tribesmen could build a pathway to the sky for the old ones to return once the winter was over and a more adequate food supply of summer was available. But just as the pathway was about to be finished, Coyote tore it loose at the bottom and, like the Ashanti tower, it came crashing down. The dead could never return.

Eschatological° Myths   Some myths are concerned with end time. Usually in end-time myths the suffering of this world is ended, and a "paradise" is recovered. These eschatological stories often have savior figures—persons who will come and guide the people back to God or who will themselves reestablish a new heaven on earth. The Hebrew messiah represents the first of these types. He will come to lead mankind, especially the Hebrews, into the kingdom of God *on earth* where, as the Prophets Isaiah and Micah foresaw it:

. . . the mountain of the house of the Lord shall be established as the highest of the mountains, and shall be raised above the hills; and all nations shall flow to it, and many people shall come, and say: "Come let us go up to the mountain of the Lord, to the house of the God of Jacob; that he may teach us his ways and that we may walk in his paths.''

For out of Zion shall go forth the law, and the word of the Lord from Jerusalem. He shall judge between the nations and shall decide for many peoples; and they shall beat their swords into plowshares, and their spears into pruning hooks; nation shall not lift up sword against nation, neither shall they learn war anymore. *(Isaiah 2:2–4; Micah 4:1–3 RSV.)*

The messiah as depicted by Christian end-time theology is of the second type—this messiah (at least as pictured in the Book of Revelation) will come as a destructive force destroying the evil world and then creating a new heaven and a new earth.

The Book of Revelation in the Christian scripture is a classic end-of-time mythology. It tells us that there is in Heaven a scroll inscribed with the destiny of the world. It is sealed with seven seals, and only Christ can break the seals and open the scroll. As Christ opens each seal a catastrophe occurs and the inhabitants of earth undergo terrible pain and suffering. After the breaking of the seventh seal, seven angels blow seven trumpets and one after another seven more catastrophes occur, even more devastating than the first seven. Then war breaks out in Heaven and God's forces, led by the angel Michael, assail Satan's forces. Satan is soon cast down from Heaven to earth where he immediately begins to vent his wrath on God's people. But this is not to continue. Seven more catastrophes are visited on earth. Then Christ, the Word of God, comes from Heaven and, leading an army of saints, defeats the Beast, the old Devil, and incarcerates him for a thousand years. During that thousand years the martyrs live with Christ on earth in the city of Jerusalem. But the end is not yet for after a thousand years Satan breaks loose again to rampage and destroy and to gather the nations of the world in an attack on Christ and the martyrs in the holy city. But again Satan fails. He is defeated— this time forever—and thrown into the lake of fire. Then from all over the earth, from all past time, the dead are resurrected and gathered for judgment—the evil persons being consigned eternally to Satan's Hell, the good to live eternally with God in a new heavenly Jerusalem.

At the end of the nineteenth century the Western tribes of American Indians were swept by an eschatological myth. A Nevada Paiute Indian, Jack Wovoka, received a vision. In his vision the Great Spirit revealed to Wovoka an Indian heaven where all Indians were young and happy. And this new heaven, this new world, was coming soon. Inspired by Wovoka's preaching, the Ghost Dance Religion began—a religion that was soon embraced not only by the Paiute, but by the Cheyenne, the Arapahoe, and the Sioux. Some Indians (especially the Sioux) came to believe that when the paradise-time came for the Indians, it would also be a time of destruction and annihilation for that devil who had destroyed the Indians' former days of joy and plenty—the hated white man. This myth shattered, and the Ghost Dance with it, in 1890, in

South Dakota, in the massacre of Sitting Bull and 150 other Sioux at Wounded Knee.

In some religions that are cyclical rather than historical (religions in which there is an endless repetition of world happenings rather than a single beginning and a final ending), the myths report how the Gods participate in this process of "eternal return." In Vishnu Hinduism, for example, God Vishnu incarnates in an animal or human form and comes to earth to guide humans in times of cultural devolution and waste. Also, frequently, in cyclical, eschatological myths, the God dies and is resurrected again and again, as, for example, spring being resurrected from the death of winter, or day being resurrected from the death of night, or a new year from the death of the old.

According to one Greek myth, there never was a more beautiful female creature than Persephone, the daughter of Zeus, king of Olympus, and Demeter, the corn Goddess, the Goddess of crops and harvests. Indeed, Persephone was so beautiful that the passions of Hades, Lord of the Dead, were enflamed beyond restraint. He seized this wondrous female, carried her off to the Underworld, and used her for his pleasure. Persephone's mother, Demeter, was so distraught by this abduction and rape that she wandered about the earth bewailing her loss, and the earth became a place barren and cold. Finally, because the situation was becoming unbearable, and the earth and mankind were threatened with extinction, Zeus intervened. He made a deal with his brother Hades. Hades could have the girl for four months each year, but for the rest of the year she must be returned to her mother on earth. So it is that each year, with the return of Persephone, spring comes and once again the earth becomes fertile and life-giving. But when each fall Persephone returns to Hades, Demeter's joy dissipates again into the coldness of winter.

MYTH-RITUAL AS DRAMA AND SYMBOL

Myths are not exhausted with the telling thereof. They are not simply stories. They are dramas—participation dramas. The participation character of a religious drama can be seen in the performance of the Christmas story dramas enacted in Christian churches and Sunday schools each year at Christmas time. While a narrator reads the Nativity accounts from Matthew and Luke (the myth), the scenes of the Nativity (what God did for mankind) are performed with ritualistic, if sometimes awkward, actions and postures by selected members of the congregation. This is an almost classic example of religious folk ritual. The myth, the dramatic narration of the divine-human encounter, and the ritual acts, the stylized actions of that encounter, are combined to effect an experience of wonder and joy in all who "behold and believe."

An important observation should be made at this point. The enactment of the Christmas story is not simply a drama, but a folk drama. It is a drama of participation. The actors, the narrator, and the auditors are all caught up in the movement and life and spirit of the event; which is to say that, although the ritual is often spectacular, it is not intended to be a spectacle. It is a vehicle of involvement in which all the community of worshippers are communicants. They are all partakers because they all participate.

In a different setting this participation aspect of ritual is exemplified in the Jewish celebration of Passover. On that ceremonial evening the Jewish family gathers at the festive table. One of the children asks the traditional question, "Why is this night different from all other nights?" Then the head of the family answers, "We were slaves unto Pharaoh in Egypt and the eternal our God led us from there with a mighty hand." So begins the participation drama of Passover in which ritual acts and myth/narration combine to re-create the sense of God's presence and God's support in Jewish life.

This ritual/action-myth/narration relationship can be seen also in two accounts of animal sacrifice as recorded in the book of Leviticus. First, chapter 9, verses 8–11:

> So Aaron came near to the altar and slaughtered the calf, which was his sin-offering. The sons of Aaron presented the blood to him and he dipped his finger in the blood and put it on the horns of the altar. The rest of the sin-offering, the fat, the kidneys, and the long lobe of the liver, he burnt in the altar as the Lord had commanded Moses.

Second, chapter 17, verse 6:

> The priest shall fling the blood against the altar of the Lord at the entrance of the Tent of the Presence, and burn the fat as a soothing odor to the Lord.[5]

Lord Ragland,° regarding these Levitical accounts, writes, "Those two descriptions are of the same rite, whereas the latter is in the form of a simple instruction [a director's instruction, so to speak], the former is a myth, that is to say, an account of the rite told as a narrative of what someone once did."[6]

Myths, apparently, can become unlatched from their appropriate rituals and continue independent careers of their own either as fairy tales, folk tales, or legends. Also, apparently, although perhaps less successfully, rituals can continue even after their original meaning or mythic narration has become unhinged. People knock on wood, throw pinches of salt over their shoulders, place an evergreen tree at the topping-out (the final steel framing) of a new, tall building, with no memory of, or narration of, the meaning or authority for such action. From such examples it appears that when religious rituals lose their original meaning (their mythos) they either cease to exist or become trivial.

Religious Symbols   As participation drama, ritual preserves and communicates religious stories and meanings. Thus, it is a religious symbol. Paul Tillich, in his *Systematic Theology,* makes some interesting observations about the nature of symbols. He asserts that "symbol and sign are different . . . while the sign bears no necessary relation to that to which it points, the symbol participates in the reality for which it stands."[7] Elsewhere in the same volume he states:

> The denotative power of language is its ability to grasp and communicate general meaning. The expressive power of language is its ability to disclose and communicate personal states. . . . Most speaking moves between these two poles: the more scientific and technical, the nearer the denotative pole, the more poetic and communal, the nearer the expressive pole.[8]

This is to say that denotation is the central function of signs, whereas expressive communication is the central function of symbols. A sign is arbitrarily assigned to convey information. A flashing red light at a street corner means stop. A green light could be used equally well. But symbols are not so, for the function of symbols is not to convey precise meanings, but to transport aesthe-noetic° experiences, and once they arrive at full symbolic status, they cannot be arbitrarily changed. They cannot be substituted simply through common agreement. For example, although the American flag does have a kind of denotative function in that it points at this country instead of that one, it is not simply a sign of this country, for it represents, depicts, excites, participates in the whole spectrum of the history and life of this nation. The symbol speaks to the American beholder of the total reality (fact and spirit) of America, of which the symbol itself is a part. It is both a piece of gaudy cloth and a nation, and it is more the latter than the former. Ritual is symbol, not sign. The concern of ritual is not to put on a show, or even simply to convey a message, but to participate in a total event that, although it is historically distant, recurs in the present enabling worshippers to experience that mighty occurrence as if they were there. They are with the shepherds and the wise men, seeing the fantastic birth in its simplicity and importance; they are at the Cross and at the Tomb witnessing; they are with Moses crossing the sea, standing at the mountain.

Theology and philosophy of religion may deal in signs—analyzing, criticizing, systematizing—but ritual is an art form. It speaks to the heart to elicit those reasons that "reason does not know." In saying this, we do not mean that ritual is irrational, or even unrational, or that theology and philosophy are inimical to ritual. Ritual simply speaks differently from theology and philosophy. It uses its own logic, which is the logic of evocation and nuance, as does any art form.

Myth or Ritual or Theology, Which Came First?   There is debate over which came first, the ritual or the myth. Which preceded the other, the reverent performance or the story of the ancient, divine action that prompted the reverent performance? Prehistoric facts are too far away to justify one claim or the other. But the facts discernible in living primitive societies indicate the likelihood that neither necessarily came first. Rather both appear to rest upon prior belief systems—upon religious beliefs already declared and accepted by the tribe. It may be, as Annamarie de Waal Malefijt proposes, that "myth and ritual are related not because they . . . complement and reinforce each other, but because both are based on dogma."[9]

Believing something about themselves and their world people behaved reverently and authenticated their reverent behavior by identifying it within their theology—their general patterns of social and religious beliefs. Such a suggestion puts not only ritual and myth as primordial forms of religious behavior, but puts theology at the beginning also. Theology, *logos* of *theos*, words about God, is not to be dismissed as some kind of intellectual strait-jacket imposed upon the "feeling" of religion long after religion emerged from the emotions of humans and flowered in rituals and myths. Rather, it is to think that people believed and spoke their beliefs to themselves from the very beginning, and in terms of their "belief-words" they did their religion. They made religious dramas (rituals), and those dramas narrated the action of the divine powers in establishing (and reestablishing) the life, customs, institutions, beliefs, and dogmas of their community life. It may be that before our prehistoric man (of Chapter 3)* went to the swamp and found his Tree, he already lived in a system of beliefs about the powers of his world, a belief system that structured his life and community into a world of ordinary and superordinary things. He was not simply an animal reacting to an environment, but a man who had begun to "make sense" of his social system, to make sense of his mundane environment, and to make sense of the tremendous, mysterious, fascinating, numinous world of sacred things. It may be that he was already in a condition of theology into which his tree ritual fit comfortably. A ritual that he would one night at the campfire be challenged to defend and would do so by searching his theologized soul for a vision of how long before, at the dawn of time, when the Old Man walked the earth, he came to the swamp and finding it loathsome and dangerous made the Tree and put it there for hunters to see and touch and be made strong for the evils of the swamp.

We have no evidence for believing that prehistoric people were not thinking beings who had theologies that informed their lives and structured their religious rituals. Paul Tillich holds that theology is as old as religion. Thinking pervades all the spiritual activities of mankind. Indeed, is not mythical narration itself theology—words about God? E. O. James° in his *Myth and Ritual in the Ancient Near East* points out that:

> even the native tribes of Australia, though they have no recorded history, have traditions which presuppose a very definite continuity with the past when inexora-

*See pages 34–35.

ble laws, customs and organizations were given to their tribal ancestors in the . . . Dream-time of long ago, when the culture heroes lived on earth and determined the existing structure of society. . . . Thus, history, in the sense of the course of significant events, is an integral part of the tribal tradition in terms of the myth and ritual which preserve the network of social relations and the state of tribal equilibrium and stability.[10]

Bronislaw Malinowski, in his chapter "Myth in Primitive Psychology," makes the same point when he states that among primitive people myth/ritual conveys much more than is contained in the story being dramatized. The myth/ritual drama fits into a larger structure of belief that the primitive person has learned in the context of his tribal life. "In other words, it is the context of his social life, it is the gradual realization by the native of how everything which he is told to do has its precedent and pattern in bygone times, which brings home to him the full account and the full meaning of his myths of origin."[11]

In this regard, Joseph Campbell° identifies the myth-ritual-theology configuration as a vitally functioning meaning-system that: (1) creates in humans a sense of awe before those powers and circumstances that lie outside their control; (2) enables them to understand better the natural order around them; (3) gives them a framework in which they can see their society as coherent and meaningful; and (4) gives them a way of understanding their own inner lives.[12]

Myth-Ritual-Theology in the Making Cargo Cults, because they are new phenomena, may give us a clue to the closeness of the mythical, ritualistic, and theological aspects of emergent religions.

In a speech made at the California Institute of Technology and subsequently published in *Business Week,* Ruben Mettler recalled a day in the late 1940s on a small island in the South Pacific when he encountered a Cargo Cult for the first time. The islanders had taken over an abandoned airfield and were acting out what they had seen the American GIs do there during World War II. The natives were wearing cast-off GI uniforms, marching about with wooden guns, manning the control tower, watching the sky. One man was wearing a set of earphones carved out of wood, speaking into a wooden microphone, and making marks on a clipboard. They were trying to make magic—the same magic the GIs had made so the silver airships would come with their rich cargoes. As Mettler says,

> The cargo cultists saw that our GIs were able to call down bounties from the sky apparently without doing any real work, merely by talking into little boxes, signalling with flags, marching in formations, or even sitting at tables with vases of flowers and sipping ceremonial libations from tall glasses. Lacking any understanding of the elaborate production, distribution, transportation, and communication technology that make possible this abundance of goods, the cultists attributed it all to what they saw and tried to achieve the same results by ritual imitation.[13]

Cargo Cults have emerged repeatedly since colonial times among natives of the South Sea Islands and in different forms in Southeast Asia and Africa. The cults are messianic° in character and express a cultural distress. Primitives have glimpsed the promised land—the cargo that comes in white men's ships, and great silver birds—and they are no longer at peace with what they have and with who they are. In the South Sea Islands, before World War II, but especially during the war, natives watched the activities of their white bosses and rulers and were disconcerted by the white men's powerful culture. They heard the white men talk about "kago" (pidgin for "cargo"), and they saw the kago come, and it was fantastic. The coming of cargo came to have a very important significance for those primitive people. It represented the coming of "the good time" when they would be like the whites and enjoy what the whites enjoyed—the coming of the millenium, the glorious end of this time and beginning of the deliverance time.

Ruben Mettler's "Cargo People" were the products of the activities of the American military forces in the South Pacific during World War II. The white men, dressed in uniforms, marched about, talked into boxes, signed papers, drank libations, had flowers in vases on their tables, gave orders—and the cargo came. But where did it come from? The natives thought about these things and concluded that it came from the white man's dead ancestors across the sea (even as the natives had ancestors across the sea). The white man had discovered how to communicate with the dead. How to perform pleasing rituals—marching, posturing, saluting, writing magic on clipboards, speaking magic into black boxes, making flower offerings. Now the white man was gone and it was the native's turn. So he dressed up in old GI cast-away uniforms. Marched with stickguns over his shoulder. Manned the control tower, and sent magic messages to his own ancestors. Also, it was noted that white men liked to keep vases of fresh flowers. Thinking there might be some particular magical importance in this, the natives often not only decorated their own houses with flowers, but decorated whole villages with flowers. Also, in the Cargo Cult movements in Melanesia, the natives often destroyed their own wealth—their crops and livestock. The old order was to be completely ended so the new order could begin.*

In the Cargo Cults the aim was to destroy the old, in an act of faith, for something new. To do this they employed simultaneously, at the very beginning, theology, myth making, and ritual, and they did so in a passion for what they considered would be true salvation. By the truth of their myth, the adequacy of their theology, and the correctness of their rituals, they would go

---

*To get rid of the old order and have the new one begin, is, of course, not only a Melanesian theological concept. It is the main theme in the Christian's Book of Revelation. In a less violent way it was a part of the theology of the Ghost Dance movement of American Indians in the 1870s. The Ghost Dancers believed that if they danced for five days, washed in the river, and fulfilled other ritual prescriptions, the dead would come back, the old way of life be restored, the whites driven from the Indian lands.

from poverty and second-rateness to cargo and first class. What more could anyone want?

KINDS OF RITUALS

The major rituals of society and cults are stylized human behavior depicting symbolically and dramatically the authority for socially acceptable or socially demanded values. There are secular rituals for various social purposes; religious rituals for various religious purposes; and "double-valence" rituals, mixing both secular and religious elements.

Secular Rituals   It was November 22, 1963; the time was 2:38 P.M. (CST); the place, Love Field outside Dallas, Texas. In the rear compartment of Air Force One was a casket holding the body of the thirty-fifth president of the United States. Forward in the gold-upholstered conference room, in the presence of Mrs. John F. Kennedy and twenty-six other persons, Sarah Hughes, district judge, read from the Constitution of the United States, and Lyndon B. Johnson, holding a Bible in his left hand, his right hand raised, repeated after her the last thirty-six words of Article II, Section I. And so the torch was passed; the fallen reins gathered up. The government had been reasserted in proper constitutional form—*in a ritual*: "I do solemnly swear that I will faithfully execute the office of the President of the United States, and will to the best of my ability preserve, protect and defend the Constitution of the United States. So help me God."

On other, more happy days, the inauguration of the president and the oath have occurred in more elaborate pageantry. But elaborateness is not the point. The point is that to assert the meaning of the nation in the mind of its citizens, to give solidarity to the diversity that is the United States, rituals are performed. The ritual of inauguration is real and vital and alive. It literally makes a person the president, and more, it makes that person *our* president. The ritual was given to us by our great cultural heroes—the Founding Fathers. When they inaugurated the first president, he too said: "I do solemnly swear. . . ."

The celebration of the Fourth of July and of Thanksgiving Day are rituals of the same secular social stripe. Each in its ritualized form authorizes and solidifies the society with an aura of ancient purpose reborn and serves as a basis for public religion.

Such rituals are predominantly secular in nature. Presidents do close the oath with the words "So help me God"; their main concern, however, is not to get supernatural assistance but rather to make a "reverent noise" at an auspicious time. In fact, these religious words are not constitutional; they do not appear in Article II as part of the prescribed oath. Thanksgiving Day purports to be more religious in intent; its religiousness, however, does not appear to run very deep, not much deeper probably than table grace. And the Fourth of July makes no religious pretense at all.

There is an argument that would disavow what is here called "sectarian rituals." Sociologist Robert Bellah argues that there is a civil religion in America composed of the various official statements and rites performed by the United States government, including the statements of belief in God affirmed in the Constitution; on the coinage of the realm; in the declarations of the Founding Fathers; in the "religious" celebrations of Memorial Day, Thanksgiving Day, and the Fourth of July; and in the occasional prayers of the president for some divine favor for the nation.

However, we shall here contend that what Bellah calls a civil religion is not a religion so much as the religious authenticating and celebrating of the nation. By using the Judeo-Christian heritage (heavily interpreted as Deistic or Protestant), the national story and symbols (the mythology) are given a religious aura. But this is not a religion so much as a sanctifying, authenticating, and celebrating of a nation. A real religion deals with the transcending of finitude. It addresses the nonmanipulable and horrendous circumstances of personal life and meaning. It is a salvation affair. That civil religion affects real religion is obvious, as real religion obviously affects civil performance, but the appropriation of some religious symbols and rituals, and even some religious attitudes, does not transform the body politic into a functioning religion. One may dress a chimpanzee in a child's clothes, but the act does not create a child.[14]

Peter Berger stated his doubt that civil religion (that is, "an amalgam of beliefs and norms that are deemed to be fundamental to the American political order") could ever replace genuine religion. He wrote:

> I am impressed by the intrinsic inability of secularized world views to answer the deeper question of human condition, question of *whence, whither,* and *why.* These seem to be ineradicable and they are answered only in the most banal ways by *ersatz* religions of secularism.[15]

Double-Valence Rites   Some rituals seem to be "somewhat" secular and at the same time "somewhat" religious. They have a secular purpose but are also obviously and essentially based in things sacred, for example, the socially vital, theologically based "rites of passage" of primitive people. The inaugural ritual is a mechanism for passing political authority from one person to another. In many places the same kind of function is performed to signify, authorize, and make real the passing of a person from childhood to adulthood. Such rituals are called "rites of passage."

For example, in the Lake Eyre country of southeastern Australia there is a tribe of people called Dieri. Whenever a Dieri boy or girl reaches puberty, rites of passage are performed to transform the boy into a man and the girl into a woman. In the case of males the rites have a prelude that consists of a ceremonious knocking out of the boy's two front teeth with a wooden chisel and a service of circumcision and naming. At a later time and without warning the boy is led out of the camp by some older men. They surround him and tell him to

> close his eyes. One of the old men then binds the arm of another old man tightly with a string, and with a sharp piece of flint lances the vein about an inch from the elbow, causing a stream of blood to fall over the young man until he is covered with it, and the old man is becoming exhausted. Another man takes his place, and so on until the young man becomes quite stiff from the quantity of blood adhering to him.[16]

In this way the spirit and wisdom of the old men transform the boy into a man by making him of one blood with them. Next the blood-covered boy is gashed on the neck and back to make scars—a lasting evidence of his initiation into manhood. At the completion of this rite, he is given a bull-roarer: a paddle-shaped slab of wood with a long string attached. The bull-roarer when whirled around the head creates a mysterious noise, which the boy and the womenfolk had often heard before, but never understood. But the bull-roarer is not to be regarded as a simple trick to frighten women and children. It is believed to have supernatural power and to speak to all living things. It is the symbol and voice of the Mura-muras (the ancient tribal heroes) who first gave the tribe its sacred laws, traditions, and rituals. The boy, now become man, is never to show the bull-roarer to any woman or tell her about it.

Finally, the initiate is sent alone into the bush where he is to remain until his wounds have healed and he has rehearsed many times the lessons he has heard during this long ritual of initiation. And he has heard many things during this time, for throughout the entire ritual there had been a narration recited by the older men, who had carefully explained the supernatural origin of each rite performed. Their recitation began with a retelling of the tribal myths in regard to the ritual being performed. The boy was admonished in his tribal duties. The totemic rules and relationships were defined with exactness. The tribal morality thus comes to each member of the community with the full weight of religious sanctions behind it.

Another double-valence ritual that can lean either toward the secular side or the religious side is the marriage rite—a rite that can be effectively performed by a judge, a justice of the peace, a sea captain, a Jewish rabbi, a Greek Orthodox priest; that can take place in a courtroom, a courtyard, a swimming pool, a chapel, a temple, or a cathedral; that can be accompanied by a matron of honor, bridesmaids, a best man and groomsmen, a weeping mother, a relieved father, organ music, songs, candles, fertility rice, and a staggering amount of champagne; a rite that is always made official by a signed, sealed, and courthouse-recorded certificate.

But it can also be a most holy sacrament, for this public declaration, which authenticates a relationship basic and essential to society, can declare itself to be "performed in the sight of God." The state insists that marriage is a legal arrangement of necessity to the stability, tranquility, and continuation of society. But the church, with a backward look to its mythos, declares that what occurs is not simply a society-fostered arrangement, more or less endorsed by two families, or even a vow of love between two persons, but an "honorable estate instituted by God" even in the beginning of time, and "is, therefore not to be entered into unadvisedly, but reverently, discreetly and in the fear of God."

Religious Ritual   Although all rituals have valuable social and political implications, some are so overwhelmingly concerned with religious things that they must be regarded as sacred or cultic* rather than sociopolitical. We shall look at two of the truly cultic types of ritual and see them as they reflect the mythos and theology of two widely different religious cultures: Roman Catholic Christianity and Zen Buddhism. First the myth—Christian and Buddhist; then the myth dramatized—the ritual.

The Myth: A Faith Story in Christianity   As Christians tell their sacred story, it all began when the angel Gabriel came to a young Israelite woman and told her that she had been selected to be the mother of a very special child. She, said the angel, had been blessed above all other women.

The time arrived for the child to be born and he was born in a stable in Bethlehem, and shepherds came, and wise men came, to celebrate the marvelous birth; and angels sang and the world was filled with joy. But this child was destined to know sorrow, and suffering, and violent death, because he had come to redeem mankind from sin and damnation.

In his "growing-up" days he lived with his mother Mary and her husband Joseph, a carpenter, and was a dutiful child. But finally the time came for him to be about his heavenly "father's business."

In the desert a kinsman was preaching, "Repent for the Kingdom of God is at hand." Jesus went out to that place, was baptized there, and began his mission. He gathered about him disciples, both men and women, and an inner group of twelve who accompanied him everywhere. He preached in Galilee, calling men and women to renounce their earth-bound ambitions and set themselves right with God. He preached a new and radical law of love—a law of unending forgiveness. And he healed those who were ill, and fed those who were hungry, and, finally, directed his footsteps to Jerusalem where his fate would be sealed on a cross.

But first there were scenes to be played out: the scene of his coming into the city riding on a donkey; the scene of his preaching in the temple yard, and his driving the merchandizers from that holy place; the scene in nearby Bethany where he was anointed with oil, symbolic of his coming death and burial; the scene in the Upper Room during the Passover celebration when he gave the

---

* Cultic pertains to a system of religious behavior, especially the rites and ceremonies of worship.

inner-twelve a new and holy ritual for all time. Also there were the scenes of agony in the garden, the betrayal by one of the twelve, the arrest, the trial, and of his stumbling, falling trip to the place of execution called the Skull; and of his death and the emptiness in the world—until on a bright third morning the tomb was empty and the word went out, "He is risen!"

The Myth: A Faith Story in Buddhism Five and a half centuries before Jesus of Nazareth was born another child was born; this time in India about 100 miles from the town of Benares—the child of a nobleman named Gautama, who named this man-child Siddhartha. At Siddhartha's birth angels did not sing, as in the story of Jesus, but wise men came and prophesied. They told Siddhartha's father that this child was indeed special; that he could become the emperor of all India. But this would happen only if he were dissuaded from becoming—the other potential of his destiny—a yellow-robed monk.

Siddhartha's father, of course, wanted the best for his son, which he, of course, believed would be emperor, not monk. So he conceived a fantastic scheme. He would see to it that his son grew up never experiencing the sordid things that so distress sensitive human beings and sometimes sent them searching in religion for the meaning of life and death. The nobleman father built three palaces where his son, during various seasons, could live in comfort. He also arranged that Siddhartha have as companions only young, healthy, happy people. He even arranged that whenever the boy traveled along the roads and highways servants went ahead of the prince's chariot and cleared the way of any old, sick, poor people who chanced to be there.

So successful was the noble father in keeping the seamier sides of life away from his son that Siddhartha grew to young manhood utterly unaware of the real condition of human existence. Further, his life was made even more joyous by his marriage to a very lovely girl, who, in due time, expanded his joy by giving him a child of his own. Siddhartha was on his way to empire.

But the Gods chose otherwise. Seeing the illusion that Siddhartha's father had created to protect his son from the true nature of life, and from the promise of true religion, they chose to intervene. They would awaken the prince to his true destiny. So one day as Siddhartha rode along in his chariot one of the Gods descended, but not in the form of a God, in the form of a decrepit old man. Seeing this the prince asked his chariot driver to tell him what it was; and thus Siddhartha learned for the first time that there was suffering and misery in the world. On another day the prince driving along saw a second sight—another God in the form of a loathsomely diseased man. And on another day—a third sight—a dead man being carried along on a bier. These three sights robbed the young prince of his peace of mind. He said, "I also must be subject to decay and am not free from the power of old age, sickness, and death. Is it right that I should feel horror, revulsion, and disgust when I see another in such plight?"

After these three startling experiences, Siddhartha became so depressed that nothing could console him. And then he beheld a fourth sight. One day on the highway he saw a yellow-robed monk walking. Siddhartha engaged this monk in conversation and was so impressed, especially by the serenity of the man, that he vowed to turn from princely living and search for the treasure of religious peace.

Leaving home, parents, wife, child, he went in quest of this true destiny. First he traveled to the city of Rajagaha and became a disciple of first one and then another holy man. With them he studied philosophy and practiced yoga discipline. But it proved disappointing. He learned much, but nothing that released him from his human anxieties.

So he left and turned to a different way of religious searching. He became an ascetic. In a grove near the town of Uruvels he began a discipline of severe self-denial that went on, and on, and on, until he was little more than skin and bones. But again failure.

After spending six years pursuing salvation, first in the way of philosophy, and second in the way of ascetic discipline, with no spiritual results, Siddhartha came to his common sense and gave up the quest. He would go home. But on his way there he stopped at a place near Budhgaya and went into a grove where he sat down under a tree to rest, a tree that would later be called the "Tree of Knowledge" (the Bodhi° or Bo-tree) because it was there that Siddhartha Gautama suddenly experienced enlightenment. It was there that his religious quest ended. It was there that he became Buddha—the awakened one.

In Catholic Christianity the calendar of faith begins with Advent, the four Sundays before Christmas. The liturgy of Advent heralds the coming of the Christ child. From Christmas to Easter, Christ's life is remembered, especially in the Lenten preparation for the representation during Holy Week of the Crucifixion and Resurrection. The remainder of the Christian year, from Pentecost to Advent, commemorates not a single life, but human life as it is reflected in the Bible and in the history of the church.[17]

Rituals That Enact the Jesus Myth (Roman Catholic)   The annual rituals of many Christian churches constitute a reliving of the atonement (the at-one-ment) of humans with God through the birth, life, death, and resurrection of Christ. This cycle of reliving begins about four weeks before the winter solstice with the season of Advent, and climaxes on the first Sunday after the first full moon following the vernal equinox, which is Easter. From this cycle of rituals, which tells the complete story of Christ's life from before his birth to after his death and resurrection, we shall give special attention to only three rites—those of Palm Sunday, Holy Thursday, and Good Friday as practiced by Roman Catholic Christians. The rites of Holy Thursday and Good Friday represent, in a sense, the quintessence of the Christian myth as viewed by Catholics. Eucharist and sacrifice are what the whole thing is about: God giving himself *for* and *to* mankind.

The ritual year celebrating the story of Jesus—birth, death, resurrection—begins four Sundays before Christmas in what is called the Advent Season. This is the time when "true believers" prepare for the great celebration of Jesus' birth on December 25. The birth is followed on the following Sunday with a celebration commemorating the Holy Family. Twelve days after Christmas (January 6) Epiphany is celebrated. Epiphany commemorates the manifestation of the divine nature of Christ to the Gentiles as represented by the coming of the wise men (the Magi). The ritual year, after an interval, shifts from the advent, birth, and recognition of Jesus, to the passion and resurrection of Jesus. This cycle of rituals begins with Ash Wednesday—the day emphasizing mortality: ashes to ashes, dust to dust. After Ash Wednesday there are five Sundays of Lent, each intended to make people more and more conscious of the sacrifice of Christ for humans. These days of sacrifice, the days of passion, begin with Palm Sunday (also called Passion Sunday) and continue for seven days with special emphasis on Holy Thursday and Good Friday.[18]

The Passion ritual begins with the coming of Christ to Jerusalem on the Day of the Palms. Before the Mass of Palm Sunday there is a rite in which not bread and wine are consecrated, but branches of the palm and olive trees. This rite begins with the priest and his assistants entering the church intoning a collect, lesson, and Gospel, as in a regular Mass. They chant the Preface and Sanctus of the music of the Mass for the Dead. The priest then blesses the branches with incense and holy water, recalling in his prayer not only the palms with which Christ was greeted as he came to Jerusalem for the last time, but also the olive branch brought to Noah by the dove as a sign of the end of the Flood and the beginning of a new covenant with mankind. The palms are distributed to the people who gather outside the church. The church door, representing the Gate of Jerusalem, is closed. Inside the church the cantors begin to sing a hymn, "All glory, laud and honor, To thee, Redeemer King." The door is then opened and the procession enters the church singing "Hosanna in the highest. . . ."

During the Palm Sunday Mass, at the time for chanting the Gospel, the clergy and the choir sing the story of the Passion according to Matthew. In the masses celebrated on Tuesday, Wednesday, and Friday the passion stories according to Mark, Luke, and John are presented.

Thursday is different because it is the ritual of the Lord's Supper as reportedly it was first given on the first Holy Thursday. This rite celebrates the institution of the Mass itself. The actual ritual of any Mass has two parts—part one for the catechumen (those under instruction in basic doctrines of Catholic Christianity in preparation for admission among the faithful of the church), and part two for the faithful. The first part is adapted from the Jewish synagogue service and consists of prayers and readings. The real Mass begins with part two. It is composed of Offertory, Consecration, and Communion. The Offertory is the presentation of the bread and the wine, which at this state represents the offering by the faithful of themselves to God. In the Consecration the priest assumes the role of Christ and repeats the actions that occurred at the Last Supper, including Christ's words that declared the bread to be his true body and the wine to be his true blood. In the final division of the Mass, the Communion, the priest and the faithful gather at the altar and consume the sacred body and blood, as reportedly the Apostles did in the Upper Room. (Traditionally in a Catholic Mass, the bread, in the form of a wafer is placed by the priest on the communicant's out-thrust tongue. Only the priest drinks the wine.)

That this central ritual is not simply a commemoration of a divine action in the distant past, but the re-creation of that action in the present, is declared in the belief that when the priest speaks Christ's words, "This is my body. . . . This is my blood," the ordinary bread and wine of the Offertory are believed to be literally transformed (transubstantiated) into the actual body of Christ and blood of Christ, with only the appearance of bread and wine remaining.

During the Mass of Holy Thursday, the priest consecrates a special host that, when the Mass is over, is placed in a monstrance° on one of the side altars where throughout the night of Holy Thursday the faithful take turns keeping vigil, as did the sleepy Apostles with Christ in Gethsemane.

For Holy Thursday the purple altar cloths signifying the Passion of Christ are replaced with snowy white cloths that speak of the beauty and gladness of Christ's giving of himself in the eucharistic gift of Holy Communion. After vespers Thursday night these snowy cloths of gladness are stripped from the altar, recalling how Christ was stripped before his crucifixion. The priest, having laid bare the altar of God, then turns to his people and taking a vessel of water and a towel washes their feet, recalling how Christ, the night before he died, washed the feet of his disciples.

Then the fateful day arrives—a bad day called "Good"—the day of crucifixion. On this Friday the priest, dressed in somber black, on a bleak, bare altar, performs the Mass of the Presanctified.° The time is hushed and agonized. The Passion in this ritual drama is the one according to John, from the agony in the Garden of Gethsemane to the burial in the tomb. When the account is finished, the priest takes a large wooden crucifix veiled in black and holds it up before the people. The crucifix is slowly unveiled and a chant sung.

Behold the wood of the cross,
on which hung the Savior of the world.

Unveiled, the cross is placed before the altar. The priest removes his shoes, kneels, and kisses the cross. Then the people form a procession that proceeds up the center aisle of the church. Before arriving at the cross they go down on their knees three times, as, according to the biblical story, Christ fell three times as he carried his cross to Golgotha.

When Christ dies on Friday afternoon, the ritual drama of Passion ends. The candles are snuffed out, the sacred host removed from the sanctuary, the church (the world) is empty—waiting.

We have looked at the Catholic tradition for our illustrations of religious rituals because the Catholic tradition can afford us such an elaborate display of rites that are, at the same time, somewhat familiar to us in our Western world. Examples from Judaism's elaborate rituals could afford us a similarly familiar array. The Protestant tradition, especially the part that developed out of the left-wing (peasant) movement of the Reformation, is much less extensive and formalized, but here also there are ritual ceremonies with accompanying narrations (myths). Even the extremely spontaneous Pentecostals, gathering for a spiritual service, are ritual-myth guided. The service may seem to be a formless succession (even confusion) of singing, preaching, exhorting, praying, but it is a deadly serious reenactment and reliving of the "birth of the church" in the first coming of the Holy Spirit fifty days after the Resurrection of Christ. It is Pentecost relived, even to the ecstasy of divine seizure and "speaking in tongues."* The action of a Pentecostal service may be more spontaneous than the action of a Catholic Mass, but it is no less ritual-myth.

We should also note that it is neither the amount of action nor the formality or spontaneity of the action that makes the ceremony a religious ritual. There are some powerful rituals constituted of "sitting quietly, doing nothing," as in a Quaker Meeting or in Zazen.°

A Ritual That Reflects the Siddhartha Gautama (the Buddha) Myth   Once, a long time ago, the great Gautama, after years of anguished searching for the true religion, gave up the search, the struggle, the action, the effort, and sat down under a tree. He sat quietly, doing nothing, as in "Sitting quietly, doing nothing, Spring comes, and the grass grows by itself."[19] And suddenly the search that Gautama was no longer making was concluded in the Great Enlightenment. Gautama's Buddhahood was accomplished, and a new, magnificent religion for mankind was born. That is the myth. It has been, since then, accoutered with the most elaborate rituals imaginable, but also with a profound ritual of practically no elaboration at all—the Zazen.

Zazen (literally, "seated meditation") is the central ritual of the meditation religion called Zen Buddhism as it is practiced in the monasteries in Japan. This service takes place in the meditation hall (*Zendo*), which is the central building with a wide platform down the length of either side. Its only adorn-

---

* The Day of Pentecost described in Acts was not really a glossolalia experience, although many people appear to hold that view. On Pentecost, according to Acts 2:6, the Apostles spoke and were understood by everyone. Their speaking was not esoteric, but universal. They spoke in known tongues, not unknown tongues.

ment is the shrine of the Buddha (*Butsudan*) standing in the center of the hall with, perhaps, a spray of flowers set before it. At the time for meditation the monks enter the hall in a procession and take their seats on the platforms in two rows facing each other across the narrow room. They sit in the traditional lotus posture, legs crossed, feet upon the thighs, hands resting in the lap, palms upward, eyes fixed upon the floor. The head monk goes forward and prostrates himself before the shrine. He then lights a stick of incense to mark the time. The head monk then takes his seat on the platform and the Zazen begins. No one speaks. There is no sound in the room except that which drifts in from outside. Breathing is regulated so as to be slow, without strain, with the outbreathing emphasized slightly by a push from the belly rather than the chest. Two attendants walk slowly back and forth between the two lines of seated men. Each attendant has a stick. Any time one of them sees anyone sitting improperly or dozing, he stops before the offender, bows cere-moniously, and proceeds to belabor him with the warning stick, until the offender has been "massaged" again into full wakefulness. When the incense has burned out, the head monk sounds a bell. It is time for relaxation and exercise. The monks get up from their lotus-posture sitting, form a column and begin to march swiftly and quietly around the room. After this exercise, they return to their meditation during the burning of another incense stick. These periods of Zazen continue for three hours.

The obvious purpose of the Zazen ritual is to revitalize and relive the enlightenment of the Buddha, which in Zen Buddhism is called *Satori*.° Satori is a state of mind in which the usual object-subject dichotomy of ordinary living is dissolved abruptly, and the "enlightened one" intuits directly that all things are Buddha-reality. All things are harmoniously one. This "way of being" is not learned in the usual sense of learning, that is, thought out. Indeed, thought-out learning (thinking) is the antithesis of Satori; it is its nemesis. One achieves enlightenment (bodhi) as Gautama himself achieved it: sitting quietly, doing nothing, in a most unordinary and mind-shattering fashion.

Our concern here is not to explore the nature of Zen (for such an exploration the student is advised to read Alan Watts's° *The Way of Zen* or his *Spirit of Zen* and especially D. T. Suzuki's° *Studies in Zen*); our aim is simply to illustrate a form of ritual-myth, which, following the primordial experience of the founder of Buddhism, is quiet, unostentatious, and non-Western.

TARGETS OF RITUAL

Rituals are performed for a variety of reasons—to celebrate the changing of the seasons, to effect a miraculous change in the world, to accomplish a spiritual change in a person, to establish a relationship of communion between the worshipper and the divine, to make the land fertile, to make the rains come, and so on. The various types of ritual can be, for convenience, classified functionally as (1) metatechnological, (2) sacramental, or (3) experiential.

Metatechnological Function   In both ancient and modern times, ritual has been used to introduce supernatural or extranatural power into natural processes. In other words, it has functioned to produce magic and miracles. We have observed this sort of thing in the religious practices of the Trobriand Islanders. Another example is the Sun Dance of the Indians of the North American plains. This dance was performed to assure the return of the buffalo for the fall hunt, and to protect the tribe from its enemies. The ritual involved fastings, self-torture, sun gazing, dancing, singing, and praying, with the entire tribe taking part in the service. Its purpose was to bring supernatural force to the assistance of the Indians in situations that were critical to their life-style and to some degree precarious. We have observed, also, that with the advance of modern scientific technology in agriculture and medicine, this type of ritual has become less and less performed in modern cultures. It is still performed in primitive cultures and in other places where modern technology is in short supply. Also, there are vestiges of it in technologically advanced cultures. There are faith healers in America, and numerous people who act on the belief that "prayer changes things." To the degree that people engage in rituals intended to infuse divine power into natural process, ritual with a metatechnological function operates.

Sacramental Function   As the metatechnological function of ritual aims to bring power into the natural environment, the sacramental function aims to bring divine power into the human soul. In this sort of ritual the believer receives divine "grace," which is purity, perhaps, or integrity or merit, and usually—and most important of all—life after death. The worshipper gets what God has: eternal life. We have noted an early form of this kind of ritual in the Egyptian cult of Osiris. The Egyptian worshipper ate the sacred body and drank the sacred blood and performed other reverent acts in order to become Osiris and so enter the life of the Blessed Immortals. This kind of ritual was also very common in the Greek mystery religions, for example, in the Eleusinian, Dionysian, and Orphic cults. In such cults the initiate underwent a preparatory purification, was introduced to the mystic secret, beheld sacred objects, and observed an enactment of the divine story performed as a ritual drama. The worshipper was then received into full cultic membership and privileged to become like the God; that is, immortal. This great power came to the initiate in many cults by drinking a sacred wine (the blood of the God) or eating the flesh of a divine animal (the body of the God), or doing both. In these ritual acts there occurred an infusion of divine power. The participant became like the God. Christianity, when it arose in the Gentile world, was greatly impressed by this notion of sacramental worship. In his letter to the Church of Rome, Paul presented a dramatic account of how the inner life of the Christian was transformed by the ritual of baptism.

> Through baptism we have been buried with [Christ] in death, so that just as he was raised from the dead through the Father's glory, we too may live a new life . . . you must think yourself as dead to sin but alive to God, through union with Christ Jesus (Roman 6:4, 11)[20]

This type of ritual became a major form of Christian religious activity and remains so in the Catholic Church. The Catholic Church is basically a treasury of seven sacraments through which divine power is brought into inner lives of people and through which they obtain a power like that of Christ—to live again after death.

Experiential Function   Often the aim of ritual is to vivify the awareness of the presence of God. The worshipper seeks to experience God as if they were face to face. In an extreme form this sort of ritual effects an overwhelming sense of oneness with God. In this dimension it is usually called mysticism. More often experiential ritual seems to establish not a sense of identity of God and the worshipper, but a sense of community. In Sufi° dancing, for example, Allah is believed to be present. The dance is an activity of God. Also, according to the preamble of the Constitution on the Sacred Liturgy, promulgated by the Second Vatican Council in 1965, Christ "is present in the sacrifice of the Mass, not only in the person of His ministers" but also in the elements of the Eucharist—in the bread and wine. Ritual as expressing the community of God and mankind has always been a central dynamic of Judaism. Quite as characteristic as their ethical-monotheism has been the Jews' awareness of God in their lives—speaking to them out of a burning bush, from the smoke of Mount Sinai, in the voices of the Prophets, and the ceremonies of the Temple, and the prayers of the synagogue, and the lighting of the Sabbath candles. To know that God is with them, and that God has a burden and a mission for them, is to summarize three thousand years of Jewish life and worship.

The targets aimed at in experiential ritual are to feel the intimate presence of God in the life of the "true believer" and to have a sense of personal conversion, of forgiveness, and of renewal because of this experience.

SUMMARY COMMENT

Theology and ritual (rationalizing and dramatizing a mythos) are two phenomenal features of religion. Indeed, these aspects of religion are sufficient for a full-blown religion. To know the God (or Gods) and to demonstrate that knowledge with thoughtful attention and with acts of reverence, propitiation, and even adoration are sufficient for religion. The supernatural must be known, and the supernatural must be properly respected with worshipful attitudes and ceremonial dramas. Theology and ritual, especially in primitive religions, are the essential means of coming into right relation with the divine

NOTES

[1] Morris Adler, *Likrat Shabbat,* comp. and tran. Rabbi Sidney Greenberg (Bridgeport, Conn.: Prayer Books Press, 1975), p. 85.

[2] The terms "rite" and "ritual" are closely related and often interchanged in usage. Thus we hear of the rite of matrimony and the ritual of matrimony. More technically a rite is the prescribed form for a ceremony, and a ritual is a collection or book of rites; for example, the ritual of Holy Week in the Christian tradition is composed of the several rites (ceremonies) performed during that week—the rites for Palm Sunday, Holy Thursday, Good Friday, and Easter.

[3] The word "myth" comes from Greek *mythos* and means tale or story.

[4] Mircea Eliadé, *Myth and Reality,* tran. W. R. Trask (New York: Harper & Row, 1963), pp. 5−6.

[5] The New English Bible.

[6] Lord Ragland, "Myth and Ritual," *Myth: A Symposium,* ed. T. A. Sebeok (Bloomington, Ind.: Indiana University Press, 1965), p. 122.

[7] Paul Tillich, *Systematic Theology,* 3 vols. (Chicago: University of Chicago Press, 1951), vol. 1, p. 239.

[8] Ibid., p. 123.

[9] Annamarie de Waal Malefijt, *Religion and Culture* (New York: Macmillan, 1968), p. 186.

[10] E. O. James, *Myth and Ritual in the Ancient Near East* (New York: Barnes and Noble, 1958), pp. 18−19.

[11] Bronislaw Malinowski, *Magic, Science, and Religion* (New York: Free Press, 1948), p. 93.

[12] See Joseph Campbell, *The Masks of God: Occidental Mythology* (New York: Viking, 1964), pp. 518−523.

[13] Ruben F. Mettler, "The Cargo Cult Mentality in America." Quoted from the September 22, 1980 issue of *Business Week,* by special permission. Copyright © McGraw-Hill, New York, N.Y., 1980. All rights reserved.

[14] For more on this question, see Robert Bellah, "Civil Religion in America," with commentaries by D. W. Bragan, Lee Pfeffer, John Witney, and Phillip Hammond, in *The Religious Situation,* ed., Donald R. Cutler (Boston: Beacon Press, 1968), pp. 331−393. Also in *Daedalus,* vol. 96, no. 1 (1967) and John F. Wilson, *Public Religion in American Culture* (Philadelphia: Temple University Press, 1979).

[15] Peter L. Berger, *Facing Up to Modernity* (New York: Basic Books, 1977), p. 160.

[16] A. W. Howitt, *The Native Tribes of South-East Australia* (New York: Macmillan, 1904), p. 650. See also J. B. Noss, *Man's Religion,* 3rd ed. (New York: Macmillan, 1963), p. 38.

[17] Roger Schmidt, *Exploring Religion* (Belmont, Calif.: Wadsworth Press, 1980), p. 162.

[18] For a beautifully handled description and statement on Christian Rituals see Alan Watts's° *Myth and Ritual in Christianity,* 3rd ed. (Boston: Beacon Press, 1970).

[19] From a Japanese Zen-Buddhist poem.

[20] *The Complete Bible, An American Translation,* tran. J. M. Powis Smith, Old Testament, tran. Edgar J. Goodspeed, New Testament (Chicago: University of Chicago Press, 1939).

Chapter 13

MORALITY

"Ye have heard that it was said by them of old
time, Thou shalt not kill; and whoever shall
kill shall be in danger of the judgment."

Jesus[1]

"If God does not exist, then anything is permitted."

Fyodor Dostoevsky°

In Fyodor Dostoevsky's *Brothers Karamazov*, brother Ivan declares: "If
God does not exist, then anything is permitted." Many people mimic this
notion: "If there is no God, why should a person be good? If there is no threat
of Hell, what would stop us from all sorts of evil? Without God, mankind is
doomed to utter moral collapse." But this is a pseudo-danger. Everything is
not permitted not because religions do not permit it, but because society does
not permit it. The moral dimension of human existence is not basically
religious. It is basically social. Despite what the German philosopher Immanuel Kant° said to the contrary (which we shall examine subsequently)
religion and morality are not synonymous realities. Whether or not Émile
Durkheim° was correct in identifying society as the origin of religion, he was
certainly right in his contention that it is from society that religious moral
codes originate.* "Thou shalt not have other Gods before me" may have been
"invented" by the Hebrew's God Yahweh, but "thou shalt not kill" came
long before the Mount Sinai Ten Commandments. Unless the Hebrews had
imposed the rule prohibiting indiscriminate killing (and the Egyptians also)
long before Moses delivered the divine message there would not have been a
"Hebrew nation" to deliver it to.

The term "religious technique," as we are using it, means a way of doing
religion. Theology, as we observed, is one of the things done when people do
religion. It is a technique. Also, ritual is one of the things done by people when
they do religion. It is another technique. Morality, we are saying, is a third
technique employed in religion. Keeping the moral rules laid down in any
given religion is another way of performing to achieve religion, and benefit

*See pages 40–43.

from the values available in religion. One of the things demanded by moral religions is that the persons involved live according to certain moral rules and principles. Religious morality is one of the ways used to please the God, or live in harmony with the God, and thereby come to enjoy the benefits promised by the religion. A moral religion is one in which, either directly or indirectly, the God is concerned with moral relations among people. It is a religion in which the Divine Being "cares" about how Smith treats Jones, and with how Jones and Smith behave in the community, and with how the community relates to both of them.

Although morality can be a tremendously important technique in religion, it is not a necessary technique. As Rem Edwards puts it, "If we 'look and see' what is actually there in the religions of man, we will find that in some there is no morality at all. . . ."[2] There are religions that do not employ morality as a technique. Such religions are not immoral religions; they are amoral religions.* An amoral religion is any religion in which morality is not a specific technique in doing the religion. *Any religion that does not have a specific set or system of moral demands as a technique for effecting religious values can be called an amoral religion. In such religions the Gods care only that they be acknowledged and properly respected.* Although such religions do not present a system of moral teachings, they are not without moral influence. They may affect the moral standards of the community, but will do so indirectly.

THE MORAL INFLUENCE OF AMORAL RELIGIONS

Amoral religions do not have codes of ethics to impose on the believing community, the community of faith, yet they may still effect moral behavior indirectly through the moral influence of the shamans. In many primitive (primordial type) religions the shaman is not only a person of primary importance in metatechnological affairs, but has a major role in maintaining social order in the community. He often operates not only as a religious leader, but also as the tribe's principle lawyer and judge, using his authority as shaman to solve social and moral problems. I. M. Lewis,° in his *Ecstatic Religion,* gives several illustrations of this. One is from the Akawaio Caribs of Guiana in northern South America. The Akawaio Caribs believe that bad things happen to the tribe when someone violates a taboo and displeases the supernatural spirits. When the spirits begin to cause trouble (for example, when an epidemic occurs or the food supply is threatened), the shaman must first diagnose the cause. This is done by holding a public seance. Transporting himself into a trance state, the shaman lets the spirits take over his personality. Through him they become investigators searching for the culprit who by

---

*The people whose religions are amoral are not themselves amoral, or immoral, but are people who get their morality from a different source—from the social structure in which they live.

breaking the taboo has brought trouble into the community. The spirits ask searching questions, and honest answers are demanded. And these questions and answers are all on the public record. Everybody is there listening. Also the people at the seance can participate by asking their own questions. In this way, smoldering quarrels and enmities are ventilated, social festers are lanced and drained, gossip and scandal are confirmed or denied, actions explained and justified, accusations openly considered. Sometimes the spirits, using the shaman's voice, deliver sermons "on the importance of correct conduct, denouncing moral failings, condemning transgressions, and generally reducing their victims to acquiescent contrition by a skillful combination of suggestive probes, satire, and sarcasm. . . ."[3]

The religious seance thus becomes a procedure for bringing into the open all sorts of hidden social and moral problems. Once the problems are exposed, the spirits proceed to pronounce judgment, through the mouth of the shaman. If the seance is a good one, their judgments are the consensus of the community. Thus a religion that embraces spirits who have no real interest in human morality—a religion that is amoral—is effecting a strong influence on the tribe's harmony, solidarity, and ethics.

PRIMITIVE MORAL RELIGIONS

Not all primitive religions are amoral. Some make specific moral demands, have ethics as part of the religious system. This characteristic may have been acquired through contact with another more advanced religion, or it may be indigenous.

External Source   Sometimes a primitive religion acquires a moral dimension through its contact with a religion of a more advanced culture. The outsiders come and the primitives' life-style is assaulted by either propaganda or temptation.

The Giriama tribe of Kenya in eastern Africa illustrates the process of moving from amoral religion to moral religion under the impact of social change and external religious influence. In the 1920s the Giriama began to change their former marginal farming culture into a serious cash-crop culture. With this change they began to trade extensively with the Muslim Swahili and Arabs of the coast. As this occurred, a lively interest in Islamic ways developed among the Giriama. However, most of the Giriamas did not immediately convert to Islam; rather, they came to embrace Islamic beliefs and moral demands in a circuitous fashion. Many of the Giriama began to be plagued, at least so they believed, by Muslim demons. Spirit possessions occurred that could be exorcised only by adopting Islamic methods. The plaguing spirits "appeared in the guise of malign peripheral demons with no moral relevance,"[4] but to get rid of them the Giriama had to become followers of Islam with its many moral demands. Interestingly, these Muslim converts became identified as "therapeutic Muslims." They were, for therapeutic reasons, both primitive and Muslim at the same time. Being Muslims, therapeutic or otherwise, laid heavy moral demands upon them and infused their religion with morality.

Indigenous Moral Religions   Many primitives have acquired their moral religions from someone else, but some have not. Moral religion, as all religion, reaches back to origins in primitivism. Moral religions arose naturally in those primitive societies that contained not only spirit worship but also ancestor worship.

A shaman may be master not only of spirits (supernatural beings of nonhuman origin) but also of souls (supernatural beings of human origins—ancestors). Often there are actually two religious cults in the same primitive society: the cult of spirits with its shamanistic medicine and the cult of ancestors with its shaman medium. Also, often, the same shaman functions in both cults. The spirit cult is primarily concerned with problems arising from nonmoral causes: a broken taboo, black magic performed by an enemy witch doctor, a foreign spirit invasion. The ancestor cult is concerned with moral delinquencies: incestuous relationships, adultery, homicide.

The Kaffa people of southwest Ethiopia, although they are mostly nominal Christians in the Church of Ethiopia, hold fast to an old, indigenous ancestor cult that operates to preserve and enforce the moral demands of their old-time religion. Each patrilineal clan of the Kaffas is led by a shaman (called Alamo) who acts as a medium for the souls of his patrilineal ancestors. "In this he functions as a diviner, diagnosing the cause of sickness and misfortune within his group in terms of ancestral wrath incurred by its members when they sin."[5] The ancestors are concerned with maintaining the solidarity and cohesion of the clans and tribe. Each Friday the Kaffas consult with the shaman, asking him questions on matters of importance to them. The next day they return to the shaman who, having consulted with the ancestors, answers some or all of the questions asked. Also, when needed, the ancestors are consulted to diagnose and prescribe cures for illnesses and other kinds of misfortune. If the ancestors inform the shaman that the cause of distress is to be attributed to moral misconduct or neglect on the part of one or more of the members of the clan, the shaman, in the name of the ancestors, demands that the guilty make appropriate propitiating sacrifices to the offended ancestors.

Kaffa ancestors demand moral rectitude. They were doing so long before the Kaffas became, as well, members of the Ethiopian Christian church. Their moral religion was an indigenous religion. They did not acquire it from someone else.

In some religions the angry ancestors themselves assail the offending humans and punish them with sickness and misfortune and tragedy. In other religions, however, it is not the ancestors who punish but, rather, foreign demons and devils. In this situation, when people sin by breaking the moral rules, the ancestors, who normally protect the family and tribe, withdraw their protection and the wayward ones are left at the mercy of foreign malevolents. This is the way it is with the Korekore Shona people and the Zezura Shona people of southern Zimbabwe (formerly Rhodesia).

Withdrawal of supernatural protection was also a "primitive Hebrew" notion. In the Book of Judges (2:11–15) we are told that when the ancient Israelites forsook their father's God and followed the Gods of other people, the anger of Yahweh was kindled against them and *he delivered them into the hands of their enemies.* As we can see, with the primitive Hebrews a different instrument of punishment was used: not demons and devils, but human despoilers and enemies. Also, and more important, we can see that it was a different punisher: not an ancestor, but a spirit—*the* spirit: God Yahweh.

At this point, we begin to deal with a different type of moral religion; namely, a religion whose God makes the moral demands and a religion that uses morality as a major technique. In such religions, one must employ not only theology and ritual to fulfill the religious requirements, but must also live by a moral code. This moral code has been revealed or discerned to be a demand made either directly or inferentially not by ancestors, but by the dominant spiritual reality behind all life and society: by the High God. Here morality is seen as a necessary technique, if not *the* necessary technique, to "please the God" and accomplish the values of religion, that is, to be saved.

THE TECHNIQUE OF MORALITY

Along with the right theology and correct ritual, morality became, in the advanced religions, a third technique for pleasing the Gods and achieving the values of religion.

Probably the ancient Egyptians were the first people to identify moral law with divine demand. This identity of morality as a technique in religion was well advanced in the religion of Osiris, by at least 2500 B.C. For a person to enter the world of the immortals (Khenti-Amenti) he had to be (besides ritualistically initiated) clean of hand and pure of heart. According to the Egyptian *Book of the Dead* a human soul had to face both god Osiris and the Gods of the forty-two Egyptian nomes. Each of these Gods was an avenger of a particular sin or crime. The soul had to make a negative confession, declaring what it had not done, in order to avoid their condemnation. The following, according to the *Book of the Dead*,[6] is part of the confession that had to be made.

> Hail to thee, great God, lord of Truth. . . . Behold, I come to thee, I bring to thee righteousness. I knew no wrong. I did no evil thing. . . . I did not do that which the God abominates. . . . I allowed no one to hunger. I caused no one to weep. I did

not murder. I did not diminish food in the temples. . . . I did not take away the food-offerings of the dead. . . . I did not commit adultery. . . . I did not diminish the grain measure. . . . I did not lead the weight of the balances. I did not deflect the index of the scales. I did not take milk from the mouth of the child. I did not drive away the cattle from their pasturage. . . . I did not dam the running water [and thus divert from others the waters of the irrigation canals at the time of the inundation]. . . . I did not interfere with the God in his payments. I am purified four times. I am pure.[7]

Clearly the Egyptians came to recognize that the techniques of religion were not limited to knowing the Gods and reverently acknowledging them; the techniques also included keeping the moral laws of the Gods.

Apparently the same understanding of religion and morality was accomplished in ancient Babylon, for we find that in the seventeenth century B.C., the great God Shamash presented King Hammurabi with a code of laws, as God Yahweh later did to Moses. Apparently in both Egypt and Mesopotamia morality became a major dimension in religious life. But it was in that little turbulent country between the great nations north and south that the connection between morality and religion was most significantly made for the subsequent religions of the Western world. We should remember, however, that Abraham had intimate connections in Mesopotamia, and Moses in Egypt.

The Hebrews came to see God as a moral being who was pleased when people worshipped him by emulating his morality. They conceived of the moral law as an essential form of religious behavior. God was pleased or displeased by the way people related to one another. Already by the year 1000 B.C. the moral dimension was important enough in Hebrew life to be a mandate even for kings. For example, in 2 Samuel, chapters 11 and 12, there is an account of Yahweh's displeasure with King David's disregard for the rights of one of his subjects. We read that King David seduced the wife of one of his soldiers, Uriah the Hittite, while Uriah was away fighting in one of David's wars. When the wife, Bathsheba, was found to be pregnant, David called Uriah home from the battlefront hoping the unsuspecting husband would take pleasure with his wife and later think the child was his. But Uriah refused to enjoy the pleasantries of home life while his comrades bore the discomforts of war. He refused to enter his own house. David, being thus frustrated in his initial chicanery, sent Uriah back to the front carrying sealed orders to General Joab. The orders instructed Joab to expose Uriah in battle that he might be killed. The deed was done, and David took Bathsheba into his palace as his wife and she bore him a son. But "the Lord sent Nathan to David" to condemn him and to predict the death of the child as a punishment for David's immoral behavior. And, indeed, the child did die shortly thereafter because, as the author of 2 Samuel put it, "the thing which David had done displeased the Lord." One might question whether David's adultery and complicity in Uriah's murder were more reprehensible than God's infanticide, but this is not the point. The point is that as early as 1000 B.C. Yahweh was being conceived as a God who was concerned with people's moral behavior. God *did* care how ''Jones'' treated ''Smith'' (David treated Uriah). The degrees of refinement in that caring were now just a matter of historical development. The Hebrews had come to believe that God had laid upon them a moral law as well as a ceremonial law. They wrote the laws of God into their Bible and that Bible became the Old Testament scripture of the Christian world.

The Hebrews continued their idea of the religious importance of right knowledge and correct ceremony, but they increasingly laid special emphasis on ethical living until, in the words of the Prophet Micah, we hear pronounced (as an ideal at least) the complete domination of morality as the technique for pleasing God.

> With what shall I come before the Lord and bow myself before God on high?
> Shall I come before him with burnt offerings, with calves a year old?
> Will the Lord be pleased with thousands of rams, with ten thousands of rivers of oil?
> Shall I give my first-born for my transgressions, the fruit of my body for the sin of my soul?
> He has shown you, O man, what is good; and what does the Lord require of you *but to do justice, and to love kindness, and to walk humbly with your God.   Micah 6:6−8 RSV (author's italics)*

Along with their Hebrew precursors, Christians asserted that God could be offended not only by wrong belief and incorrect worship but also by violating people in any way abhorrent to the divine morality. Along with knowledge and ceremony, morality became a means of achieving the high morale possessed by one who lived securely in God.

THE MORAL DIMENSION

It is the general contention of religious systems of the consummate type[8] that there is not only a moral order in the social world but a moral order in the structure of the universe itself. It is generally contended that human behavior is so geared to life in its largest dimensions that any violation of human beings has not only individual and social implications but metaphysical implications as well. As Winfred Garrison put it, there is a basic structure of morality in human life ''which is beyond the power of society to make or modify,'' and this structure is

> first, that there shall *be* codes of conduct, backed by conscience and a sense of ''oughtness,'' so that human community shall not exist in a state of moral chaos or nihilism; second, that these codes, whether derived from custom, enactment, or revelation, shall implement the fundamental truth that man himself has unique value and shall demand behavior consistent with man's essential worth and dignity. These requirements are fulfilled by the second terms of Jesus' summary of the commandments: ''thou shalt love thy neighbor as thyself.''[9]

A RULE OF THUMB

Most of the consummate religions not only assert the claim of universal moral order, but they all have, somewhere in their teachings, a rule of thumb for keeping the universal moral order. This rule-of-thumb formula in Christianity is called The Golden Rule: "All things whatsoever ye would that men should do to you, do ye even so to them." Other world religions have substantially the same rule:

> *In Hinduism:* "Do not to others, which if done to thee would cause thee pain."
> *In Buddhism:* "In five ways should a clansman minister to his friends and familiars—by generosity, courtesy, and benevolence, by treating them as he treats himself, and by being as good as his word."
> *In Judaism:* "What is hurtful to yourself, do not do to your fellow man."
> *In Taoism:* "Regard your neighbor's gain as your own gain and regard your neighbor's loss as your own loss."
> *In Confucianism:* "Do not unto others what you would not have them do to you."
> *In Sikhism:* "As you deemest thyself so deem others."
> *In Jainism:* "In happiness and suffering, in joy and grief, we should regard all creatures as we regard our own self."
> *In Zoroastrianism:* "That nature only is good when it shall not do unto another whatever is not good for its own self."

IMMANUEL KANT'S POSITION

Immanuel Kant went so far as to say that religion is nothing other than "recognizing our duties as divine commands." This epistemologically tough philosopher found his evidence for religion, God, human freedom, and life after death from the fact that humans as humans have moral natures. Roughly Kant argued so: People possess moral natures, which thrust upon them a sense of obligation. They are obliged by their own consciences to seek holiness, that is, perfect obedience to the highest good, to the highest virtue. In responding to this inborn "categorical imperative," people are necessarily driven to certain reasonable inferences about the nature of the world in which they live. Their consciences demand that they pursue the highest virtue. Each person is to pursue holiness. But no human can hope to achieve perfect holiness, because (1) each person is imperfect. Human beings, despite the moral center of their lives, are sensual and rebellious. (2) People live in a world that is obviously not under the control of moral principles. In short, each person is a sinner and nature or history is unjust or at least amoral. Humans, creatures possessing a sense of justice, live in a world that is not always just. If their moral life under these circumstances is not to be taken as a farce, they must postulate the existence of: (a) their own free moral will, (b) a life after death where the injustices of this life can be balanced, (c) a supreme being of perfect Good Will to whose will humans respond when they strive to fulfill their duty to the moral law. Freedom, life after death, and God cannot be "known" by logical structures, but through practical reason each can claim to be an ingredient of moral faith. Kant makes "practical reason" (moral consciousness) superior to "pure reason" (scientific and philosophical intelligence) in matters of religion. God, the Supreme Being of Good Will, is a necessary postulate of mankind's innate moral nature, and religion is the "recognition of duties as divine commands."

JAMES'S PRAGMATIC ARGUMENT

The American philospher William James,° in his essay "The Moral Philosopher and the Moral Life,"[10] makes an interesting practical plea for the existence of a transcendent moral order, that is, for a self-conscious God who is morally demanding. James's argument is that religion includes the dimension of morality primarily for the promotion of morale. First, James points out that wherever there is a conscious being there is also a moral order. "The moment one sentient being . . . is made a part of the universe, there is a chance for goods and evils really to exist. Moral relations now have their *status* in that being's consciousness. So far as he feels anything to be good, he *makes* it good. It *is* good for him."[11] In a world where there are a vast number of sentient beings, representing an even vaster number of desires, the ethical philosopher must try to discover what hierarchy of desires and obligations ought to take precedence and have supreme weight in the ordering of individual and social relations. To define the supreme good, the ethical philosopher must trace the "ought" to its source in some existing consciousness, for there can be no morality that does not ground itself in some self-conscious mind. To be sure, one may conclude that morality takes its foothold in the universe if only through human life, for "whether a God exists, or whether no God exists . . . we form at any rate an ethical republic here below."[12] But if we do not reject the ordinary person's belief that there is a moral order independent of people, we must place this independent moral order also in a *thinking mind*. If there is a transcendent, extrahuman moral order, then there is a sentient God in whose mind that moral order is grounded, for the seat of "oughtness" simply cannot exist in a vacuum.

Second, the question is: Is there such an order? A moral order independent of people? And James proposes that there had better be, or, at least it is better if we believe there is. To avoid social chaos and personal disorientation, people impose upon themselves rules for living—mores, legal and ethical codes, general moral attitudes. Now, there are people who fall in line with the rules for living simply to avoid the discomfort of social disapproval. But there are other people differently oriented who embrace ethical discipline, not so much for their own benefit as for the benefit of a "hoped for world" not yet born. They dream wild dreams like the notion that humans are born with certain unalienable rights, that people will one day actually beat their swords into plowshares, that pain and hunger and crime and cruelty and violence will some day be conquered; and for such dreams they are willing to sweat and bleed and even die. James divided these two kinds of people into what he called the "easy-going-mood" and the "strenuous mood." He further held that the capacity for the strenuous mood may lie in all people, but it is not always easy to arouse. It "needs the wilder passions to arouse it, the big fears, loves and indignations; or else the deeply penetrating appeal to some one of the higher fidelities, like justice, truth, or freedom."[13] Especially it needs belief in God. To be sure, in a merely human world life is lived in an "ethical symphony," but, as James states, "it is played out in a couple of poor octaves."[14] The strenuous mood of high ethical living is not really called out simply for the needs of everyday, nine-to-five; or for the sake of posterity, for those people who will be alive 100 or 200 years from now. All this is too finite. It lacks the excitement of the infinite demand that is aroused when people believe they live and act not merely for their own sake, or for the sake of future generations, but in and for the moral expectations of an infinite demander. When convinced that there is a God calling on individuals to live in high moral commitment, people get inspired by life as in no other way. As James put it, "every sort of energy and endurance, of courage and capacity for handling life's ills, is set free in those who have religious faith."[15]

James held that people need to believe in a God who expects them to live morally, even heroically. Indeed, James proposed (as we observed earlier) that even if no such God existed, the need is so great that we "would postulate one on a pretext for living hard, and getting out of the game of existence its keenest possibilities of zest"[16]—as, perhaps, we have.

James concludes his essay with some advice to moral philosophers: "In the interest of our ideal of systematically unified moral truth, therefore, we would-be philosophers, must postulate a divine thinker, and pray for the victory of the religious cause."[17]

In this kind of thinking, William James (against the Kantian position) supports the contention that morale and not morals is the central function of religion. Using morality, motivated by a strenuous belief in God's moral will, religion affirms and demonstrates that in religious people there is a center of gravity that balances the inward life against the outward winds of adversity enabling them to take the frustrations of life with poise, the comedies of life with good grace, and the challenges of life with an energy that bespeaks not of finitude but of infinity.

TYPES OF MORAL DECISIONS

Generally moral decisions are made in three alternative ways—by legal decision, or by antinomian decision, or by situational decision. These three ways are stated informatively and briefly in the opening chapter of Joseph Fletcher's° 1966 publication *Situation Ethics, the New Morality*.[18]

Legalism   In legalistic ethics moral decisions are made according to moral laws and the rules and regulations derived from those laws. For example, Jews, especially those of ancient times and of modern orthodoxy, live by the Torah (law) and its "correct" interpretation—the Talmud. After Jesus' day, and after Paul's ministry, legalism asserted itself and became the dominant ethical way of Christianity. Islam, also, is a legalistic system.

If God-Yahweh gave his commandments and statutes and ordinances to Moses and commanded him to teach them to his people, and God-Allah did the same for Muhammad, and other Gods for other people, what else can one do but live by them. If this is a moral, God-created universe, living by the divine morality can be the only way. If the sixth Commandment says, "Thou shalt not kill," and the seventh says, "Thou shalt not commit adultery," then by moral law, on principle, you shall neither kill nor commit adultery. Not kill anything? Anybody? Not even in self-defense? Not even in war? Well . . . perhaps . . . sometimes. Which means that the legalism "thou shalt not kill" must be considered "legalistically" according to the exact case involved. Often the moral principle must be interpreted according to contextual circumstances, which is called casuistry (from the Latin *casus*, "choice" or "case"). For killing there are legalistic exceptions to the rule, for adultery (in legalism) apparently no exceptions.

The laws and rules of legalistic ethics are derived from revelation, as in the cases of Moses and Muhammad; from oral tradition, as in primitive cultures; from rational interpretation of nature or natural law, and of canon law, as in Roman Catholicism; and from the Bible, as in Protestantisms.

Referring to this system Fletcher, a situational ethicist, quotes Cardinal Newman as saying: "The Church holds that it were better for the sun and moon to drop from heaven, for the earth to fail, and for all the many millions who are upon it to die of starvation in extremest agony . . . than that one soul, I will not say should be lost, but should commit one single venial sin."[19]

A legalistic system does give stability and unity to a social system, which is what, after all, ethics is basically all about—to ensure social order rather than anarchy. But at times the moral demand implies not only commands and prohibitions, but also punishments, some of which can be cruel and unusual. According to a Hebrew holy law one is not to "suffer a witch to live" (Exodus 22:18). According to Muslim holy law the hand of the thief is to be cut off. To be sure, the strict legalist may be truly sorry that the moral law requires at times such harsh punishment, but is it not essential that right be done, the laws of God be kept, the moral fabric of society be upheld, even if the heavens fall? To this question there are, Fletcher states, two types of ethicists who say, "no!"—the antinomians and the situationalists.

Antinomianism   The antinomians (*anti*, "against," *nomos*, "law") enter the moral decision-making situation with no moral principles or roles whatsoever. They do not have any moral principles, divine or otherwise, with which to judge a moral-decision situation. They have only the situation. An ancient example of antinomianism can be discerned in early Christian communities. Apparently some people began to believe that the coming of the Holy Spirit had freed them not only from the Jewish law, but from the usual moral restraints imposed on fleshly appetites. Their spirits were free. Morally it no longer mattered what their bodies did.*

A variation of this antinomianism is discernible in Paul's correspondence with the church at Corinth. Some of those people, having rid themselves of the Torah law of the Jews, insisted that there was now no law commanding them. Their moral choices rested solely on spiritual guidance in each moral-demanding situation. They considered themselves spirit-guided (*pneumatikoi*). One does not need preestablished principles and laws if moral choices are guided by God's spirit. Some persons (both ancient and modern) believe that there is a "moral faculty" or "moral intuition" that empowers persons to make proper moral choices, if they so desire.

Certain modern existentialist philosophers are antinomian not by choice, but by, they believe, necessity. They hold that there is no moral order made up in advance. There is no divine morality, and, indeed, no ultimate meaning to human life. We live in a coldly indifferent universe, they say. Whatever morality there is, is what humans invent, and that is primarily self-centered and selfish. Jean-Paul Sartre saw the real situation of human existence as being utterly incoherent. His novel *Nausea* makes distressingly clear the true situation as he saw it, the situation of anxiety inherent in a world where there is no real meaning. To pretend that there is meaning and order and purpose in life is, according to Sartre, to live in "bad faith," to live in an illusion of wishful thinking. In every moment of moral choice, he writes, "we have no excuses behind us and no justification before us."[20] He emphatically rejected the notion of general principles for human guidance and, even more, the notion of universal moral laws.

Situation Ethics   Joseph Fletcher,° in the mid-1960s, became the unofficial spokesman for a movement of "modern ethics," which is, in fact, not especially modern.† The fundamental notion in situation ethics is that there is one commanding principle in ethics; namely, love, which is to be the final arbiter in every ethical situation. As Fletcher states it:

> Situation ethics goes part of the way with natural law, by accepting reason as the instrument of moral judgment, while rejecting the notion that the good is "given"

*This is a form of Gnosticism,° which is a philosophical theology that defines a radical dichotomy between flesh and spirit.
†Other supporters of modern, or contextual, or situation ethics are Emil Brunner, Karl Barth,° Rudolf Bultmann,° Reinhold Niebuhr,° Gordon Kaufman, Paul Tillich,° and John A. T. Robinson.

in the nature of things, objectively. It goes part of the way with Scriptural law [legalism] by accepting revelation as the source of the norm while rejecting all "revealed" norms or laws but the one command—to love God in the neighbor. The situationist follows a moral law or violates it according to love's need. . . . Only the commandment to love is categorically good.[21]

In situation ethics a person must examine the circumstances involved in the case of moral decision. Usually one can follow the established rules (the rules available through legalistic ethics or the socially acceptable rules of moral behavior), but these rules are always to be interpreted, and when necessary set aside, by the fundamental principle that one is "to love God in the neighbor." You may catch the thief, but an automatic hand chopping cannot be the immediate and inevitable, or probably ever, answer to dealing with the thief in a truly moral manner. Perhaps the proper course of moral action would be a loving concern for rehabilitation, or as Hajj had it—let him ride out of town on your donkey. It is hard to conceive how one could kill in a loving manner, but Dietrich Bonhoeffer, a modern Christian ethicist, was executed because of his attempt to commit murder: He plotted to kill Adolf Hitler. Every situation must be dealt with as a unique situation. Make your moral decision lovingly, but also make it in the total context of the immediate situation. It may be morally sound that one Hitler should die that a holocaust might stop.

And what of the giant, legalistic proscription on adultery, on the breaking of the marriage regulations so essential to human societies—primitive, ancient, modern, Eastern, Western, everywhere? The situationist declares that that too depends on *agapé*, the loving of God by loving the neighbor. As an argument for the sometime moral rightness of adultery or, probably, in this instance, fornication, Fletcher refers to N. Richard Nash's play *The Rainmaker*. In this play, as depicted on the stage and in the movie, there is a scene where:

> the morally outraged brother of a lonely, spinsterized girl threatens to shoot the sympathetic but not "serious" Rainmaker because he makes love to her in the barn at midnight. The Rainmaker's intention is to restore her sense of womanliness and her hopes for marriage and children. Her father, a wise old rancher, grabs the pistol away from his son, saying, "Noah, you're so full of what's right you can't see what's good." I nominate the Texas rancher as co-hero with the cab driver.[22]

The cab driver reference made by Fletcher goes like this: A man arrived in St. Louis during a presidential campaign. His cab driver, not beyond campaign battles, volunteered that he and his father and his grandfather were all straight-ticket Republicans. The visitor then said, "I take it then you will be voting for Senator So-and-So, the Republican candidate for senator." "No," said the driver, "there are times when a man has to push principles aside and do the right thing." That man, according to Fletcher, was a grass-roots, situationist hero.

Morals and Morale   The importance of moral discipline (religious ethics) cannot be gainsaid in religion. But morality is not a substitute for religion or the summation of religion. It is a technique in religion. Kant told us that religion is the recognition of our moral duties as divine commands; Matthew Arnold° once said that it is "morality tinged with emotion"; A. E. Haydon° said that it is the "shared quest of the good life." But they were all wrong. The function of religion is not to make people morally good, but to give them transcendence; to deal with their sense of finiteness; to give them hope, courage, and confidence as they face the human condition. Religion is *morale* centered. Ethical living may be the fruit of religion (as Paul and Calvin saw it), or a way to religion (as in Judaism and Catholicism), but it is not why people do religion. We expect "high religion" to express itself in high ethical standards. High religion produces high ethical values, just as some farms produce excellent hybrid corn. But it only confuses the facts to define religion as ethics and morality, as it would confuse the facts to define a farm as a place where hybrid corn is grown. Again, we may refer to the account of Jesus in Gethsemane. Surely he was just as moral when he went into the garden as when he came out of it, but the same cannot be said for his morale. He went in terrified; a man desperately in need of the hope, confidence, and courage that come from religion. He prayed not for moral perfection but for religious courage and, apparently, if we can trust the accounts, he got it.

NOTES

[1] Matthew 5:21, AV.

[2] Rem B. Edwards, *Reason and Religion* (New York: Harcourt Brace Jovanovich, 1972), p. 54.

[3] I. M. Lewis, *Ecstatic Religion* (Harmondsworth, England: Penguin, 1971), p. 161.

[4] Ibid., p. 130.

[5] Ibid., p. 144.

[6] cxxv, Theban Recension.

[7] J. H. Breasted, *Development of Religion and Thought in Ancient Egypt* (New York: Scribner's, 1912), pp. 299–300. From 18th Dynasty "Papyrus of Nu."

[8] See Chapter 8 for consummate religious systems.

[9] Winfred Garrison, *Protestant Manifesto* (Nashville, Tenn.: Abingdon, 1952), p. 67.

[10] William James, "The Moral Philosopher and the Moral Life," in *Essays in Pragmatism* (New York: Hafner Pub., 1951).

[11] Ibid., p. 70.

[12] Ibid., p. 75.

[13] Ibid., p. 85.

[14] Ibid., p. 85.

[15] Ibid., p. 86.

[16] Ibid., p. 86.

[17] Ibid., p. 86.

[18] Philadelphia: Westminster Press, 1966.

[19] J. H. Newman, *Certain Difficulties Felt By Anglicans in Catholic Teaching* (New York: Longmans, Green, 1918), p. 190; quoted in Joseph Fletcher, *Situation Ethics, the New Morality* (Philadelphia: Westminster Press, 1966), p. 20.

[20] Jean-Paul Sartre, *Existentialism*, tran. B. Frechtman (New York: Philosophical Library, 1947), p. 27.

[21] Fletcher, *Situation Ethics, The New Morality*, p. 26.

[22] Joseph Fletcher, *Situation Ethics*, pp. 13–14. See also N. Richard Nash, *The Rainmaker* (New York: Bantam Books, 1957), p. 99.

PART FOUR

Religion as Experience

. . . Black-winged Night
Into the bosom of Erebus [the son of
  Chaos] dark and deep
Laid a wind-born egg, and as the seasons
  rolled
Forth sprang Love, the longed-for, shining,
  with wings of gold.

Aristophanes°

IV   With all this (and especially in the conviction that there is a divine order basic to life) religion turns out to be for people not simply a method of dealing with religious problems (those horrendous, nonmanipulable circumstances of life), but is itself an experience of great satisfaction and immense personal worth. Religion is not only something people "do" and "use"; it is also something that happens to them. It is an experience—a highly treasured experience, and even, at times, an experience of sheer ecstasy. [See page 7.]

Chapter 14

RELIGION: EXOTERIC EXPERIENCE

Celebration is
Greeks dancing Epiphany
or sparrows at dawn.
W.C.T.

THE RELIGION POSIT

First we should observe an obvious thing. In the face of religious problems (horrendous, nonmanipulable problems) or intense *numinous* experiences, persons do not go out and invent theologies and rituals and moral codes. These techniques of religion are already provided by the religious heritages into which the individuals are born. With rare exceptions, the religions accepted by people are those they find already operating. The most that usually happens are some simple modifications by the child of "the family religion." Children internalize, privatize, individualize, the posit of religion they have inherited and learned in their parents' house and world. They may change some details (even become a Presbyterian instead of a Baptist), but seldom do they change any of the essential features. A person is born Muslim and usually stays that way, or Jewish and stays that way, or primitive and stays that way. The religion one espouses is usually an accident of birth. It comes from the parents by a kind of emotional and intellectual osmosis. One's need for religion is human, but the answers to that innate need begin with the postulates and practices of the religion into which one is born, and usually remain there.

The sociogenetic character of religion is especially discernible in primordial type religions. In these religions membership is "natural" rather than voluntary. One does not choose a religion, or join it. Indeed, there is no religion to join. There is only a religion to be born into. In an Indian tribe, for example, religion, as part and parcel of tribe and totem, is involved in every aspect of each Indian's existence—birth, social status, marriage, work, death. It is impossible to be born and reared in a primitive community without being, in every direction, immersed in religion.

RELIGION AS SHARED EXPERIENCE

The social character of religion is obvious also when religious rites are public and collective, when, for example, people go to church or synagogue for

249

religious services. This is especially obvious in those religious communities (systems) with strong communal rituals, such as the Roman Catholic and Greek Orthodox° churches. Even more than in theological belief, participation in community rituals can provide the cohesiveness that gives groups their distinctive characters and in which religious experience for individuals most vividly occurs. For example, in Judaism it is not so much the holding of theological beliefs, but of participation in the ritual and commitment to acceptable community behavior that marks a Jew as a faithful Jew. The fundamental question is not do you believe like a Jew, but do you act like one in your religious behavior; do you feel like one. Jews are incorporated into their faith primarily by religious practice (orthopraxis)° rather than by affirmation of beliefs (orthodoxy).° To be Jewish is less a private confession of faith than an observance of the traditional communal worship forms. The high celebration of Yom Kippur,° the Day of Atonement, for example, is not so much a private purging of sin as it is a corporate purging. Not Isaac but Israel prays for forgiveness. The prayers of Yom Kippur are "we" prayers, not "I" prayers.

> May it therefore be Your will, O Lord our God and God of our fathers, to forgive *us* for *our* sins, pardon *us* for *our* iniquities, and to grant *us* atonement for all *our* transgressions.[1] (author's italics)

In primitive societies, where kinship is the primary determinant of social relations, the divine reality, the holy, is often experienced as a social (family) relationship. The Oglala° Sioux, for example, address the Great Spirit as Grandfather, the earth as Mother, the sky as Father, and the six points of direction (north, south, east, west, earth, and sky) as Grandfathers.[2]

In Confucianism, where kinship is also the primary determinant of social relations, *Li* (propriety), which Confucius° declared "is the principle by which ancient kings embodied the laws of heaven and regulated the expressions of human nature," is vitally important in the religio-social relationships and experiences among human beings. These relationships and experiences are five in number: the relationship and experience between father and son, husband and wife, older brother and younger brother, elders and juniors, ruler and subject. In the *Book of Rites* (in Chinese *Li Chi°*) the Five Relationships are described as:

> Kindness in the father, filial piety in the son
> Gentility in the elder brother, humility and respect in the younger
> Righteous behavior in the husband, obedience in the wife
> Humane consideration in elders, deference in juniors
> Benevolence in rulers, loyalty in ministers and subjects*

If the ten attitudes expressed in the Five Relationships are kept in social life, Heaven will look favorably upon humankind. So claimed Confucius. Neither

---

*It is doubted that Confucius actually developed such a schematic treatment of the Five Relationships, but they logically flow from his teaching.

quarrels nor injustices will exist. There will be peace at home and abroad, as there is peace in Heaven.

PRIVATE DIMENSION OF A SHARED EXPERIENCE

We are saying, then, that religion is a private experience with a social-communal matrix. Earlier we argued (especially in Chapters 1 and 3) that religion arises from human frustration. It moves to overrule anxiety and meaninglessness. It structures life with sustaining morale. It culminates in commitments and aspirations and moral demands of the highest order. It discerns and depicts God. But we have also suggested along the way that anyone sensitive to deep religious experience would not want to settle for only this much, for it does not account for the private aspects of religion (for the sentiments, passions, love, spiritual knowledge, elation, ecstasy) that are to the believer, the worshipper, the mystic, the most precious and definitive characteristics of all. Even if we could solve technologically all of the problems of human finitude, there would still be devotees of religion, for there would still be those who had discovered that religion is not only something that people do, but something that happens to them. It is an experience, even an ecstasy. Concerning this, I. M. Lewis,° opens his book *Ecstatic Religion*, declaring emphatically: "Belief, ritual, and spiritual experience: these are the cornerstones of religion, and the greatest of them is the last."[3] Having looked at the first two cornerstones—belief/theology and myth/ritual—we shall now look at the last, without which religion would be no more than a business or game.

In trying to discern the dimension of experience in religion, we shall observe, first, several expressions of religious experience that are predominantly exoteric in character, that is, open to external observation and description: religion as sensuous, religion as sexual, religion as love, and religion as charity/agapé. Second, in the next chapter, we shall observe several religious experiences that are esoteric in character, that is, privately personal: religion as a noetic experience (the inner knowledge of conversion) and religion as an ecstasy (divine seizure, worship, and mysticism).

SENSUOUSNESS

That religion is accoutered with sensuousness is abundantly obvious. People's greatest (and sometimes not so great, but always sincere) artistic efforts have been directed to making religion a sensuously attractive experience. Magnificent buildings, exquisite colors, elaborate pageantry, superb dramatics, the best of music and dancing and poetry: indeed, the superior artistic accomplishments of mankind grace and enhance the sensuous enjoyment of religion. Even the more drab traditions of Christian pietism and Protestant evangelicalism have heightened sensuous enjoyment with lively hymns and vividly sensuous, even sensational, preaching.

I have a sharp memory of my own shocked discovery of the importance of the olfactory sense in my own religious life. Reared a Roman Catholic, I eventually left that church and became an evangelical Protestant, but for some reason I never "felt religious" in a Protestant service of worship. Yet I could simply enter a Catholic church and sense immediately something mysteriously religious. I became aware of this odd circumstance, and even wondered occasionally if the "Catholic God" were not depriving me because of my desertion of "Holy Mother the Church." And then one day as I entered a beautiful Catholic cathedral and felt that usual experience of religiousness I had the presence of mind to ask myself why. And immediately I knew why. It was the smell: the lingering odor of incense and burning candles. It smelled right! The thing wrong with a Methodist church was that it did not smell religious. Sensuousness is certainly part of the religious experience.

As we have already noted at length in Chapter 12, ritual and myth are artistic forms. Frederick Streng,° in his *Understanding Religious Man,* calls this liturgical art visual theology. This is the art that self-consciously attempts to express the content of a given religious tradition. It "includes especially the images of gods, saviors, and saints, and the architecture of holy places."[4] In this kind of art, the artist, like the prophet, tries to become a medium through which God, or infinite reality, is manifested to people. Through dramatic action, the action of God is exposed. For example, in religious dance, God's movements are shown.

> Dancing in a circle or in a long, serpentine line dramatized the divine actions of creation or the battle between the powers of life and the dark forces of nature. The movements and verbal expression in the archaic drama and dance were based on formal elements revealed not only in these art forms but also in the myth and other rituals. Here one could dance a prayer.[5]

Various religious traditions have different styles of artistic expression. In Christianity, for example, much of the art focuses on Jesus Christ, on his image, on his cross, on various stylized images that represent Christ—a lamb, a babe, a fish. In Hinduism, the foci of religious art are widely scattered. There are many images and forms "to depict the infinity of the divine."

> The "otherness" of God is expressed also through various suggestions of the "nonnatural": multiple arms or many eyes, or skin that is gold or dark blue. Perhaps the unique Hindu quality is best expressed in the image of the union of opposites in the combination of Gods and Goddesses (for example, Shiva and Shakti).[6]

Islamic art exemplifies another style of religious art. Here, following the biblical restrictions on divine images, the Muslim artist has developed the fantastic art of Arabic design. Beginning with a simple mosaic design, the design is repeated, until it begins to generate variations of the original design *ad infinitum*. God, who in Islamic thought is intricately involved in the lives and fates of people, emerges visually not as an anthropomorphic God but as a magnificent pattern, an infinite design.

Streng also takes note of the fact that among some religious thinkers (Paul Tillich,° Jacques Maritain,° Ananda K. Coomaraswamy, and D. T. Suzuki°) and in some religious traditions, art expresses religion not in directly religious subjects but in ordinary, everyday subjects.

> *Any* aesthetic performance, regardless of explicit content, arises from the pressure of life's experiences which are grounded in ultimate reality. It is this ultimate ground and spiritual essence in which the artist and observer participate when each is sensitive to beauty.[7]

A young professor of philosophy was once questioned by an irritated sophomore student to justify why he, the student, should be expected to read and struggle with something like Plato's° *Timaeus* or Kierkegaard's° *Unscientific Postscript*. The professor replied to this question with a question: Why have a bowl of flowers? One would expect that a philosophy professor would tell the student that both Plato and Kierkegaard had something worthwhile "to say" to him, but the professor chose to hint at a deeper answer. Perhaps, even in concrete experiences, it is possible to experience ultimate and profoundly religious things.

Plato and Kierkegaard may not be ordinary and concrete experiences for many people, but the drinking of tea surely is for anyone, and the drinking of tea can be, according to Japanese custom, both an art form and a religious experience. The noted Zen interpreter D. T. Suzuki illustrated this in his book *Zen Buddhism* in which he describes a tea ceremony that takes place in a tearoom in one of the temples attached to Daitokuji, the temple that is the headquarters for the tea ceremony.

The tearoom is itself no more than a straw-thatched hut, but it is a place where a person or a few friends can go to sit quietly to sip a cup of tea and put out of the mind for awhile the worldly cares that so often depress the spirit and make life a hassle instead of a joy. There is one white chrysanthemum in a flower vase, and a soothing fragrance emitting from an incense burner, and the sound of boiling water coming from a tea kettle suspended on a tripod frame over an open fire. Suzuki explains that the sound is really not so much that of water boiling as of steam escaping from the heavy iron kettle, "and is most appropriately likened by the connoisseur to a breeze that passes through a pine grove. It adds greatly to the serenity of the room, for a man here feels as if he were sitting alone in a mountain-hut where a white cloud and the pine music are the only consoling companions." In such a place, declares Suzuki, talking quietly with friends, or just relaxing silently, the mind can be wonderfully lifted above the perplexities of life. Suzuki then asks gently, "Is it not something, indeed, to find in this world . . . a corner . . . where one can rise above the limits of reality and even have a glimpse of eternity."[8]

Here is an art form that is simply doing something well and sensitively, which reveals and heals and saves, and which is, thereby, an expression of and an experience of religion sensuously operating in ordinary human life. Similarly a farmer plowed his fields in straight furrows not merely because that made planting and harvesting more efficient and easier but because, as the farmer expressed it, "A straight plowed field is a pretty thing to see. It's like going to church."

SEXUALITY

That religion expresses itself sensuously is abundantly obvious. That it has sexual expressions is, perhaps, not so obvious, but it is also a fact.

The excitement and mysteriousness of sexuality must have been both fascinating and awesome to primitive and ancient people. The all-pervasive nature of the sex instinct, its imperious demands, its mystery, its pleasures must have brought it early into the ambit of religious belief and ritual. The startling nature of sex must have appeared quite magical to the primitive mind, as indeed it often does to the civilized mind. Everywhere throughout nature the miracle of fertility operated extravagantly, displaying abundance of new life in animals, plants, and women. Around such a phenomenon it was natural that an aura of religiousness would develop, and in many cases a priesthood to systematize it. Once ritualized, phallic worship influenced many aspects of religion from the defloration of virgins, to the ritually depicted fecundation of the Earth Mother by the Sky God in the annual rites of spring, and to the elaborate programs of temple prostitution carried on in such places as Babylon, Corinth, and, even for a while, in Jerusalem.

Without pursuing this matter unnecessarily far, we shall observe a few examples of sexuality in several of the world religions, past and present.

First, in Greece: Sexuality among the Gods   In numerous creation myths the sex act accounts for the origin of the world. In Greek and Roman mythology, for example, the primordial chaos was affected by Love, and from this Earth and Sky were formed. Earth and Sky then mated and gave birth to the Elder Gods (the Titans). Two of these Elder Gods mated and bore five children: Zeus, Poseidon, Hades, Demeter, and Hera, who along with their children became the Gods of Mount Olympus. All of whom were like Greeks twelve feet tall, with all the virtues and vices of Greeks exaggerated, including an appetite for sex. Of all the Gods, Zeus was the most powerful. He was the supreme ruler of humans and Gods, but for all his power he had some weaknesses. The Fates and Destiny often opposed him successfully. He was not omniscient. He was sometimes fooled by both Gods and humans. Also, he had a propensity, if not a weakness, for shapely females, both divine and mortal. Out of this "propensity" Zeus had numerous love affairs that resulted in some famous progeny (both divine and human): the Three Graces, the Nine Muses, Diana, Apollo, Mercury, Minerva, Hercules, Perseus, and others. Zeus was actually married to Hera, and they had three offspring: Mars; Hebe, the Goddess of youth; and Vulcan. As might be expected, Hera was justifiably jealous of Zeus's escapades, and some of Zeus's female companions felt Hera's wrath even beyond what they actually deserved. The nymph Callisto was one.

Callisto was a nymph of rare beauty who belonged to the company of Diana the Huntress. One day Callisto lay down for a rest in a forest glade. Zeus spied her and was immediately smitten with passionate desire. He transformed himself into the form of Diana and wakened the slumbering nymph. Unsuspecting at first, Callisto permitted this "Diana" to embrace her, but quickly the lovely nymph was alarmed by an ardor too intense to be considered sisterly. She began to fight desperately, but to no avail. Zeus had his way. When Diana discovered that Callisto was no longer a virgin, she drove the poor nymph from her company. And then, when Callisto gave birth to Zeus's child, Hera, who had discovered her husband's infidelity with the nymph, moved in for her revenge. She turned the hapless nymph into a shaggy bear. Callisto's son, named Arcas, grew to manhood and himself became a hunter. One day while hunting in the forest he came upon a bear and was about to kill her. But at the last moment, Zeus, finally contrite, intervened. Sending a whirlwind to catch up mother and son, he set them down among the stars in the heavens, where they can still be seen: the Great Bear and the Little Bear.

On the female side of divine sexuality there was, of course, the famous and infamous Aphrodite. She was not an Olympian by birth (or even a Greek), but probably had her origins in the fertility Goddess Ishtar of Mesopotamia. The Greek myth had it that she was born from the foam of the sea near the island of Cyprus and was taken as a visitor to Olympus by gentle Zephyr, where she so charmed the Gods with her beauty that they all wanted to marry her; but Zeus gave her to the ugliest of all the Gods, his son, the lame Vulcan. This may not have been exactly what Aphrodite wanted, for she soon fell into the habit of being unfaithful to her husband, or, perhaps, it was not spite that led her astray but her warm-blooded nature. Nevertheless, stray she did, and on one occasion quite embarrassingly so.

It was Apollo who first became aware that Aphrodite and Mars were meeting clandestinely, even in the bedroom of the house where she and Vulcan lived. Apollo reported this to Vulcan, who was at first angry, and then vengeful. He devised a punishment in the form of an embarrassment. Vulcan, who was the most inventive and dexterous of the Gods, proceeded to fabricate a net of bronze with links so fine that they were invisible to the naked eye. This he spread over his marriage couch, and then hid himself nearby. When Aphrodite and her lover slipped into the room and began to make love on that bed, Vulcan quickly drew the net tight and imprisoned the two lovers in shameful embrace. He then threw open the doors of the bedchamber and invited all the Gods and Goddesses to view the spectacle. (It was reported that the Gods and Goddesses of Olympus all liked this story very much, and kept it alive as a choice piece of gossip.)

This may resemble an X-rated movie. Our purpose, however, is not pornographic but to illustrate that in some religions, among some Gods, sexuality was a very active dimension.

Second, Religious Prostitution   We have already observed that fertility ceremonies were performed annually in the Baal religion of ancient Palestine. The same kind of fecundation rituals were common practically everywhere in the ancient and primitive world. In addition to such sexually involved religious practices as fertility rites, rites of passage (from childhood to adulthood), virgin defloration, and marriage, there developed also in many religions the practice of temple prostitution. As we observed, not even the Yahweh-worshipping moral-minded Hebrews escaped this sort of thing. In the days of Manasseh, especially, Jerusalem was invaded by the fertility Gods, and along with those Gods, temple prostitutes, both male and female.[9] Nevertheless, overt sexuality was rarely more than a peripheral aspect of the Hebrew religion, and temple prostitution was short lived. Manasseh's son Josiah in 621 B.C. put a stop to it when he made a sweeping reform in favor of Yahweh worship. The same was not so of Israel's great northern neighbor.

In the cult of Mylitta (the Babylonian Aphrodite), prostitution was fully endorsed as a formal part of public worship. There were temple prostitutes, and there was also sexual congress for religious reasons between men and women who were not normally religious prostitutes. The Greek historian Herodotus has given a graphic, perhaps eyewitness, account of one aspect of this sex-centered worship.

The Babylonians have one most shameful custom. Every woman born in the country must once in her life go and sit in the precinct of Aphrodite and there have intercourse with a stranger. Many of the wealthier sort, who are too proud to mix with the others, drive in covered carriages to the precinct, followed by a goodly train of attendants, and there take their station. But the larger number seat themselves within the holy enclosure with sheaths of string about their heads, and here there is always a great crowd, some coming and others going; lines of cord make out paths in all directions among the women, and the strangers pass along them to make their choice. A woman who has once taken her seat is not allowed to return home till one of the strangers throws a silver coin into her lap, and takes her with him beyond the holy enclosure. When he throws the coin, he says these words: "I summon you in the name of the goddess Mylitta." The silver coin may be of any size; it cannot be refused, for that is forbidden by law, since once it is thrown it is sacred. The woman goes with the first man who throws her money, and rejects no one. When she has had intercourse with him, and so satisfied the goddess, she returns home, and from that time on no gift however great will prevail with her. Such of the women who are tall and beautiful are soon released, but those who are ugly have to stay a long time before they can fulfill the law. Some have waited three or four years in the precinct. A custom very much like this is found in certain parts of the Island of Cyprus.[10]

We should make a special observation about the sex act as a religious act. There is a categorical difference between people's engaging in sexual debauchery and their performing a religious rite in which sexuality is present or even predominant. Sexuality in religion creates its own "occult atmosphere," whereas sexuality in debauchery does not. There was a vast difference between an ancient Roman orgy and an ancient fertility ceremony. In a Roman revel, which was a large drinking bout interspersed with other sensual pleasures, the aim was pure pleasure and at best might have had some kind of cathartic value, a means of letting off steam. In the cultic rites that employed sexuality, the aim was not sexual pleasure, but religious ecstasy. This latter type of performance was a supernatural occasion and in it sex was used as a means of heightening a religious mystery. The purpose was not to enjoy sexual excitement, but to experience religious emotions. The Maenads (raving women) of a certain form of the Dionysian religion, who danced with bodies convulsing in orgasmic frenzy, were said to be not "in sex" but rather to be in "enthusiasm," which, in the Greek meaning of the word, means "God-possessed." Even in the medieval witches' Sabbats, the indications are, as reported, that the participants were in "enthusiasm," in a state of trance and dissociation.

Third, Sexuality and Islam   In the Muslim Qur'an both sensual enjoyment and sexual pleasure are promised as the rewards of the true believers. In Paradise the righteous "shall be in a pleasing life, in a lofty garden, whose fruits are nigh to cull—'Eat and drink with good digestion, for what ye did aforetime in the days that have gone by' "(The Infallible). "Verily, the pious [shall be] in gardens and pleasure, enjoying what their Lord has given them . . . . Reclining on couches . . . wed to large-eyed maids" (The Mount).

Fourth, Repressed Sexuality   Christianity, with its austerity, has had a history of driving the sexuality of religion underground, into the subconscious. An elderly, very lovely nun of the Catholic Church, while addressing a large audience, spoke of the joy of being part of a religious order. She pictured vividly the fact that unlike most women, she would be buried in her "wedding dress," in the habit of her order, which was, according to her, the gown she was wearing the day she became "the bride of Christ." There was nothing untoward or immodest in her remarks. She was simply reporting that wives can be virgins and remain so if they are married to God. Indeed, that God can be related symbolically in marriage is solemnly declared in the very act of the marriage ceremony.

> Dearly beloved, we are gathered here . . . to join this man and this woman in holy matrimony, which is an honorable estate, instituted by God, and signifying unto us the mystical union which exists between Christ and his Church.

In this same kind of reference the Song of Songs° (Solomon's Song) is of interest here. It is a passionate, poetic dialogue between a dark-skinned woman of great beauty and a magnificent white-bodied man, and it is a part of the Jewish Bible and the Christian Old Testament. What this poem is supposed to be has been given a number of interpretations. It has been called an allegory of the relationship between the divine and the human. (If so, it is an exceedingly sensual and sexual one.) It has been called a drama celebrating the marriage of Solomon to Pharaoh's daughter. It has been called an epithalamium° composed for a royal wedding. It has been called a love poem. Some scholars believe that it was originally a fertility rite in a fertility cult° popular in the Near East, and in Jewish history, performed even as late as the fifth century B.C. The cult was concerned with the union of the Baal of Heaven and the Mother Earth Goddess. Involved in the cult were ritual practices intended to promote the return of the vegetation and the assurance of a good harvest. A prominent feature of the cult was the death and resurrection of the God. He died in the spring as the sown seed or in summer at the parching of the vegetation by the blistering sun. When this happened his wife and lover, the Goddess, sought him in the underworld, and when she found him and he was restored, they celebrated their marriage in a joyous fashion. Whichever interpretation one subscribes to, one must admit that sex and religion are closely related in this scripture, as they are in the marriage ceremony and also, at least with some, in the chastity of nuns.

Fifth, Yahweh Remains Asexual   In spite of aberrations (for example, permitting such things as fertility cults and temple prostitutions to occur in Israel), the Jews were first among religion builders to emasculate God, to remove sexuality from the Godhead. God Yahweh stood aloof and alone, without consort, without phallic symbolism. To be sure, as the God of creation he was the inventor of the sexual process, but he never himself engaged. He said, "Be fruitful and multiply," and he called his creation "good." Sexuality was divinely ordained. Only the misuse of sex was evil. As a part of God's law, Jews are supposed to marry and enjoy the intimacies of sexual pleasure. Indeed, some rabbis tell us that the Sabbath is not properly kept unless husband and wife make it joyous with coitus. Lovemaking is proper and good; it is ordained of God, but in no direct, personal way is it an activity of God.

One reason why Christianity was such a scandal to Judaism was the purported impregnation of Mary by God's Spirit. To propose that Mary's pregnancy was something that God did to her was blasphemy in the extreme. For 1,200 years the Hebrew religion had struggled against the sexuality of pagan Gods. It is not surprising, then, that they were not about to revert to a former "evil in the sight of the Lord."

It should be noted that although the founders and protectors of Judaism avoided the phallic symbol as a symbol for God, they, on numerous occasions, used a marriage metaphor in reference to Yahweh. The Prophet Hosea, for example, who is often called the prophet of love, tells a beautiful story of a marriage that shattered in the perversity of a wayward wife who deserted husband and children and ran off with another man. Before long she and her lover fell on hard times and she turned to prostitution and finally was seized to be sold into slavery to pay their debts. The husband, who still loved his wife in spite of her violation of their marriage, learning of her situation, rescued her by buying her back. He then restored her to her former position as wife and mother in his home. All she had to do was repent her ways and become a faithful wife. Hosea's account was a metaphor of the relation between Yahweh and Israel. God, the loving husband, would restore Israel, his whoring wife, if only Israel would repent and live in fidelity.

In numerous places in the Jewish scriptures, Yahweh is depicted not in the role of fertility God, not as a God of sexuality, but as a husband to a people— to Israel. He is seen not in the dimension of sexuality but in the dimension of love.

LOVE

The fact of sensuousness in religion and the endorsement of sexuality is not to be denied. Aphrodite° (sexuality) is a part of religion although at times she may be disguised. Also, Eros° (love) is part of religion. Eros is the God of those who are "in love," not merely "in sex." Love as Eros is both different from sexuality and more than sexuality. C. S. Lewis,° observing how Eros differs from Aphrodite, says in his *Four Loves:*

> Now Eros makes a man really want, not a woman, but one particular woman. In some mysterious but quite indisputable fashion the lover desires the Beloved herself, not the pleasure she can give.[11]

Speaking of Love in the context of religion, William Evans states in his article in *The International Standard Bible Encyclopedia:*

> Love, whether used of God or man, is an earnest and anxious desire for, and an active and beneficent interest in, the well-being of the one loved.

Although sexuality is part of Eros as it exists between man and woman, it is not all of Love, or even the essential part. And where love exists between friend and friend, neighbor and neighbor, God and human (as affection, brotherhood, agapé), sexuality is scarcely a characteristic at all.

In Love it is the person himself/herself who is precious and desired and loved, not simply what that person can do for the lover in the way of furnishing pleasure. Simply wanting pleasure and using another person as the vehicle for that pleasure is far different from being in love. To be in love is to desire a person, not a thing; it is wanting to see that person happy, to give that person happiness. In such a relationship sexual pleasure and even friendship are simply additional boons in the relationship.

However, Love does not only flow from the lover's passion to give; it also is motivated by the lover's need for "nesting." It is when the beloved returns love that the capacity of Love is fully demonstrated, and the desired *miracle* occurs. A lover finds joy in simply loving, but finds something even more joyous when the beloved responds in kind. A mutual penetration takes place, a common ground of being is accomplished, and the two lovers are no longer alone in the world, or alone in themselves. There is a nesting in each other. The story of the creation of the first woman from the rib of the man may not be scientifically factual, but it is superbly true metaphorically. God had placed Adam alone in the Garden of Eden, and Adam was lonely. So God created all sorts of possible companions for him—singing birds, lithely beautiful animals, fascinatingly colorful fish in the pond. But Adam remained locked inside himself in a world of things out there: a lone and lonely subject, in a world of objects, until *She* was formed, bone of his bones, flesh of his flesh. And with her coming, loneliness ended. And this, we are informed, is why a man and a woman leave parents and the world out there and cleave to each other, "and they become one flesh," yes, and one spirit.

In religion it is God, or someone or something that God loves, who is the beloved. As examples of this one might note (1) the biblical commandment: "And thou shalt love the Lord thy God with all thy heart, and with all thy soul, and with all thy might." In this it is God himself who is to be loved. But (2) in the teachings of the rabbis it is especially God's law (Torah) which is to be loved. Indeed, it is said that if one could either believe in God or keep God's Holy Law, but not both, that person should keep the law, for God wants more that people should love the law than that they should love him. Also (3) in Christian tradition it is Christ who is truly the beloved, Christ who is the object of the believers' greatest devotion. Interestingly, certain "Death of God" theologians contended, and perhaps accurately, that Christianity could survive without God, but not without the beloved Jesus. It is obvious that Christians love what God loves; namely his Son. And (4) Christians are not the only people who love the manifestation of God on earth; the Hindu disciples of Vishnu-Krishna° do the same.

How one loves the beloved God is, of course, affected by the tradition in which the loving happens and by the individual doing the loving. Some love adoringly, as the worshippers of Krishna and Christ. Some love loyally, as the Jews who keep the law that God loves. Some love sentimentally: they walk in the garden alone, with dew on the roses; they talk and walk and have an adolescent love experience. Some fall down weeping in the torn love of Good

Friday and the devastation of Crucifixion. Some love God by loving spouse, child, neighbor, stranger, enemy, and all who are in need: "When did I see you hungry? thirsty? naked? in prison?" (See Matthew 25:31–46.)

Concerning this last kind of God love (loving God by loving people), we might note, again, that the Jewish-Christian command to love one's neighbor as oneself, and to do unto others as one would be done by, is to be found in virtually the same form in all of the major religions of the world. The reason for loving others, at least in the Near Eastern religions, is because God loves them. And equally, the reasons for loving God is because God loves us. The writer of the letter called First John puts it as follows:

> Dear friends! Let us love one another, for love comes from God. Whoever loves is a child of God and knows God. Whoever does not love does not know God, because God is love. This is how God showed his love for us: he sent his only Son into the world that we might have life through him. This is what love is: it is not that we have loved God, but that he loved us and sent his son. . . .
> . . . if this is how God loved us, then we should love one another.[12]

God loved his lost children and sent his Son, so say the Christians. Out of love for mankind Krishna came, and the other Avatars° of Vishnu also, so say the Hindus. Once a Jew wrote God's love for Israel in a passionately vivid account preserved today in the eleventh chapter of the Book of Hosea.

When Israel was a child, I loved him,
And out of Egypt I called my son.

How can I give you up, O E'phriam!
How can I hand you over, O Israel!

My heart recoils within me,
My compassion grows warm and tender.

I will not execute my fierce anger,
I will not again destroy E'phriam
For I am God and not man,
The holy One in your midst,
And I will not come to destroy.[13]

CHARITY/AGAPÉ

Important as it is, Eros/Love is not the last word in love. There is, some claim, a love that is devoid entirely of the dimension of need on the part of the lover. It is completely gift love, and God is the giver; God is the lover. With no need to be loved, God simply, openhandedly, loves. Rain falls on the just and unjust alike. Krishna comes for everyone, as does Christ. God's saving message through the Prophet Muhammad is for all mankind. The Buddha's wisdom is open to all people. Israel's ultimate kingdom is not for Jews only.

It is contended that God loves because it is God's nature to love. God *is* love, and his loving is always outbound, toward people. And in many cases it is not even in the intention of the Giver. God gives without forethought, without knowing, simply because he is what he is. According to Greek mythology, the primal chaos was first stirred by Love; from thence all else emerged. According to Hindu philosophy, God Brahman is, and all else is simply himself given. In other systems of religious thought, God gives intentionally, lovingly: he gave Moses to the Hebrews in his loving desire to rescue them from bondage in Egypt; he gave himself in his Son, the Christians say, to suffering and death, because he loved mankind.

This love has a name of its own. It is called Charity or Agapé; both words in original usage mean love. Charity/Agapé is gift love, especially the divine gift of life: life now, and in many religions, life to come.

Charity/Agapé is not limited only to God's action. People too can love givingly, and when they do, they are, in many religious traditions, being most like God. In the New Testament letter called First John (4:10), it is declared that "God is love and whoever lives in love lives in him." And one who lives in love at times not even knowing it is perhaps more like God than when that person plans and works to be charitable. There is a story told about a young man and a Methodist bishop riding on a train in the club car with several other men. None of them knew the others. But several of the men soon identified themselves as businessmen and began to talk about lucrative businesses. One wished he could get into the oil business; another wished he had gone into plastics; another sang the praises of IBM. One said that he just wished he had ten million dollars and would not have to be in any business at all. Finally the young man upset by the lack of human concern, the lack of idealism, that he found among the talkers, blurted into the conversation that he only wished that he could live his life knowing that he was helping people. In the embarrassed silence that followed, the bishop interposed a slightly different point of view. He said, "To want to live your life knowing that you are helping people is a most admirable ambition. There is only one greater." The young man asked him what could possibly be greater. And the bishop replied: "To live your life doing good without knowing it."

Be that as it may, there would be one tremendous benefit in having a God who not only loved, but loved purposefully. Such love would go even beyond the nesting love of Eros, and would provide the saving love of divine forgiveness and acceptance. Jacques Maritain makes the point in his *Existence and Existent*. First, he points out that a person is known inwardly, as he really is, only by himself, if at all. Other people see him as an "it," as an object. To be known as an "it," as an object is to be forever unknown and wounded in one's identity.

It is to be always unjustly known—whether the *he* who sees condemns . . . or whether . . . the "he" does honor. . . . A Tribunal is a masquerade where the accused stands accoutered in a travesty of himself. . . . The more the judges stray from the crude outward criteria with which formerly they contented themselves, and strive to take account of degrees of inner responsibility, the more they reveal the truth of him whom they judge remains unknowable to human justice. Interrogated by such a tribunal, Jesus owed it to Himself to remain silent.[14]

We have suggested that this wound of broken identity can be at least soothed in the nest of Eros/Love. Maritain proposes that it can be healed in the embrace of God's love. Only God knows a person in his subjectivity, in his inwardness. Only to God is a person open and known. And even if God condemns for what he knows, the broken identity is repaired. The person is understood. The idea that we are known completely, that no secrets are hidden, may reduce us at first to fear and trembling, because of the evil that is inside us. But, as Maritain proposes,

> on deeper reflection, how can we keep from thinking that the God Who knows us and knows all those poor beings who jostle us and whom we know as objects, whose wretchedness we mostly perceive—how can we keep from thinking that God Who knows all these in their subjectivity, in the nakedness of their wounds and their secret evil, must know also the secret beauty of that nature which He has bestowed upon them? . . . To know that we are known to God is not merely to experience justice, but is also to experience mercy.[15]

Being known, our identity is healed; being seen in both evil and beauty, we are forgiven and accepted, not for a little while, as with our beloved, but forever with God.

NOTES

[1] Abraham E. Milligram, *Jewish Worship* (Philadelphia: Jewish Publication Society of America, 1971), p. 306.

[2] See John G. Neihardt, *Black Elk Speaks* (New York: Pocket Books, second edition 1972), pp. 2, 4, 5, 21–27.

[3] I. M. Lewis, *Ecstatic Religion* (Middlesex, England: Penguin, 1971), p. 11.

[4] Frederick J. Streng, *Understanding Religious Man* (Belmont, Calif.: Dickenson, 1969), p. 85.

[5] Ibid., p. 86.

[6] Ibid., p. 86.

[7] Ibid., p. 87.

[8] D. T. Suzuki's account of this tea ceremony, including the two brief quotes used here, can be found in his *Zen Buddhism* (Garden City, N.Y.: Doubleday Anchor, 1956), pp. 293–294.

[9] See 2 Kings, 23:7.

[10]*History of the Persian Wars*, tran. Geo Rawlinson, 2 vols. (Chicago: Regnery, 1949), vol. 1, par. 199.

[11]C. S. Lewis, *The Four Loves* (New York: Harcourt Brace Jovanovich, 1960), p. 135.

[12]1 John 4:7–11, Good News for Modern Man (New York: American Bible Society, 1966).

[13]Hosea 11:1–9, RSV.

[14]Jacques Maritain, *Existence and the Existent,* tran. L. Galantiere and B. Phelon (Garden City, N.Y.: Doubleday, Image, 1960; second edition, 1948), pp. 83–84.

[15]Ibid., p. 85.

Chapter 15

RELIGION: ESOTERIC EXPERIENCE

I found, circled with
chaos, in stillness centered,
the hurricane's eye.

W.C.T.

Religious experience occurs in a special kind of consciousness, often called the mystical consciousness. It is a consciousness that results when the believer and the essence of a divine reality unite in some kind of incarnation. This can occur in an incarnation of *possession,* as in Shamanism, where a person is seized and invaded by the divine reality; or it can happen in an incarnation of *presence,* as in worship, where one simply senses the nearness, the availability, the presence of the supernatural or extranatural divine reality; or it can happen in an incarnation of identity, as in *mysticism,* where the normal human consciousness bursts asunder and a new egoless, ineffable consciousness expands the human mind into a divine mind.

We shall look directly at these three kinds of religious experience (possession, worshipful presence, mystical identity), but first we shall take time to observe that the religious experience is noetic in character. It is not simply an ecstasy, but a way of knowing. Besides the kind of rationalized knowledge that theology affords, there is, in the experience of religion, a directly intuited knowledge: esoteric knowing, intuitional knowing, which without formal logic or dialectics makes known its "truth" directly, forcefully, and usually irresistibly.

ESOTERIC KNOWING

In addition to the empirical and rational methods of obtaining knowledge, which we observed in Chapter 9, and knowledge from revelation, which we observed in Chapter 11, there is another kind of knowledge that arises out of inner and immediate experience. One knows, for example, what it is to have a toothache, or what it is to be afraid, or to be in love, or to think, or to be saved. This kind of knowledge might properly be called "enlightenment." A light in the mind gets turned on and one "sees" things one has never seen before. One knows something directly that could not possibly be known in any other way. This is esoteric knowing. It is subjective and private, and it is tremendously significant. It is the kind of knowing that informs and certifies certain values: for example, aesthetic values, that certain music is beautiful; and ethical values, that human beings have rights; and religious values, that God is real and that one has been spiritually renewed.

The knowledge indigenous to religious experience occurs primarily in the private awareness of a human consciousness, and this is especially so in the case of mysticism. Mysticism is esoteric knowing of the highest order. But because we shall examine mysticism later in this chapter, we shall defer at this point to another kind of religious experience in which enlightenment occurs—conversion—and will observe three examples of it. One example is of an Eskimo conversion and enlightenment; one is a Hindu conversion and enlightenment; and the other is the autobiographical account written by John Wesley° of his own conversion and enlightenment.

Conversion Knowing   The Danish Arctic explorer and ethnographer Knud Rasmussen° records the following account told to him by an Eskimo shaman who, as a neophyte, had gone into solitude in the wilderness in search of divine inspiration. There, he told Rasmussen,

> I soon became melancholy. I would sometimes fall to weeping and feel unhappy without knowing why. Then for no reason all would suddenly be changed, and I felt a great inexplicable joy, a joy so powerful that I could not restrain it, but had to break into song, a mighty song, with room for only one word: Joy, Joy! And I had to use the full strength of my voice. And then in the midst of such a fit of mysterious and overwhelming delight I became a shaman. I could see and hear in a totally different way. I have gained my enlightenment.[1]

The Eskimo shaman experienced enlightenment, which is an inner knowing, a vision of ultimate truth. This report is not unlike that told of the great Siddhartha Gautama, founder of Buddhism. Gautama too went into solitude searching for divine inspiration. For six years he was an unsuccessful searcher. He tried, perhaps too hard, by giving himself rigorously first to the practice of meditation and then to severe ascetic discipline—the two common paths to salvation in India. But none of it was of any avail. Then one day, after years of enormous effort, he gave up trying and sat down under the Bodhi-tree.° There it abruptly happened: suddenly, completely, he knew the answer. He experienced enlightenment, and with it liberation. Siddhartha suddenly knew something he had never known before. He knew a principle of life that at once both shattered human reality and re-formed it new. There is a story that Gautama, after he had become enlightened (that is, Buddha), was asked if he were a God. He said, "No." Then he was asked if he were a saint. Again he said, "No." Finally he was asked, "Then what are you?" And he answered, "I am awake." His conversion was an awakening, a discovery of transforming knowledge. He saw a new way, and seeing it became a new man—a liberated man.

The account of John Wesley's esoteric experience is of the same life-shaking character as that of the Eskimo shaman and the founder of Buddhism, although it is, with a certain British reserve, dramatically understated in Wesley's *Journal*. Like the Buddha and the Eskimo, John Wesley too was a searcher after divine light. He was a professor at Oxford University who in a kind of low-key religious frenzy gave up his position and traveled to the New World searching for something he did not find. Except he saw it, as it were, afar off, in the faith of the simple Moravians (Peter Bohler,° in particular) he met on shipboard. But he did not get it himself until, on his return to London, he let himself be persuaded to go to an anabaptist-type° meeting. The following is part of the entry of Wesley's diary for May 24, 1738:

> In the evening I went very unwilling to a society in Aldersgate Street where one was reading Luther's preface to the Epistle to the Romans. About a quarter before nine, while he was describing the change which God works in the heart through faith in Christ, I felt my heart strangely warmed. I felt I did trust Christ, Christ alone for salvation; and an assurance was given me that He had taken away *my* sins; even *mine*, and saved *me* from the law of sin and death.[2]

Transforming Knowledge   Another important thing to observe about this kind of knowledge is that it does not just inform the mind; it transforms the life. Or, probably more correctly, it is not the knowledge that transforms, but the coming of the knowledge. Something happens (conversion, for example) and when it happens the person, as he is "informed" is also "transformed." It is the transformation, the happening, that makes the difference. We shall now proceed to examine more closely the religious "happenings" of possession, presence, and identity.

THE POSSESSION GAME

Joseph Campbell,° in his *Masks of God: Primitive Mythology* points out that "the mask in a primitive festival is revered and experienced as a veritable apparition of the mythical being that it represents—even though everyone knows that a man made the mask and that a man is wearing it."[3] This primitive ability to be seized with belief is not simply a primitive ability. Sophisticated, civilized persons are also capable of being so seized with belief. For example, in the celebration of the Eucharist,° the Catholic knows that he is eating bread, and often rather palate-sticking, tasteless bread at that, but he "plays" the part of believing until he is seized with the believing. It is not unlike children pretending that there are ghosts in the bedroom until there really are ghosts in the bedroom. Even when the religious practices are known to be different from what they represent, they become religious practices when the game of "as if" takes on the aura of "as is," and the person behind the mask does not simply represent the God, but *is* the God. The bread does not simply remind one of Christ; it *is* the Christ. The person involved must be seized by the game if that game is to count as real religion.

Some people have difficulty "psyching" themselves from the attitude of "as if" to the attitude of "as is." Their modern skepticisms must be purposefully set aside. They must ease themselves into the game, let the ritual aura take over, before they can return to the capacity of childlikeness, which has been all but lost in the machinations of a modern world that makes few accommodations (except during festival times) for the innocence of true believing. This, however, is an affliction that affects only those people who have come to live in the modern, twentieth-century world of science, business, and technology. Much of the rest of the world (and the world of the past) has no such difficulty.

KINDS OF DIVINE POSSESSION

Professional Possession   Everywhere in the phenomenon of religion, we observe persons who are caught up in a frenzy of religious excitement. They become what is called spirit-possessed or demon-possessed. Sometimes this possession has a professional character. The persons possessed are possessed on purpose at their own command. In 1 Samuel, we read how in the days of Samuel and Saul and David there were "companies of prophets" who met at the hill shrines in Palestine and led by lute and harp and fife and drum were filled with "prophetic rapture" and danced naked and in ecstasy. There are, of course, today the Near Eastern dervishes,° that is, the members of various Muslim orders of ascetics, some of whom practice the achievement of collective ecstasy through whirling dances and the chanting of religious words. And there are in all primitive communities shamans and Shamanism.[4] I. M. Lewis° in his book, *Ecstatic Religion,* tells us that shamans are priests who have become possessed by or possess one or more spirits. They are masters of spirits, which they summon at will to assist in their religious duties.

> A shaman is a person of either sex who has mastered spirits and who can at will introduce them into his own body. Often in fact, he permanently incarnates these spirits and can control their manifestations, going into controlled states of trance.[5]

In addition to professional ecstatic seizure, there has also been, throughout religion and religious history, a more general form of spirit possession that we shall refer to as compensatory seizure. It is compensatory in the sense that although it may seem to be demonic and undesirable, it is often, in fact, an experience full of compensations for the person possessed.

Victim and Compensatory Possession   As we have seen in our consideration of the demonic, most of the people in bygone days, and many people today, accept the idea of demons possessing human beings as obviously (even by observation) true. Sometimes demons even possess human beings sexually; for example, the sons of God (angels) in Genesis "who came in unto the daughters of men, and they bore children of them," the incubi and succubi who seduced both men and women. Also the "victims" did not always consider themselves especially victimized. Possession is not always regarded as something terrible. Indeed, often possession instead of being depriving is compensatory. In getting at this aspect of spirit possession, I. M. Lewis points out that many instances of what appear to be demonical illnesses as viewed by primitives are, by primitive women, transformed into both compensatory events and therapeutic ecstasies.

Lewis is convinced that spirit possession and possession cults are strongly motivated by the unconscious need to protest the inferior status imposed on the cultists by the general society in which they live. This, he thinks, is especially true where women are concerned. Those forms of possession regarded initially as illnesses are virtually restricted to women, and they are "thinly disguised protest movements directed against the dominant sex."[6] When pathogenic spirits come possessing they seem to do so capriciously, with no apparent rhyme or reason. They do not come to punish the wicked. They have no concern for moral behavior. They do not defend the society's ethical code. As this is the case, one would expect to find that the spirits are indiscriminate in their selection of human prey, but Lewis points out that this is not usually the case. The spirits "show a predilection for the weak and the downtrodden . . . the underprivileged and oppressed." The phenomenon of possession is especially prevalent among women in those cultures where women are arrogantly repressed by male domination.

In such cultures the women, far more than the men, are assailed with illnesses caused by spirit possession. But in this context, Lewis makes the interesting observation that in many cases the "added misery" is in fact a blessing in disguise. The woman is compensated by the attention she gets in her "illness," and, one might suspect, from the domestic inconvenience caused her husband and the expense he must bear to get her cured, that is, to get her demon exorcised.

From Lewis we get some indication of this sort of thing as it occurs among the Somali people of northeast Africa who live in what is now called the Somali Republic. The Somalis are Muslims. Their culture is completely male dominated. Somali women are to be at all times weak and submissive. But being weak and submissive does not always have its rewards in responsive male gentleness and concern, for the Somali culture is rigidly puritanical. Any open display of affection and love between men and women is regarded as unmanly and sentimental and must be suppressed. Furthermore, as polygamy is permissible, a wife may be at any time affronted by the establishment of another, younger, more attractive wife in the household. As elsewhere in Islam, Somalis believe that demons (jinn) lurk everywhere ready to attack and possess unwary persons. Some of these demons are thought to be female, desiring dainty foods, luxurious clothing, jewelry, perfume, and other finery; and perhaps not surprisingly, women are the prime targets of these spirits. The spirits are called *sar*, and the afflicted woman is said to have been seized by the sar. The sar spirits demand various forms of luxurious gifts. These requests are voiced through the lips of the afflicted woman and uttered with an authority that the woman normally would not dare to assert. The spirits, also, have their own language which is interpreted, for a fee, by a female shaman. It is only when the costly demands have been met, as well as the expense involved in mounting a cathartic dance attended by other women and directed by the shaman, that the victim can be expected to recover, and even then the recovery may be only temporary.

Because the men believe in sar spirits, they are inclined to accept the idea of sar possession of their women. However, sometimes the men become skeptical and begin to suspect the genuineness of some of the seizures. Normally the husband will endure a few bouts with the sar spirits, but if they happen too often and his wife becomes a regular member of a circle of sar devotees, the husband's patience may wear out, and he may begin to exorcise his domestic problem himself. "If a good beating will not do the trick (and it often seems effective), there is always the threat of divorce." That usually works, so Lewis reports.

We are saying, then, that the spirit possession, even when regarded as an illness, as an affliction, may effect a sense of power and importance in the life of the possessed that is not otherwise possible.*

Ecstasy Possession   The greatest rewards of spiritual possession, however, are not found in a few trinkets or in a temporary psychological lift that comes from escaping briefly from repressive social restraints. It comes in the ecstasy of a consciousness that has become dislocated and fled to some ethereal heights or has been taken over by an enlightening and joy-giving spiritual being. We referred to the "conversion" of the Eskimo shaman as he expressed it to Knud Rasmussen. From melancholia and weeping suddenly the Eskimo, about to become a shaman, was transported into a great, inexplicable joy. In the midst of mysterious and overwhelming delight, he became a shaman. He could experience things in a totally different way, and this had happened, he went on to say, "in such a manner that it was not only I who could see through the darkness of life, but the same bright light also shone out of me, imperceptible to human beings but visible to all spirits of earth and sky and sea, and these now came to me to become my helping spirits."[7]

Francis Thompson° speaks with bitter-sweet eloquence of the tragedy of resisting the conquest of divine possession; of those who flee the pursuing

---

*Various explanations are given for the phenomenon of mental dislocation or possession. Sometimes it is explained naturalistically, sometimes supernaturalistically. For example, the frenetic dancing that seized whole communities in Europe in the fifteenth century was diagnosed in Holland as demonic possession and was exorcised, while in Italy it was diagnosed as resulting from the bite of a tarantula spider; thus the name Tarantism.

spirit "down the nights and down the days . . . down the arches of the years," pleading outlaw-wise, running from the hound of heaven;

> From those strong Feet that followed, followed after.
>   But with unhurrying chase
>   And unperturbed pace,
> Deliberate speed, majestic instancy
>   They beat—and a Voice beat
>   More instant than the Feet—
> "All things betray thee, who betrayest Me."[8]

It is the joy that comes in submission, in being possessed by the pursuing spirit, that is the reward the shaman seeks, and Jacob wrestling in the night, and Gautama, pale and emaciated, sitting under the Bodhi-tree, and Wesley outward bound for the colony of Georgia.

The experience of divine possession is so intimate that it is often symbolized as a marriage. We have already observed this in the interpretation that sees Hosea's story of the husband and the wife as being the relationship between God and Israel, and sees the Christian wedding ceremony as signifying the mystical union that exists between Christ and his church. But beyond this is the idea that the relationship is not simply symbolic marriage, but actual marriage. Lewis gives two accounts in which this is the situation. First, taking his information from Verrier Elwin's *The Religion of an Indian Tribe* (London, 1955), he reports that a man of the Saora Tribe of Orissa, in India, claims that he married a spirit girl who presented him, in the course of time, with three fine spirit boys, the celestial counterparts of his earthly children.[9] Lewis also published in his book a copy of a Voodoo marriage certificate that records the mystical union of a woman with her spirit mate Damballah. The certificate officially records that on January 6, 1949, at three o'clock, Damballah Toquan Mirisse and Madame Andremise Cetoute appeared before the Registar of Port-au-Prince and were "united by the indissoluble bond of the marriage sacrament." The marriage was certified according to Article 15.1 of the Haitian Code, and witnessed by persons whose names appear thereon.

PRESENCE AND IDENTITY

Worshipful Presence   Some people would hold that Whitehead's statement, quoted at the beginning of our study (see p. 3), that religion is what people do with their own solitariness would more correctly be what happens to each person in that solitariness. Religion is not what we do when we are alone, but what happens to us when we are alone, or more accurately what we become when we are *truly* alone. It is not simply being by yourself, but being in spiritual solitude. It is the soul stillness of the Psalmist when he said, "Be still and know that I am God." It is worship or, in its more extreme dimension, mysticism.

Worship should not be confused with worship service. All organized religions have forms and rituals that are called "worship," but our concern is not with forms and rituals but with human experience: an experience of rapt, and even enraptured, attention in which the worshipper feels in intimate personal relations with divine being. The worship service may foster this experience, and even religious ecstasy, but it does not constitute the experience. Worship is not stylized performance, but a personal engagement. Worshippers are involved not simply with their physical behavior, but with their mental and emotional life as well. They feel "caught up" in a heightened awareness of religious values. They sense the reality of something mysterious and awesome, which is, at the same time, congenial, sustaining, and concerned. They feel enlivened and enlightened and joyous, even to the point of tears. Worship is not something easily defined, nor does it occur in all people, nor at different times, with the same intensity or significance. Indeed, at times it seems to be little more than a religious kick, evoked by the sight of a crucifix, or a church steeple, or the sound of a stirring hymn, or even a cheap, popular song of religious sentiment, effecting little more than a brief, sentimental exhilaration. But, at other times, it can be an atunement to mystical consciousness, which becomes sheer religious ecstasy.

Religious Mysticism To understand worship as more than "religious kicks," it might be helpful to look at it in one of its extreme forms—in the form called mysticism. This degree of religious experience is not common. Not everyone truly experiences it. But it is universal; it is an experience that has been reported in all ages and in all religions, and the reports have always added up to the same kind of experience. Christians may describe it in Christian terms, Hindus in Hindu terms, Buddhists in Buddhist terms, but no matter what terms are used, they all describe the same basic experience: one in which the mystic becomes lost in ultimate being, in God, and enjoys an indescribable bliss. The mystical experience itself is (1) an experience in which the consciousness is flooded with an awareness of the interrelatedness and unity among all things: a spiritual ecology which gives all things, including the mystic and God, a common identity, and (2) an experience of bliss and contentment that passes all human understanding. In the words of the Hindu *Mandukya Upanishad,*° it is an experience "beyond the senses, beyond all understanding, beyond all expression . . . it is pure unitary consciousness, wherein awareness of the world and of multiplicity is completely obliterated. It is ineffable peace. It is the Supreme Good."[10]

TWO FORMS OF MYSTICISM: EXTROVERTIVE AND INTROVERTIVE

If the unity and ecstasy of mysticism are accomplished by turning outward to the world, the mysticism is, according to Walter T. Stace° in his *Teaching of the Mystics,* extrovertive in form. If it is accomplished by turning inward and, through meditative discipline, penetrating to the deepest level of human consciousness, it is, according to Stace, introvertive in form.

Extrovertive mystics continue to perceive the world of people and trees and skies and houses and butterflies, but they see them transfigured in such a way that not only physical and biological unity is apparent, but a spiritual ecology as well. Of this experience Meister Eckhart° wrote: "Here all blades of grass, wood, and stone, all things are One." And another mystic, Jacob Boehme,° wrote: "In this light my spirit saw through all things and into all creatures and I recognized God in grass and plants." A modern mystic, Sokei-an Sasaki, gave the following account of his experience:

> One day I wiped out all the notions from my mind. I gave up all desire. I discarded all the words with which I thought and stayed in quietude. I felt a little queer—as if I were being carried into something, or as if I were touching some power unknown to me . . . and Ztt! I entered. I lost the boundary of my physical body. I had my skin, of course, but I felt I was standing in the center of the cosmos. I spoke, but my words had lost their meaning. I saw people coming toward me, but all were the same man. All were myself! . . . no individual Mr. Sasaki existed.[11]

This extrovertive form of mysticism is, apparently, a consciousness in which the world is transfigured and unified in one ultimate being.

Introvertive mysticism is much more extreme than extrovertive mysticism in that in this form the egos of the mystics are completely suspended. The experience of unity and ecstasy occurs, but, apparently, mystics *do not know that they* are experiencing it. They are not experiencing unity and ecstasy; they *are* unity and ecstasy. They are not experiencing God; *they* are God. By arduous techniques (self-mastery), mystics systematically shut off all the normal sensory-intellectual experiences. They do not feel anything, see anything, hear anything, think anything, experience anything. When this state has been truly accomplished, the emptied consciousness is abruptly flooded with pure, nonobjectified experience, and the mystic enters perfection, beauty, joy, love, ecstasy, God and is completely lost to himself or herself. Out of this kind of mystical experience, the Flemish mystic Jan Van Ruysbroeck,° afterwards when he had returned to the mundane world of normal mortals, wrote:

> In the abyss of this darkness, in which the loving spirit has died to itself, there begin the manifestations of God and eternal life. For in this darkness there shines and is born an incomprehensible Light, which is the Son of God, in whom we behold eternal life. And in this Light one becomes seeing; and this Divine Light is given to the simple sight of the spirit, where the spirit receives the brightness which is God Himself, above all gifts and every creaturely activity, in the idle emptiness in which the spirit has lost itself through fruitive love, and where it receives without means the brightness of God, and is changed without interruption into the brightness which it receives . . . this brightness is so great that the loving contemplative, in the ground wherein he rests, sees and feels nothing but an incomprehensible

Light; and through the Simple Nudity which enfolds all things, he finds himself and feels himself, to be that same light by which he sees, and nothing else.[12]

Extrovertive mysticism can happen quite spontaneously. One is walking or sitting or standing quietly, and suddenly it happens. As Sasaki says it: Ztt! and it happens. But this is not the case with introvertive mysticism. Introvertive mystical experience is accomplished only with disciplined preparation and effort. By arduous effort the yogis of India become proficient in turning off their thoughts and feelings, and entering samhadi. Christian mystics in Catholic monasteries have their own techniques. They usually call their techniques "prayers," but they are not prayers in the crude sense of asking God for something. They are more like the meditations of the Indian mystics. These techniques do not come easily. It is not easy to stop thinking, seeing, hearing, feeling, remembering. It is not easy to empty the consciousness of all sensory intellectual contents; thus few of us are mystics of this more arduous type.

Mysticism and Religion   It is generally assumed that mysticism is a form of religious experience, but this may not be true. It can be argued that mysticism may be a nonreligious fact and that its connection with religion is after the fact. In other words, an autonomous mystical experience may be so loaded with religious significance that it is appropriated and used to support and explain religion. It can be argued that when the mystical experience is stripped of all religious interpretations (such as those identifying it with Nirvana, or God, or the Absolute), what is left is simply the experience of undifferentiated unity. The world of things is transfigured so that unity shines through. This may be an important existential fact, but it is not, perhaps, necessarily a religious fact. It becomes a religious fact only when the unity is interpreted as being God or some mode of the divine order.

For our purpose here, however, it is probably enough simply to recognize that, at least, religion has taken mysticism unto itself, and that mysticism speaks relevantly to religion in a number of important ways: (1) Religion is concerned with repivoting human life from self-centeredness to God-centeredness, and mysticism is a process in which the self seems to fall away into union with an infinite and absolute one (often called God). (2) Life often seems broken. Mysticism makes it seem whole. (3) Human beings crave identity. Mysticism fuses them into a meaningful whole with what seems to be all reality, or true reality. (4) Life is laced with tragedy and sadness. Mysticism lifts one above tragedy and sadness. As we have observed, religion is concerned with overcoming basic human frustrations; mysticism, according to mystics, does just that, transporting one into an experience of peace, blessedness, and joy. In such things, and more, mysticism relates naturally to religion, if not necessarily to it.

There is, however, a problem that should not be passed over without some examination, for there is a crucial point at which mysticism is not in perfect accord with religion, especially with the religions of the Western World.

According to Judaism, Christianity, and Islam, mysticism at times almost approaches a heresy, because mystics often insist that in the mystical experience they become one with God. This is acceptable to certain Asian religions where it is believed that in the end (in salvation) this is exactly what happens to people. They are merged with the beatitude of infinity. They enter Nirvana and become indistinguishable from Brahman. But among Jews, Christians, and Muslims there has always been an I-Thou relationship between humans and God, a distance of difference and, indeed, it is sacrilegious to think otherwise. The great Western religions have always proclaimed unequivocally that God is always and only God and that humans are his creatures. When Sasaki says that he must now recognize that he was "never created," he may be explaining something congenial to the Zen Buddhist religion and of metaphysical importance, but it certainly smacks of heresy to Jew, Christian, and Muslim. There is a dualism in Western religion that is not comfortable with the mystical experience of absolute unity. St. Paul may say, "I live, yet not I but Christ liveth in me," but this is not the usual way that Christians think of themselves or of Paul. Not even in Heaven do people become God. In fact, to aspire to such grandeur was in some way the guilt of both Lucifer and Adam. The Jews say, "Hear, O Israel, the Lord our God, the Lord is one," and they mean it—and so do the Christians. With equal obstinacy the Muslims declare: "There is but one God, Allah." To proclaim a unity of human and God is congenial to pantheism, where everything is somehow a projection of God, but only uneasily so to theism, where God is a person separate and alone. In the West, mysticism takes some additional explaining. The fact is that although Christian mysticism has always been acknowledged by Christians, the Christian mystic has usually lived under some suspicion of heresy.

Whether or not mysticism is a unique experience or simply another form of religious experience, it is crucially involved in the religious experience and demands consideration in any definition of religion.

Worship   There are only a few mystics in the world, even in all history. Few people ever really lose themselves completely in an ecstasy of union with the infinite ground of ultimate and mysterious being (with God), but there are many people who lose themselves at least a little bit in a similar experience. They worship.

> Far off the noises of the world retreat;
> The loud vociferations of the street
> Become an indistinguishable roar.
> So, as I enter here from day to day,
> And leave my burden at this minster gate,
> Kneeling in prayer, and not ashamed to pray,
> The tumult of the time disconsolate
> To inarticulate murmurs dies away,
> While the eternal ages watch and wait. *H. W. Longfellow, "Divina Commedia"*

Many people turn aside from the hurry and confusion of every day and in a quiet moment, while ages wait, feel themselves as "I" to "Thou" with God. In this experience (as in the experience reported by the mystics) there is a fading of self-centeredness, but seldom, as in mysticism, is there a suspension of self-awareness. Jones is always Jones, and God is God. There is continued polarity: worshipper *and* divine object, I *and* Thou; there is no suspension of the ego. There is a feeling of community with God, but no loss of the feeling of multiplicity of life. The object/subject relationship remains. All things do not become one, although they may become intimately, even exquisitely, related.

Early in this book we said that humans are the religion-doing animals, and we examined why they do religion, and what they do when they do it, and we observed some of the practical benefits received in doing it. But in these last two chapters, we have been saying that religion is, for all this, something superbly more.

Even if, through some supertechnology, all of the practical values now available only through religion could be technologically produced for people, religion would yet be sought and treasured by those who had discovered its profounder dimensions. It would remain exciting and precious in the lives of those who waited on the Lord and mounted up with eagle wings, for those who found his footprint "just where one scarlet lily flamed,"[13] for those who took on love and charity and forgot themselves in fullness of living, and, perhaps, most precious of all, for those who were still and knew God.

NOTES

[1] Knud Rasmussen, *The Intellectual Culture of the Iglulik Eskimos* (Copenhagen, 1929), p. 119.

[2] John Wesley, *The Journal of John Wesley* (London: Epworth Press, 1938), vol. 1, pp. 475–476.

[3] Joseph Campbell, *The Masks of God: Primitive Mythology* (New York: Viking, 1959), p. 21.

[4] The word "shaman" comes from the reindeer-herding people, the Tungus of Siberia, and literally means "one who is excited, moved, raised."

[5] I. M. Lewis, *Ecstatic Religion* (Harmondsworth, England: Penguin, 1971), p. 51.

[6] Ibid., p. 31.

[7] Rasmussen, *The Intellectual Culture of the Iglulik Eskimos*, p. 119.

[8] For the full text of this fine poem see *The World's Great Religious Poetry*, ed. Caroline Miles Hill (New York: Macmillan Company, 1942), pp. 45–49.

[9] I. M. Lewis, *Ecstatic Religion*, p. 60.

[10] Quoted by Walter T. Stace, *The Teachings of the Mystics* (New York: New American Library, Mentor, 1960), p. 20.

[11] Sokei-an Sasaki, "The Transcendental World," Zen Notes, 1, no. 9 (1954): 5.

[12] Jan Van Ruysbroeck, *The Adornment of the Spiritual Marriage*, tran. C. A. Wynachenek (New York: Dutton, 1916).

[13] Bliss Carman, "Vestigia," verse 1, line 4. For copy of poem, see *The World's Great Religious Poetry*, ed. Caroline M. Hill.

Afterword

GETTING IT IN SHAPE

And he who sat upon the throne said,
"Behold, I make all things new."
Revelation 21:15

In 1965 Harvey Cox° published a book that announced the demise of religion. It had died, so Cox proclaimed, in the turning of the world into a secular city. "The age of the secular city, the epoch whose ethos is quickly spreading into every corner of the globe, *is* an age of 'no religion at all.' "[1]

A year later Thomas Altizer° and William Hamilton° wrote a book that announced the demise of God. Altizer and Hamilton had looked inward and discovered that the world was suffering from an absence of the experience of God, or at least they were. They proclaimed, somewhat inconsistently, that although "God had died in our time, in our history, in our experience," he really died when he willingly poured himself into the person of Jesus of Nazareth, and died with Jesus on the Cross. Other "Death of God" advocates of the Jewish tradition apparently concluded that God had died at Auschwitz. In his book *After Auschwitz,* Richard Rubenstein raised the question poignantly: How can a Jew believe in God? He concluded that after Auschwitz, he, for one Jew, could not; that he was living at the time of the death of God.

> If I believed in God as the omnipotent author of the historical drama [the death camps] and Israel as His Chosen people, I had to accept [the] conclusion that it was God's will that Hitler committed six million Jews to slaughter. I could not possibly believe in such a God nor could I believe in Israel as the chosen people after Auschwitz.[2]

Cox's death of religion was politely received by the American intelligentsia, and widely read by it, but not widely read by everyone else. But the proclamation of God's death struck the fancy of certain news journals and for a while it got wide publicity and much popular attention. But today neither Cox's *The Secular City* nor the books of the Death of God school command much attention, and we are, perhaps, in a position to make some sober observations about the flurry of religious excitement.

First it is somewhat surprising that a Death of God announcement in the twentieth century got viewed as "news," when the same kind of announcement had been made much more logically and philosophically on a number of occasions much earlier. One can go back as far as the second century B.C. when Carneades, the head of the Second Platonic Academy, examined the evidence and concluded not that God had died, but that God could not possibly ever have existed. In the eighteenth century, the Scottish philosopher David Hume° made the same argument even more systematically than had Carneades. And after Hume there were Schopenhauer and Feuerbach° and Nietzsche° and Freud°—all presenting brilliant arguments proving that God and religion had surely passed out of the picture for anyone bright enough to read their books on the subject.

The second observation to make is that apparently when the modern-day announcements were made, as in earlier times, nobody listened. Robert Ellwood° in his little book on the Jesus People has asserted that what happened was that everybody played a game called "Fool the Prophets."

> "Fool the Prophets" has been played on a sweeping scale in American popular and political culture in the sixties and seventies. Never have predictions and projections been more plentiful and precise. Never have the people who make popular culture taken more apparent delight in confounding the prognostications by finding something else to do.[3]

Lots of people heard what the "prophets" were saying clearly enough: Religion is gone, replaced by technology, megalopolis, and secularism. God is gone, dead gone; and we must learn to live not in the experience of the absence of God, but in the absence of the experience of God. *But nobody listened.* Religion did not end, and God seems to have come back alive from Argentina or wherever else he was hiding. Evidence to this effect can be seen in recently taken polls that indicate that although church and synagogue attendance has declined over the past few years, a large portion of the American population still goes to church or synagogue once each week. Also, apparently God is alive and well in American hearts and minds. Pollsters report that among adult Americans belief in God, on a scale of 100, registers in the high 90s. In Europe this belief is less impressive but still high.*

The Reshaping of Religious Expressions　Another observation to make about the current shape of things is that Harvey Cox, Thomas Altizer, William Hamilton, and other "radical theology" people did not mean exactly what they said or mean it exactly as they said it. When Cox said, in effect, Religion is dead, he really must have meant: *Religion is dead. Long live religion!* And the others must have meant, similarly: *God is dead. Long live God!* What they were doing was proposing that certain kinds of religious expressions and feelings were gone, and that it was time to redo religion for the world of today. And in such proposing they were not doing anything especially new or even radical. Redefining religion is probably as old as the second generation of the

---

*Recent Gallup polls show that something like 40 percent of all adult Americans claim to be "born again" Christians. See especially George Gallup, Jr., and David Poling, *The Search for America's Faith* (Nashville, Tenn.: Abingdon, 1980).

first religion of mankind. Once started, the next generation surely had to redefine it to make it fit some modified contemporary situation.

Any time there is sufficient reason, the case of religion is restated. Sometimes a person coming at the right time is sufficient reason, for example, Moses, Gautama, Jesus, and Muhammad. Sometimes a major cultural change is sufficient reason. When Paul and the other Apostles left Palestine and moved their religion into a different cultural setting, the faith got restated. It was made to talk sense not to Jews only, but also to Ephesians and Colosians and Athenians and Romans. And when it became sophisticated enough to appeal to educated people, it was reinterpreted by St. Augustine in Platonic modes of thought. When in the thirteenth century Aristotelian philosophy became the science of the day, Christianity was restated by St. Thomas in the rational forms of Aristotle's logic. When modern states began to rise in Europe, the Christian church decentralized and nationalized and talked a theology congenial with the newly emerging mercantile and industrial economies. When modern science introduced heliocentric and evolutionary theories, Christian theology at first fought it and then joined it. Christian theology today is simply not the theology of Jesus, or Paul, or Augustine, any more than the world of today is the same as that of Jesus, or Paul, or Augustine. Religion does not die, but its form changes. Sometimes almost imperceptibly, sometimes dramatically, sometimes drastically, religion takes on new shapes as it presents its old message in a new way.

Principles of Reshaping   It is impossible to tell how the forms of religion (or techniques, as we have called them) will change in the next 10, 50, 100 years, but they will change. What does not change is the fact of religion in the lives of people. Human finitude does not change. The joy of religious experience does not change. But the answers and expressions given and experienced constantly change and are today changing rapidly. Our world (replete with new computer calculations, controls, and communication; with air travel and extraterrestrial explorations; with atomic energy, and atomic bombs, and international economic intricacies) is simply not the world of our ancesters of even a generation ago. And when the world changes, the world's religions reform themselves to restate their message in the languages and thought patterns of the new day.

Everywhere new styles of religion are being tried, both independent of and inside established denominations. The future of any style cannot be predicted, but a historical perspective may give us some insight into the dual forces that seem to govern all religions as they move through history. Religion expresses itself in two ways: as rational, culture-related thought and activity; and as emotional, inner-directed experience. The rational pole emphasizes the ideas, vocabulary, and the established scientific and philosophical world view in which it operates. It is, properly, historically worldly. The other pole of the same religion is seen as basically unique and not to be corrupted by any foreign "modern language." At any given time both of these antagonistic poles are alive and straining against each other. Religion has its extremely rational moments. It also has its extremely emotional moments. Its long-run success comes when some degree of balance is maintained between the two. An imbalance usually occurs when the culture shifts.

Our culture has shifted. There is an imbalance between the poles, between rationalism, a willingness to let the *head* take charge; and emotionalism, an unwillingness to let the head overrule the *heart*. Perhaps more precisely and technically, we should say, as Robert Linder points out, the contemporary struggle is between "liberals who are willing to accommodate to the new scientism, even in matters of faith, while conservatives draw the line at certain fundamental essentials no matter what modern science happens to be saying at the moment."[4]

Today liberalism, on the one hand, and conservatism, on the other, are standing opposed to each other as an internal split in both the Catholic and Protestant divisions of Christianity. Similar tensions and splits are to be seen in Judaism (both in America and in Israel), in Buddhism (for example, in Vietnam), in Hinduism, in the religions of Japan, and surely in China. Indeed, today religion everywhere seems to be caught between the old ways and the new ways. How these tensions all around the world will be resolved no one can possibly predict.

A deeper penetration of the religious situation, however, as we have pursued it in this book, informs us that it is the style that changes, the shape that changes, not the need for, or the fact of, religion in people's lives. Religion as such remains constant today and tomorrow, as it was yesterday.

NOTES

[1] Harvey Cox, *The Secular City* (New York: Macmillan, 1965), p. 3.
[2] Richard L. Rubenstein, *After Auschwitz* (Indianapolis: Bobbs-Merrill, 1966), p. 46.
[3] Robert S. Ellwood, *One Way* (Englewood Cliffs, N.J.: Prentice-Hall, 1973), p. 1.
[4] Robert Linder, from private correspondence.

Appendix 1

DATA BANK FOR RELIGIOUS STUDIES

Religion, from the looks of it, is a many splendored thing. It covers the full range of human life and activity. It encompasses art, thought, literature, and emotion. It is a social structure. It is a political dynamic. It is both a reason for peace, and a stimulant for violence. All of which means that to investigate adequately what religion is involves a wide variety of scholarly disciplines. This accounts for the fact that courses in what are now called religious studies departments in many colleges and universities utilize the research and methods of many different disciplines, including theology, philosophical theology, biblical criticism, history of religions (comparative religion), social and behavioral sciences, and archaeology.

Most of these disciplines are new developments. Modern biblical criticism began in the middle years of the eighteenth century; sociology of religion and history of religions in the nineteenth century; and psychology of religion and biblical archaeology in the twentieth century. Philosophical theology is a different matter. Theology (words about God and religious things) presented in philosophical form (according to rational principles and arguments) goes back in Christian history to the early centuries, beginning with such important early church leaders as Origen° of Alexandria (c.185–254) and St. Augustine° of Hippo (354–430).

These several disciplines are important bases of information for defining religion, and therefore, some comments about each seem in order.

PHILOSOPHICAL THEOLOGY

In the Ancient World Important early Christians like Paul were primarily concerned with getting the "Jesus story" told and delineated theologically. They were not philosophers in the sense of using philosophical criteria in their arguments for the new faith. They had not come head-on against such philosophers of the ancient world as Plato or Aristotle. Indeed much early Christian theology was hammered out in conflict not with Greek and Roman philosophy, but with Jewish opponents, and the Jews were not (with a few exceptions, such as Philo° of Alexandria) philosophers. The early nonphilosophical presentations of the Christian witness continued in the works of the so-called Apostolic Fathers: such second-century church leaders as Clement I, bishop of Rome; St. Ignatius, bishop of Antioch; Barnabus, the author of an important letter on theology written about 117–119; St. Polycarp, bishop of Smyrna, martyred about 156. These Fathers of the Church, while addressing themselves to Hellenistic° threats, based their arguments on "inspired truth" not on rational philosophical argument.

It was in the third century that leaders in the Christian church became not simply witnesses to the Christian faith, but philosophical theologians using philosophical categories and methods, and even synthesizing Greek philosophical concepts with the Christian intellectual (faith) system. These teachers are today called Apologists,° and of their number Origen of Alexandria possessed by far the most systematic and philosophically capable mind of the Christian teachers of his time.* He assimilated into his exposition of the Christian dogma elements from Plato,° Aristotle,° Philo,° the Neo-Platonists,° and the Gnostics.° Indeed, he and his teacher Clement, both teachers in Alexandria in Egypt, helped renew the intellectual and philosophical prestige of the ancient capital of Egypt.

After Origen a number of Christian theologians† devoted their energies to dealing with internal theological tensions especially relating to doctrines of the Trinity and the divine-human nature of Christ.

The most exciting of these Patristic Fathers, as they came to be called, was St. Augustine (354–430). Augustine was the greatest of the early speculative philosophical theologians. His system of Christian theology, both Christian revelation and Platonic philosophical in character, was the systematic theology of early Catholicism that carried forward to the Middle Ages and beyond, in tremendous influence, even to today. Augustine is not only a giant among Christian theologians, but he stands firmly among the world's greatest philosophers. His philosophical theology covered a vast range of speculative thought. He examined, for example, the concepts of God, human soul, ethics, dialectic,° theology, cosmology, and psychology.

But for all his philosophical interest in religion, Augustine never did define accurately the difference between philosophy and theology. That distinction was left to another giant of philosophy and theology: the mastermind of the thirteenth century— St. Thomas Aquinas° (c. 1225–1274). Like all the early church fathers, St. Augustine esteemed Plato above Aristotle, but eventually (with Thomas Aquinas) Aristotle would have his "Christian day" also.

IN THE MEDIEVAL WORLD: SCHOLASTICISM° IN THE MIDDLE AGES

Sometime before the eleventh century there was a decline in philosophical theology because of the opposition of church authorities. This opposition occurred partly because a man named Erigena, born in Ireland early in the ninth century, had attempted to find a rational basis for the union of reason (philosophical thought) with revelation. Only he pushed too far—or so thought the church leadership—and for a while philosophical theology was discouraged. However, by the eleventh century this prejudice had declined, as can be seen in the importance given to the work of St. Anselm° of Canterbury (1033–1109).

Anselm, often called the "father of Scholasticism," did two things of lasting worth in philosophical theology. He said, "I believe that I may know" (credo ut intelligam), by which he proposed that one can see and know (study) religion or God, or

---

*Other apologists were Justin Martyr (100–160), Athanagoras (died c. 180), Tatian (late second century), Theophilus (late second century), Irenaeus (140–202), Hippolytus (early third century), Tertullian (c. 160–240), and Clement of Alexandria (died 217).
†Such as Athanasius of Alexandria (died 373), Gregory of Nyssa (c. 331–394), Basil (died 379), Gregory Nazianzen (born 330), and Cyril of Alexandria (died 444).

both, more correctly by standing firmly in faith rather than by standing outside just looking at it objectively. Anselm's other famous contribution to religious thought (both then and now) was his ontological argument for the existence of God.*

Because of an increase in information about Plato and Aristotle acquired through Christian contacts with Islam,† especially in Spain where the Muslims still ruled, Christian theology took a new direction in the eleventh century. This new direction included the making of summaries, systematic theologies, by important philosophical theologians.** The most important of these summaries was that of St. Thomas Aquinas—*The Summa Theologica*. With Thomas the Christian theology got a powerful dose of philosophy that continues to this day, especially in Catholic thought. Thomas took the position that through reason (philosophical investigation) one can know of religion and religious things. God's existence can, for example, be proved through reason, namely, empirical investigation of the world around us.‡ This is natural theology. But such things as the personal nature of God, Jesus Christ as Savior, the Trinity, the Virgin Mother, are not items that are discoverable through natural investigation and reason; they depend on revelation. All this is to say that Thomas delineated sharply the fields of philosophy and theology. The subject matter of philosophy he restricted to everything that lies open to argument. The purpose of philosophy he declared to be the establishment of such truth as can be discovered and demonstrated by the use of human reason. On the other hand, the subject matter of theology is the content of faith, or, in other words, it is revealed truth that reason is incapable of discovering or demonstrating and about which there can be no argument. Nevertheless, the two fields overlap. Since no truth can contradict reason, the "mysteries" of faith cannot be unintelligible but are simply beyond our finite, human understanding. They, therefore, can be reasoned about and, in part at least, are within human comprehension. The existence of God, for example, can be demonstrated by reason apart from revelation. Other theological points, too, are susceptible of rational demonstration. Indeed, a good part of philosophy—the most important part in fact—is devoted to matters of theological interest and forms a *natural theology,* as Aquinas called it, to be distinguished from *revealed theology.*[1]

The philosophical theology of Thomas Aquinas found an able opponent in the gifted, "subtile doctor," as he is often called, John Duns Scotus° (c. 1266–1308). Duns Scotus accepted Thomas's distinction between theology and philosophy and then proceeded to relegate philosophy to a position of little significance in religion. Unlike Thomas, who placed intellect at the forefront in religion, Duns Scotus placed the human will in that posture. It is the will that is primary in religion, not the mind. Thomas taught that salvation (ultimate happiness) was to be sought in contemplation of the "divine essence." It was an intellectual affair. Duns Scotus rejected this and taught that final happiness (salvation) was to be attained in an act of perfect love. It was an affair of the will.

---

*See pages 154–156.

†Aristotle especially, whose works were pretty much lost to the Christian world, was reintroduced into Europe through contacts with Islam where his works had been more extensively preserved. This rediscovery of Aristotle in the West began to occur in the eleventh century.

**For example, summaries by Alexander of Hales (died 1245), Albert the Great (c. 1206–1280), Bonaventura (1221–1274).

‡See pages 152–153.

In the controversy of Aquinas and Duns Scotus we can see a split that runs through the history of Christian philosophical theology: How does one come to final truth and ultimate salvation? Does one discover ultimate truth by careful thinking (reason), as Thomas would propose; or is it the way of inner feeling, experience, intuition (faith), as Duns Scotus put it? One type of theologian will say: "Thinking, reasoning, philosophizing is the way!" Another will reject this saying, "Feeling is what counts. Intuition is the way. The truth of religion is not that it thinks right, but that it feels right!"

With the work of William of Occam°* (c. 1280–c. 1349) the affinity between philosophy and theology further declined. Occam argued that reality cannot be conceived as being universal; rather, it is individual. What we know are specific facts. All real knowledge is based on intuition. Abstraction does not give a true picture of reality. One should cut away all unnecessary theologizing and hypothesizing; one should employ "Occam's razor."°† All knowledge is based on experience. Furthermore, in knowledge we do not perceive the object directly, but through our senses. It comes to us as an appearance (a "sign" Occam called it) of itself. Occam was a skeptic in the sense of restricting the powers of reason. He did not deny the possibility of certainty. He simply argued that the intellect could not furnish it. In the list of truths that human reason cannot prove, he lists: the human soul, the existence of God, the infinity of God, the immediate creation of the universe by God.

In the sixteenth century, beginning with the Protestant Reformation, philosophical theology declined in importance. Neither the reforming Protestant nor the Counter-Reformation° Catholics relied on philosophy to support religious faith. The Protestants did their arguing on the basis of direct Bible authority, and on the doctrine of "salvation by faith alone." The Catholics based their Counter-Reformation case on apostolic authority.

The late sixteenth and early seventeenth centuries, the time of both Martin Luther (1483–1546) and Nicolaus Copernicus° (1473–1543), was a time of bitter theological controversy on the continent of Europe and in England. Protestants and Catholics were at each other's throats, and neither Protestant nor Catholic reformers and counterreformers took any account of the new science and philosophy that were developing. But there were features in Protestant thought that helped set the stage for a new philosophical-theological stance in the eighteenth century. First, Scholastic thought was already highly rationalistic, relying on truth deduced from first principles. Second, the times were divisive. Thought was going in many directions and there arose a desire to find some common ground upon which persons of reason could agree despite their theological differences.[2]

---

*Also Ockham.
†Also called the Law of Parsimony. The law reads, *Entities are not to be multiplied except as may be necessary.* It means that we are not to explain things in a more complicated fashion than necessary. For example, if existence can be explained in terms of natural causes, do not add supernatural explanations. Do not compound hypotheses unnecessarily. Although Occam himself remained a man of faith, this kind of thinking paved the way to later materialistic skepticism.

The Modern World   Philosophy returned full speed into Western thought with René Descartes° (1596–1650). His *Discourse on Method* with its famous *Cogito ergo sum* (I think; therefore, I am) laid the foundation for modern rationalistic philosophy.* In his little book *Meditations on First Philosophy*, he harkened back to St. Anselm and presented his own version of the ontological argument.† He also argued that matter and mind are absolutely different. Matter is devoid of all mind, and mind is absolutely immaterial. This view of mind and matter gave Descartes some claim to being the founder of modern philosophy, for his concept of the immaterial nature of mind proved suggestive to modern idealist (mind-based) philosophy, and at the same time, his divorcing of matter from mind was important to the development of subsequent naturalistic and materialistic philosophies.

But actually it was not Descartes who first represented the emancipation of the modern thinker from the medieval thinker; it was Girodano Bruno who lived half a century earlier (c. 1548–1600). Descartes was in spirit at least still part of Scholasticism. Indeed, he literally went back to Anselm for his ontological argument. But not Bruno. Bruno was a "modern" in a world not quite ready for him. It cost him his life.

Born in Nola, in southern Italy, Bruno entered a monastery at age sixteen. But by the age of eighteen he was having grave doubts about orthodox Catholicism/Christianity. When he was thirty he fled the monastery and went to Rome. From that time on he became a perpetual exile, wandering from place to place. For a while he took refuge in the south of France and taught at the University of Toulouse. He went to Paris and at the University of Paris was an admired teacher. He also spent time in London and Oxford, but he despised the English. Back in Paris he attacked the Aristotelian philosophy that St. Thomas had so much admired and had given prominence in Catholic theology. Then Bruno made a fatal mistake. He set forth in clear and forceful language the new Copernican° world view. This view, heralding the coming of the modern world, was an unwelcome pronouncement in the late sixteenth century. Bruno was arrested by the Office of the Inquisition° and after a protracted trial was burned at the stake. Bruno died, but a new world was on its way.

Descartes had made his case for God by relying on reason alone—formal, deductive, *a priori°* reasoning. For example, he said one could demonstrate the existence of God on purely rational grounds and on innate ideas.[3] The Englishman John Locke° (1632–1704) found such logic completely unacceptable. He held that all knowledge must be based on experience. People are born, he said, devoid of any ideas. Human minds at birth are *tabula rasa* (blank tablets) upon which experience writes. All ideas, without exception, are derived from experience. The existence of God, for example, can only be demonstrated on empirical grounds.°**

---

*Other philosophers of modern rationalistic philosophy are Baruch Spinoza, George Berkeley, Immanuel Kant, Friedrich Schleiermacher, Auguste Compte, Rudolph Lotze, and Albrecht Ritschl.
†See pages 154–156.
**Locke argued that the existence of human beings necessitates a creator at least equal to the creation. This argument actually went back to St. Thomas and Aristotle.

Locke made another argument that proved influential in later philosophical theology. He pointed out the danger of "wish thinking." People are apt to believe what they want to believe not because it is true, but because they want to believe it. According to Locke, "They are sure because they are sure; and their persuasions are right because they are strong in them." What they believe "is a revelation, because they firmly believe it; and they believe it because it is a revelation." Locke did not deny the reality of biblical revelation. Rather he insisted that such revelation did not replace empirical investigation and conclusion. God made all truth reasonable; therefore "reason must be our last judge and guide in everything."*

Locke attempted to apply empirical, scientific principles to the Christian faith. He desired to show Christianity in a "reasonable light," using the reason of empirical investigation, not of logical deduction.

Descartes, Bruno, Locke, all seventeenth-century thinkers, stood on the threshold of the modern world. But in philosophical theology it was the giants of the next century who crossed that threshold,† especially Immanuel Kant,° Georg Hegel,° and Friedrich Schleiermacher.° But first we should note David Hume° (1711–1766) who as much as anyone else took the first major step.

In 1739, David Hume's *Treatise on Human Nature* was published in London. He expected it to make quite a stir, but it did not. Yet it should have for it announced the arrival of an intellect that would shake philosophical thought to its very foundations. Hume's starting point was radical empiricism, and his conception of the purpose of philosophy was critical examination. His own critical examination led him to conclude, first, that the human mind is simply its own contents.

Thus, an analysis of the mind would be no more than an inventory of its contents, namely, perceptions. Perceptions Hume declared to be of two types: *impressions*—the more lively perceptions experienced when one sees, hears, wills, loves, and the like; and *thoughts* or *ideas*—the faint images of perceptions. This means, among other things, that when thinking about the world and the world's God, we are all caught in an "anthropomorphic trap." We think of the divine according to our own experience, but our experience—our consciousness—is only a bundle of perceptions, and these perceptions tell us about ourselves, perhaps, but not about the world and its God.

Second, Hume made the startling announcement that "cause and effect" is simply our perception of the successions in phenomena. We perceive "A" followed by "B." If this happens over and over, we say that "A" causes "B." But Hume pointed out that we do not perceive "A" causing "B," only "B" following "A." He stated that "the knowledge of this relation (causality) is not . . . attained by reasoning *a priori*; but arises entirely from experience, when we find any particular objects are *constantly* conjoined with each other."[4]

---

*Other important philosopher-theologians who joined in this effort to base religion empirically include William Chillingworth, John Tillotson, John Toland, Matthew Tindal, G. E. Lessing, and François Marie Arouet (pen name Voltaire).

†In the eighteenth century, called the Age of Enlightenment, Christian thought got its really modern dimensions. More than anything else, this was a century of revolt against authoritarianism and it marked the emergence of individual reason and personal conscience as the primary arbiters of truth and action.

Third, Hume's moral philosophy restricted the role of reason as a moral criterion. Instead, moral distinctions were seen as being determined by one's sense of the agreeable and the disagreeable. The following is Hume's ultimate analysis of moral value, which, he held, was situated in sympathy:

> No man is absolutely indifferent to the happiness and misery of others. The first has a natural tendency to give pleasure; the second, pain. This everyone may find in himself. It is not probable that these principles can be resolved into principles more simple and universal. . . .[5]

Fourth, in *The Natural History of Religion,* one of his two sustained studies of religion,* Hume directed his attack particularly against two generally held beliefs that he believed could not be supported by empirical evidence. One was the supposition that belief in *one* God is a universal human instinct. He held rather that it was not reason that lay behind belief in God, but fear. Fear of the unknown causes at work in nature produced the tribal deities of primitive people. Furthermore, he held, that even after the idea of a supreme God was accomplished, popular religion always remained more or less polytheistic. The other object of Hume's attack was the notion that the so-called high religions have been socially beneficial. Rather he found that they not only resulted in superstition and fanaticism, but also in a system of duties that weakened the human attachment to principles of justice and humanity. And even more important, Hume held that "high religions" subvert integrity and knowledge. To participate in such a religion people must force themselves to endorse beliefs whether or not they believe them to be true. Thus, "unlike the inescapable human propensity to causal inference and the belief in an order of nature upon which all action depends, ordinary religious belief is a form of make-believe which, treated as religious obligation, becomes a chain of hypocrisy which leads by degrees to dissimulation, fraud and falsehood."[6]

With this sort of criticism, Hume started a string of new explosions in philosophical theology in a new world. One of those explosions came in the work of the extraordinary German philosopher Immanuel Kant who admitted that he was awakened from his dogmatic slumbers by David Hume. It was Hume's analysis of causality that undermined Kant's certainty about things philosophical and religious. He could no longer accept the tenets of rationalism or believe in the axioms of an ontological philosophy. To answer Hume became the main goal of Kant's philosophical thinking.

Immanuel Kant (1724–1804) wrote two books on the source of human knowledge. In his *Critique of Pure Reason,* he skeptically dismantled the ancient tools of reason. He argued that neither rational thought nor empirical evidence gives us assured information because both reason and experience are themselves given form by the nature of the human mind. Our minds shape what we know. We do not directly experience the world. We experience it through our minds. We know the world as it appears to us. The *Ding-an-sich* (thing in itself) may be quite different.

In his second critique, *Critique of Practical Reason,* the prospect for assurance in knowing became markedly advanced. Here he explored the conditions of moral experience. Through the "practical reason" much can be known. For example, consciousness (a dimension of practical reason) informs me that *I ought* to perform certain actions and avoid others. A little thought convinces me that this "oughtness" is

---

*The other being *Dialogues Concerning Natural Religion.*

universal. It is true for everybody, everywhere. In its abstract form this "categorical imperative" demands that I so act that I can will that the maxim on which I conduct my actions should become a law for everyone—a universal law. This *moral law*, because it is universal and unchanging, must rest on a necessary foundation. And it does. It is autonomous. It rests on its own foundation. It is not imposed by external motive or deduced by rational speculation. It is, rather, imposed on the will by the practical reason, and it is revealed in immediate consciousness.

Moral experience, then, is direct. It is imperative. It is based in itself. Furthermore, since morality is real, certain other deductions can be made: (1) The will is free; otherwise morality would be unreal. (2) There must be life after death to balance the moral scales that are too often out of balance in this life where innocence often suffers and evil is rewarded. And (3) there must be God to see to the final moral equity.

Kant based religious faith not on reason, but on the experienced fact of human conscience. He, therefore, could define religion succinctly as the recognition of duties as divine commands.

Kant based his theological synthesis on moralilty: Religion is duties recognized as divine commands. Georg Wilhelm Friedrich Hegel (1770–1831) saw religion differently, not as a thing of the will (morality), but of the intellect. Religion was finally, for Hegel, pure philosophy, a philosophy of absolute idealism.

Hegel held that God (the Absolute) is not a thing, not a being, not a substance, but a *process*. God is the world-process, which is the process whereby the inherent plan or character of that process is becoming explicit—is coming to full self-realization. Now *self*-realization implies *self-consciousness*; therefore, the world process (the absolute existence) must be conceived as a process of evolving self-consciousness that will finally culminate in complete self-knowledge. Seen in pure philosophical terms, God is Spirit that is the process of life. Without the world, God is not fully God. There is no distinction to be drawn between the Spirit (God) and the process of self-fulfillment.[7]

Hegel proposed that by three steps we can rise to the heights of Absolute Spirit: by art, by religion, and by philosophy. In art the Spirit (God) may be symbolized, but not accomplished. In religion objective nature may be presented as the manifestation of Spirit. In this (1) God may be regarded as transcendent to the world, as a changeless, eternal being who exists apart from the world that he created; or (2) God may be conceived of as an incarnate or immanent creative power in the world; or (3) God may be seen as the infinite to which the finite (world) returns.[8] But the philosophical vision of God stands higher than that of either art or religion. Philosophy, combining the glorification of God found in art with religion's assertion that the finite world is a creation of God, proclaims the Absolute Spirit to be the world-process in which God is, in fact, fulfilling his own self-realization, is, in fact, becoming finally and fully God.

Although not at first sympathetic to Christianity, Hegel eventually concluded that Christianity was the best form of religious expression for in it alone can be seen the dialectical (back-and-forth) process by which Spirit (God) works out to full expression in history. God is a God of history not simply as Jews and Christians first supposed (as simply the creator of the world and the determiner of its destiny), but as the very immanent process of that world and its history. Hegel realized that Christianity does not yet present itself in proper philosophical and contemplative form. It does, in fact, present itself in sensuous dimension, in moralizing and aesthetic forms, but eventually, he held, such forms must be transcended *(aufgehoben)* into pure thought *(Begriffe).* Christianity must finally escape all historical analogies and become Absolute Idea. It must finally recognize that salvation is not an affair of morality or feeling, but a direct cognitive contemplation of God.

Another evidence of Hegel's eventual endorsement of Christian theology is to be seen in his insightful interpretation of the Fall as presented in the Old Testament story of Adam and Eve. He presented the Fall not as an isolated incident in the long ago, but as a human advance beyond innocence in the direction of ultimate knowledge (salvation). Animals live "in innocence" with God, functioning simply as God has designed them. But humans move beyond innocence and become beings of self-consciousness. They become beings of true spirit, of intellect. The Genesis story of Adam's Fall is simply the myth of the transcendence of human brute animal to Homo sapiens.° In Hegel's own words: "The Fall is therefore the Mythus of Man—in fact, the very transition by which he becomes man." This quote is from Hegel's *The History of Philosophy,* tran. J. Sibree (New York, 1944), p. 321.

Kant saw religion as a way of behaving—a matter of ethics. Hegel saw it as a way of thinking—a matter of metaphysics. Friedrich Schleiermacher° (1768–1834) made a radical shift. He said religion "cannot be an instinct craving a mass of metaphysical and ethical crumbs."[9] Rather, he held that feeling was the peculiar faculty of the religious life. By feeling in this situation Schleiermacher meant the immediate, intuitive consciousness "that our being and living is a being and living through God." For Schleiermacher religion rested in the feeling of infinity that we all have, and of our feeling of dependence on that infinity. He wrote:

. . . the self-identical essence of piety is this: the consciousness of absolute dependence, or, which is the same thing, of being in relation with God.[10]

Toward the end of the eighteenth century in Europe there came to prominence a generation of thinkers and artists (the Romantic Movement) who saw things differently. They were in revolt against the current rationalistic Zeitgeist.° They threw wide the door of personal, emotional experience. Among these philosophers and artists were such men as Byron, Blake, Wordsworth, Coleridge, Beethoven, Chopin, Balzac, and Goethe. They responded to life with "romantic" enthusiasm. Friedrich Schleiermacher was also a person of such sentiments.

Schleiermacher's work led to some radical changes in modern theology. After Schleiermacher religion would be viewed more scientifically. New dimensions of depth psychology would be added. New critical examinations of religious traditions and history would be made. More critical examinations of scripture would be encouraged. There would be a deemphasizing (and even dismissal) of certain Christian doctrines that no longer seemed essential, such as, the Virgin Birth, the Trinity, the Second Coming. A comparative study of religion, and the scientific analysis and classification of religious phenomena would be fostered. All of this, of course, explains why Schleiermacher is called the "father of modern theological liberalism." It also makes him initially responsible for the rejection of modern Liberalism by modern Neo-Orthodoxy.[11]

The Twentieth Century Initiated by Hume, Kant, Locke, and Schleiermacher, by Copernicus and Darwin, and by the whole explosion of science and technology in the modern world, certain philosophers and theologians have tried to interpret religion (and particularly Christianity) so that it "can make sense" once again, this time in a new Zeitgeist—that of the twentieth century. At least three directions of modern philosophical theology have been (and are being) tried: (1) liberalism of a personalistic orientation; (2) liberalism of an immanentalistic,° nonpersonalistic, nature-mystic dimension; and (3) a negative reaction to all forms of liberalism called the new orthodoxy—Neo-Orthodoxy.

First, we should note that liberal theologians of both types (personalists and immanentalists) are not biblical literalists or doctrinal conservatives. They hold the Bible to be a book of tremendous religious and spiritual worth. It is to be taken seriously, but not literally. It is a book (a whole series of books covering 1,500 years of the living of a people of religious genius—the ancient Hebrews) that was written long before the age of modern science. It is not a book of science and should not be used as one. It is a book of inspiration and direction for holy living. For that it should be used seriously, devotedly, thankfully, joyously. As for Christian tradition, it, too, should be taken seriously. It is the basic faith story. It is the sustaining root. But it is not sacrosanct.°

Second, liberal theologians of both types view God in the dimensions of twentieth-century knowledge: God of a universe fantastically larger, and older, and more mysterious, and magnificent than ever dreamed in ages past; God of a world where the earth is practically nothing (a second-rate planet of a fifth-rate star), but where human life makes it a center of infinite worth.

This much liberal theologians agree on, but they are about to part company, for when they go on to say what God is like, they go their separate ways. One group says, "God is like a great person, a supernatural, personal being." The other group says, "God is like a great creative event, a process of creative activity discernible in the motions of the heavenly bodies, the evolution of the species, the coming of the springtime, the birth of a child, as well as a moment of joy too stunning to be spoken." One group may be called personalistic theists; the other group immanentalist naturalists.

Personalist Theism The primary concerns of personalistic theists* are to define God's nature, to identify the relation of God to humans and to the world, and to identify the purpose of God for humans in the world. They answer these concerns by declaring that this is "a world of persons with a Supreme Person at the head"[12] . . . "a Supreme Person who embodies the highest goodness . . . [and is] . . . the source both of

---

*Scholars of this tradition include Dean A. C. Knudson, H. P. Van Dusen,° H. F. Rall,° Walter M. Horton,° Edgar Sheffield Brightman,° R. T. Flewelling,° Bordon Parker Bowne,° William Adams Brown.°

existence and value."[13] God is, for personalistic theists, the independent and self-existent cause, ground, or creator of the cosmos, and is thus transcendent to it. At the same time, as the driving force of the universe, God is somehow immanent in it. God is

> the immanent force or drive which appears to be pushing, or pulling, the process of evolution onward and upward toward even more significant forms of reality in the direction of a Realm of Values. This upward nisus is God's purpose.[14]

God is thus seen as both transcendent to the world and immanent within it.

The goal of human existence, from this theistic viewpoint, is the perfection of individual and social life.[15] In his critique of recent theism, William Henry Bernhardt writes:

> Briefly stated, Theism believes that the purpose of God, so far as it affects this planet, is the creation and development of ideal persons in an ideal society. . . .
>
> [Life on earth] exists for personal ends, and may be called the theater of human activities, the stage on which man plays his part in response to Divine promptings.[16]

Immanentalism or Naturalism   Liberal theologians of an immanentalistic or naturalistic type generally (1) dismiss the concept of supernaturalism. All reality falls within the natural order, even God. (2) God is seen as the basic dynamic and direction of the natural order—of the world. (3) Religion is held to be the attention, devotion, and trust that humans give to God's sustaining power, and as the spiritual support and joy they receive from that relationship.

As seen by Alfred North Whitehead:° (1) The world is a process of channelized activity. As "activity" it can be seen as always changing; as "channelized" it can be seen as offering stability in flux. (2) It is, also, an ecological process. All things hang together. Everything is what it is because of its relatedness to everything else. (3) And not only is everything related to its environment (even its universal environment), but it appropriates that environment into itself. It prehends the world. In the microcosm there is the macrocosm; in the macrocosm there is the microcosm. (4) Also everything is moving toward concretions (realities) of increased complexity and of increased harmony. Nature is, thus, both a physical system and an aesthetic system. (5) The world process is also a system of possibilities—things appear; there is consistency (patternfulness) in their appearance; novelties emerge—there is God. God is that which (a) contains possibilities; (b) creates things; (c) preserves values. In what Whitehead calls God's Primordial Nature, God contains all possibilities, everything that might possibly be. In this same nature, God is the ordering of activities, and the principle and/or power of concretion (creation). God, according to Whitehead, possesses also a Consequent Nature. This is God as a living being in which and through which the actual world has its individual existence. This is God prehending the world, influencing its development, knowing it, conserving its values.

Harvey Potthoff° identifies the religious aspects of such a philosophical theology. He writes: "It is my belief that there is a basis for human hope and a clue to man's most appropriate direction of expectation in the way things are—*in the character of the whole of which we are part. . . .*"[17]

Potthoff believes that one knows the world and the world's God not only by objective scientific and philosophical investigation, but also by direct, personal experience. God is to be seen not only in the patterned processes of the whole universe, but also in the answering and fulfillment of religious questions and needs. Persons act toward God in trust and devotion, and they are answered with the experience of deliverance, the experience of integrity and presence, the experience of trust, the experience of forgiveness, the experience of healing, the experience of freedom, the experience of love that accepts and brings wholeness, the experience of claim and summons to a life of moral commitment, the experiences that lead some persons to affirm the reality of God as the Real Other and to witness the meaning and experience of God's continuing revelation.[18]

Neo-Orthodoxy   Following World War I, with the general and widespread disillusionment that it fostered, especially in Europe and particularly in Germany, there developed a countermovement to liberal theology. The movement was initiated by Karl Barth° (1886–1968),* a theologian of such stature that he is often equated with St. Augustine, whom he greatly admired, and with Friedrich Schleiermacher, whom he both admired and rejected.

A central principle of Neo-Orthodoxy is epistemological transcendence, which means that in no way can humans discover God. Philosophy is out. Philosophical theology is out. Theology straight is out. Even the Bible taken literally is out, and taken in liberal interpretation is even more out. God is to be known only through God. God is known in an act of grace that God bestows, if and when God chooses to bestow it. God reveals himself if and when he chooses to do so; and even this revelation is a mystery of a mystery for it not only signifies the hiddenness of God, but also his becoming manifest in a hidden or nonapparent way. Barth returned philosophical theology to theology *period,* and to theology that does not truly speak the God-word, but to theology and Bible that speak "God's Word so far as God lets it be His word."[19]

Neo-Orthodoxy was intended to correct what Barth and others† found no longer tenable—modern Protestant Liberalism. Barth called for a break with philosophy, science, and culture because he believed that these all blunted and distorted the Christian message in order to accommodate it to the modern world.

With Barth we put an end to philosophical theology, but only for Barth and other Neo-Orthodox adherents. Even though his attempt to divorce theology from philosophy is more radical and thoroughgoing in the twentieth century than Duns Scotus's attempt in the thirteenth century, it will not prove to be more successful. Even if not always friendly bedfellows, philosophy and theology have been wed for a long time in a marriage of convenience, if not always love. They will continue so.

SACRED LITERATURE—SCRIPTURE

Primary sources of information for the study of religion are, of course, the sacred writings of the consummate religions of the world—the Vedas of Hinduism, the Tao Te

---

*In the first half of the nineteenth century in Denmark, Søren Kierkegaard had made a passionate cry against substituting philosophy (in his case Hegel's philosophy) for religious experience. Kierkegaard in theology can rightly be considered the father of Neo-Orthodoxy, for the themes of his major works run like a binding cord through the early writings of the German theologians whose program came to be known as the "theology of crisis." The "crisis" was both in the times they lived and in the way they believed that God broke through with His saving grace in certain moments of human crisis.

†Emile Bruner (1889–1966), Rudolf Bultmann° (1884–1976), George Merz (1892–1959), Fredrich Goganten (1887–1967), and Reinhold Niebuhr (1892–1971).

Ching of Chinese Taoism, the Qur'an of the Islamic faith as well as the Jewish and Christian scriptures.*

Important also to religious studies are the extensive critical studies of the Old and New Testaments that have developed in the last 250 years. These studies attempt to view the Judeo-Christian scriptures not kerygmatically, but historically. That is to say, attempts are made to place the various writings of these scriptures in their original times and ask such questions as: What were the living conditions that caused this document first to be written (or spoken if it was originally a part of oral tradition)? What was the author primarily concerned to say? Who were the people for whom he spoke or wrote? What kind of world did they live in, or did they think they lived in? What was their *Zeitgeist?*

Apparently whatever conditions prompted the production of sacred writings, they soon became, after the passing of their authors, not simply reports about religious things made by such religious authorities as Moses, Isaiah, Jesus, Paul, Mark, John, and Muhammad, but also authorities in themselves. Once the living leader was gone, and those who knew that leader face to face were gone, the words of the leader (now in written form, if not before) became, so to speak, depersonalized. As Lindsay Longacre° in his *Old Testament–Its Form and Purpose* puts it: When all living contact was lost with the authors (oral and written) of the sacred writings and these "leaders receded into the past, their figures took on heroic proportions," and their writing and preaching "tended to become a sort of constitutional document serving as part of the official basis of a movement which had developed into an organic institution."[20] And this position, Longacre further points out, seems to be the position taken by most Jewish and Christian believers even today: The sacred writings are authoritative scriptures above and beyond any critical questioning. They are kerygmatic and final. But the problem is that they are very ancient, written in a different age, in a different world, and not always to be simply and directly understood even kerygmatically.

Sacred or not, scriptures are historical documents and amenable to historical examination and criticism, and in the middle of the eighteenth century this sort of study began to take place. Certain biblical scholars began to study the Judeo-Christian scriptures in a discipline that came to be called "historical criticism" or "higher criticism." They began to do what we identified in Chapter 1 as phenomenistic study. "This period finds its essential characteristic in its endeavor to recover the facts of the first period"—the time of the initial writing.[21] It attempts to return to the historical settings of the original presentations and writing of the "sacred documents."

Beginning with the French physician Jean Astruc° in the middle of the eighteenth century and continuing in the works of such scholars as Johann G. Eichhorn,° Wilhelm Martin Leberech De Wette,° Hermann Hupfield,° George Von Ewald,° and Julius Wellhausen° we have a tremendously influential development of critical information regarding the Judeo-Christian scriptures, especially concerned with identifying dates of writing, styles of writing, historical matrices of writings, and the like.

This scholarship that began largely with the Old Testament studies moved, of course, finally emphatically into the New Testament studies. Just after World War I, two German scholars in particular made seminal contributions in this effort: Martin Dibelius° of Heidelberg University and Rudolf Bultmann of Marburg University.†
They zeroed in on the oral forms that lay behind the written Gospels and began the

---

*It is with these writing sources (scriptures) that theologians also are primarily concerned.
†Martin Dibelius's *From Tradition to Gospel* was published in 1919. Two years later Rudolph Bultmann's *History of the Synoptic Tradition* was published.

effort to get back to the voices that did the original speaking. They and a battery of other scholars have carried the methods employed earlier in Old Testament historical criticism into the study of the New Testament. The results have been a whole new nonkerygmatic way of understanding the sacred scriptures as one of the phenomena of the Christian tradition. For additional comments on sacred literature see Chapter 11.

HISTORY OF RELIGIONS (COMPARATIVE RELIGION)

The history of religion is a rich source of material for understanding what religion is. Applied to Western religions, modern historical study methods have emphasized free and critical examination of Judeo-Christian scriptures and a similar examination of the theological and historical dimensions of Judaism and Christianity. And since the nineteenth century, the study of history of religions, employing comparative methods, has turned its attention to all of the religions of mankind. The result has been a wealth of information for explaining the meaning of religion not only in the Occident, but in the Orient as well, and, indeed, for explaining the meaning of religion itself.

History of religions is a study that seeks to understand what religion is by engaging in a comparative study of religions—primitive, ancient, and modern. Before this new type of study, through most of Christian history, Christian leaders and scholars have usually placed other religions someplace between ignored and despised. Judaism was an exception. It was not to be ignored or despised, but corrected. But in the 1870s, and since that time, something new has developed: a comparative study of religions to discern their similarities and differences, and this, usually, in an effort to comprehend the origins and essential character of religion as such—to get at *religion: what is it?*

Friederich Max Müller° (1823 – 1900) launched the science of comparative religion (history of religions) in 1870 when he delivered four lectures on the science of religion at the Royal Institute. In doing this he "made the first systematic and integrative attempt to understand the nature of religion in a scientific manner."[22] With these lectures, and especially with their publication in 1873,[23] the way was opened for interest in what Müller was doing and encouragement for his continuing that effort. He did continue it eventually translating and editing some fifty-one volumes of *The Sacred Books of the East.*

At the same time that Müller, a philologist° was initiating studies in comparative religions through comparative linguistics, Edward Tylor,° an ethnologist,° was beginning his comparative culture studies in primitive religions. He identified animism° as the original form of religion, and his findings were published in 1871 in his important work *Primitive Culture.*[24]

At the same time that Müller and Tylor were engaging in their comparative studies, Cornelius Tiele of Leiden wrote the article on "Religion" for the ninth edition of the *Encyclopaedia Britannica* (1875). For more than 100 years of publication, the *Britannica* article on "Religion" had been a discussion of Christian theology. This time (in tune with the new science of religion movement) the article was an impartial description of religious behavior from earliest primitive animism to the consummate religions of Buddhism, Christianity, and Islam.

Another contributor to the development of the new movement was Robert R. Marett.° He made important comments about the origins of animism, speculating insightfully about how the idea of souls and spirits first developed in human thought.[*]

The history of religious studies was greatly assisted by other developing disci-

*See pages 30–32.

plines occurring at the same time, especially Egyptian hieroglyphics° and the initiation of archaeological activities in Mesopotamia by Austen H. Layard° (1817–1894).

The first scholar in America to publish in the new history of religions discipline was James Freeman Clarke° (1810–1888), who wrote two volumes each called *Ten Great Religions*.[25] And the study was greatly advanced in America by the prolific work of Morris Jastrow, Jr.° (1861–1921), author of *The Study of Religion*.[26] Jastrow, like Tiele, examined Christianity and Judaism with the same objective appreciation that he gave to other religions, not more, not less.

At this same time other religious studies scholars were challenging the exclusion of Christianity from comparative studies, but were, at the same time, finding ways to continue the idea of Christian superiority. Among these scholars were Wilhelm Schmidt° (1866–1954), Rudolf Otto° (1869–1937), and Nathan Soderblom° (1866–1931).

But other scholars were more skeptical of Christianity's superiority among world religions, for example, James George Frazer° (1854–1941), Franz Boas° (1858–1942), and especially Max Weber° (1864–1920), whose contributions to modern religious studies have been outstanding. Weber described convincingly how religions were initially shaped by the charismatic character of their founders and how religions both shape and are shaped by the way people normally live—by their attitudes and beliefs and social and economic systems. Weber examined Protestantism and the economics of capitalism in both Europe and America. He also studied the Eastern religions of Confucianism and Taoism through which he was better able to get in focus the differences between Eastern and Western patterns of life and religions. By looking at what was different he better explained what was familiar.[27]

In more recent times two important scholars in the history of religions have been Joachim Wach° (1898–1955) and Mircea Eliadé,° who is currently teaching at the University of Chicago.

History of religions scholars draw from a variety of sources—philology, ethnology, sociology, psychology as well as history—as they work to identify religions especially in the dimension of human experience.[28]

SOCIAL AND BEHAVIORAL SCIENCES

Religious phenomena are studied by three social and behavioral sciences, all of which arose in the nineteenth century—psychology, sociology, anthropology.

Psychology   Psychology of religion focuses on the way individual human needs are met through religion. The inner, private character of religious experience especially lends itself to psychological study.

In 1879, Wilhelm Wundt° established the world's first psychological laboratory in Leipzig, Germany. In America such laboratories were established by E. B. Titchener and William James at the universities of Cornell and Harvard. James especially had a keen interest not only in psychology, but in philosophy and religion as well, and his book *Varieties of Religious Experience* (his Gifford Lectures of 1901–1902) remains a classic in the field of religious studies.*

---

*In writing *The Varieties of Religious Experience* James was indebted to Edwin D. Starbuck, who had compiled an extensive research collection of reports of religious experience, many of them extreme and bizarre. For more on Starbuck's contribution to religious studies see his *Look To This Day* (Los Angeles: University of Southern California Press, 1945).

James based his generalizations on observable data. He was interested in establishing a scientific understanding of religion by employing both philosophical and psychological principles in his investigations. J. H. Leuba° and J. B. Pratt° have worked with a similar dedication in employing observable verifiable data to the study of the psychology of religion.

Recent experimental psychology, especially of the behavioral type, has been generally indifferent to religion. However, other modern psychologists interested in the development of human personality (for example, Carl Jung,° Gordon Allport,° Erich Fromm°) and those persons concerned with the discipline of psychoanalysis continue a lively interest in religious phenomena.

Sociology   Sociology of religion examines the role that religion plays in society. If the etymology° of the word "religion" is taken as a clue, this relation is vital to one of the two major purposes of religion. The term "religion" derives from two Latin terms— *religare,* which means "to bind"* and *relegere,* which means "to gather." The inference may be reasonably drawn that religion is intended to bind one to that which is holy, and at the same time to gather persons into a social system, a sacred community. Religion (from *relegere*) implies social structure.

Indeed, humans cannot be religious, or even human, in complete isolation. We are what we are to a large extent (both as religious and as human) because of our societal connections. As John Donne° declared: "No man is an Island;" we are all "part of the main." We are gregarious animals. The social character of humans has profound implications for the study of religion. As J. Milton Yinger° puts it: "Seen culturally, religion is part of the complex of prescriptions and proscriptions that guide the interaction of men in all societies."[29]

Sociology, both launched and named by Auguste Compte° (1789–1857), began with a critical interest in religion, with a concern for religious beliefs and practices. Since Compte's time sociologists have usually agreed that social patterns and social values influence extensively religious beliefs and practices. Emile Durkheim° (1858–1917), a sociologist, in his *Elementary Forms of Religious Life,* and Sigmund Freud° (1859–1939), a psychologist, in his *Totem and Taboo,* both argue that religious beliefs and practices are totally the products of social intercourse. They argue that religion is actually a symbolizing of society. It is simply society *writ large.* The "city of God" is really the "city of humans" seen through utopian glasses. Not everyone agrees with this. The important anthropologist E. E. Evans-Pritchard° insists that there is no proof for believing that religion is simply "a symbolic representation of the social order" as Durkheim and Freud contended.

That societal structure and values may affect religion is not the only part of the story. Apparently religion also affects society. At least Max Weber saw it that way in his *Protestant Ethic and the Spirit of Capitalism* he identified the profound influence of the ethics of Calvinistic Protestantism on the rise of capitalism.†

In 1912, the brilliant German scholar Ernst Troeltsch° published the *The Social Teachings of the Christian Churches.* In it he analyzed the influence of Christianity

---

*The Latin term *religio* means "the bond between humans and gods."
†Weber also made sociological analyses of the religions of India, China, and ancient Israel.

upon the ancient, medieval, and modern world. Troeltsch's work has influenced later scholars to explore not just Christianity, but all religions as creative dynamics in their particular social and cultural systems. The contemporary scholar Joachim Wach is one such person.[30] He admits that Troeltsch has seriously influenced his thought, but gives Max Weber credit for being the first person to develop a truly systematic sociology of religion.[31]

Of the social dynamic in relation to religion Reinhold Niebuhr wrote:

One important source of religious vitality is derived from the social character of human existence; from the fact that men cannot be themselves or fulfill themselves within themselves, if not in an affectionate and responsible relation to their fellows. It is this fact, rather than the fiat of any scripture, which makes the law of love the basic law of man. This law is not of purely religious origins, and indeed it is not necessary to be religious to ascertain its validity.

Reinhold Niebuhr, "The Religious Situation in America," in *Religions and Contemporary Society*, ed. Harold Stahmer (New York: Macmillan, 1963), p. 146.

Obviously sociologists have contributions to make in answering *religion—what is it?*

Anthropology   Beginning with Charles Darwin's *Descent of Man* (1871)* and Edwin B. Tylor's *Primitive Culture* (1875) anthropology has maintained an interest in primitive societies. The scholarly product of this interest is important in religious studies.

Also, the comparison of cultures done in cultural anthropology is especially valuable to religious studies. In the twentieth century (beyond its genetic and evolution concerns of the nineteenth century) anthropology has become concerned with examining the many varieties of human culture and the general patterns of human culture as well as with the place of persons (the function of individuals) in the many structures and processes of society.

Such study is important to the understanding of religious people in the structures and processes of society in both its secular and religious dimensions.

BIBLICAL ARCHAEOLOGY
Biblical archaeology is important to religious studies because: (1) it accumulates data about ancient religious beliefs and practices in Canaan and later Roman Palestine, (2) it makes available a broader and more accurate understanding of social structures and cultural institutions in ancient Israel, and (3) provides the entire cultural context for the emergence of the Bible and other early Jewish Christian literature.†[32]

---

*Darwin's earlier great work was of course, his *On the Origin of Species* (1859).
†For this succinct statement of the importance of biblical archaeology, I am indebted to James Strange.

NOTES

[1] In his monumental philosophical theology, *The Summa Theologica*, Thomas synthesized the more or less fragmentary truths that during the preceding centuries the schoolmen had slowly gathered together, and the elements of thought that during the early part of the century in which he lived had been derived from Greek and Islamic sources. In so doing he, among other things, formulated the first complete system of Christian Aristotelianism, determined the place between faith and reason, and constructed one of the most masterful statements of Christian philosophical theology ever created.

[2] One seventeenth-century attempt to give rational universalism to religion was undertaken by Edward, Lord Herbert of Cherbury (1583–1648), called the father of Deism.° Lord Herbert believed that certain principles were innate in humans. They had been imprinted by God. Thus, rational agreement could be arrived at among all people despite any divergence in religious tradition. Herbert held that in religious beliefs there are five innate principles: (1) the existence of God; (2) God ought to be worshipped; (3) the practice of virtue is the chief part of the worship of God; (4) people have always had an abhorrence of crime and are under obligation to repent their sins; and (5) there will be rewards and punishments after death.

[3] See pp. 155–156.

[4] *Hume's Works*, vol. 4 (London: Green and Grosse, 1889–1890), p. 24.

[5] Ibid., p. 208 n.

[6] David Hume, *Dialogues Concerning Natural Religion by David Hume*, ed. Henry D. Aiken (New York: Hafner, 1951), p. ix.

[7] These ideas are found especially in Hegel's *Phenomenology of the Spirit* (1807). See especially the Preface and Introduction.

[8] *Phenomenology of the Spirit*, CC, VII, B.

[9] Friedrich Schleiermacher, *On Religion: Speeches to its Cultured Despisers*, tran. John Oman (New York: Harper & Row, 1958), p. 31.

[10] Friedrich Schleiermacher, *The Christian Faith*, ed. H. R. Mackintosh and J. S. Stewart (Edinburgh, 1948), p. 12.

[11] Other important scholars of the nineteenth century who affected philosophical theology were Søren Kierkegaard° (1813–1855), Ludwig Feuerbach° (1804–1872), Albrecht Ritschl° (1822–1889), Friedrich Nietzsche° (1844–1900), and Josiah Royce° (1855–1916).

[12] Bordon Parker Bowne, *Personalism* (Boston: Houghton Mifflin, 1908), p. 277.

[13] Edgar Sheffield Brightman, *Introduction to Philosophy*, (New York: Henry Holt, 1925), p. 329.

[14] H. P. Van Dusen, *The Plain Man Seeks for God* (New York: Scribner's, 1933), p. 105.

[15] Edgar Sheffield Brightman, *Moral Laws* (New York: Abingdon, 1933), pp. 242–255.

[16] William Henry Bernhardt, "The Logic of Recent Theism," *The Iliff Review*, 4, 1 (1947):42.

[17] Harvey Potthoff, "The Reality of God," *The Iliff Review*, 24, 2 (Spring 1967):10. See also Potthoff, *God and the Celebration of Life* (Chicago: Rand McNally, 1969) and William Calloley Tremmel, "Harvey H. Potthoff: A Theology for Today," *The Iliff Review*, 38, 1 (Winter 1981): 23–40.

[18] Potthoff, "The Reality of God," pp. 14–16.

[19] Karl Barth, *Church Dogmatics* (New York, 1936), vol. 1, p. 123.

[20] Lindsay B. Longacre, *The Old Testament—Its Form and Purpose* (New York-Nashville: Abingdon-Cokesbury Press, 1945), pp. 200–204.

[21] Ibid., p. 204.

[22] Charles H. Long, "The History of the History of Religions," in *A Reader's Guide to the Great Religions*, ed. Charles J. Adams (London: Collier Macmillan Publishers, 1977), p. 471. This essay by Long (pp. 467–477) is an excellent outline of this subject.

[23] *Introduction to the Science of Religion: Four Lectures Delivered at the Royal Institute in February and May, 1870* (London: Longmans, Green, 1899).

[24] See E. B. Tylor's two-volume work *Primitive Culture*, first published in 1871. It is available now through Harper Torchbooks (New York: Harper & Brothers, 1958).

[25] James Freeman Clarke, *Ten Great Religions* (Boston: Houghton Mifflin, 1971).

[26] Morris Jastrow, Jr., *The Study of Religion*, The Contemporary Study Series, ed. Havelock Ellis, no. 41 (New York: Scribner's, 1902).

[27] See Max Weber's *The Protestant Ethic and the Spirit of Capitalism*, tran. T. Parsons (London: George Allen & Unwin, 1930); and "The Protestant Sects and the Spirit of Capitalism," in *From Max Weber: Essays in Sociology*, tran. Hans H. Gerth and C. Wright Mills (New York: Oxford University Press, 1946), pp. 302–322; and Weber's *The Religions of China, Confucianism and Taoism*, tran. Hans H. Gerth (New York: Free Press, 1951).

[28] See William A. Clebsch's presidential address at the American Academy of Religion Annual Meeting, 1980, "Apples, Oranges, and Manna: Comparative Religion Revisited," *Journal of the American Academy of Religion*, March 1981.

[29] J. Milton Yinger, *The Scientific Study of Religion* (New York: Macmillan, 1970), p. 203.

[30] See Joachim Wach, *The Sociology of Religion* (Chicago: University of Chicago Press, 1944).

[31] Other students of the Weber theme are R. H. Tawney, *Religion and the Rise of Capitalism* (London: John Murray, 1926); V. A. Demant, *Religion and the Decline of Capitalism* (New York: Scribner's, 1952), and H. R. Niebuhr, *The Social Sources of Denominationalism* (New York: Holt, Rinehart and Winston, 1929).

[32] Informative works in this important area are G. E. Wright's *An Introduction to Biblical Archaeology* (New York: Doubleday, 1960) and his *Biblical Archaeology* (Philadelphia: Westminster Press, 1957); Yigael Yadin's *The Art of Warfare in the Light of Archaeological Study*, tran. M. Pearlman (New York: McGraw-Hill, 1963); *The Old Testament and Modern Study* (Oxford: Clarendon Press, 1951); Eric M. Meyers and James F. Strange, *Archaeology: The Rabbis and Early Christianity* (Nashville, Tenn.: Abingdon, 1981).

Appendix 2

HOW WE KNOW— EMPIRICALLY, RATIONALLY, INTUITIVELY

EMPIRICAL KNOWING—KNOWLEDGE FROM EXPERIENCE

We know some things because we see, taste, touch, or hear them; that is, we sense them. Someone who is asked, "Is it raining outside?" may go out and look about and discover that the sun is shining and no water droplets are falling. With this evidence that person can declare, "It is not now raining outside." The proposition is supported by empirical evidence. Evidence here means a structure of experience that informs a critical consciousness concerning the truth or falsity of a proposition. Experience is the basis of empirical knowing.

RATIONAL KNOWING—KNOWLEDGE FROM LOGICAL REASONING

Besides knowledge from sense experience, there is knowledge established directly from the operation of deductive reasoning. It is rational knowledge. Reason itself, proceeding formally from established premises, can establish conclusions that cannot be false. Take, for example, the classic syllogism: *All men are mortal. Socrates is a man. Therefore, Socrates is mortal.* This syllogism is absolutely valid. No other conclusion can be drawn. Again, if the statement "All the pictures are hanging on the wall" is true, then the statement "None of the pictures is hanging on the wall" is false. Or if the statement "Some of the pictures are not hanging on the wall" is false, then the statement "All the pictures are hanging on the wall" is true. This kind of thinking is very impressive. Unlike empirical reasoning, which may be persuasive but seldom absolute, this formal logical operation appears to be indubitable.

INTUITIVE KNOWING—KNOWLEDGE THROUGH DIRECT, UNREASONED PERCEPTION

Unlike the rational and empirical ways of knowing (which are especially the ways of talking and knowing in science and philosophy), the intuitive (or some prefer, the aesthetic) way of knowing is not based in cogitation so much as in direct experience. The intuitive approach to knowing concentrates on direct perception. I "know" a Bach fugue not by reasoning about it, but by listening to it. I know it directly, as I know a love experience, or a toothache, or a moment of fear. I know a poem not by analyzing it, but by reading it. And if I spend enough time reading enough poems, I can tell, again without analyzing, whether or not it is a good poem and even can tell which is the better of two good poems. For example, one who knows haiku* can tell in direct perception that the great haikuist Matsuo Basho° was exactly right when he corrected his student one day. They were going through a field when Kikaku, seeing the darting dragonflies, composed a poem.

> Red dragonflies!
>> Take off their wings,
>>> And they are pepper pods!

"No, no," cried Master Basho, "you have missed it. It should be:

> Red pepper pods!
>> Add wings to them,
>>> And they are dragonflies!"

We know that Basho was right just as he knew that Kikaku had missed perfection. We intuit it, as he did. The knowing of intuition is spontaneous and self-affirming. It is a moment of direct seeing, direct knowing—a sudden insight.

To be sure, intuitive knowing (and/or propositions arising from such experience) cannot gain the verification status of empirical knowledge or the formal validity of logic, but as Pascal° once proclaimed, "The heart has reasons that reason cannot know." Intuitive knowing may have little in the way of verification method, but it makes up for what it lacks in this regard with its powers of persuasion.

*Haiku is a type of Japanese poetry of a fixed seventeen-syllable form that usually simply points to a thing in nature, or pairings in nature, that the poet has observed.

Appendix 3

THE ONTOLOGICAL ARGUMENT ASSAILED

Neither Anselm nor Descartes escaped criticism of their ontological arguments. The monk Gaunilo of Marmoutiers immediately argued with Anselm's technique, saying that by using it one could arrive at absurd conclusions. One could, for example, prove the existence of an absolutely perfect island. All one would have to do would be to conceive of an absolutely perfect island, an island than which no greater could be conceived. Such an island, by Anselm's reasoning, would have to exist. But Anselm replied, saying that the element missing in Gaunilo's island refutation was the element of necessity. An island (or any other ordinary object) is part of the contingent world, and can be thought of as contingent, and therefore, as not existing. But this is not true of God. In his second formulation of the ontological argument Anselm demonstrated that God could not be conceived of as not existing. Thus Gaunilo's argument might be cogent against perfect islands, but not against a perfect God.

It has been widely believed that Immanuel Kant devastated the ontological argument by showing that there is no necessary connection between the concept or idea of an absolutely perfect being and the objective fact of an absolutely perfect being.* Kant argued that as "an idea" the predicate angularity does belong to a triangle, and the predicate existence does belong to God. As a concept, in each case, the appropriate predicate is necessarily linked to the subject. But, Kant argued, it does not follow from this analytical necessity that these subjects with their predicates actually exist. If there actually is a triangle that is not simply an idea, then its angles will be of a certain character; and if there actually is an infinitely perfect being that is not simply an idea, it will have existence as one of its perfections. "To posit a triangle, and yet to reject its three angles, is self-contradictory," said Kant in his *Critique of Pure Reason*, but, he went on to say, "there is no self-contradiction in rejecting the triangle altogether with its angles. The same holds true of the concept of an absolutely necessary being." Kant was arguing that we can have the *idea* of a triangle, which would have to include all necessary predicates; but the idea might be only an idea. It need not have an objective counterpart anywhere outside the idea. There could conceivably be the idea of a triangle without there being any "real," nonmental triangles. The same is true of God's existence. If we are going to think of an absolutely perfect being, we must think of it as

---

*Some philosophers (Charles Hartshorne and Norman Malcolm, in particular) point out that Kant missed the mark as Gaunilo had done. He attacked Anselm's first formulation, but missed the second formulation.

existing, but thinking it exists does not make it exist, except in thought. An idea, Kant pointed out, is not made more perfect by the "objective" existence of what is conceived. External existence does not add anything to the perfection of the idea of God, or any other idea. For example, the idea of a hundred dollars is not made more perfect, or even changed by the existence of a hundred "real" dollars in one's pocket. The ontological argument, Kant insisted, does not prove the "real" existence of God. It only proves that existence is a necessary predicate if one is going to *think* of an absolutely perfect being.

Norman Malcolm argues that Anselm's critics, including Kant, have missed the point in supposing that the proposition "God necessarily exists" is equivalent to the proposition "If God exists then he necessarily exists." *If God exists* implies the possibility of contingency. He might not exist. But Anselm's proposition places God in the category of absolute necessity. The whole of his argument is that God is not a contingent being, as Anselm most emphatically informed Monk Gaunilo. By the very nature of Anselm's argument, God possesses necessary existence; therefore, to say, as the Kantian attack does, that God necessarily exists, but it is possible he may not exist is to state a contradiction. Indications are that Anselm's deductive theological argument has not been summarily removed from theological contention. His deductive theology survives and even resuscitates.

BIBLIOGRAPHY OF SELECTED READINGS

Chapter 1   A Definition
Bernhardt, William H. *A Functional Philosophy of Religion.* Denver, Colo.: Criterion Press, 1958. A functional definition of religion. See especially Chapter 14. (Copies available through the Iliff School of Theology, 2201 S. University Boulevard, Denver, Colo. 80210.)

Chapter 2   The Religious Animal
Doniger, Simon, ed. *The Nature of Man in Theological and Psychological Perspective.* New York: Harper & Row, 1972. Essays by theologians and psychologists on the nature of mankind.

du Noüy, Pierre Lecomte. *Human Destiny.* New York: Longmans, Green, 1947. A biologist sees evolution as now transferred from the physical realm to the spiritual realm.

Feifel, Herman, ed. *The Meaning of Death.* New York: McGraw-Hill, 1959. Essays by scientists, philosophers, and theologians discussing the problem of death.

Frazier, A. M. *Issues in Religion.* 2nd ed. New York: Van Nostrand Reinhold, 1975. See especially R. M. Rilke, "Chamberlain Brigge's Death," and F. Dostoevsky, "Underground Man."

Fromm, Erich. *Man for Himself.* New York: Fawcett World Library, 1973; first publication, 1947. A study of humanistic ethics that also contains a psychological analysis of modern mankind. See especially Chapter 3.

––––––. *Psychoanalysis and Religion.* New Haven, Conn.: Yale University Press, 1950. On the nature and function of religion.

Kaufmann, Walter. *Existentialism from Dostoevsky to Sartre.* Cleveland: World, Meridian Books, 1965. See especially Albert Camus, "The Myth of Sisyphus," a beautiful and brief commentary on human emptiness and the moment of salvation.

Kierkegaard, Søren. *Concluding Unscientific Postscript.* Translated by David Swenson and Walter Lowrie. Princeton, N.J.: Princeton University Press, 1971. An extended critique of Hegel's philosophical system, presenting themes that play a major role in twentieth-century theology.

––––––. *Fear and Trembling.* Translated by Walter Lowrie. Princeton, N.J.: Princeton University Press, 1973. An excellent single volume introduction to Kierkegaard's thought.

Maslow, Abraham. *Religious Values and Peak Experiences.* Columbus, O.: Ohio

State University Press, 1962. A consideration of religion and human personality with special reference to peak experiences.

Mead, George H. *Mind, Self and Society*. Chicago: University of Chicago Press, 1947; first publication, 1934. A classic statement on the nature of mind and self as emergents from social intercourse, by one of the most seminal thinkers of modern times.

Stace, Walter T. *Time and Eternity*. Princeton, N.J.: Princeton University Press, 1952. See especially "What Religion Is," pp. 3–8.

Tillich, Paul. *The Courage To Be*. New Haven, Conn.: Yale University Press, 1962; earlier publication, 1952. A statement on the nonmanipulable aspects of religion and on the courage of religion—courage in-spite-of. See especially pp. 32–63.

————. *Theology of Culture*. New York: Oxford University Press, 1964. Especially Chapter 1, identifying religion with the metaphor "depth"—religion is that which concerns humans deeply; it is their ultimate concern.

Tremmel, William C. "The Converting Choice." *Journal for the Scientific Study of Religion* 10 (Spring 1971), pp. 17–25. On the nature of conversion.

Weiss, Paul. *Nature and Man*. New York: Holt, Rinehart and Winston, 1947. Humans and their problems are one with the rest of nature.

Whitehead, Alfred N. *Religion in the Making*. Cleveland: World, Meridian Books, 1969; first publication, 1926. A fine statement by one of the finest minds of the twentieth century.

Chapter 3 Origins of Religion: Primitive

Albright, William F. *From the Stone Age to Christianity*. Baltimore: Johns Hopkins University Press, 1940. A review of history, sociology, and archaeology as they relate to understanding the Bible.

Campbell, Joseph. *The Hero with a Thousand Faces*. Princeton, N.J.: Princeton University Press, 1968; first publication, 1949. A comparative study of hero cults.

————. *The Masks of God: Primitive Mythology*. New York: Viking, 1959. On the nature and function of mythology and its significance for religion.

Codrington, R. H. *The Melanesians: Studies in Their Anthropology and Folk-Lore*. New York: Dover, 1972; first publication, 1891. A report on the preanimistic character of primitive religion.

Eliadé, Mircea. *The Sacred and the Profane: The Nature of Religion*. Translated by W. Trask. New York: Harcourt Brace Jovanovich, 1968. A well-known historian of religion explores religion as a manifestation of the sacred.

James, Edwin O. *Prehistoric Religion: A Study in Prehistoric Archaeology*. New York: Barnes & Noble, 1961. A picture of prehistoric religions by a renowned historian of religion.

Jensen, Adolf E. *Myth and Cult Among Primitive People*. Chicago: University of Chicago Press, 1963; first publication, 1951. An ethnological interpretation of primitive cultures.

Lessa, W. A., and E. Z. Yogt, eds. *Reader in Comparative Religion: An Anthropological Approach*. 3rd ed. New York: Harper & Row, 1972. Essays by ten social scientists on the origins of religion.

Norbeck, Edward. *Religion in Primitive Society*. New York: Harper & Row, 1961. An anthropological statement on the place of religion in primitive society.

Toffler, Alvin. *Future Shock*. New York: Random House, 1970. A best-selling book on contemporary technology and modern world change as they affect institutions and people.

Tylor, Edward B. *Religion in Primitive Culture*. New York: Harper & Row, 1958; first publication, 1871. A pioneer figure in the field of primitive religions identifies the origins of religion with animism.

Chapter 4   Other Speculations

Berger, Peter L. *Rumor of Angels*. Garden City, N.Y.: Doubleday, 1970. A sociologist's attempt to go beyond cultural relativism and find a basis for accrediting the reality of religion.

————. *The Sacred Canopy*. Garden City, N.Y.: Doubleday, 1969. An analysis of religion as a social "construct," as a way that society constructs its own reality and provides itself with symbols of order.

————. *Facing Up to Modernity*. New York: Basic Books, 1977. A lucidly written examination of various social dimensions of modern American life—including religion—from the perspective of sociology.

Bettis, Joseph Dabney, ed. *Phenomenology of Religion*. New York: Harper & Row, 1969. A collection of essays by modern thinkers who represent several ways of employing phenomenological methods in religion. See especially "An Introduction to Phenomenology," by the editor, and "What is Phenomenology," by Maurice Merleau-Ponty.

Durkheim, Émile. *The Elementary Forms of Religious Life*. Translated by J. W. Swain. Atlantic Highlands, N.J.: Humanities, 1964; first publication, 1915. A pioneer student in the field of sociology identifies religion as a natural product of socialization. See especially Chapter 7 and conclusions.

Feaver, J. C., and W. Horosz, eds. *Religion in Philosophical and Cultural Perspective*. New York: Van Nostrand Reinhold, 1967. See especially Peter Koestenbaum's chapter "Religion in the Tradition of Phenomenology" for a definition of phenomenology and several examples of phenomenological method in religion.

Freud, Sigmund. *The Future of an Illusion*. Garden City, N.Y.: Doubleday, Anchor, 1961; first publication, 1927. Freud's insightful proposal that religion is an unhealthy neurosis and God a surrogate father.

————. *Totem and Taboo*. Translated by James Stachey. London: Routledge & Kegan Paul, 1961; first publication, 1950. Freud's identification of the origin of religion with the Oedipus Complex.

James, William. *Varieties of Religious Experience*. New York: Random House, Modern Library. The Gifford Lectures on Natural Religion, given in Edinburgh, 1901–1902. A pioneer study and classic in the psychology of religion.

Lang, Andrew. *The Making of Religion*. New York: AMS Press, 1968; first publication, 1898. See especially Chapters 9 and 10 on the origin of the idea of God in primitive religions.

Otto, Rudolf. *The Idea of the Holy*. Translated by J. W. Harvey. London: Oxford University Press, 1924. A classical statement of religion as the feeling of numinous reality, as God, an inner experience from an outside source.

Schmidt, Wilhelm. *High Gods in North America*. Oxford, England: Clarendon Press, 1933. The Upton Lectures in religion given at Manchester College, Oxford.

————. *The Origin and Growth of Religion*. Translated by H. J. Rose. London:

Methuen, 1931. Schmidt argues that the earliest peoples believed in a supreme being in a monotheistic sense.

Chapter 5   Religious Response to the Human Condition

Camus, Albert. *The Fall*. Translated by J. O'Brien. New York: Random House, 1956. An outstanding twentieth-century statement of the existentialist point of view.

————. *The Plague*. Translated by Stuart Gilbert. London: Penguin Books, 1968. A novel that wrestles with the facts of evil and human heroism.

Evans-Pritchard, E. E. *Witchcraft, Oracles and Magic Among the Azende*. Oxford: Oxford University Press, 1968. A study based on three expeditions among the Azende people from 1926 to 1930. See especially Part 4 on magic, sorcery, and magicians, pp. 387–423.

Frazer, James G. *New Golden Bough*. Edited by T. H. Gaster. New York: Macmillan, 1959. This is an abridgment of Frazer's extensive pioneering work, in which, among other things, he presents his theory of magic as the genesis of religion.

Hill, Douglas. *Magic and Superstition*. London: Hamlyn, 1968. A readable, extensively illustrated publication on magical practices and superstitions.

Lewis, C. S. *Miracles: A Preliminary Study*. New York: Macmillan, 1963; first publication, 1947. A persuasive statement in support of metatechnological (miraculous) intervention into the natural processes of human life.

Malinowski, Bronislaw. *Magic, Science and Religion*. Glencoe, Ill.: Free Press, 1948. On the character and interrelationships of magic, technology, and religion in a primitive culture. See especially the title essay.

Mouss, Marcell. *A General Theory of Magic*. Translated by R. Bain. London: Routledge & Kegan Paul, 1972; first publication in French, 1950.

Noss, John B. *Man's Religions*. 6th ed. New York: Macmillan, 1980; first publication, 1949. See especially the statement on magic in Chapter 1, "Primitive and Bygone Religions."

Roszak, Theodore. *The Making of a Counterculture*. Garden City, N.Y.: Doubleday, 1969. In the last chapter of his analysis and in his interpretation of the modern counterculture movement, Roszak presents an insightful apologetic for shamanism; the maker of magic does more than just perform metatechnological feats.

Chapter 6   God

Bertocci, Peter A. *Introduction to the Philosophy of Religion*. New York: Prentice-Hall, 1951. A personalistic statement of God and religion. See especially Chapter 18, "How, Then, Shall We Think of God?"

Brightman, Edgar Sheffield. *The Problem of God*. New York: Abingdon, 1930. A statement about God being both transcendent to the world and immanent in it, God as not a supremely peaceful being, but one who must struggle with a "given" element in his own nature.

Harrington, John B. *Issues in Christian Thought*. New York: McGraw-Hill, 1968. Harrington has gathered statements/essays by important modern religion scholars in the disciplines of history, theology, and philosophy.

Hartshorne, Charles. *The Divine Reality*. New Haven, Conn.: Yale University Press, 1964; first published, 1948. God conceived of as immanent, temporal, changing, and related to the world intimately. See especially pp. 22–34.

Hartshorne, Charles, and William L. Reese. *Philosophers Speak of God*. Chicago: University of Chicago Press, 1963; first publication, 1953. A monumental work on the idea of God. See especially the Introduction, p. 1025. See also the sections on E. Brightman, M. Buber, M. Iqubal, W. James, A. Schweitzer, S. Radhakrishna, A. Watts, A. Whitehead, and H. Wieman.

Hick, John. *Evil and the God of Love*. London: Macmillan, 1966. A searching study of theodicies from St. Augustine's day to our own.

James, William. *Essays on Faith and Morals*. New York: Longmans, Green, 1943. James talks about God from a pragmatist's point of view. See pp. 82–84, 103–141.

————. *A Pluralistic Universe*. New York: Longmans, Green, 1909. See pp. 181, 268–319.

Kaufmann, Walter. *God, Ambiguity, and Religion*. New York: Harper & Row, 1958. God's existence cannot be proved. The idea of God is essentially ambiguous. Religion is a matter of loyalty and tradition.

Maringer, J. *The Gods of Prehistoric Man*. Translated by M. Ilford. New York: Knopf, 1960; earlier publication, 1952. An account of what is known of the Gods of preliterate people.

Plantinga, Alvin, ed. *The Ontological Argument*. Garden City, N.Y.: Doubleday, Anchor, 1965. An examination of Anselm's argument by philosophers from the eleventh to the twentieth century.

Sartre, Jean-Paul. *Existentialism and Humanism*. Translated by P. Mairet. London: Methuen, 1957; first publication, 1948. See especially comments on Atheistic Humanism.

Taylor, John V. *The Go-Between God*. New York: Oxford University Press, 1979. An insightful book on the actions of God as seen in the concept of the Holy Spirit.

Teilhard de Chardin, Pierre. *The Phenomenon of Man*. Translated by B. Wall. New York: Harper & Row, Torchbooks, 1965; first publication in French, *Le phenomene humain,* 1955. An important work that identifies the emergence of humans in the evolutionary process, and God, or God action, as the complexification, direction, and Omega Point of the evolutionary process.

Whitehead, Alfred N. *Adventure of Ideas*. New York: Macmillan, 1933. See especially pp. 356–357.

————. *Process and Reality*. New York: Macmillan, 1929. See especially pp. 517–533.

————. *Science and the Modern World*. New York: Macmillan, 1929. See especially Chapter 11, "God," and Chapter 12, "Religion and Science."

Wieman, Henry Nelson. *The Source of Human Good*. Carbondale, Ill.: Southern Illinois University Press, 1964; first publication, 1946. Wieman speaks of the processes of creation and the production of good from living events. This process Wieman is willing to call God; God is creative event.

Chapter 7   The Devil's Due

Brother Francesco Maria Guazzo. *Compendium Maleficarum* (Handbook on Witchcraft). Edited by The Reverend Montague Summers. Translated by E. A. Ashwin. New York: Barnes & Noble, 1970. A facsimile reprint of a 1608 document showing "the iniquitous and execrable operations of witches against the human race, and the divine remedies by which they are frustrated."

Douglas, Mary, ed. *Witchcraft Confessions and Accusations*. London: Tavistock, 1970. See especially the article by Norman Cohn entitled "The Myth of Satan and

His Human Servants''; an important statement on the origins of the Devil concept and on the "fantasy of witchcraft."

Franklyn, Julian. *Death By Enchantment.* London: Hamish Hamilton, 1971. A balanced, readable statement of the phenomenon of witchcraft.

Guazzo. See Brother Francesco Maria Guazzo.

Kelly, Henry Ansgar. *The Devil, Demonology and Witchcraft.* Garden City, N.Y.: Doubleday, 1974. See especially Chapters 1 and 2 on the development of the concept of the Devil in Western tradition and Chapter 4 on demonic possession and exorcism.

Kluger, Rivkah Schärf. *Satan in the Old Testament.* Translated by Hildegaard Nagel. Evanston, Ill.: Northwestern University Press, 1967. A scholarly and penetrating examination of the idea of Satan, first published in German in 1948.

Littell, Franklin H. *The Crucifixion of the Jews.* New York: Harper & Row, 1975. How can Christendom claim credibility in the face of the deafening silence of church leaders before the brutality of the Holocaust?

Milton, John. "Paradise Lost." The presentation of this great poem in volume 4 of *The Harvard Classics* is especially recommended because it introduces each of the twelve books of the poem with a summary of the action taking place in that book. The *Classics* were published in New York by Collier Press in 1909.

Murray, Margaret Alice. "Witchcraft." *Encyclopaedia Britannica.* 14th ed. A statement on the nature of witchcraft, including Murray's theory on the origins of witchcraft.

Russell, Jeffrey B. *The Devil.* Ithaca, N.Y.: Cornell University Press, 1977. Russell's work examines the idea of evil in several cultures, and then concentrates on the idea of the Devil as it was formulated in late Judaism and early Christianity.

———. *Satan.* Ithaca, N.Y.: Cornell University Press, 1981. Russell examines the concept of Satan as expressed by the early church fathers from Clement to Augustine.

———. *Witches in the Middle Ages.* Ithaca, N.Y.: Cornell University Press, 1972.

Rudwin, Maximilian. *The Devil in Legend and Literature.* New York: AMS Press, 1970. See especially Chapter 1 on the legend of Lucifer.

Watts, Alan W. *The Two Hands of God.* New York: Macmillan, 1963. An examination of the myths of polarity, for example, the Yang-Yin of Taoism, the Brahma-Shiva of Hinduism, the God-Devil of Christianity.

Chapter 8   God Coming of Age

Burtt, Edwin A. *Man Seeks the Divine.* New York: Harper & Row, 1957. An insightful examination of the religions of the world.

Campbell, Joseph. *The Masks of God: Occidental Mythology.* New York: Viking, 1964. Especially the conclusion of the volume on the four functions of mythology.

———. *The Masks of God: Oriental Mythology.* New York: Viking, 1962. Development of mythology in India, in China, and in Japan. The myth of "Eternal Return" versus the myth of "Cosmic Restoration."

Comstock, W. Richard, ed. *Religion and Man: An Introduction.* New York: Harper & Row, 1971. A substantial survey of the religions of the world by six scholars: Robert Baird, Alfred Bloom, Janet K. and Thomas F. O'Dea, Charles C. Adams, and W. R. Comstock.

Loew, Cornelius. *Myth, Sacred History and Philosophy*. New York: Harcourt Brace Jovanovich, 1967. A survey of the pre-Christian religions of the West.

Martin, Malaehi. *The Encounter*. New York: Dell, A Delta Book, 1971. See especially Book I, pp. 3–166, "The Priceless Moments." A succinct statement of the Kairotic episodes in Judaism, Christianity, and Islam.

Noss, John B. *Man's Religions*. 6th ed. New York: Macmillan, 1980. For details on world religions both East and West.

The World's Great Religions. New York: Time, 1957. A collection of articles appearing in *Life Magazine* in 1955: February 7, Hinduism; March 7, Buddhism; April 4, Chinese faiths; May 9, Islam; June 3, Judaism; and December 26, Christianity.

Chapter 9 Theology

Brown, Robert McAfee. "Story and Theology." In *Philosophy of Religion and Theology*. Edited by J. W. McClendon, Jr. Tallahassee, Fla.: Florida State University Press, 1974. On theology as autobiographical witnessing.

Castaneda, Carlos. *The Teachings of Don Juan: A Yanqui Way of Knowledge*. Berkeley, Calif.: University of California Press, 1968. How a Yanqui Indian teacher, a spiritual master, works with a pupil to transmit religious knowledge. See especially pp. 14–34.

Descartes, René. *Meditations on First Philosophy*. Translated by Laurence J. Lafleur. Indianapolis: Bobbs-Merrill, 1960. See especially meditation number three, on the existence of God, proved by the innateness of the idea of perfect being in the mind of man; and meditation number five, on the existence of God, proved by a reformulation of Anselm's ontological argument.

Diamond, Malcolm L. *Contemporary Philosophy and Religious Thought*. New York: McGraw-Hill, 1974. An examination of modern philosophical discussions concerning religious issues—theology and verification, religious experience, existentialism, arguments for God, religion, and ultimacy.

Frazier, A. M. *Issues in Religion*. 2nd ed. New York: Van Nostrand Reinhold, 1975. See Chapter 12, "Anselm: The Ontological Argument," "Aquinas: The Five Ways," "Kant: The Moral Argument."

Hick, John. *Faith and Knowledge*. 2nd ed. Ithaca, N.Y.: Cornell University Press, 1966; first publication, 1957. Some of the problems of religious knowledge. This is a lucid examination of epistemology and religion.

Hick, John, and Arthur McGill, eds. *A Proof of God's Existence: Recent Essays on the Ontological Argument*. New York: Macmillan, 1965. Essays defending and criticizing the ontological argument.

Hospers, John. *An Introduction to Philosophical Analysis*. 1967, first publication 1953. An analysis of important contemporary philosophical problems, such as meaning and definition, knowledge, truth, determinisim-freedom, religion, ethics.

Hume, David. *The Natural History of Religion and Dialogues Concerning Natural Religion*. Edited by A. W. Clover and J. V. Price. Oxford: Clarendon Press, 1976. The *Dialogues* is a brilliant critique of the proofs of God's existence.

Miller, David I. *Gods and Games*. New York: Harper & Row, 1972. Especially p. 183 on Campbell's function of mythology; and Chapters 3 and 4 on the theology of play; pp. 99–108 on the origins of religion; and pp. 80–91 on theology.

Otto, Max. *The Human Enterprise*. New York: Appleton-Century-Crofts, 1940. In Chapter 11, Otto argues for the good human effects of not believing in God; that is, in a Western personalistic God.

Perrin, Norman. *The New Testament*. New York: Harcourt Brace Jovanovich, 1974. A scholarly introduction to the books of the New Testament.

Ramsey, Ian T. *Religious Language*. New York: Macmillan, 1963; first publication, 1957. An effort to show the use of contemporary language analysis in theology.

Shelby, Donald J., and James King West. *Introduction to the Bible*. New York: Macmillan, 1971. A solid general introduction to the Old and New Testament.

Tremmel, William Calloley. *The Twenty-Seven Books That Changed the World*. New York: Holt, Rinehart and Winston, 1981. An introduction to the writing of the New Testament.

Wiesel, Elie. *Night*. New York: Avon, 1972; *Souls on Fire*. New York: Random House, 1973; *Ani Maamin*. New York: Random House, 1974. In these three stories (and half a dozen others that are all thinly veiled autobiography), a Jew, whose baccalaureate was from Auschwitz and Buchenwald, tells stories that are superb, and something more. They are theology, which, in agony, move from a God of divine indifference to a God who, however hidden, suffers in and with his creation.

Chapter 10   Salvation Theology

Brightman, Edgar S. *Philosophy of Religion*. Englewood Cliffs, N.J.: Prentice-Hall, 1940. See especially pp. 395–404 on arguments for and against immortality.

Epicurus. "Epicurus to Menoeceus." In *Ethics*, edited by Oliver A. Johnson. New York: Holt, Rinehart and Winston, 1974. On death without fear.

Head, Joseph, and S. L. Cranston, eds. *Reincarnation in World Thought*. New York: Julian Press, 1967. An extensive survey of reincarnation in the thought and practices of mankind.

Lamont, Corliss. *The Illusion of Immortality*. 4th ed. New York: G. P. Unger, 1965; first publication, 1935.

Langley, Noel. *Edgar Cayce on Reincarnation*. Edited by Hugh L. Cayce. New York: Paperback Library, 1967. Accounts of people who have lived more than once, from the files of a noted American clairvoyant.

Larson, Martin A. *The Religion of the Occident*. Paterson, N.J.: Littlefield, Adams, 1961. See especially Chapter 1, on the original God—Osiris.

Pope, Marvin H. *Job*. Garden City, N.Y.: Doubleday, 1973; first publication, 1965. A scholarly examination of the thesis that Job is a theodicy of "reverent agnosticism." See especially the Introduction, pp. xv–lxxxv.

Stendahl, Krister, ed. *Immortality and Resurrection*. New York: Macmillan, 1965. See especially Oscar Cullmann's "Immortality of the Soul or Resurrection of the Dead," the Ingersoll Lectures of 1955, comparing Semitic reincarnation with Greek immortality.

Wood, Ernest E. *Patanjali, Practical Yoga Ancient and Modern*. Hollywood, Calif.: Welshire Books, 1973; first publication, 1948. A new translation of Patanjali's yoga aphorisms.

Chapter 11   Revelation and Scripture

Baillie, John. *The Idea of Revelation in Recent Thought*. New York: Columbia University Press, 1956. Lectures on contemporary Protestant views of revelation.

Bultmann, Rudolph. *Jesus Christ and Mythology*. New York: Scribner's, 1958. In this little book a major biblical scholar explains what he means by "mythology" and "demythologizing."

Carnell, Edward J. *The Case for Orthodox Theology*. Philadelphia: Westminster Press, 1959. See especially pp. 97–102 and 110–111, a discussion of biblical revelation from a conservative Christian perspective.

Champion, Selwyn C., and Dorothy Short, eds. *Readings from World Religions*. Greenwich, Conn.: Fawcett, 1963; first publication, 1951. Selections from the scriptures of twelve consummate religions.

Edgerton, Franklin, tran. *The Bhagavad Gita*. Cambridge: Harvard University Press, 1944. A scholarly translation and interpretation of this classic religious poem.

Fosdick, Harry E. *The Modern Use of the Bible*. New York: Macmillan, 1925. A classic statement of the nature and use of the Bible as seen in Liberal/Modernist Protestantism.

Frost, S. E., Jr., ed. *The Sacred Writings of the World's Great Religions*. New York: McGraw-Hill, 1972. Selections from the sacred writings of thirteen living religions.

Hamilton, Edith. *Mythology*. New York: New American Library, Mentor Book, 1971. A compact, readable account of classical mythology.

Lessa, William A., and E. Z. Yogt, eds. *Reader in Comparative Religion: An Anthropological Approach*. 3rd ed. New York: Harper & Row, 1972. See especially Section III, "Myth and Ritual."

Sebeok, Thomas, ed. *Myth: A Symposium*. Bloomington: University of Indiana Press, 1965; first publication, 1955. Essays by nine modern scholars.

Watts, Alan. *Myth and Ritual in Christianity*. Boston: Beacon Press, 1968; first publication, 1953. A description of the Christian year as seen in its symbolic/ritual forms.

Chapter 12   Myth and Ritual

Campbell, Joseph. *The Masks of God: Occidental Mythology*. New York: Viking, 1964. See especially pp. 518–523, on the fourfold function of myth.

Cutler, Donald R., ed. *The Religious Situation in 1968*. Boston: Beacon Press, 1968. See Chapter 8, "Civil Religion in America," by R. Bellah; Chapter 16, "Secularization and the Sacred," by Huston Smith; Chapter 17, "The Secularization of the Sacred," by Joseph Campbell; Chapter 19, essays on ritual by K. Z. Lorenz, Julian Huxley, Erik H. Erikson, Edward Shils, and William F. Lynch.

Eliadé, Mircea. *Myth and Reality*. Translated by W. R. Trask. New York: Harper & Row, Torchbooks, 1963. Especially Chapter 1, "Structure of Myths."

———. *Rites and Symbols of Initiation*. Translated by W. R. Trask. New York: Harper & Row, Torchbooks, 1965; first publication, 1958. A survey of the rites of passage in religions, both primitive and consummate.

Chapter 13   Morality

Buber, Martin. *I and Thou*. Translated by R. G. Smith. New York: Scribner's, 1965; first publication, 1936. According to this Jewish, Hasidic-inclined, existentialist philosopher, the relationship between God and humans and humans and humans must be a relationship not of person to thing, but of person to person. See especially pp. 8, 75–83.

Fletcher, Joseph. *Situation Ethics: The New Morality*. Philadelphia: Westminster Press, 1966. A new way to conceive and practice religious ethics.

Heschel, Abraham J. *God in Search of Man*. New York: Meridian Books, 1961. A Jewish philosophy on three ways to God: the world, the Bible, and sacred deeds (mitzvat).

Hospers, Joseph. *Human Conduct: Problems of Ethics*. New York: Harcourt Brace Jovanovich, 1972; first publication, 1961. See especially Chapter 6, "Kant's Ethics of Duty," pp. 264–296.

James, William. *Essays in Pragmatism*. New York: Hafner Publishing Co., 1951. See especially the essays on "The Moral Philosopher and Moral Life," and "The Will to Believe."

Marty, Martin E., and Dean G. Peerman, eds. *New Theology No. 3*. New York: Macmillan, 1966. See especially James M. Gustafson's article "Context Versus Principles: A Misplaced Debate in Christian Ethics," an examination of the modern debate in Christian ethics; a debate which, on the one hand, rests ethical decisions in the existential ethical situation, and, on the other hand, in the objective moral principles given in the tradition.

Ramsey, Paul. *Nine Modern Moralists*. Englewood Cliffs, N.J.: Prentice-Hall, 1962. See especially Chapter 5, "Reinhold Niebuhr: Christian Love and Natural Law."

Chapter 14 Religion: Exoteric Experience

Lewis, C. S. *The Four Loves*. New York: Harcourt Brace Jovanovich, 1960. A beautifully written and insightful study of love as affection, friendship, eros, and charity/agapé.

Lewis, I. M. *Ecstatic Religion*. Harmondsworth, England: Penguin, 1971. An examination of the emotional states of religious people.

Marty, Martin E., and Dean G. Peerman, eds. *New Theology No. 3*. New York: Macmillan, 1966. See especially Tom F. Driver's article on the "Sexuality of Jesus," an examination of the Christian tradition of disassociating Jesus from sexuality.

Streng, Frederick. *Understanding Religious Man*. Belmont, Calif.: Dickenson, 1969. See especially religion and art forms, pp. 84–91.

Suzuki, D. T. "Zen Buddhism." In *Selected Writings of D. T. Suzuki*, edited by W. Barrett. Garden City, N.Y.: Doubleday, 1956. See especially Chapter 10, on painting, swordsmanship, and the tea ceremony.

van der Leeuw, G. *Sacred and Profane Beauty: The Holy in Art*. Translated by D. E. Green. New York: Holt, Rinehart and Winston, 1963; first publication, 1932. The religious significance of dance, drama, architecture, pictorial arts, and music; art as a sacred act.

Wach, Joachim. *The Comparative Study of Religion*. New York: Columbia University Press, 1958. See especially Chapters 2, 3, and 4, on the nature of religious experience.

Chapter 15 Religion: Esoteric Experience

Bassuk, Daniel. "The Secularization of Mysticism: An Analysis of the Mystical in Rufus Jones and Martin Buber." Ph.D. dissertation, Drew University, 1974. Available from the University of Michigan Microfilms, No. 74–27, 897.

Buttrick, George A. *So We Believe, So We Pray*. Nashville, Tenn.: Abingdon, 1951. A study of prayer.

Huxley, Aldous. *The Perennial Philosophy*. New York: Harper & Row, 1945. A statement of "the metaphysics that recognizes a divine reality substantial to the world."

Johnson, William, S. J. *The Still Point: Reflections on Zen and Christian Mysticism*.

New York: Fordham University Press, 1970. See especially Chapter 8, "Defining Mysticism."

Jones, Rufus. *Pathways to the Reality of God*. New York: Macmillan, 1931. A Quaker mystic discusses the many ways that people have come to God.

Koestler, Arthur. *The Invisible Writing*. New York: Macmillan, 1970; first publication, 1954. The autobiography of a modern contemporary mystic.

Otto, Rudolf. *Mysticism East and West*. Translated by B. Bracey. New York: Collier Books, 1962; earlier publication, 1932. A comparative analysis of the nature of mysticism East and West.

Stace, Walter T. *Mysticism and Philosophy*. Philadelphia: Lippincott, 1960. See especially the section on mysticism.

————. *The Teachings of the Mystics*. New York: New American Library, Mentor, 1960. Especially Chapter 1, "What is Mysticism?"

Watts, Alan W. *Behold the Spirit: A Study in the Necessity of Mystical Religion*. New York: Random House, 1972. Watts argues that the dimension of feeling, so prevalent in Eastern theology, must be included in Western theology, which is overly intellectual and dualistic, pp. 132–173.

————. *Psychotherapy East and West*. New York: Pantheon Books, 1961. Watts's study shows how Eastern philosophers long ago faced the problem of human existence in a hostile world, an understanding yet to be achieved in the West.

Writings of Several Mystics

Blakney, Raymond Bernard, tran. *Meister Eckhart, A Modern Translation*. New York: Harper & Row, 1957. German mystic, 1260–1328.

Gicovate, Bernard, tran. *San Juan la Cruz*. New York: Twayne, 1971. St. John of the Cross, 1542–1591.

O'Brien, Elmer, S. J., tran. *The Essential Plotinus*. New York: Mentor, 1964. The writings of a great mystic of antiquity.

Peers, E. Allison, ed. and tran. *The Complete Works of St. Teresa*. New York: Sheed & Ward, 1946. Spanish mystic, 1515–1582.

Scholem, Gershom G., ed. *Zohar, The Book of Splendor*. New York: Schocken, 1949. Basic readings from the Kabbalah, a book of Jewish mysticism.

Afterword Getting it in Shape

Altizer, Thomas, and William Hamilton. *Radical Theology and the Death of God*. Indianapolis: Bobbs-Merrill, 1966. Independent but concurring statements by two Christian theologians on the need for a new kind of theology.

Bedell, George, et al. *Religion in America*. New York: Macmillan, 1975. An excellent examination of religion in America, with pertinent documents included.

Cox, Harvey. *The Secular City*. New York: Macmillan, 1965. This author celebrates the rise of urban civilization and the collapse of traditional religion, exulting in a new freedom of secularization.

Ellwood, Robert S., Jr. *Religious and Spiritual Groups in Modern America*. Englewood Cliffs, N.J.: Prentice-Hall, 1972. Brief, readable statements on the many new religious and spiritual groups in America.

Herberg, Will. *Protestant Catholic Jew*. Garden City, N.Y.: Doubleday, Anchor, 1960. A survey of the place of religious immigrants in American culture.

King, Martin Luther, Jr. *Why We Can't Wait*. New York: Harper & Row, 1974. See especially King's "Letter from Birmingham Jail—April 16, 1963," his protest to his fellow clergymen of the South.

Kraemer, Hendrik. *World Culture and World Religions: The Coming Dialogue*. Philadelphia: Westminster Press, 1960. The impact of Eastern and Western religions upon each other.

Littell, Franklin H. *From State Church to Pluralism*. Garden City, N.Y.: Doubleday, Anchor, 1962. An examination of the movement of religion in America from state establishment to voluntaristic pluralism.

Needleman, Jacob. *The New Religions*. New York: Pocketbook, 1972; earlier publication, Garden City, N.Y.: Doubleday, 1970.

Newman, Joseph, ed. *The Religious Reawakening in America*. Washington, D.C.: U.S. News and World Reports, 1972. A survey of attitudes and actions in contemporary American religious life.

Raschke, Carl, "New Gnosticism?" In *Philosophy of Religion and Theology*, edited by David Griffin. Tallahassee, Fla.: American Academy of Religion, 1973. Some critical comments concerning recent Asian invasions into Western religions.

Rubenstein, Richard L. *After Auschwitz*. Indianapolis: Bobbs-Merrill, 1966. A radical Death of God statement in the Jewish tradition.

BIOGRAPHICAL NOTES AND GLOSSARY
of People and Things

> "The time has come," the Walrus said,
> "To talk of many things:
> Of shoes—and ships—and sealing-wax—
> Of cabbages—and kings . . ."
> Lewis Carroll, "The Carpenter" (stanza 2)

A term marked by ° within an entry is a cross reference to the entry of that title.

Abū Bakr A close associate of Muhammad. At the death of Muhammad, The Companions (so-called because they were the group most closely associated with the Prophet) chose Abū Bakr as caliph. Abū Bakr, in his brief reign of one year, established the first armies of Islam destined to assault the outside world. Apparently Abū Bakr also ordered Muhammad's secretary, Zaid ibn Thabit, to make a collection of the Prophet's revelations.

Achilles The hero of Homer's *Iliad*, son of Peleus and Thetis. Achilles was protected from death except for one fatal weakness. Through his heel he was vulnerable, and from a wound in the heel, he died.

Aesthe-noetic Pertaining to those things known by both perception and thought.

Age Middle Stone (Mesolithic). See Middle Stone Age.

Agnostic One who disclaims any knowledge of God; or more technically, one who holds it impossible to have knowledge of God and ultimate things.

Agnosticism The belief that certain truths are unattainable and that only perceptual phenomena are objects of exact knowledge. In theology a theory that does not deny God but denies the possibility of knowing God.

Allport, Gordon Willard American psychologist, born in Montezuma, Indiana, in 1897. Educated at Harvard, and the European universities of Berlin, Hamburg, and Cambridge. He taught at Robert College, Istanbul, Turkey, and at Dartmouth College and Harvard. Allport was also director of the National Opinion Research Center, a member of the National Commission for UNESCO, and a Visiting

Foreign Consultant to the Institute of Social Research, University of Natal (South Africa). Among his many published books is his 1950 work *Individual and His Religion*. Allport died in 1967.

Altizer, Thomas Born in 1927. Educated at the University of Chicago, he was one of the primary voices in the 1960s Death of God Movement. Drawing upon nineteenth-century artists and philosophers, Altizer traced the idea of the death of God and its implications for the modern world in his book *The Gospel of Christian Atheism*, published in 1966.

Anabaptist (*Ana*, "again"; *baptizen*, "to baptize" in Greek) A member of one of the radical movements of the Reformation of the sixteenth century that insisted that only adult baptism was valid and held that true Christians should not bear arms, use force, or hold government office.

Animism The belief that all objects have a life or vitality, or an indwelling soul. *Anima* is a Latin word meaning "breath" or "soul."

Anselm Born in Aosta in Lombardy, in 1033. He entered the monastery of Bec in Normandy. In 1078 he became the abbot of Bec, and in 1093 the Archbishop of Canterbury. He died in 1109. Throughout his career Anselm tried to improve the moral condition of the clergy. His three main works are *Monologium*, which deals with the being of God; the *Proslogium*, which contains his famous ontological proof for the existence of God; and the *Cur Deus Homo*, which presents his doctrine of atonement and indicates how humans can be saved through Christ.

Anthropomorphism Attributing human feelings and characteristics to nonhuman objects.

Aphrodite The Goddess of love and beauty in Greek mythology, identified with the Roman Venus. Also called Cytherea.

Apologist A person who argues in defense or justification of another person or cause.

A posteriori Denotes reasoning from facts or particulars to general principles, or from effects to causes.

A priori (1) Proceeding from a known or assumed cause to a necessarily related effect; (2) describing knowledge not derived from experience. Knowledge that is *prior* to experience. Knowledge based on hypothesis or theory rather than experience, e.g., $2 \times 2 = 4, 3 + 1 = 4, 8 \div 2 = 4$. Knowledge statements made before or without examination, not supported by factual study.

Aquinas See Thomas Aquinas.

Aristophanes An Athenian dramatist. His dates of birth and death are uncertain, probably from 448 B.C. to 380 B.C. He wrote many satirical comedies, eleven of which are extant.

Aristotle Greek philosopher, born in 384 B.C. He was a student of Plato, tutor of Alexander the Great, author of works on logic, philosophy, natural science, ethics, politics, and poetics.

Arnold, Matthew Born in 1822, in Satcham, near Staines, Middlesex, England. He was educated at Winchester, Rugby, and Oxford. He was an ethicist, a teacher of ethics, and a professor and chairman of poetry at Oxford. He wrote many volumes of poetry. He died in 1888.

Artifact An article produced or shaped by humans, for example a tool, weapon, or ornament of archaeological value or historical interest.

Ashanti A former kingdom and British protectorate of western Africa, now a region of central Ghana. Population about one million.

Astruc, Jean French physician and Bible student. In 1753, Astruc initiated a new biblical scholarship when he began to consider the several names for deity used in the Old Testament.

Athanasius, Saint (293?–373) Patriarch of Alexandria. He worked as deacon and secretary to Bishop Alexander of Alexandria and became bishop himself in 328. He led the fight against the Arians who considered God, the Father, as superior to Christ, the Son. Athanasius was influential at the first ecumenical council at Nicea in 325. His view of the nature of Christ became the orthodox position of Western Catholic Christianity.

Aton The one God of the universe of the Egyptian religion of Pharaoh Amenhotep IV, who changed his name to Ikhnaton (light of Aton). Aton was symbolized by the sun. Ikhnaton came to the Egyptian throne in 1375 B.C. He died in 1358.

Augustine, Saint (Aurelius Augustinus) Augustine was born in North Africa in A.D. 354. He died in 430. He taught rhetoric at Carthage and at Rome. He was a serious student of the Manichean theology (a mixture of Zoroastrianism and Christianity) and Platonic philosophy. Influenced by his mother (an exemplary Christian later sainted—Monica) and by St. Ambrose, Augustine became a Christian in 387. He then dedicated his time to the study of the Christian scriptures and to the task of instituting a systematic inquiry concerning God and the human soul. In 395 he was made Bishop of Hippo in North Africa. His best known works are *Confessions* and *The City of God*. Augustine was a primary theologian in the history of Christianity and of equal prominence as a philosopher in Western thought.

Avatar An incarnation of a divine being, such as Krishna in the Hindu religion. Krishna is said to be the eighth incarnation of the God Vishnu.

Ayer, Alfred Jules Born in 1910. Educated at Eton and Oxford, Ayer served in the Welsh Guards and in Military Intelligence during World War II. He taught at Wadham College, Oxford, and the University of London and was Wykeham Professor of Logic at Oxford. Ayer is a leading authority in the modern philosophical movement called Logical Positivism.

Baalim (Baals) Plural of Baal. Fertility Gods of ancient Semitic peoples.

Barth, Karl Born in Basel, Switzerland, in 1886. He studied at the University of Berne under his father who was a professor of church history and New Testament. Barth attended a number of universities studying under a number of outstanding liberal theologians (Harnack, Gunkel, Weiss, Hermann). In 1909 he became a minister in the Swiss Reformed Church. In the next twelve years he broke with the liberal theology and set out on the work of his significant career—the formulation of a new orthodox Christian theology. His efforts were remarkably successful. He became one of the dominant theological voices of the twentieth century. He died in 1968.

Baruch An associate-disciple and secretary of the Prophet Jeremiah, recorded in the Book of Jeremiah in the Jewish Bible (the Old Testament).

Basho, Matsuo Born in 1644. The father of Japanese haiku (a seventeen-syllable poem). In 1686, Basho wrote what is probably the best known haiku in the Japanese language: *Furu-ike ya kawazu tobi-komu mizu-no-oto*—literally,
Old pond/frog-jump-in/water-sound
> Old pond:
>> frog-jump-in.
>> Plop!

Bassuk, Daniel Born in 1938. Educated at the universities of Chicago, Columbia, Southern California, Drew, and at Union Theological Seminary. He is an assistant professor in the Department of Religious Studies at the University of South Florida. Bassuk's expertise is in Oriental religions.

B.C.E. Before the common era, a substitute form for **B.C.** (Before Christ).

Becket, Thomas à Known as St. Thomas à Becket. He was born probably in 1118 and died in 1170. He was appointed Archibishop of Canterbury by Henry II in 1162. Henry had hoped Becket would stand as a force for the king against the pope, but Becket took his ecclesiastical responsibilities seriously. The conflict between king and archbishop resulted finally in Becket's assassination.

Beelzebub (also Beelzebul) A demonic figure (sometimes equated with Satan) found in ancient Hebrew literature. In a Christian account, the Gospel of Nicodemus, probably from the fourth century, Beelzebub is identified as the supervisor of Hell. In Milton's *Paradise Lost*, Beelzebub is the fallen angel next in power to Satan. In Hebrew, Beelzebub is *ba' 'al zebūb*, which means "Lord of the flies." He is identified as the God of Ekronites.

Bellah, Robert N. Born in Altus, Oklahoma, in 1927. Educated at Harvard. Bellah taught at McGill University in Montreal and then at Harvard. In 1967 he was appointed professor of sociology at the University of California, Berkeley. He is also director of the Institute of International Studies and the Center for Japanese and Korean Studies. He wrote an influential article titled "Civil Religion in America" in which he proposes that the beliefs and practices of Americans constitute a "civil religion."

Bernhardt, William Henry Born in Chicago in 1893. Educated at Nebraska Wesleyan, Northwestern University, and the University of Chicago. In 1929 he began teaching at the Iliff School of Theology in Denver, Colorado, and he continued on the Iliff faculty until his retirement in 1966. After retirement he joined the faculty of the University of California in San Diego. Bernhardt was a philosopher of religion who identified with modern Protestant Liberalism. He founded *The Iliff Review*, and was the author of two books—*A Functional Philosophy of Religion*, on the nature of religion, and *The Cognitive Quest for God and Operational Theism*, on the nature of God-talk—and many important articles. He died in 1979.

Bertocci, Peter Anthony Born in Elena, Italy, in 1910. Educated at Boston University, Harvard, and Cambridge, he taught at Bates College and Boston University. Bertocci was a modern liberal theologian of the personalistic type.

Boas, Franz (1858–1942) German-born American anthropologist; especially a student of North American Indian tribes.

Bodhi In Hindu the term means "enlightenment." The bodhi tree was the tree, in Hindu tradition, under which Gautama was sitting when he received his spiritual enlightenment. Also called bo-tree.

Bodkin As used in Shakespeare's *Hamlet*, a dagger or stiletto.

Boehme, Jacob Born in 1575. A German mystic. He was a man of tolerance who saw the "light of God" as not confined to one faith or sect. He held that nothing more is needed but to lead a gentle life with God, to be merciful and reject evil.

Böhler, Peter A Moravian preacher whose counseling with John Wesley during a sea voyage to the New World was critical in Wesley's spiritual crisis. Without Böhler's influence, Wesley might not have experienced his conversion at the meeting in Aldersgate Street, May 14, 1738.

Bo-tree See Bodhi.

Bowne, Borden Parker (1847–1910) Born in Leonardville, New Jersey. He was educated at the University of the City of New York and at the universities of Paris, Halle, and Göttingen. He taught at the University of the City of New York and Boston University. Bowne attempted to synthesize the facts and methods of modern science with idealistic (liberal personalistic) philosophy. His work had a liberalizing influence primarily on Methodist thought. It was continued in the works of E. S. Brightman and Albert C. Knudson. Bowne's ideas laid the philosophical groundwork for much liberal theology in America.

Braithwaite, Richard B. Born in Banbury, England, in 1900. Educated at Kings College, Cambridge, in physics, mathematics, and philosophy, he became Knightbridge Professor of Moral Philosophy at Cambridge, and president of both The Mind Association and the Aristotelian Society. His main interests have been in philosophy of science and in the interpretation of religious belief in such a way as to make it empirically tenable.

Brightman, Edgar Sheffield (1884–1953) Born in Holebrook, Maine. Educated at Brown University and Boston University, he studied also at the universities of Berlin and Marburg. He taught at Nebraska Wesleyan and Boston University. A liberal theistic philosopher, Brightman took the personhood of God as central in his thinking. He wrote some 14 books and more than 200 articles and became a leading exponent of personalistic theism.

Brown, Robert McAfee Born in Carthage, Illinois, in 1920. He studied at Amherst College, Union Theological Seminary, and Columbia University and taught at Macalaster College, Union Theological Seminary, and Stanford University.

Brown, William Adams Born in New York City in 1865. Educated at Yale, Union Theological Seminary in New York, and the University of Berlin, he became a professor of systematic theology and applied Christianity at Union Theological Seminary. He was a leading voice among twentieth-century liberal theologians. He did not argue over the questions of God's existence because he held that belief in God was a matter of experience, not of logic. What he did do was focus on the figure of Christ as the revealer of the moral attributes of God. He died in 1943.

Buber, Martin Austrian-born Israeli philosopher and theologian. Buber was born in Vienna in 1878 and reared in Lwow in the Ukraine by his grandfather, Solomon Buber, a man of wealth and Hebrew scholarship. Martin Buber became acquainted with Hasidic Judaism and later became an important interpreter of this kind of Judaism. He studied at the universities of Vienna, Leipzig, Zurich, and Berlin. In a mystical fashion, Buber interpreted Jewish history as the ever-present encounter of God's call ("Hear, O Israel, the Lord our God is one Lord" Deuteronomy 6:4) and Israel's willing acceptance or obstinate refusal to respond. He died in Jerusalem in 1965.

Bultmann, Rudolf Born in 1884, in Wiefelstede, Germany, the son of an Evangelical-Lutheran pastor. Bultmann studied at the universities of Tübingen, Berlin, and Marburg. He taught New Testament at Marburg University beginning in 1912. Between 1916 and 1920 he taught at Breslau, where he wrote his influential *Die Geschichte Der Synoptischen Tradition* (The Story/History of the Synoptic Tradition). Bultmann returned to Marburg University, where he remained until 1951, at which time he became emeritus. He died in 1976.

Calvin, John (1509–1564) A Swiss reformer, scholar, and religious leader. While a student in France, he became an ardent supporter of the reformation doctrines of Martin Luther. His life threatened, Calvin took refuge in Switzerland, where at Geneva he led in the establishment of a new form of city government in which the power was in the hands of the clergy; there, also, he wrote his formidable theological volumes called *The Institutes of the Christian Religion*.

Campbell, Joseph   American mythologist. Born in 1904. Educated at Dartmouth and Columbia and at universities in Europe. He was a student of literature, mythology, philology, and art history. His important publications include three volumes entitled *The Masks of God* and the book *Hero with a Thousand Faces*.

Camus, Albert   Born in Mondovi, Algeria, in 1913. After earning a degree in philosophy, he worked at various jobs, including journalism. In the 1930s he ran a theatrical company and wrote fiction. During the war he was an activist in the French Resistance, editing an important underground paper, *Combat*. Among his major works are two widely praised works of fiction, *The Stranger* (1946), *The Plague* (1948); a volume of plays, *Caligula and Three Other Plays* (1958); and two books of philosophical essays, *The Rebel* (1954) and *The Myth of Sisyphus* (1955). Camus was awarded the Nobel Prize in Literature in 1957. At one time a close companion of **Jean-Paul Sartre**, Camus broke with him when Sartre made common cause with Communism. He died in 1960.

Canaanite   Canaan in biblical times was the name for that part of Palestine between the Jordan River and the Mediterranean Sea. A Canaanite was a non-Hebrew inhabitant of Canaan.

Carman, Bliss   Born at Fredericton, New Brunswick, Canada, in 1861. He graduated from the University of New Brunswick and later attended the universities of Edinburgh and Harvard. He moved to the United States in 1890, where he became an important figure in the editorial and literary world. He wrote more than thirty books of both prose and poetry. He died in 1929.

Carroll, Lewis   The pen name of Charles Lutwidge Dodgson, an English mathematician and author. He was born in 1832, attended Christ Church, Oxford, and became a teacher of mathematics. In 1856, using his pseudonym, he began to write for a comic newspaper. A speech defect kept Carroll from becoming a minister, but he was ordained a deacon at Oxford and often enjoyed preaching to children. He became recognized as a mathematician, but his first love was children—and storytelling. His book *Alice's Adventures in Wonderland* was published in 1865, *Phantasmagoria* in 1869, *Through the Looking-Glass* in 1872, and *The Hunting of the Snark* in 1876. He died in 1898.

Carruth, William Herbert   Born in Osawatomie, Kansas, in 1859, Carruth was a poet, educator, and author. He wrote *Letters to American Boys*, in 1907; *Each in His Own Tongue and Other Poems*, in 1909; and *Verse Writing*, in 1917. He was editor of *Kansas in Literature*.

Chandogya Upanishad   The Upanishads are philosophical interpretations of the basic Hindu scriptures called Vedas. The *Chandogya* is an early prose form of Upanishadic philosophy.

Clarke, James Freeman   Born in Hanover, New Hampshire, in 1810. He was educated at Harvard College and Cambridge Divinity School and was pastor of the Unitarian Church in Louisville, Kentucky, from 1836 to 1839. He moved to Boston and in 1841 established the Church of the Disciples and served as pastor there for forty-one years. He also taught at Harvard as professor of natural religion and Christian doctrine and lectured there on ethics and religion. He wrote extensively including eight volumes entitled *Events and Epochs in Religious History*. Clarke died in 1888.

Codrington, Robert Henry, D.D.   Clergyman, missionary, anthropologist, philologist, Codrington was educated at Wardham College, Cambridge, and graduated from there in 1852. In 1855 he was elected fellow and in 1856 was ordained into the Anglican ministry. He went to Melanesia as a missionary. Back in England, he wrote an eight-volume work, *The Melanesian Languages,* which was published in 1885.

Cohn, Norman   Born in London in 1915. Educated at Christ Church, Oxford, he taught at the University of Durham in Durham, England, and the University of Sussex in Falmer, England. In the United States Cohn has taught at Stanford University in California and Wesleyan University in Middletown, Connecticut. He has written a number of interesting works, including one on Siberian legends, one on Millenarians (a mystical anarchist movement of the Middle Ages), and one called "The Myth of Jewish World-Conspiracy."

Complex   See Oedipus Complex.

Compte, Auguste (1798–1857)   French philosopher. The most important academic thinker in the first half of the nineteenth century in France. Compte was born in an orthodox Christian family, but as a young man he turned from Christianity and propounded what has come to be known as philosophical positivism. The critical aspect of positivism is the denial of the validity of metaphysical speculation, and its rejection of final causes and of the idea of the absolute. Knowledge, according to positivism, is confined to observable facts and the relations among facts. Compte's ambition was to become a regular professor at the École Polytechnique, but he failed in his ambition. Rather he was forced to make a meager living as a private tutor.

Concomitant   Existing or occurring concurrently, at the same time.

Confucius (551–479 B.C.)   Original name was Kung Chiu, also long known in China as Kung Fu-tse. Confucius was a philosopher and teacher and founder of the Confucian religion.

Constantine (Flavius Valerius Aurelius Constantinus)   Born probably in A.D. 280. He is called Constantine the Great and was Roman emperor from 306 to 337, when he died. Constantine adopted Christianity in 312 after winning a battle against a formidable opponent, Maxentius, who also claimed to be emperor. Years later Constantine told his friend Bishop Eusebius, the first church historian, that before his battle with Maxentius he had seen a vision in the heavens—a cross of light with the inscription, "Conquer by this." Under a Christian banner he had entered the battle and won and, thereupon, had accepted Christ. From Constantine on, in the Western World, Christianity enjoyed the benefits of political favor and political power.

Copernican   See Copernicus.

Copernicus, Nicolaus (1473–1543)   His Polish name was Mikolaj Kopernik. An astronomer who enunciated the principle of heliocentric planetary motion, which says the earth rotates on its axis and, with other planets in the solar system, revolves around the sun. This is the revolution that shook the Western World from the ancient and medieval period into the modern age.

Counter-Reformation   A reform movement within the Roman Catholic Church during the sixteenth century and the first half of the seventeenth century. In response to the Protestant Reformation, the Catholic Church began a renovation of itself. It purified old monastic orders and established new ones, brought about an improvement in the morals of the clergy and laity, reorganized the church for better discipline, and even reduced to some degree the political and ecclesiastical authority of the pope.

Cox, Harvey Gallager, Jr.   Born in Chester County, Pennsylvania, in 1929. Educated at Harvard University, Cox served as director of religious activities at Oberlin University in Oberlin, Ohio. Ordained to the ministry in the American Baptist Church, he served on the Baptist Home Mission Society and taught at Andover Newton Theological School, Newton Center, Massachusetts. In 1965 he was appointed to the faculty of the Harvard Divinity School. His most notable publications are *The Secular City* (1965) and *Feast of Fools* (1969).

Cro-Magnon   An early race of modern humans characterized by robust physique. Remains were found in a cave in southern France.

Cullmann, Oscar   Born in 1902. A continental Protestant theologian who has taught New Testament and early Christianity at the University of Basel. He has also taught at the Sorbonne in Paris and at universities in the United States. He is the author of many scholarly works.

Cult   See fertility cult.

Deism   In theology, Deism identifies the belief that God totally transcends, is totally different from the world (his creation), and has no intimate relation to it. Deism was a strong trend in theology in England and France during the seventeenth and eighteenth centuries. It was also an important influence in the days of the American Revolution and the writing of the Constitution and Bill of Rights.

Dervish (Persian *dārvish*, "mendicant" or "beggar")   A member of various Muslim orders of ascetics, some of whom practice the achievement of collective ecstasy by performing whirling dances and chanting religious words.

Descartes, René (1596–1650)   Born in La Haye, in Touraine, France. He studied at the Jesuit college of La Flèche and throughout his life maintained friendly relations with his teachers, his greatest regret being that they never accepted his philosophy. After college he went to Paris. In 1617 he took service as a volunteer in the army of Prince Maurice of Nassau. Maurice was a student of science and mathematics and gathered in his camp at Breda a distinguished group of scientists. Descartes attached himself to this group. From this period came his early writings on music, mathematics, and his *Pensées*. He left the army of Maurice for that of the Elector of Bavaria. While in winter quarters at Neuburg on the Danube, in 1619–1620, he experienced the mental crisis of his life and discovered, as he tells it, "the foundations of a wonderful science"—the principle, namely, that all geometrical problems may be solved by algebraical symbols (analytic geometry). It was in this same mental crisis that the notion of universal methodic doubt first occurred to him as well as the thought that "the mysteries of Nature and the laws of Mathematics could both be unlocked by the same key." Tired of soldiering, he took up residence in Holland and devoted himself to his favorite studies, astronomy, physics, chemistry, anatomy, and medicine. While in Holland most of his important books were published—*Discourse on Method* (1637), *Meditations on First Philosophy* (1641), and *Principles of Philosophy* (1644). Descartes exercised a profound influence on his own and subsequent generations. His doctrines left their imprint on the theology, science, and literature as well as the philosophy of the seventeenth century. Indeed, it is hardly an exaggeration to say that his thoughts determined the whole course of the development of modern philosophy.

Deutero-Isaiah   The name given to the author of chapters 40−66 of the Book of Isaiah. This author was a Hebrew living during the Hebrew captivity in Babylon, 586 B.C.−539 B.C. Chapters 1−39 of Isaiah were by an earlier writer (eighth century B.C.) in Judah—Isaiah. Deutero means "second," Isaiah means "salvation of the Lord."

De Wette, Wilhelm Martin Leberech (1780−1849)   Professor of theology at the University of Basel. From a study of Hebrew institutions De Wette concluded that the reforms of King Josiah recorded in the biblical book called 2 Kings were the same as those cited in the Book of Deuteronomy. He concluded that the book referred to 2 Kings (11:8−12:13) was the Book of Deuteronomy. Knowing Josiah's dates, De Wette could date the "discovery" of Deuteronomy as 621 B.C.

Dewey, John (1859−1952)   Born in Burlington, Vermont. He studied at the University of Vermont and Johns Hopkins University in Baltimore, Maryland, receiving his doctorate in 1884. He taught at Michigan University and in 1894 joined the faculty of the University of Chicago where he influenced especially the development of the School of Education. In 1904 he moved to Columbia University and became the most noted professor at that institution. Dewey was a leading figure in the development of the American philosophy called "Pragmatism."

Dialectic   The art of arriving at truth by disclosing the flaws in the opposite argument and overcoming them. A process of change whereby an idea entity (thesis) is transformed into its opposite (antithesis) and preserved and fulfilled by it.

Dibelius, Martin   Born in Dresden, Germany, in 1883. Dibelius was professor of New Testament at Heidelberg University beginning in 1915. His work *Die Form-geschicte Des Evangelius* (the form-history of the Gospels), published in 1919, greatly advanced the study of New Testament form criticism. He died in 1948.

Dickinson, Emily (1830−1886)   American poet whose works were not published until after her death. Dickinson's delightful ability to put words together is evidenced in this poem: "To make a prairie it takes a clover and a bee—/One clover, and a bee,/ And reverie./The reverie alone will do/If bees are few."

Diocesan   Pertaining to a diocese, that is, a district under the jurisdiction of a bishop.

DNA (Dioxyribonucleic acid)   The basic molecular structure of life. It is a polymeric chromosomal constituent of living cell nuclei that determines individual hereditary characteristics. It is found in cell nuclei (in the chromosomes only) and provides the model of a genetic "template" complex enough to contain all the information needed to direct the formation of an organism. It is (in the Watson-Clark model) envisioned as a double helix with connecting links that contain genetic information in bits of coded information. In other words, it is the genetic information for the construction of a living being.

Donne, John (1573−1632)   English clergyman and poet during the reign of James I. Born in London. His father was a wealthy merchant. Donne was educated at Oxford, spent time in Italy and Spain and took a voyage to the Azores. He wrote poems, essays, and sermons that were especially popular in his own day, and he still holds considerable influence in the literature of England.

Dostoevsky, Fyodor Mikhailovich (1821−1881)   Russian novelist. He wrote such classical works as *The Idiot* and *The Brothers Karamazov*.

Duns Scotus, John (called "Doctor Subtilis") Born in 1266 or 1274, place uncertain, probably England. He entered the Franciscan Order and studied at Oxford. From 1294 to 1304 he taught at Oxford. In 1304 he moved to Paris to teach. In 1308 he moved to Cologne where he died that same year. At both Oxford and Paris, Duns Scotus enjoyed a reputation as a teacher of unequaled worth.

Durkheim, Émile Born in Alsace in 1858. He is credited as founder of the science of sociology. In 1887 he was appointed to the first chair of sociology in France. He taught at Bordeaux, where he laid the groundwork for a comprehensive analysis of social systems. Eventually he became a professor of sociology at the Sorbonne. In religion, Durkheim's primary contribution is his theory ascribing social origin and function to religion. His primary work in this area was *The Elementary Forms of the Religious Life* (1912). He died in 1917.

Eckhart, Meister (1260–1320) Born in Germany. He entered the Dominican Order and eventually became head of that order in the territories of Saxony and Bohemia. He was a Christian mystic. A profoundly philosophical, original, and independent person, he got in trouble with the church hierarchy because of some of his writings, but he died before he could be tried for heresy.

Eddy, Mary Baker (1821–1910) American religious leader. Founder of the Church of Christ, Scientist (Christian Science).

Edwards, Rem Blandon Born in Washington, Georgia, in 1934. Educated at Emory University and Yale University, his specialties are ethics, epistemology, and philosophy of religion. He has taught at Jacksonville University and the University of Tennessee (Knoxville).

Eichhorn, Johann (1752–1827) A German scholar who analyzed the flood story (Genesis 7:1f) and concluded that it is a composite of at least two accounts. He considered many books of the Old Testament to be spurious, and in the New Testament questioned the authorship of 2 Peter and Jude and doubted that Paul had written Timothy and Titus. He also suggested that the Gospels might have been based upon translations and editions of a number of original Aramaic gospels.

Eliadé, Mircea Born in Bucharest, Romania, in 1907. He was educated in Bucharest, doing his doctoral dissertation on Yoga in 1932. He lived in India, principally in Calcutta, studying Sanskrit and Indian philosophy with Professor Surendranath Dasgupta. He taught in Bucharest. In 1940 he was sent to the Romanian Legation in London as cultural attache. He then went to Lisbon, and in 1945 to Paris as a visiting professor at the École des Hautes Études of the Sorbonne. From there he went to the University of Chicago where he has been ever since. Eliadé is well known as a writer (of both fiction and nonfiction), a historian of religion, and an Orientalist. His works in phenomenology° of religion are widely read; especially, *The Sacred and the Profane* (1959), *Cosmos and History* (1959), and *Yoga, Immortality and Freedom* (1958).

Ellwood, Robert Scott, Jr. Professor of religion at the University of Southern California. Born in Normal, Illinois, in 1933. Educated at the University of Colorado (Boulder), Berkeley Divinity School (New Haven, Connecticut), and the University of Chicago. Ellwood served as an Episcopal minister in Nebraska before joining the faculty at the University of Southern California (USC) in 1967. He holds the Bishop James W. Bashford Chair of Oriental Studies at USC and is the Director of the East Asian Studies Center. Ellwood has written extensively on contemporary religious movements and religious phenomena.

$E = MC^2$ According to Albert Einstein there is an equivalence between mass and energy. This means that if there is sufficient energy to make up the mass of a particle, or group of particles, it is possible to convert that energy into mass; i.e., new particle(s) will be produced out of "nothing."

Empathy To understand so intimately that the feelings, thoughts, and motives of one person are seemingly experienced by another.

Enoch In Genesis 4:17–18, Enoch is the eldest son of Cain and the father of Irad. In Genesis 5:18–21, Enoch is the son of Jared and the father of Methuselah. This later Enoch "walked with God," and then suddenly disappeared "for God took him" (Genesis 5:24).

Epicurus Born on the Island of Samos, about 341 B.C.. He moved to Athens where his largely self-taught philosophical education was accomplished. He also took part in political and community affairs. He traveled widely. In 310 B.C., Epicurus established a school of philosophy in the city of Mitylene. He later returned to Athens and established a school in a garden. He lectured informally to an audience of not only freemen, but of women and slaves as well. He wrote an important work in thirty-seven volumes called *On Nature*. Unfortunately only fragments of the work are now extant.

Epiphany A Christian festival held on January 6 in celebration of the manifestation of the divine nature of Christ to the Gentiles as represented by the Magi (Zoroastrian priests).

Epistemology Concerning the validity and limits of knowledge. It deals with the theory and method of how knowledge is attained.

Epithalamium A nuptial song or poem in honor or praise of the bride and bridegroom.

Eros The God of love in Greek mythology, son of Aphrodite.

Eschatology Greek *eskatos*, "last" and *logos*, "study." The branch of theology that deals with ultimate things: for example, death, judgment, Hell, and end of time.

Ethnologist One who studies ethnology, an anthropological study of socioeconomic systems and cultural heritage, especially of cultural origins and cultural changes.

Ethnology The anthropological study of socioeconomic systems and cultures. In Greek *ethnos* means "people."

Etymology The study of the origin and development of words; the derivation of words.

Eucharist Christian sacrament commemorating Christ's Last Supper. Also, called Communion.

Eusebius (Surname Pamphili) Lived about 260 to about 340. In the early fourth century, Eusebius, Bishop of Caesarea, undertook to write the first history of the Christian church, *Historia Ecclesiastica*. Subsequent generations have relied heavily on this work for information concerning the early church after the writing of the books of the New Testament.

Evans-Pritchard, E. E. Born in 1902 in England. He taught at Oxford and engaged in anthropological expeditions in Africa. He became professor of sociology at the University of Egypt in Cairo in 1930 and in 1935, research lecturer at Oxford. Later he taught at Cambridge and again at Oxford. Among other things, Evans-Pritchard attempted both a summary and a critique of prevalent intellectual, psychological, and sociological attempts to reach the core of religious experience.

Existential Here used in the sense of human experience and existence. Existentialism is a nineteenth- and twentieth-century philosophy that centers in the uniqueness and isolation of individual persons in an indifferent or even hostile universe. It is a philosophy that emphasizes human freedom of choice and responsibility for choices made.

Fertility Cult A religious cult or set of religious rituals intended to effect or promote fertility, especially in agricultural produce and herd animals.

Fertility Rites Religious rituals intended to stimulate fertility, especially in food animals, and crops. These rites were often overtly sexual in nature, including human copulation. In such cases it was a form of imitation magic. Man and woman mating ceremoniously caused, by magical means, sky and earth to mate and bring forth abundance.

Feuerbach, Ludwig (1804–1872) Born in Bavaria, Feuerbach studied at Heidelberg and Berlin. In Berlin he listened to the lectures of Friedrich Schleiermacher° but preferred those of Georg Hegel,° who was also at Berlin. Eventually he took his doctorate under Hegel. He was appointed *privatdozent* (an instructor) in philosophy at Erlangen, but his controversial lectures, especially one titled "Thought on Death and Immortality," cut short his university teaching career. He became a private tutor. Although tremendously influenced by Hegel, Feuerbach decided that his great teacher had failed to understand the role of sense-experienced in knowledge. Further, Feuerbach saw Hegel as simply another of a long list of unsuccessful Christian apologists. Feuerbach said that "Hegelian philosophy is the last ambitious attempt to reestablish lost, defeated Christianity by means of philosophy." Whereas Hegel saw a person as a being in which God reveals himself, Feuerbach turned this on its head: "If it is only in human feelings and wants that the divine 'nothing' becomes something, obtains qualities [as Hegel proposed], then the being of man is alone the real being of God—man is the real God." (From *Kleine Philosophische Schriften*, tran. M. L. Lang, 1950, p. 56.) Of his many writings, the following are especially important: *The Essence of Christianity* (1841), *The Philosophy of the Future* (1843), and *The Essence of Religion* (1848).

Fletcher, Joseph F. Born in Newark, N.J., in 1905. Educated at West Virginia University, Berkeley Divinity School, University of London, and Kenyon College. He lectured at Workingmen's College, London, and at St. Mary's, Raleigh, N.C. He was dean of the Graduate School in Applied Religion, in Cincinnati, Ohio, and Paine Professor of Social Ethics, Episcopal Theology School, Harvard.

Flew, Antony Gerrard Born in 1923. Flew is a professor of philosophy, an author, and an editor of scholarly works. He became a lecturer at Christ Church, Oxford, in 1949. In 1954 he became a lecturer in moral philosophy at the University of Keele, Keele, Staffordshire, England. In 1954 he became a member of the editorial board of *The Sociological Review*. Antony Flew, R. M. Hare, and Basil Mitchell engaged in a "parable debate" on theology and falsification, discussing whether or not God-talk can be meaningful. The debate is often called the University Discussion. It began with John Wisdom's° parable about the invisible gardener.

Flewelling, Ralph Tyler Born in DeWitt, Michigan, in 1871. He studied at the University of Michigan, Alma College, Garrett Biblical Institute, and Boston School of Theology. Ordained in the Methodist Episcopal Church, he was appointed pastor of First Methodist Church, Boston. In 1917 he shifted from the ministry to education as chairman of the Department of Philosophy at the University of Southern California (USC), Los Angeles. At USC he was instrumental in founding the School of Philosophy and was appointed head of the school in 1929, a position he held until 1945. Flewelling was an exponent of the philosophy of personalism as set forth in the writings of Borden Parker Bowne. According to Flewelling, "Personalism affirms that the only real unity of which we are directly aware is the unity of the free and conscious self. The self survives the passing events of experience . . . and makes itself the centre of its changing world. That there is any higher unity is due to the fact that one is not alone, but is surrounded by a world of self-conscious intelligences, themselves comprehended in synthesis by a supreme personal intelligence" (from Flewelling's article "On Personalism" in the *Hasting's Encyclopedia of Religion and Ethics*). Flewelling died in 1960.

Franklyn, Julian   British author, lecturer, educator. Born in London in 1899, he was active in the field of parapsychology. He became an expert in London cockneys and their slang; he was also an expert in heraldry, holding membership in the Heraldry Society and the Society of Genealogists. He edited the *Survey of Occult* (first published in 1935). His book on witchcraft, *Death By Enchantment*, was published posthumously in 1971. He died in 1970.

Frazer, Sir James George   Born in 1854. He was educated at the universities of Glasgow and Cambridge in anthropology and the classics. After a brief session teaching at Liverpool, he went to Cambridge and remained on that faculty throughout his teaching career. He wrote a multivolumed work titled *The Golden Bough* in which he gathered a great amount of information on magic and folklore from all parts of the world. Based on his belief in evolution and his opinion that magic is a simpler form than religion, Frazer argued that magic came first, followed by religion, and finally by science. Frazer died at Cambridge in 1941.

Freud, Sigmund   Born of Jewish parents in Freiburg, Moravia (formerly Austria, now Czechoslovakia), in 1856. Freud was reared and educated in Vienna. He studied medicine and worked for a number of years in the physiological laboratory of Ernst Brücke, who was his teacher. In 1881 Freud received his doctorate in medicine, and shortly thereafter he took a position in Vienna's Allgemeine Krankenhaus (general hospital). In 1885 he went to Paris to continue his studies, especially with reference to the use of hypnosis in the treatment of hysteria and other nervous disorders. Returning to Vienna he entered private practice while also lecturing at the University of Vienna. During his early years of private practice, Freud employed hypnosis as a method of treatment, but eventually he discarded it and developed a technique employing the free flow of ideas, which he called "psychoanalysis." Freud died in Vienna in 1939.

Fromm, Erich (1900–1980)   Educated in Germany with a doctorate from Heidelberg University, he taught in Germany at the Psychoanalytic Institute of Frankfurt University. He went to the United States in 1934 and was naturalized as a citizen in 1940. In the states he taught at Columbia University, Bennington College, and other colleges. Fromm was a social humanist who strove to understand human existence by breaking down the barriers he found between individuals and schools of thought. He culled data from Marxist, socialist, and Freudian psychology, and applied psychoanalytical thinking to social and cultural problems in the twentieth century. Arguing that psychoanalysis should not be divorced from morality, he sought to show how to deal with the alienation and despair brought on by this modern technological age.

Frost, Robert (1874–1963)   American poet. Frost is to be counted among America's foremost poets. He wrote and published more than 300 poems—none more insightful than "Mending Wall" or more poignant than "The Death of the Hired

Hand." See *Complete Poems of Robert Frost* (New York: Holt, Rinehart and Winston, 1962).

Geddes, Alexander (1737–1802) A liberal-minded, Scottish, Roman Catholic priest. He concluded from his critical examination of the Old Testament that the Pentateuch (first five books of the Bible) had not been written by Moses, as formerly supposed, but had been written not before the days of David (c. 1000 B.C.), or after Hezekiah (c. 700 B.C.). Some material in the Old Testament might go back as far as Moses, but Moses was certainly not the author of the books as they now exist.

Gilles de Rais A soldier of Charles VII of France, and the chosen protector of Joan of Arc in battle. He was accused of treason and witchcraft, tried, proclaimed guilty, and executed.

Glossolalia From Greek *glossa*, "tongue" and *lalein*, "to talk or babble." One dictionary definition calls glossolalia a fabricated nonmeaningful speech. Many people claim that such gibberish does have meaning if it can just be translated. Usually called "talking in tongues."

Gnosticism From the Greek word *gnosis*, "knowledge." Gnosticism is a system of religious or philosophical teaching that claims that spiritual truth and salvation are attainable only through mysterious and secret methods. Salvation comes through special, esoteric knowledge and practice.

Greek Orthodox (Eastern Orthodox Church) The body of modern churches, including the Greek and Russian Orthodox, derived from the church of the Byzantine Empire and acknowledging the Byzantine rite and primacy of the patriarch of Constantinople.

Greeley, Andrew Born in Oak Park, Illinois, in 1929. Educated at St. Mary of the Lake Seminary and the University of Chicago, Greeley is a controversial Catholic priest whose work has brought both criticism and acclaim: criticism from persons (including some of his ecclesiastical superiors) whom he attacks with some regularity, and praise from some sociologists who admire his work on how immigration and political patterns have affected church structures in America. He teaches at the University of Arizona and at the same time directs the National Research Center, situated in Chicago, an organization that he founded in 1961. Greeley also publishes extensively both scholarly books and scholarly articles and has written several novels. One, entitled *The Cardinal Sins*, some believe, is a barely disguised attack on the late John Cardinal Cody, who was head of the archdiocese of Chicago and one of Greeley's bitterest enemies. This extremely popular book (unlike most of Greeley's more scholarly works) may not be, except financially, much to brag about. One literary critic has stated in print that *The Cardinal Sins* is "going to give trash a bad name."

Hajj (also Hadj) A pilgrimage made by Muslim men to Mecca during the holy month of Ramadan. Each devout Muslim male desires to make this journey at least once in his lifetime.

Hamilton, William A contributor to the literature of the Death of God Movement that flourished briefly in the 1960s. Born in Evanston, Illinois, in 1924 and educated at Oberlin, Princeton, Union Theological Seminary, and the University of St. Andrews, Hamilton taught at Hamilton College, Colgate, Rochester Divinity School, New College (in Sarasota, Florida), Portland State University, and the University of Rochester.

Harnack, Adolf Von (1851–1930) A Protestant liberal theologian. Born in Dorpat,

Estonia and educated at the University of Leipzig, Harnack held professorships at the universities of Giessen, Marburg, and Berlin. He wrote a number of influential books. After a careful study of the development of the church in relation to the environment, he published his findings in *The Mission and Expansion of Christianity in the First Three Centuries* (1908). His most influential statement of liberal Protestant theology is to be found in his work entitled *What Is Christianity?* (1957).

Hasidim (also Hassidum, Chassidim)   A sect of Polish Jewish mystics, begun about 1750, who opposed the formalistic Judaism of that time. The sect still continues not only in Poland, but also in New York City, Israel, and elsewhere.

Hayden, Albert Eustace   History of religions scholar. Born in Brampton, Ontario, Canada, in 1880 and educated at McMaster University and Chicago University, he served as pastor of the First Baptist Church at Dresden, Ontario, at Fort William, and at Saskatoon, Saskatchewan. He joined the faculty of the University of Chicago in 1919 and taught there until 1945.

Hector   A Trojan prince killed by Achilles in Homer's *Iliad*.

Hegel, Georg Wilhelm Friedrich   Born in Stuttgart, Germany, in 1770. At age eighteen he entered the theological seminary at Tübingen where he studied Kant and Rousseau. He spent 1793–1800 as a private tutor in Berne and at Frankfurt-am-Main. In 1801 he entered the University of Jena. In 1805 he was appointed professor there. In 1807 his *Phenomenology of the Spirit (Mind)* was published; it was his first important contribution to speculative philosophy. After several years in Nuremberg (as rector of the Gymnasium) where his book *Logic* was published (1816), he became a professor of philosophy at Heidelberg. In 1817 his *Encyclopedia of Philosophic Sciences* was published. The next year he moved to the University of Berlin where he spent the rest of his life. From his lectures given between 1823 and 1827 came his *Aesthetics*, *Philosophy of History*, *Philosophy of Religion*, and *History of Philosophy*. In 1831 Berlin was stricken with a cholera epidemic. On November 14, Hegel contracted the dread disease. He died the next day.

Heidegger, Martin   Born in 1889. His academic career was mainly at the University of Freiburg. He is to be credited with the technical formulation of the central doctrine of existential philosophy—existence precedes essence in the human dimension. His major work is *Sein und Zeit (Being and Time)*. Heidegger died in 1976.

Hellenistic   Relating to Greek history or culture from the time of Alexander the Great (356–323 B.C.) into the first century B.C.

Hermeneutics   The scholarly discipline of interpretation, especially that branch of theology that determines the rules whereby scripture is interpreted.

Herodotus   A Greek historian who lived in the fifth century B.C. He was called the father of history.

Heschel, Abraham Joshua   Born in Warsaw, Poland, in 1907. He was educated in Germany, taking his Ph.D. at the University of Berlin in 1934. He taught in Poland, Germany, England, and the United States. In England, in 1940, he founded the Institute of Jewish Learning. Beginning in 1940 he taught at Hebrew Union College in New York City. After 1945 he was professor of Jewish ethics and mysticism at Jewish Theological Seminary. Among his writings are *God in Search of Man* and *Man Is Not Alone*. Heschel died in 1972.

Hesiod   Greek poet of the eighth century B.C.

Hick, John   Born in 1922. An English analytic philosopher and Presbyterian clergyman. He has taught at Cornell University, Princeton Theological Seminary, and Birmingham University in England.

Hieroglyphics   Picture writing as found, for example, in ancient Egyptian and Mexican artifacts.

Hobbes, Thomas (1588−1679)   An English materialistic philosopher who wrote the *Leviathan*, which outlines his doctrine of political absolutism that makes the state supreme. It is a most comprehensive and systematic exposition of totalitarianism. Hobbes held that the natural condition of life is one of constant warfare, and that the human condition is "solitary, wolfish, brutish and nasty." For any kind of peaceful existence people agree to abide by certain laws. They make a contract that then becomes absolutely binding. The social contract gives all power to the sovereign (the government). Once the contract has been made all democratic power is ended, which, Hobbes held, is good because, in his view, democracy is one of the worst forms of government.

Hocking, William E. (1873−1966)   Educated at Harvard University. He studied in Germany and taught at Harvard. Hocking was a consistent and prominent defender of idealist philosophy and liberal religion.

Homer   Greek epic poet believed to have been the author of the *Iliad* and the *Odyssey*.

Homo Naturalis   In contrast to Homo sapiens, Homo naturalis would be a creature of nature, instinct guided, rather than a creature of thought and imagination, "wisdom" guided.

Homo Sapiens   Greek, *Homo*, "man"; *sapiens*, "wise." Humans as distinct from other organisms. The only extant species of the genus *Homo*.

Horton, Walter Marshall   Born in Somerville, Massachusetts, in 1895. Educated at Harvard and Union Theological Seminary, he was an instructor at Union Theological Seminary from 1922 to 1925. He then joined the faculty of the Graduate School of Theology, Oberlin College, where he taught systematic theology. He was also an occasional lecturer at Strasbourg University (Germany), Doshisha University (Japan), United Theological College (India), and Chicago Theological Seminary.

Hume, David   Born in Edinburgh, Scotland, in 1711. He was educated at Edinburgh University in classics and in Greek and Roman philosophy. He worked in a merchant's counting house in Bristol, then went to France for two years where he wrote *The Treatise on Human Nature*, which was published later in London. This work was not received with enthusiasm. Indeed, Edinburgh University refused employment to anyone who professed such opinions. Hume became involved in a diplomatic career that took him to Turin and Vienna, Holland, Germany, and Italy. In 1748 his *Enquiry into the Human Understanding* was published; in 1751, *Enquiry into Morals*; and in 1752, *Political Discourses*. In 1763, Hume, working for the ambassador Lord Hertford, was made secretary of the embassy in Paris. He returned to Edinburgh in 1766, where he was made Undersecretary of State for Scotland. However, for all his political career, Hume was destined to be remembered as an outstanding philosopher and critic of philosophy. In his highly skeptical work he reduced mind as well as matter to mere phenomena and denied the ontological nexus between cause and effect. He died in 1776.

Hupfield, Hermann   A German Old Testament scholar. As a result of Hupfield's studies published in 1853, it became apparent that traits of three documents or literary traditions are to be found in the books of Genesis, Exodus, Leviticus, and

Numbers. (See also in this biographical listing, DeWette, Von Ewald, and Wellhausen.)

Husserl, Edmund (1859–1938) A German philosopher. He is founder of a modern philosophical method called "phenomenology," a reaction against empiricism and the pretentions of modern science. In their places it emphasizes the *essence* of phenomena. It is used especially in the study of the social sciences, mathematics, art, and religion. Husserl taught philosophy at Göttingen University and at Freiburg University. During the Nazi regime he was persecuted because of his Jewish faith. Important books of Husserl include *Logical Investigations* (1900) and *Formal and Transcendental Logic* (1929).

Huxley, Sir Julian Sorrell Biologist. Born in England in 1887, he attended Eton and Balliol College, Oxford. He lectured in zoology at Balliol; at Rice Institute (Houston, Texas); at New College, Oxford; King's College (London); and McGill University in Montreal, Canada. He has produced educational films. He was made a Fellow of the Royal Society in 1938 and was knighted in 1958. He is the grandson of the celebrated British Darwinian biologist Thomas Huxley (1825–1895), and the brother of the novelist and critic Aldous Huxley (1894–1963).

Ikhnaton (also Akhenaton) The name taken by Amenhotep IV (an Egyptian pharaoh, 1375–1358 B.C., and husband of Nefertiti) when he accepted a theology of universal monotheism under the God Aton,° symbolized by the sun. Ikhnaton may have been the world's first monotheist monarch. However, his efforts were overthrown in the years after his death. The priests of God Amen managed to reestablish the old religion.

Immanentalistic Immanentalism is a doctrine that holds that God is completely within the natural world. It denies the reality of what is usually called the supernatural.

Inquisition, Office of the Officially called The Holy Tribunal of the Inquisition. An authority established by the Roman Catholic church after the Crusades for the purpose of dealing with heresy; that is, with movements and beliefs other than those endorsed by the Roman Catholic hierarchy.

Islanders See Trobriand Islands.

Jacks, Lawrence Pearsall Born in Nottingham, England, in 1860. Educated at the universities of Nottingham, London, Oxford, Göttingen, and Harvard. In 1903 he joined the faculty of philosophy at Manchester, and in 1915 became the principal of Manchester College, Oxford. From 1902 to 1947, Jacks was editor of the *Hibbert Journal*. He was a student of parapsychology, with an interest in psychical phenomena as they pertained to philosophy. Apropos of this interest he was a member of the Society of Psychical Research, London, from 1909 to 1955, and president of that organization in 1917–1918. He wrote some thirty books on religious subjects including *Mad Shepherds and Other Studies; Among the Idol Makers;* and *Religious Perplexities*. Jacks received honorary degrees from the universities of Oxford, Liverpool, Harvard, Glasgow, McGill, and Rochester. He was a Unitarian clergyman. He died in 1955.

Jacob's Sons Reuben, Simeon, Levi, Judah, Issachar, Zebulum, Dan, Naphtali, Gad, Asher, Joseph, Benjamin.

James, Edwin Oliver Born in 1886. In 1933 he joined the faculty of history and philosophy of religion at Leeds University. A recognized anthropologist and history of religions scholar, James has written a number of books on primitive religion and is a contributor to the *Encyclopedia of Religion and Ethics*.

James, William Born in 1842, in New York City. He died in New Hampshire in 1910.

His father Henry James, Sr., was a writer on religious topics. His brother Henry was a gifted novelist. William received his formal education in the United States, England, France, Switzerland, and Germany. He studied medicine at Harvard and was granted an M.D. degree in 1869. He was appointed to the Harvard faculty in 1889 and remained on that faculty until 1907. His first appointment was as instructor in physiology, but he was also greatly interested in psychology and in 1910 he published a classical work *The Principles of Psychology*. After that he turned his attention to philosophy. From about 1892 to 1903 his philosophical interest focused largely on religious questions. Then he began to give serious attention to philosophy from an American point of view and became one of the several founders of modern Pragmatism. He was one of the truly exciting thinkers and writers that America has produced. He had a vast range of interests but was always especially interested in empirical methods even when studying philosophy. He recognized the plurality of truth, a position that lies at the heart of pragmatic philosophy. He was always sensitive to the religious dimensions of human experience.

Jastrow, Morris, Jr. (1861–1921) Philologist and archaeologist. Born in Warsaw, Poland, he came to America with his parents in 1866. They settled in Philadelphia. He graduated from the University of Pennsylvania in 1881, and from 1881 to 1885, he studied at the universities of Breslau, Berlin, Leipzig, Strasbourg, and Paris. He became a recognized authority on Semitic religious languages. He was chairman of the Department of Arabic and Rabbinical Literature at the University of Pennsylvania from 1886 to 1892.

Jehovah (Yahweh) See Yahweh.

Jerome, Saint (340?–420) Latin scholar and doctor of the Catholic Church. Commissioned by the bishop of Rome, he translated the Bible into Latin. This translation became known as the Vulgate. Vulgate comes from Latin *vulgātus*, which means "common" or "popular." It is now used in revised form as the Roman Catholic authorized version of the Bible.

Joan of Arc, Saint (1412–1431) Her French name was Jeanne d'Arc, and she was also called the Maid of Orléans. She was the daughter of a prosperous peasant family. In her early teens she began to hear voices, which she believed came to her from God and saints and angels. Her voices led her to support her French king, Charles VII, against the English in the One Hundred Years' War. She became a military leader and, in accordance with her prophesy, the English were defeated in an important battle. But later Joan fell into the hands of the English. She was accused of being a witch, tried, found guilty, and burned at the stake. She was canonized (made a saint) by the Roman Catholic Church in 1920.

Johnson, James Weldon (1871–1938) Poet and novelist, born in Jacksonville, Florida. For eleven years Johnson was Secretary of the National Association for the Advancement of Colored People. He has been widely acclaimed for his contributions to black culture.

Jones, Ernest A Welshman and medical doctor, born in 1879. He was educated at Lanovery College in Wales, and at the universities of London, Paris, and Munich. He founded and edited the *International Journal of Psycho-Analysis*. His articles were published extensively in scientific journals. He wrote an important book on Sigmund Freud and two books on religion—*On the Nightmare* and *Psycho-Analysis of the Christian Religion*.

Jung, Carl Gustav (1875–1961) Born in the small village of Kesswil on Lake Constance in northeastern Switzerland. He studied at the University of Basel where his grandfather had been a distinguished professor of medicine. In 1905 he became a lecturer in psychiatry at the University of Zurich and senior physician at the Psychiatric Clinic. In 1909 he lectured at Clark University in Massachusetts. In 1912 he visited the United States again and lectured at Fordham University. Jung's contributions to an understanding of the human psyche have been extensive. His concepts of the collective unconscious, archetypal personality, extroversion and introversion; his inquiries into the functions of thought, insight, and feeling; and his investigations of the roots and meanings of dreams all have been of far-reaching influence. It is probably safe to say that among the giants of modern psychological thought, Carl Jung stands second only to Sigmund Freud.

Kalpa   The period of world existence. From the time the world begins its emanation from Brahman to the time of its return into the quietude of Brahman. A period that repeats over and over, taking each time some 4,300,000 years to do so.

Kant, Immanuel   A German of Scottish descent, born in Königsberg in 1724 and died there in 1804. Kant never traveled farther than forty miles from the place of his birth. In 1770 he was appointed professor of logic and mathematics at the University of Königsberg. Of Kant's place in philosophy, William Turner writes:

> His philosophy is . . . the watershed from which streams of thought flow down in various courses into modern liberalism, agnosticism, and even materialism. To this source may also be traced . . . the movement toward nondogmatic Christianity.*

Kant's writings stimulated much subsequent discussion on theory of knowledge, metaphysics, ethics, and religion. His major works include: *The Critique of Pure Reason* (1781, rev. 1787), one of the most celebrated masterpieces of modern philosophy; *Prolegamena* (1783), a popular statement of Kant's philosophy; *Foundations of the Metaphysics of Morals* (1785); *Metaphysical Foundations of Natural Science* (1786); *Critique of Practical Reason* (1788); and *Critique of Judgment* (1790).

Kelly, Henry Ansgar   Born in Fonda, Iowa, in 1920. He was educated at St. Louis University and Harvard University. Kelly specialized in medieval Renaissance literature and intellectual history. He joined the faculty at the University of California, Los Angeles, in 1967.

Kierkegaard, Søren (1813–1855)   Although Kierkegaard lived in the first half of the nineteenth century, he was a twentieth-century philosopher. He is known today as the father of twentieth-century existentialism. He was born in Copenhagen, Denmark, and studied theology at the University of Copenhagen. Hegel's philosophy was *the* philosophy in the Denmark of Kierkegaard's day, and Kierkegaard's work must be seen in large measure as an effort to eradicate Hegelian theology. Indeed, Kierkegaard's works are a sustained attack on all forms of rational theology, whether the moral idealism of Kant or the absolute idealism of Hegel.

Kikaku (1661–1707)   Haikuist. First student of Matsuo Basho. Perhaps his best poem is the one about a naked beggar: *kojiki kana tenchi wo kitaru natsu-goromo—* "Beggar Heaven-and-Earth-is-wearing summer clothes," which in poetic form is:

---

*William Turner, *History of Philosophy* (Boston: Ginn and Company, 1929, second edition), p. 547.

There a beggar goes!
Heaven and earth he's wearing
for his summer clothes.

Kipling, Rudyard (1865 – 1936)   Born in Bombay, India. Educated in England, Kipling
returned to India as a young man to edit a newspaper. There he soon began to
publish poetry that was extremely popular. He also became a masterful short story
writer. He traveled widely in the Orient, in South America, and in North America.
It is in his "The Ballad of East and West" that we find his critique on East and West
meeting.

Oh East is East, and West is West,
and never the twain shall meet
Till Earth and Sky stand presently at
God's great Judgment Seat
. . . .

Knudson, Albert Cornelius (1873 – 1953)   Educated at the universities of Minnesota,
Boston, Jena, and Berlin, he taught at the University of Denver, Baker University
(Baldwin, Kansas), Allegheny College (Meadville, Pennsylvania), and Boston
University. Influenced by Borden Parker Bowne,° he developed his theology
according to personalistic theism (a form of modern Protestant Liberalism). He
became the chief systematizer of personalism, giving polished expressions to
liberal religious concepts that were widely accepted especially up to World War II.

Koestenbaum, Peter   Born in 1928, in Berlin. He is now professor of philosophy and
humanities at San Jose State College, San Jose, California. He spent his childhood
in Caracas, Venezuela, but has lived in the United States since 1945. He was
educated at the universities of Stanford, Harvard, and Boston. Koestenbaum is an
interpreter of phenomenology and existentialism.

Krishna   An avatar—the human incarnation of God Vishnu of the Hindu trinity of
Gods: Brahma, Vishnu, Shiva. Krishna plays a central role in the sacred writing
called *Bhagavad Gita.*

Lang, Andrew   Born in Selkirk, Scotland, in 1843. He was educated at St. Andrews
and at Balliol College, Oxford. He was elected Fellow of Merton College in 1868.
He was a writer for the London *Daily News*, a frequent contributor to periodical
literature, and editor of the English Worthies series. He wrote books on poetry and
lyrics. He was also an anthropologist and held a keen interest in mythology viewed
especially from an ethnological perspective. He wrote a two-volume work, *Myth,
Ritual, and Religion*, published in 1887. Lang died in 1912.

Laotzu (also Laotse or Lao Tan)   A Chinese philosopher, credited with the founding of
Taoism. He was born in 604? B.C. and died in 531 B.C.

La Vey, Anton Szandor   High Priest of the First Church of Satan, San Francisco. Born
in Chicago in 1930 of Alsatian-French-German-Romanian-Russian ancestry, as a
young man he joined the Clyde Beatty Circus as a roustabout. Later he was a lion
tamer, calliope player, hypnotist, palmist, phrenologist, and magician. He became
an occult devotee and teacher and played the role of Satan in the underground
movie, "Invocation of My Demon Brother." He founded the Church of Satan on
Walpurgis Night (April 30) in 1966 as a new cult celebrating carnal indulgence and
self-satisfaction and replacing God with Satan as the object of worship. Film

director Roman Polanski selected La Vey for the Devil's role in "Rosemary's Baby."

Layard, Austen Henry, Sir   English diplomat and archaeologist. Born in Paris in 1817, he studied law and in 1839, set out on travels that took him through European Turkey and various parts of the Near East. He mastered Persian and Arabic languages and, in 1845, started his archaeological explorations in the territory of ancient Nineveh and Babylon. In 1849 he published two sumptuously illustrated books both entitled *Nineveh and Its Remains*. In 1853 he published *Discoveries Among the Ruins of Nineveh and Babylon*. In 1852 Layard entered political life in England, eventually being appointed to the Privy Council (1868), envoy to Madrid (1869), and ambassador to Constantinople (1877). In 1889 he published *Early Adventures in Persia, Babylon and Susiana*. He died in 1894.

Leek, Sybil   One of the most popular figures in modern occult circles. She calls herself a white witch. Born in Midlands, England, in 1923, Leek left school at sixteen years of age and traveled to France. She settled in the United States. Leek has written extensively on witchcraft and astrology.

Leibniz, Gottfried Wilhelm (1646–1716)   Born in Leipzig, Germany. At age fifteen he entered the university of his native city, where he studied law and philosophy, and later took a doctorate of laws at the University of Altdorf. He then entered the court of the elector of Mainz who sent him as a diplomat to the court of Louis XIV in France. Leibniz became acquainted with most of the learned men of France, England, and Holland. From 1676 to his death he resided in Hannover, Germany, where he held the offices of court councilor and librarian. His major works are *Monadology*, *Principles of Nature and Grace*, *The Discourses on Metaphysics*, and *Theodicy*.

Leuba, James H. (1868–1946)   Psychologist. Born in Neuchatel, Switzerland. Leuba was professor of psychology at Bryn Mawr College from 1889 to 1933. Among his writings are *The Psychological Origin and Nature of Religion* (1909), *The Beliefs in God and Immortality* (1916), and *The Psychology of Religious Mysticism* (1925).

Lewis, Clarence Irving (1883–1964)   Edgar Pierce Professor of Philosophy at Harvard from 1920 to 1953. He specialized in questions of logic and epistemology. Much of his work culminated in his Carus Lectures, published as *An Analysis of Knowledge and Valuation* (1946).

Lewis, C. S.   Born in Belfast, Ireland, in 1889. He studied and taught at the University of Oxford and in 1954 became professor of medieval and Renaissance English at Cambridge. His religious books include *The Problem of Faith* (1940), *The Screwtape Letters* (1942), *Mere Christianity* (1943), *Miracles* (1947), *Surprised by Joy* (1955), and *The Four Loves* (1960).

Lewis, I. M.   Professor of anthropology at the London School of Economics. In 1971, Lewis published *Ecstatic Religion*, which makes contributions to the understanding of African shamanism, the classical shamanistic religions of Arctic Asia and South America, Haitian Voodoo, the cult of Dionysus (ancient Greece), and Christian mysticism.

Libido   The psychic and emotional energy associated with instinctual biological drives—sexual desire.

Li Chi (pronounced lē Jē)   The Confucian classic on the religio-ethical principles of Confucius.

Linder, Robert D.   Born in 1934. Educated at Emporia State University, Central

Baptist Theological Seminary, Iowa University, University of Geneva, and Oxford University, Linder is a professor of history at Kansas State University where he has been teaching since 1963. He is an author and editor, he has been a commissioner on the City Council of Manhattan, Kansas, and has served two terms as mayor of Manhattan. He was director of the Religious Studies Program at Kansas State University, 1979–1982. His special expertise is the history of religion and politics.

Locke, John (1632–1704)   Educated at Westminster School and Christ Church Oxford. He studied Descartes's° philosophy but never became a Cartesian himself. On leaving Oxford he entered the service of Lord Ashley (later earl of Shaftesbury) as secretary, tutor, and physician. In 1683, Locke moved to Holland, staying there for six years. He then returned to England in the service of William of Orange. He died at Oates in Essex. Locke's works were initially published in nine volumes in London (1714). Included among these volumes were the important works entitled *Essay Concerning Human Understanding, Thoughts Concerning Education, Two Treatises on Government,* and *The Reasonableness of Christianity as Delivered in Scripture.* Locke's philosophy was based on the principle that all knowledge comes from experience; there are no innate ideas.

Longacre, Lindsay B. (1870–1952)   For thirty-two years a member of the faculty of the Iliff School of Theology, Denver. He was professor and head of the Department of Old Testament until 1952 when he became professor emeritus. One of his fine hymn tunes appeared for many years as Hymn 361, "Deeper Life," in The Methodist Hymnal (lyrics by Katharine Lee Bates). Longacre wrote *A Prophet of the Spirit* (1917), *Amos, Prophet of a New Order* (1921), *Deuteronomy, A Prophetical Lawbook* (1924), and *The Old Testament—Its Form and Purpose* (1945).

Luther, Martin (1483–1546)   German monk, and founder of Protestantism. Luther theologically rejected the Thomas-Aristotelian philosophical theology of Roman Catholicism and returned to the philosophical theology of St. Augustine and the theology of St. Paul.

Macintosh, D. C. (1877–1948)   Modern liberal theologian. Born in Ontario, Canada, he studied at the University of Chicago where he became acquainted with the "Chicago School" of modernism in theology as taught by Edward Scribner Ames, Shailer Mathews, C. B. Foster, and C. B. Smith. Macintosh went to Yale in 1909 where he taught until 1938.

Maimonides, Moses (also called Moses ben Maimon)   Jewish philosopher and physician. Born in Cordova, Spain, in 1135. Codifier of the Talmud and rabbi of Cairo, Maimonides was the greatest of the Jewish Aristotelians. He wrote *Guide to the Doubting,* which is an exposition of the Aristotelian philosophy combined with Jewish teachings. To Maimonides may be traced the scientific movement in Jewish circles in the thirteenth, fourteenth, and fifteenth centuries. He also influenced the work of Baruch Spinoza (1632–1677), a Dutch philosopher and theologian, also Jewish.

Malinowski, Bronislaw Kasper (1884–1942)   Polish-born English anthropologist. He wrote a famous essay titled *Magic, Science and Religion* (1948). His observations of primitive societies led him to interesting theses regarding the origins of religious rites and their meaning for primitives. Malinowski also wrote *The Argonauts of the Western Pacific* (1922), an exhaustive study of the natives of the Trobriand Islands.

Manduka Upanishad   See Upanishad.

Marcion   He came to Rome in 138 or 139 from Sinope, a seaport in Pontus on the south coast of the Black Sea. He was a remarkable man who came to believe that the God of the Jews was an inferior God. He also believed the revelation of Jesus had been corrupted by the Twelve Apostles but preserved by Paul. In support of his beliefs, Marcion compiled the first Christian New Testament. It consisted of an edited version of the Gospel of Luke (the companion of Paul) and of Paul's letters.

Marett, Robert R.   Born in 1866. Educated at Victoria College, Jersey, and Balliol College, Oxford (M.A. and D.Sc.), he was rector of Exeter College, Oxford. He contributed to Tylor's° speculations on animism. Among his writings on religion are *Threshold of Religion* (1909), *Faith, Hope, and Charity in Primitive Religion* (1932), and *Sacraments of Simple Folk* (1933). He died in 1943.

Maritain, Jacques   Born in 1882. A French Thomist (St. Thomas Aquinas) philosopher.

Maslow, H. Abraham   American psychologist. Born in 1908, he was educated at the University of Wisconsin. He served on the Wisconsin faculty from 1929 to 1934. In 1935 he moved to Columbia University where he was a Carnegie research fellow. He moved to Brooklyn College, and then in 1951 to the Psychology Department of Brandeis University. In 1961 he delivered an important public lecture at La Jolla, California. That lecture, "Lessons from Peak Experiences," was published in the *Journal of Humanistic Psychology*, 2, 1, 1962. Another publication concerned with religion is his *Religious Values and Peak Experiences* (Columbus: Ohio State University, 1946).

Masoretic   The masora/masorah is the body of tradition relating to correct textual reading of the Old Testament.

Mead, George Herbert   Born in South Hadley, Massachusetts, in 1863. He died in 1931. Mead graduated from Oberlin College and continued his studies at Harvard. He was primarily interested in philosophy and psychology and studied these subjects in Europe. He taught at the University of Michigan. In 1893 he joined the faculty of the newly established University of Chicago where he remained until his death. Mead was one of the profound thinkers of early American Pragmatism. His important writings include: *The Philosophy of the Act* (1938), *Movements of Thought in the Nineteenth Century* (1936), *Mind, Self and Society* (1934), and *The Philosophy of the Present* (1932).

Messianic   Pertaining to a Messiah.

Metaphysics   The branch of philosophy that investigates the nature of first principles and problems of ultimate being (ontology) and the structure of the universe (cosmology). The term comes from Aristotle's treatise on transcendental philosophy that came after (*meta*) his treatise on physics.

Mettler, Ruben F.   Chairman and chief executive officer of TRW, Inc.

Middle Stone Age (Mesolithic)   Archaeological designation for culture and time between Paleolithic and Neolithic ages—roughly from 100,000 to 10,000 years ago. A time marked by the appearance of the bow and arrow and cutting tools.

Miletus   An ancient city-state in Asia Minor. An important port city of extensive trade and wealth and an important intellectual center. The founder of Greek philosophy, Thales,° lived there. In 494 B.C. Miletus fell before a Persian onslaught. After that the dominance of Milesian philosophy ended and philosophy shifted its center first to southern Italy and Sicily and later to Athens.

Millay, Edna St. Vincent (Mrs. Eugene Jan Boissevain)   Born in Rockland, Maine, in 1892. Poet and playwright. Educated at Barnard College and Vassar College, she won a Pulitzer Prize for her poetry in 1922. She wrote five plays and fifteen books of poetry. Millay lived and traveled in Europe, the Orient, and in India, and the East Indies. She died in 1950.

Milligan, Charles S.   Professor of Philosophy of Religion at the Iliff School of Theology in Denver, where he has been on the faculty since 1957. Before that he was on the faculty of Tufts University. He was born in Colorado in 1918 and was educated at the University of Denver, where he received an A.B. degree; the Iliff School of Theology, where he was granted Th.M. and Th.D. degrees; and Harvard University, where he earned the S.T.M. and Ph.D. degrees. He did postdoctoral studies at the Hebrew University and at the universities of Illinois and Basel. Milligan is an ordained minister in the United Church of Christ. He is editor of the *Iliff Review*, has written numerous articles, and is the author of *A Guide to Contemporary Philosophy of Religion*.

Moloch (also Molech)   A God of the Ammonites and Phoenicians to whom, according to the Old Testament, children were sacrificed.

Monstrance   Used in the Roman Catholic Church, a receptacle in which the host (communion bread) is held up for public display.

Montague, William Pepperell   Philosopher and educator. Born in Chelsea, Massachusetts, in 1873, he was educated at Harvard and studied also at Cambridge. He taught at the University of California at Berkeley. In 1903 he began a teaching career at Barnard College and four years later began teaching at Columbia University as well. He retired from these two institutions in 1947. He also lectured in Japan, Czechoslovakia, and Italy. He delivered the Terry Lectures (Yale) in 1930 and the Ingersoll Lectures (Harvard) in 1932. Montague died in New York, in 1953.

Muhammad (Mohammed)   Prophet and founder of Islam. Born in 570?, Muhammad was reared by his paternal grandfather 'Abd-al-muṭṭalib, and then by his uncle Abū Tālib. They were Arabs of the Hāshimite clan. He became a caravan driver for a rich Qurayshite widow whose name was Khadīja. She was fifteen years his senior, and she not only employed the young Muhammad, but mothered, loved, and finally married him. Khadīja bore Muhammad a number of children, probably three sons and four daughters. Only one daughter, Fatima, survived Muhammad. According to Muslim tradition, Muhammad received his first "prophetic call" while he was visiting a cave near Mount Hīra, a few miles north of Mecca. After his "call," and with encouragement from Khadīja, Muhammad began his ministry, first in Mecca, then in Medina. The development of the Muslim faith engendered considerable animosity at first, including a holy war between Muhammad's Medina forces and the city of Mecca. Muhammad died unexpectedly in 632.

Müller, Friedrich Max   Often called the "father of comparative mythology and history of religions," he was born in Dessau, Germany, in 1823. He studied Sanskrit at Leipzig University. At the universities of Berlin and Paris he studied philology, philosophy, and comparative religion. He went to England in 1846 to edit a translation of the Hindu scripture called *Rig-Veda*. He remained in England and taught at the University of Oxford. In 1873 his book *The Science of Religion* was published, and shortly thereafter he began a massive project of translating and editing the *Sacred Books of the East*. He became curator of the Bodleian Library at Oxford, where he remained for the rest of his life. He died in 1900.

Murray, Margaret Alice   Born in Calcutta, India, in 1863. Educated at University College, London, she lectured in Egyptology at University College and at Oxford. She became interested in witchcraft, and her writings played an important part in the twentieth-century revival of interest in it. She is most widely known for her controversial books *The Witch Cult in Western Europe* (1921), *God of the Witches* (1933), and *The Divine King* (1954). She also wrote works related to her archaeological explorations in Egypt; Malta; Hertfordshire, England; Minorca; Petra; and Tel Ajjul, Southern Palestine. Murray died on November 13, 1963, shortly after her 100th birthday.

Naturalis   See Homo Naturalis.

Neanderthal Man   An extinct human species, *Homo neanderthalensis,* who lived during the first Pleistocene Age in the Old World and is associated with Middle Paleolithic tools. Identified in 1856 from remains found in the Neanderthal, a valley near Düsseldorf, West Germany.

Neo-Platonism (New Platonism)   A philosophical theology developed in Alexandria, Egypt, in the third century A.D. based on the earlier philosophy of Plato° of Athens (427?−347 B.C.). Neo-Platonism also contained doctrines from other Greek philosophers, Oriental mysticism, and some Judaic and Christian elements.

Niebuhr, (Karl Paul) Reinhold (1892−1971)   Born in Wright City, Missouri. Educated at Elmhurst College, Eden Seminary (Missouri), and Yale University. In 1915 Niebuhr became pastor of Bethel Church in Detroit. His thirteen years as pastor there convinced him of the inadequacy of Protestant Liberalism as a theology for suffering people. He found what he thought was a better answer in the Neo-Orthodoxy of Karl Barth.° Niebuhr became national head of the pacifist Fellowship of Reconciliation. In 1928 he became professor of applied Christianity at Union Theological Seminary in New York where he taught until his retirement in 1960. His important book *The Nature and Destiny of Man* was initially presented at the prestigious Gifford Lectures at the University of Edinburgh in 1939.

Nietzsche, Friedrich Wilhelm (1844−1900)   In 1864 Nietzsche entered the University of Bonn. A year later he moved to Leipzig to continue his studies under Albrecht Ritschl. As early as age eighteen, Nietzsche had had serious doubts about Christianity. In 1869, he was appointed to the Chair of Philosophy at the University of Basel. There he began writing a number of important books, including the popular *Thus Spake Zarathustra* (1881−1883). Nietzsche hoped that through philosophy a new civilization with new values—the values of superhumans—could be achieved. This new world would be characterized by superior men (Übermensche) who live by the principle of power, the Will to Power, which Nietzsche regarded as the opposite of Christianity's glorification of inferiority. According to Nietzsche meekness, war, pain, suffering, were all good for they weed out defectives. They alone should survive who have the will to survive, who can master and tame their world.

Noss, John Boyer   Born in Sendal, Japan, in 1896. Educated at Franklin and Marshall College, the Theological Seminary Reformed Church U.S., and at Edinburgh University of Scotland, he served as a minister in Pennsylvania and as a professor and chairman of the Department of Religion at Franklin and Marshall. His most widely read book is *Man's Religions* (1949), which is now in its sixth edition.

Numinous   A word coined by Rudolf Otto from the Latin word *numen* meaning, among other things, divine power, divinity, deity. The numinous is an experience of divine power or presence.

Occam See William of Occam.

Occam's Razor/Law of Parsimony Principle of economy in ideas. An explanation should employ as few ideas (hypotheses) as possible for an adequate explanation, that is, one of both scope and precision.

Odysseus (Latin name, Ulysses) Greek mythology. The cunning king of Ithaca, a leader of the Greeks in the Trojan War, whose return home after the war was for ten years frustrated by the enmity of Poseidon, who was God of the seas (called Neptune by the Romans).

Oedipus Complex Libidinal feelings in a child (especially a male child) for the parent of the opposite sex, usually accompanied by hostility to the parent of the same sex.

Oglala A tribe of Siouan-speaking North American Indians of the Teton Dakota group, inhabiting an area west of the Missouri River in South Dakota.

Omnipotence All powerful.

Omniscient All knowing.

Ontology The branch of philosophy that deals with being.

Ordinary As used here, a noun designating a cleric, such as a bishop, with ordinary jurisdiction over a certain territory.

Origen (185?–254?) Born in Alexandria, Egypt. The oldest of seven sons and a precocious child, Origen was instructed by his father in the scriptures and Greek philosophy. Before he was seventeen years old his father was imprisoned and killed and the family property was confiscated during the persecution of Emperor Severus. After the persecution, when Origen was only eighteen years old, he was given charge of Christian instruction in the Cathedral School in Alexandria. The persecution was renewed and Origen, who boldly visited those imprisoned and even accompanied some to the place of their execution, avoided arrest only by moving his residence frequently. Later Origen visited Rome, Arabia, Greece, and Palestine. Falling into conflict with the bishop of Alexandria, he moved to Caesarea in Palestine where he continued to teach and write. During a persecution in the reign of Decius, he was arrested and tortured. His health broken, he died shortly thereafter, in his seventieth year, in Tyre.

Orthodoxy Greek *ortho*, "right" and *doxa*, "opinion." Those religious doctrines deemed correct by an established religious authority.

Orthopraxis Greek *ortho*, "right" and *prossein*, "to do." Right practice. Proper, authorized behavior or performance.

Otto, Rudolf Born in Peine, Germany, in 1869. Died in Marburg in 1937. A Protestant (Lutheran), he trained for a career in theology at the universities of Erlangen and Göttingen. He taught at Göttingen, Breslau, and Marburg. He was early influenced by Albrecht Ritschl and Friedrich Schleiermacher. These two had sought for a basis for religion that would survive the attack implicit in Immanuel Kant's *Critique of Pure Reason*. Otto wanted to find a grounding for religion given in religious experience and one that does not depend on empirical verification. It was toward this end that he wrote his classical *Das Heilige* (The Idea of the Holy) in 1917. Otto also developed an interest in non-Western and non-Christian religions. He traveled to Africa, India, and Japan and developed an interest in the inter-cultural dimensions of religious experience. He discovered, he believed, that his concept of the holy not only gave religion independence from rational and empirical categories, but also proved to be a central dimension in all religions, Western, Eastern, and primitive.

Parsimony, Law of See Occam's Razor.

Pascal, Blaise (1623–1662)   French philosopher and mathematician. Born in Clermont in Auvergne, he was educated at Paris. He was a leading Jansenist, that is, a member of a religious movement that emphasized predestination, the denial of free will, and the claim that human nature is incapable of good. He made several imporant discoveries in mathematics and physics. His work called *Pensées* (1669) consists of fragmentary reflections intended to form a system of Christian philosophy.

Passover   A Jewish festival beginning on the fourteenth day of the Jewish month of Nisan. It is traditionally celebrated for eight days. It commemorates the escape of the Jews from Egypt. See Exodus, chapter 12, for the biblical account of this escape. Jesus was crucified at the time of the Passover.

Patristic   Concerning the fathers of the early Christian church or their writings, or both. Such men as Tertulian, Origen, Jerome, and Augustine.

Patristic Period   From late second century through the fifth century. Name comes from *patrēs*, "father." The period of such Christian church leaders as Tertulian, Cyprian, Lactantius, Jerome, Ambrose, and Augustine.

Perrin, Norman   An excellent New Testament scholar and professor at the Divinity School at the University of Chicago. Born in 1920; an untimely death ended his career in 1978.

Personalizing   In this case, ascribing human characteristics to natural objects.

Phenomenology   A contemporary method of doing philosophy. The idea for phenomenology was initiated by Georg Hegel in his *Phenomenology of the Mind* (1807). The method has been developed more recently by Edmund Husserl (1859–1938). Giving up what they regard as an impossible task—the solution of the debate over what things in themselves are—phenomenologists are concerned with reporting as exactly as they can the world as experienced by humans. In religious studies this means to report as faithfully as possible religious beliefs and behavior as experienced by believers.

Phenomenon   Any occurrence or fact that is directly perceptible by the senses.

Philo   A Jew born about A.D. 25 who lived in Alexandria in Egypt and attempted to support and "modernize" Judaism by employing Hellenistic philosophical concepts to explain Jewish monotheism in a Greco-Roman world. Philo's efforts paved the way for later second-century Christian philosophical and theological efforts to accomplish the same kind of explanations for Christianity.

Philology   Study of langauge, especially, as a discipline or science.

Pietà   A painting or sculpture of the Virgin Mary holding the body of the dead Jesus; especially the Michaelangelo (1475–1564) sculpture in the Sistine Chapel in the Vatican.

Plato   Original name, Aristocles (427?–347 B.C.). Greek philosopher.

Potthoff, Harvey H.   Born in Le Sueur, Minnesota. He graduated from Morningside College (Sioux City, Iowa) with an A.B. degree and did his graduate work at the Iliff School of Theology, Denver (Th.M. 1935, Th.D. 1941). From 1937 to 1952 Potthoff was a part-time instructor at Iliff while serving as pastor of Christ Methodist Church, Denver, Colorado. In 1952 he became Professor of Christian theology at Iliff, a position he held until his retirement in 1981. He has been an active church leader in the United Methodist Church serving as a delegate to the World Methodist Conferences of 1966 and 1971. He was also a delegate to the Fourth Assembly of the World Council of Churches in Uppsala, Sweden, 1968. He was editor of *The*

Iliff Review from 1952 to 1958. Potthoff's major contribution to theology has been his insightful interpretation of Christian belief and experience in modern perspective.

Pratt, James Bissett Philosopher. He was born in Elmira, New York, in 1875, and educated at Harvard, Columbia, and Berlin Universities. He also studied native religions in India and Buddhism in China. He taught philosophy at Williams College. He died in Williamstown, Massachusetts, in 1944.

Presanctified A special eucharistic (communion) service in which the elements (bread and wine) have been consecrated in a previous service.

Propitiate To conciliate an offended power. To appease, for example, an offended God by offering prayer or sacrifice.

Pseudepigrapha Noncanonical Hebrew/Jewish religious writings from about 200 B.C. to A.D. 100. They are especially concerned with the question of evil in the world. These writings have been falsely ascribed to various Prophets and leaders of Hebrew scripture. The term is the neuter plural of the Greek word *pseudepigraphos,* which means falsely ascribed—from *pseudes* "false" and *epigrapheim* "to write on."

Ragland, Lord Fitzroy Ragland Somerset, 4th baron of Ragland (1885–1964). Born in London and educated at Eton and Sandhurst, Ragland served in the army in the Far East and Near East. After retirement, he pursued his interests in folklore and anthropology.

Rahner, Karl Born in Freiburg in Brisgau (in what is now the German Federal Republic). He entered the Society of Jesus (Jesuit) in 1922 and studied in Germany, Austria, and Holland, receiving his doctorate at the University of Munich. Rahner was ordained a priest in 1932. He taught at Innsbruck, Munich, and Münster. He was *peritus* (official theologian) at Vatican II (1962–1965).

Rais See Gilles de Rais.

Rall, Harris Franklin Born in Council Bluffs, Iowa, in 1870. He studied at Iowa State University and Yale University and then at Berlin University and Hale-Wittenberg University, where he earned a Ph.D. degree in 1899. He was ordained a Methodist Episcopal minister in 1900 and served as pastor of Trinity Church, New Haven, and First Church, Baltimore. From 1910 to 1915 he was president of the Iliff School of Theology, Denver. He also lectured at Yale University, the University of Denver, Ohio Wesleyan, and Garrett Biblical Institute, where in 1940 he was awarded the LL.D. degree. Rall died in 1964.

Rasmussen, Knud Johan Victor (1879–1933) Born in Greenland, son of a Danish missionary and an Eskimo mother. He began his ethnological studies of Eskimos in 1902 and established a trading station at Thule, Cape York, Greenland, in 1910. From Thule he led four scientific expeditions that took him to the Canadian Antarctic. He collected songs, poems, legends, myths, and tales of various Eskimo tribes that were published in some forty-four volumes.

Rauschenbusch, Walter Born in Rochester, New York, in 1861. Educated at the University of Rochester and Rochester Seminary, he served for eleven years as a minister in the Hell's Kitchen section of New York City. In 1897 Rauschenbusch joined the faculty of Rochester Theological University. Among his writings is the book *A Theology for the Social Gospel* (1917), which is a lucid statement of liberal Protestant theology. Rauschenbusch died in 1918.

Renaissance A period (fourteenth to sixteenth century) when classical art and learning had a rebirth in Europe. This period marked the transition from medieval to modern times.

Rist, Martin Born in Antioch, Illinois, the son of a Methodist minister. He was educated at Northwestern University, Garrett Biblical Institute, Iliff School of Theology, and the University of Chicago. He joined the faculty of the Iliff School of Theology in 1936, teaching New Testament and church history. He also served as librarian. His best known writing is the "Introduction and Exegesis to the Book of Revelation," in *The Interpreter's Bible*, vol. 12 (New York: Abingdon Press, 1957).

Rites, Fertility See Fertility Rites.

Ritschl, Albrecht (1822–1889) Born in Berlin. He studied at the universities of Bonn, Halle, Heidelberg, and Tübingen and became a disciple of the historian F. C. Bauer. Ritschl began his teaching career at Bonn in 1846. In 1864 he moved to Gottingham where he taught for twenty-five years. Ritschl was basically concerned not with Friedrich Schleiermacher's° "absolute dependence" as the basis of religion, but with the experience of "moral freedom" as basic. Religion rests in the experience of being liberated from the bondage of nature's blind necessity. Ritschl is to be counted among the fathers of modern Protestant Liberalism.

Royce, Josiah (1855–1916) An American idealist philosopher. He taught at the universities of California and Harvard. Royce held that science could describe, but not appreciate. Appreciation is in the province of philosophy. The real world is a mental world (the Absolute) and true morality is being loyal to this Absolute.

Rubenstein, Richard Distinguished professor in the Department of Religion at Florida State University.

Ruysbroeck, Jan van Born in Brussels in 1293. After ordination to the priesthood, he became cathedral chaplain in Brussels. At age fifty he went into spiritual retirement in a forest hermitage near Brussels. He remained there for thirty-eight years in a life of worship and contemplation. He died in 1381.

Sacralizing Making sacred.

Sacred Worthy of veneration.

Sacrosanct (From Latin *sacer*, "sacred," *sancāre*, "to consecrate"). To regard as sacred.

Sankara (A.D. 788–820) A Hindu Vedanta philosopher. Sankara held that the world and Brahman (God) do not exist separately. Nothing but the impersonal and indescribable Brahman exists. All else is illusion (is *maya*).

Sapiens See Homo sapiens.

Sartre, Jean-Paul Born in 1905. French man of letters and leading exponent of contemporary atheistic existentialism. In 1964 he was awarded the Nobel Prize in Literature, which he declined. His major philosophical work is *Being and Nothingness* (1956).

Satori A state of spiritual enlightenment sought in Zen Buddhism. It is the Japanese term for Hindu "bodhi."°

Schleiermacher, Friedrich (1768–1834) Generally regarded as the best theologian since John Calvin. His revolution in theology is equal to that of Kant in philosophy, and his theology is rightly acknowledged as the most forceful and systematic statement of Romantic and liberal understanding of the Christian religion. Educated at the University of Halle. He wrote *On Religion: Speeches Addressed to Its Cultural Despisers* in 1799 and *Soliloquies* in 1800. In 1904 he became a professor of theology at the University of Halle. In 1809 he became preacher at the Holy Trinity Church in Berlin. In 1811 he was appointed to the faculty of theology at the University of Berlin. There in 1821 and 1822 he wrote the two parts of his important *The Christian Faith* (revised in second edition in 1830). In *On Religion,* Schleiermacher developed a new conception of religion. In his *The Christian Faith* he presented a new interpretation of Christian theology.

Schmidt, Wilhelm A Roman Catholic priest born in Hörde, Westphalia, in 1868. He was educated in Holland, Berlin, and Vienna and taught in Germany, Austria, and Switzerland. Schmidt utilized the reports of Catholic missionaries who were working in the South Seas and Australia. He also became an expert in the languages of these areas. Against the ideas of such scholars as Tylor° and Codrington,° who saw religion originating in polytheism, Schmidt argued that the earliest people believed in a supreme being. They were monotheists. He attempted to document this idea in a twelve-volume work called *Der Urspring Der Gottesidee* (The Origin of the Idea of God). Schmidt fled from Germany to Switzerland in 1938. He died in Freiburg in 1954.

Scholasticism The dominant theological and philosophical school of the High Middle Ages, based on the authority of the early Latin Fathers of the Church and the philosophy of Aristotle and various Aristotelian commentators.

Scott (or Scot), Reginald (1538?–1599) Educated at Hart Hall, Oxford. In 1584 he wrote *The Discovery of Witchcraft*, a book intended to prevent the unjust persecution of poor, aged, simple-minded persons who were often in popular thinking regarded as witches. Scott attempted to undermine the incredulity that supported belief in sorcery and witchcraft.

Scotus See Duns Scotus.

Shaman A priest. One who communicates directly with spirits or Gods, or both. The term comes from Russian "shaman," a Siberian priest-mystic. Among North American Indians a shaman is usually called a "medicine man."

Shang A Chinese dynasty from 1766 B.C. to 1122 B.C. Its capital was An-yang, a city in central Honan Province.

Shiite A principal minority group in Islam composed of the followers of Ali, the cousin and son-in-law of Muhammad. Shiites regard Ali and his successors as the legitimate line of authority in Islam. They, thus, reject the line of the caliphs (beginning with Muhammad's friend Abū Bakr) and Sunni° legal and political institutions.

Sioux See Oglala.

Skull, The The hill of Calvary where Jesus was crucified. Golgotha (Aramaic *gulgultha*) means "skull." The name may have been derived from the shape of the hill.

Smith, Huston C. Born in China in 1919. After seventeen years in China, Smith came to the United States to enter college. He studied at Central College in Missouri and then at the universities of California and Chicago. He taught at the University of Denver, Washington University in St. Louis, the Massachusetts Institute of Technology, and Syracuse University. His best-known book is *The Religions of Man* (1958).

Söderblom, Nathan (1866–1931) Swedish churchman. An important leader in the ecumenical movement for the unification of Christian churches. He won the Nobel Peace Prize in 1930 for his efforts in international understanding. A pietist minister, he studied at the University of Uppsala and the Sorbonne, receiving his doctorate in 1901. He was professor of history and later vice-chancellor of Uppsala University.

Song of Songs (Song of Solomon)   A book of the Old Testament/Jewish Bible consisting of a dramatic love poem.

Squik-diddle   A nonsense word.

Stace, Walter T.   Born in London. Educated at Trinity College, Dublin University, Stace is a man of two careers—politics and education. While serving as a British civil servant in Ceylon (1910–1932), he wrote distinguished books on Greek philosophy, the philosophy of Hegel, and on aesthetics. Later, as Stuart Professor of Philosophy at Princeton University, he continued writing. In 1960 he published an important work, *Teachings of the Mystics*.

Stonehenge   A prehistorical ceremonial ruin on Salisbury Plains in Wiltshire, England; constructed sometime between 1900 and 1700 B.C. of huge upright stone slabs and lintels placed in a circular form.

Streng, Fredrich John   Born in Seguin, Texas, in 1933. Educated at Texas Lutheran College, Southern Methodist University, and the University of Chicago, his expertise is in methods of studying religion and Oriental and Western psychology. He was a Fulbright Scholar at Banaras Hindu University in 1961–62, after which he taught at the University of Chicago, the University of Southern California, and Southern Methodist University.

Sufis (sōōfē)   A member of a Muslim mystic sect. Probably called Sufis because of their wool garments. In Arabic *sūf* means "wool."

Sunni   The largest branch of Islamic people following orthodox tradition and accepting the first four caliphs as the rightful successor of Muhammad (see Shiite).

Suzuki, Daisetz Teitaro   Born in 1870 in Kanazawa, Japan. He is recognized as the foremost interpreter of Zen Buddhism in the Western World. He was educated at the Imperial University in Tokyo, but he spent most of his time at the Zen monastery in Kamakura, near Tokyo. He came to the United States in 1897. Later he returned to Japan and taught at the Imperial University and Otani University in Kyoto. After World War II he traveled and lectured in Europe, India, and the United States. He died in 1966.

Synod   A council or assembly of churches or church officials.

Synoptic   From Greek *synopsis*, "viewed together." The term is used to refer to the Gospels of Matthew, Mark, and Luke, which when viewed together are so much alike. This is not true of the Gospel of John, which is quite different from the Synoptics.

Taboo   A prohibition excluding something from use, approach, or mention, because of its sacred nature.

Tagore, Rabindranath (1861–1941)   Indian (Hindu) poet.

Taoism (pronounced "daoism"; from *tao*, "way")   A principle philosophy and system of religion of China based upon the teachings of Laotzu° or Lao Tan who lived in the sixth century B.C.

Tautology   A needless repetition of a statement in different words. In philosophy (logic) a statement that is "true" no matter what, such as, "It will either rain tomorrow, or it will not rain tomorrow."

Taylor, John V.   Anglican bishop of Winchester, England. His book *The Go-Between God* is a rewriting of the Edward Codbury Lectures in Theology that Taylor gave at the University of Birmingham in 1967. The book received the Collins Religious Book Award for the best religious book by a British author 1971–1973.

Teilhard de Chardin, Pierre Born to an aristocratic family in Socenat, France, in 1881. He joined the Society of Jesus (Jesuit) in 1899 and was ordained to the priesthood in 1911. An excellent theologian, paleontologist, and geologist, Teilhard taught at the Catholic Institute in Paris until he displeased the religious authorities by his advocacy of evolution. For this he was sent, in virtual exile, to China. There he became involved in various scientific projects. He was, for example, involved in the project that discovered the "Peking Man" (an extinct hominid primate of the genus *Sinathropus*) found at Choukoutein, near Peking, China. Teilhard could not get permission from his order to publish his writings, so his monumental work *Phenomenon of Man* was published after his death. This work integrated into Christianity some of the most advanced discoveries in modern science. Although Teilhard received worldwide acclaim, the Holy Office (an office of Catholic censorship) in 1957 ordered all of Teilhard's works removed from Catholic libraries. Teilhard died in 1955.

Thales (c. 624–546 B.C.) The father of Greek philosophy. Born in Miletus in Asia Minor, he identified water as the cause of all things and in so doing proposed to conceive of the world process in natural rather than supernatural terms and to conceive of it as basically monistic. The diversity of the world he believed was to be seen as a unified system—a scientific and philosophical endeavor that still goes on.

Thomas Aquinas The exact date of Aquinas's birth is uncertain, but it was probably about 1225. He came from a Lombard family and was born at the castle of Roccasecca near the small town of Aquino between Naples and Rome. He attended the Abbey of Monte Cassino for elementary schooling. In 1239 he became a student at the University of Naples, where he entered the Dominican Order. He studied under Albert, the Great, also a Dominican, at Paris and Cologne. In 1252 he began to lecture in Paris on the scriptures and later on *The Sentences* of Peter Lombard. In 1256 he became a regular professor of theology occupying one of the two chairs at Paris for the Dominicans. From 1259 to 1269 he taught in Italy at Anagni, Orvieto, Rome, and Viterbo. In 1269 he returned to Paris, but in 1272 he went to Naples to organize the Dominican house of theological studies. He died in 1274 and was canonized (declared a saint) on July 18, 1323. Thomas wrote two monumental summaries of theology: *Summa Theologiae* and *Summa Contra Gentiles*. He was the most important theologian of medieval scholasticism and remains to this day the foremost theologian in contemporary Roman Catholicism.

Thompson, Francis (1839–1905) An English poet. Son of a Lancashire physician, he was educated at Ushaw College near Durham, England, and then studied medicine at Owins College, Manchester. Determined to take up literature, he moved to London where he drifted finally into a life of dereliction. Wilfrid Maynell, editor of *Merry England*, a Manchester periodical, recognized Thompson's talent and began publishing his poems and helped get some books of his poetry published. His poem "The Hound of Heaven" was published in 1893.

Thoreau, Henry (1817–1862) American poet and essayist, who said, among other things, that most people live lives of quiet desperation.

Tillich, Paul (1886–1965) A major twentieth-century theologian. Born in Germany, he was educated at the universities of Breslau and Halle. During World War I, he was a chaplain in the German army. After the war he taught at the universities of Breslau, Halle, and Frankfurt. When the Nazis came to power, Tillich left Germany and went to America (1933). He taught at Union Theological Seminary in

New York, at Yale, at Harvard, at the University of California in Santa Barbara, and at the University of Chicago. His major study is contained in the three-volume work titled *Systematic Theology*.

Totem   Animal, plant, or other natural object that serves as the emblem of a primitive clan or family by virtue of an asserted ancestral relationship.

Toynbee, Arnold Joseph (1889–1975)   British historian. Born in London. Educated at Winchester and Balliol College, Oxford, he studied also in the British Archaeological School in Athens, Greece. He taught at Balliol College and the University of London. He also lectured extensively in the United States. Toynbee's twenty-three-volume synthesis, *A Study of History*, stresses forces at work in the rise and fall of civilizations.

Tremmel, William Calloley   Born in Englewood, Colorado, 1918, he was educated at Denver University and the Iliff School of Theology (Denver), and did advanced study at the University of Colorado, The University of Southern California, and the University of Chicago. In 1945 he was ordained a Methodist minister and served pastorates in Colorado and Kansas, and was Wesley Foundation Director at the University of Colorado. In 1950 he joined the faculty of Kansas State Teachers College, Emporia, Kansas. In 1956 he moved to Kansas State University in Manhattan, Kansas; and in 1969 he joined the faculty of the University of South Florida as chairman of the Department of Religious Studies. Tremmel has authored a number of books and articles, including an introduction to the New Testament entitled *The Twenty-Seven Books That Changed the World*.

Trobriand Islands   A group of small islands, about 170 miles in area, off eastern New Guinea in the Southwestern Pacific, part of the territory of Papua.

Troeltsch, Ernst (1865–1923)   The important early theoretician of the history of religions movement—a movement concerned with Christianity as a natural, historical development of late Judaism, Oriental eschatology, Greek mysteries, Gnosticism, and Stoicism. Troeltsch criticized those scholars (such as Adolf von Harnack) who tried to identify an essence of Christianity. Troeltsch held that Christianity is an open-ended historical development. Essence implies abstraction, but Christianity cannot be reduced to an abstract idea. Whatever Christianity is differs in different epochs, "and is to be understood as something involved in the totality of its active influence," Troeltsch wrote in "The Dogmatics of the Religions-geschichtliche Schule" in *The American Journal of Theology*, January 1913, pp. 12–13.

Trueblood, David Elton   A Quaker philosopher. Born in Pleasantville, Iowa, in 1900. He studied at Pennsylvania College, Brown University, Hartford Theological, Harvard and Johns Hopkins Universities, and taught at Guilford College (Greensboro, North Carolina), Haverford College (Haverford, Pennsylvania), Stanford University, and Earlham College (Richmond, Indiana).

Tylor, Edward B. (1832–1917)   An important contributor to the early discipline of history of religions. His approach to the study was ethnological, and his interest in primitive cultures led to the new science of anthropology. He wrote *Primitive Culture* in 1876.

Upanishad   Literally means "sitting by a teacher." The Upanishads are additions to the Vedas (original Hindu scriptures). They are largely philosophical discourses on religion, especially on the nature of ultimate reality.

Van Dusen, Henry Pitney (1897–1975)   A liberal theologian. Born in Philadelphia, Pennsylvania and educated at Princeton, Union Theological Seminary (New

York), and Edinburgh, he taught at Union Theological Seminary from 1926 until his retirement in 1963. He was an active leader in the YMCA, the Presbyterian Church, and the World Council of Churches. Both Van Dusen and his wife were members of the Euthanasia Society. When crippling diabetes finally overtook them, they opted to end their own lives.

Vedanta A system of Hindu philosophy that advances the Upanishad° notion that all reality is a single principle—Brahman. One's goal in life should be to transcend self-identity and realize unity with Brahman.

Vishnu-Krishna Vishnu is the second member of the Hindu trinity—Brahma and Shiva being the other two Gods of the trinity. Krishna is the human incarnation of Vishnu or, as said by Hindus, the eighth and principal avatar of Vishnu, often depicted as a handsome young man playing a flute.

Von Ewald, George Henry August (1803–1875) German theologian and Orientalist. He concluded that the first six books of the Hebrew Bible (the Old Testament) were compiled from at least four independent sources: a priestly code (P); a history of Judah, the southern kingdom (E); a history of Israel, the northern kingdom (J); the book of Deuteronomy (D).

Vonnegut, Kurt Novelist. Born in Indianapolis, in 1922. Professor at Iowa University and Harvard and distinguished professor of literature at City College, New York.

Wach, Joachim Born in Saxony, Germany, in 1898. Educated at Leipzig, Munich, and Berlin, he specialized in the history of religions, philosophy of religion, and Oriental studies. He taught at the University of Leipzig until the Nazis terminated his appointment. He then went to America and taught at Brown University in Rhode Island. Later he was appointed chairman of the History of Religions Department at Chicago Univeristy. He died in 1955.

Watts, Alan Wilson Born in Chislehurst, England, in 1915. Educated at Sebury Western and the University of Vermont, he was a religious counselor at Northwestern University and taught at the College of the Pacific, Harvard University, and San Jose State College. His specialties were Zen Buddhism, Chinese philosophy, and philosophy and psychology of religion. Watts died in 1973.

Weber, Max (1864–1920) Born in Erfort, Germany. Educated in economics, history, philosophy, and law at the universities of Heidelberg, Berlin, and Göttingen, he taught law at the University of Berlin and economics at the universities of Freiburg and Heidelberg. In 1903 Weber became associate editor of a leading journal on sociology and politics. He began to write extensively for this journal, and he wrote books on ancient Judaism, religion in China, and on the sociology of religion. His most important work is concerned with religion and economics: *The Protestant Ethic and the Spirit of Capitalism*.

Wellhausen, Julius (1844–1918) German biblical historian. In 1878 Wellhausen's two-volume *History of Israel* was published. It is based on the notion that the Old Testament does not furnish a history of Israel, but supplies the source materials from which such a history can be constructed. Among other things, he arranged and dated the documentary sources of the first five books of the Bible, using George Von Ewald's° nomenclature—J (written down c. 850 B.C.), E (written down c. 750 B.C.), D (using De Wette's° dating, 621 B.C.), and P (written sometime after the Babylonian Exile, c. 400 B.C.).

Wesley, John (1703–1791) Founder of Methodism. The son and grandson of an English clergyman, Wesley was himself ordained in the Anglican Church. He was also a teacher at the University of Oxford.

Whitehead, Alfred North (1861–1947)   British philosopher. Born at Ramsgate, Isle of Thanet, Kent, England. At age fourteen, he entered Sherborn in Dorset, one of the most prestigious schools in England. There he excelled in mathematics and Rugby. In 1880 he entered Trinity College, Cambridge, where he continued his studies in mathematics, receiving his D.Sc. degree in 1905. In 1898 he published a book on algebra, which was of sufficient quality to secure him an election to the Royal Society in 1903. His outstanding mathematical work, *The Principia Mathematica*, was written with Bertrand Russell; it was published in three volumes, 1910–1913. This work is generally regarded as one of the great intellectual accomplishments of contemporary times. In 1910 Whitehead resigned his lectureship at Cambridge. A few years later he joined the faculty of the Imperial College of Science and Technology in London, where he remained until 1924. In 1924 Whitehead was offered a professorship in philosophy at Harvard. There his important philosophical work began, starting with his *Science and the Modern World*, published in 1925. A year later he published *Religion in the Making*, and *Process and Reality* in 1929. In America Whitehead became the central figure in a golden age in philosophy. His philosophy is probably the most original ever written in English. And in theology, he is the pioneer figure in process theology. Furthermore, he wrote English in a fashion to earn him a place in English letters.

Wieman, Henry Nelson (1884–1976)   An important philosopher-theologian of the immanentalistic variety of modern Protestant Liberalism. He taught at the Divinity School, University of Chicago. Wieman was an extremist in Christian modernism. For him the Christian theological tradition was inadequate as a guide for modern people. Often Wieman is regarded as not so much a Christian theologian as a philosophical theologian free of all special tradition. He was born in Missouri, did his undergraduate studies at Park College, and his seminary work at San Francisco Theological Seminary. Then he studied in Germany at Jena and Heidelberg. He served as a Presbyterian pastor in California before moving to Harvard for additional studies. He taught at Occidental College and in 1927 was appointed professor of philosophy of religion at the Divinity School, University of Chicago, where he remained until his retirement in 1949.

Wiesel, Elie   Born in Hungary in 1928. He was deported with his family to Auschwitz when he was still a boy and then to Buchenwald where his parents and younger sister died. His book entitled *Night* is a frightening dramatization of those experiences. After the war Wiesel lived in Paris. As a journalist he traveled to Israel and the United States, where he now lives. Other stories by Wiesel are *Dawn, The Accident, The Town Beyond the Wall, The Gates of the Forest, A Beggar in Jerusalem,* and *The Oath.*

William of Occam (Ockham)   Born about 1280 in Surrey. Occam may have been a student of Duns Scotus. He taught in Paris between 1320 and 1323, and then, after quitting that position, he joined a group opposing the temporal power of the pope. For this he was imprisoned at Avignon. He escaped and took refuge at the court of Louis of Bavaria. The place and date of his death are uncertain but may have been Munich in 1349.

Wisdom, John   Born in 1904. A professor of philosophy at the University of Cambridge, Wisdom has been a leading figure among British analytical philosophers.

Wittgenstein, Ludwig Josef Johann   Born in 1889. Philosopher. One of the most creative thinkers in the twentieth century. He studied at the Technical Institute in

Berlin, and at Manchester University. He also studied with the British philosopher Bertrand Russell at Cambridge. He was appointed to succeed G. E. Moore at Trinity College, Cambridge. In 1921 he published an extremely influential work called *Tractatus Logico Philosophicus*. This work was held of highest importance by modern logical positivists. In sharp contrast to the *Tractatus,* he later wrote *Philosophical Investigations*. Wittgenstein became a British citizen in 1938. He died in 1951.

Wundt, Wilhelm Max   German psychologist. Born in Neckarau, Baden, Germany, in 1832. He received both a Ph.D. degree and an M.D. degree and joined the faculty of Heidelberg University in 1854. He became increasingly interested in the study of psychology and initiated the first university course in experimental psychology. In 1875 he transferred to Leipzig University and there in 1879 established the first laboratory to be devoted to experimental psychology. In 1881 he founded the first journal in experimental psychology. Wundt died in Grossbathen, near Leipzig, Saxony, in 1920.

Xenophanes   Born in Colphon in Asia Minor about 565 B.C. He traveled in Greece and finally settled in Elea in southern Italy, where he founded a school. Xenophanes opposed polytheism with a doctrine of the unity, unchangeableness, sublimity, and spirituality of God. He challenged the common notion of what the Gods were said to be like. In a poem he said, ''Each man represents the gods as he himself is: Negro as black and flat nosed, the Thracian as red-haired and blue eyed; and if horses and oxen could paint, they, no doubt, would depict the gods as horses and oxen'' (fragment 6, of the fragments of Xenophanes' didactic poem).

Yahweh   A name for God assumed by modern scholars to be the rendering of the four Hebrew letters (YHVH/ יהוה) that represent God's proper name in Hebrew tradition.

Yinger, J. Milton   Born in 1916, in Quincy, Michigan, the son of a minister father and a writer/speaker mother. Educated at Depauw University, Louisiana State University, and the University of Wisconsin at Madison, he taught at Ohio Wesleyan and was professor of sociology and anthropology at Oberlin College.

Yoga   A Sanskrit word meaning ''union'' or ''yoking.'' Yoga is a Hindu discipline aimed at training the consciousness for a state of perfect spirituality and tranquility. A yogi is one who practices yoga.

Yom Kippur (*yom*, ''day,'' *kippūr*, ''atonement'')   The holiest Jewish holiday, celebrating the tenth day of the month of Tishri. It is a day of fasting and prayer for the atonement of sins. Also called Day of Atonement.

Zarathustra (also Zoroaster)   The Persian (ancient Iranian) prophet who in the seventh century B.C. founded the Zoroastrian religion. Zoroaster means ''owner of old camels.''

Zazen   Meditation technique in Japanese Zen Buddhism.

Zeitgeist   The cultural-intellectual character of a given time period such as the technological-scientific character of twentieth-century America.

Zeus   The presiding God of the Greek pantheon, ruler of the heavens and father of other Gods and mortal heros.

INDEX